Speaker's Sourcebook
of
New Illustrations

Speaker's Sourcebook
of
New Illustrations

Virgil Hurley

WORD PUBLISHING
Dallas·London·Vancouver·Melbourne

Editor—Terri Gibbs

Library of Congress Cataloging-in-Publication Data:

Hurley, Virgil, 1936–
    Speaker's sourcebook of new illustrations / Virgil Hurley.
      p. cm.
    Includes index.
    ISBN 0-8499-3675-6 (alk. paper)
    1. Homiletical illustrations—Dictionaries. I. Title.
BV4225.2.H87 1995
251'.08—dc20

95-37255
CIP

5 6 7 8 9 RRD 9 8 7 6 5 4 3 2 1
Printed in the United States of America

Dedicated to Judy,
the delight of my eyes
and my earthly treasure.

CONTENTS

ACKNOWLEDGMENTS

I acknowledge my debt to Sherwood Wirt, who while speaking to a group of ministers providentially noted that Word Publishing was looking for a book of illustrations. Many thanks to Ernie Owens, retired Word Publishing executive, who first looked at the manuscript and offered continual encouragement in its rewrite. Thanks to Word Publishing for its confidence in the work. Special thanks to my wife, Judy, for her excellent workmanship, computer skills, and untiring devotion to finishing the project.

INTRODUCTION

The *Speaker's Sourcebook of New Illustrations* was developed as a tool to clarify, amplify, and enhance a speaker's presentation by using illustrations from daily activities to apply often overlooked spiritual insights. Life in many forms expresses itself all around us, and God is always at work somewhere in that expression. Sometimes it is in people at work in everyday tasks, or in forging historic decisions. Those expressions emerge like images on film—they are photographs from life.

Twin emphases undergird the book's primary importance. First, it is believable history—it really happened, or is happening. Second, it applies historical and personal events to God's person, purpose, and mission in history.

Let me suggest several ways the book can be useful. Each illustration can be used as written to make a specific point; or several, with common or contrasting themes, can be combined as a single presentation. Each illustration is written with an added spiritual application, which can be used in its entirety or as a catalyst for other spiritual insights. The Scripture texts with each illustration will provide a quick reinforcement of an existing idea or an exposition of a verse. The index will help you to find an illustration even when you only have a vague idea what you want to illustrate, and the appendix offers numerous cross-references on particular themes.

I trust that reading and using the material will be as profitable in your personal life and career as preparing it has been in mine. Like his creatures, God leaves his mark wherever he has been in life. He invites us to look . . . see . . . and be surprised where he reveals himself. To him who once lived among us and now delights in possessing vessels of clay as his personal temple, be honor and glory forever.

Virgil Hurley
July 1995

Speaker's Sourcebook
of
New Illustrations

ACHIEVEMENTS — not given their due
Deuteronomy 9:4; 2 Corinthians 4:7

Not According to Its Worth

One night in the fall of 1861, while watching campfires from thousands of bivouacs around Washington, D.C., Julia Ward Howe experienced a powerful inspiration of words and music—the melody familiar, the prose militantly biblical. They danced separately in her head at first, then together, then arm in arm. She sent the poem to the *Atlantic Monthly*, which published it in the spring of 1862. "The Battle Hymn of the Republic" became an instant sensation all over the North. Julia did not profit by it, however; she received only $5 for her classic.

Lorraine Petersen became the Sun-Maid Raisin Girl in 1915, appearing in a red bonnet, holding a basket of the fruit. The company made millions. She received $15 a week as part-time model and part-time seeder/packer for the Griffin and Skelley Packing Company. The company purchased the original Sun-Maid portrait from her for $1,700.

In seventy days General Tomoyuki Yamashita's troops in Northern Malaya advanced seven hundred miles, all the while outfighting, outwitting, and out-maneuvering General Percival. Then, with a stroke of military genius, his 30,000 men captured Singapore and its 100,000 Britons. For this stunning achievement, military commander Tojo, ever jealous, transferred Yamashita to Manchuria, a military no-man's-land. There he stayed for three years while Japan lost the war.

There is a quintessential unrewarded merit: God in Christ reconciling the world to himself—an expressed spiritual elegance the unsaved cannot fathom, an accepted spiritual glory the saved fail to esteem.

ADULTERY — fair punishment
Proverbs 5:15; Hebrews 13:4

Shouldn't the Man Be Punished Too?

Ancient Egyptians brutally punished a woman caught in adultery by cutting off her nose. Blackfoot Indians practiced the same hideous penalty, then seized the property of the offending male and gave it to the offended husband, who refused to take his wife back. The Persians lopped off both the nose and ears of the offending female. The Law of Moses demanded the death of both miscreants caught in adultery (Lev. 20:10). In the aftermath of China's Cultural Revolution, some authorities felt that the third person in the ménage à trois should be prosecuted for criminal behavior.

It seems right that both parties should be chastised since both agreed to misbehavior that mars the most sacred of all human relationships. In nearly every society, faithfulness to one's married partner has at least been taken for granted, if not actually vowed. Since the intimate marital relationship is symbolic of the union Christ has with his church, Scripture demands faithfulness from both partners.

ADVERSITY — beneficial
Proverbs 3:11–12; 2 Corinthians 12:9

Adversity, Our Friend

A queen bee lays each egg in a six-sided cell filled with the pollen and honey that will nourish the unborn offspring. She then seals the top with wax. Twenty-one days later, its food supply exhausted, the newborn wrestles, squirms, and strains to break the wax seal and emerge alive. The opening it makes in exiting is so narrow that it rubs off the membrane covering its wings, enabling it to fly. Should the wax seal be opened prematurely, the bee will emerge without a struggle—unable to fly since the membrane remains on the wings. It is soon stung to death by other bees.

Don't we invariably view adversities as obstacles? Instead, they are often like the opening torn by the exertion of the bee: the means to growth. They can uncover resources, develop strengths, and stimulate tenacity we would not otherwise have. They can bring us a joy equal to their distress. As John Bunyan wrote, "They can appear as the lion to Samson: roaring and gnashing; but, when subdued, full of honey."

God wisely designed a specific struggle to give the common bee new life. We can trust him to provide for each of us the struggles best suited to bring us rewards, not penalties. If we obey him even when it is difficult, we will grow and stretch. Perhaps we need to ask ourselves, "Do we want to walk, or fly?"

AGING — compensations
2 Samuel 19:31–37; 2 Timothy 4:8

We Can Remember What They Are

Speaking with acquaintances at a party, Clare Boothe Luce averred that "old age has its compensations." Then, giving Hollywood director George Cukor a pat on the arm, she cracked, "The trouble is, George, that you and I have forgotten what they are."

Hardly true for her or anyone else reaching advanced years, especially when old people are consistently older than yesteryear. According to Blue Cross, gains in longevity offer a ten year grace period, meaning that old age now starts at seventy-five, not sixty-five years of age. People now participate actively in sports into their eighties and beyond.

Cicero wrote a beautiful treatise on aging when he was sixty-two. Cato referred to it when he was eighty-four. The treatise's main defense is as adequate now as when written: Age does not necessarily render people unfit for work—or the body feeble or deprived of pleasures. Cicero claimed that only as a harbinger of death did advancing age pose an insoluble dilemma.

Anyone fifty plus can cheer the great orator. Christian seniors, especially, accept advancing years with expectation, for they moderate their longings for the things of this world and quicken their appreciation of spiritual graces. That spiritual anchor, long before thrown into Heaven to secure their soul, remains firmly intact. In undisguised eagerness they yearn to share God's presence as they have for so long shouldered God's purpose. They meet their future with eyes glistening and faces aglow.

AGING — welcomed
Proverbs 16:31; Colossians 1:13

Where Age Is Esteemed

No differences exist between Eastern and Western cultures like their respective attitudes towards aging. In China, when a person asks the "glorious age" of another, the younger apologize for their youth. The older offer condolences and seek to assure the younger that they still have a "glorious future" by becoming elderly. The older people get, the more enthusiastic they are about it; those fifty and beyond are accorded special respect. Fifty is magical to the Chinese.

Conversely, many American workers regret their fiftieth birthday for they suddenly become expendable. Long periods of unemployment often follow, with underemployment their fate. A rediscovery of Corinna Lindon Smith's perceptions on aging would profit us. Quoting George Santayana that the reward of aging "is to have expressed all that is latent in us," Corinna wrote that we never discharge all that is latent within us while our mind functions.

How much truer for Christian seniors! They can't ever retire from their church and their faith. They have a Samson-like strength in their convictions and can responsibly discharge obligations in local churches, on mission fields, and in Bible colleges. God brought us into the kingdom to serve until death. Until then he encourages us to continue touching human hurts and helping others.

AGING — vigor

Deuteronomy 34:7; Luke 2:36–38

Gray Can Be Golden

Quoting *The People's Almanac*, *Parade Magazine* listed a few people with major achievements after age eighty. Among them were David Eugene Ray of Tennessee, who at ninety-nine learned to read; twin sisters Kin Narita and Gin Kanie, who at ninety-nine recorded a hit single in Japan; and Paul Spangler, who at ninety-two completed his fourteenth Marathon.

Advertisers are getting the elderly in focus. The cosmetic company Maybelline, Inc. targets older women by offering a Revitalizing line and Age-Denying makeup. McDonald's offers seniors a 25 cent cup of coffee and hires 40,000 of them in its restaurants. Schumacher and Company's *Understanding Living Trusts* has sold 150,000 copies since being issued in 1990. *Modern Maturity*, the publication of the American Association of Retired Persons has an annual circulation of 22.5 million copies. The 64 million people in America over 55 hold $800 billion in their reserve—about 77 percent of the nation's assets—and most of them are willing to spend. With $300 billion in ready cash, they buy over 40 percent of the new cars and half the luxury cars sold.

Indeed, depending on our lifestyle, habits, diet, and exercise, old age need not be gloomy and disagreeable. Instead, we can say with Adam to Orlando in *As You Like It*, "Therefore my age is as a lusty winter. Frosty but kindly."

Can the church afford to ignore these senior citizens? Aren't we compelled to make special efforts to evangelize and disciple those whose very age offers substantial advantages to God's kingdom?

ALCOHOL — weak penalty

Proverbs 20:1; Titus 2:1–3

The Unpunished Sin

Drunk drivers fare poorly in other countries: in France, a loss of license, jail time and fines; in South Africa, 10 years in jail or $10,000 fine or both; in Sweden or Finland, jail and hard labor. Contrast that to the $677 fine levied against Joan Kennedy on July 4, 1988, when she was arrested for driving under the influence of alcohol. Oh, yes, she did lose her license for forty-five days and had to attend an alcohol-education program.

American laws against driving under the influence remain ridiculously understated. Drunk drivers who kill innocent motorists and pedestrians receive three to six years in prison, with parole likely much earlier, even though alcohol is linked to 94,000 deaths a year, costing society $85 billion.

Yet, beer continues to be a major advertiser in sports, accounting for 10 to 12 percent of all network sports revenue. In 1988, Anheuser-Busch sponsored broadcasts for all but one major league team, eighteen NFL teams, twenty-two

NBA franchises, and thirteen domestic NFL franchises, not counting other less significant sporting events. What an uneasy marriage: something that debilitates the body and mind sponsors activities where healthy minds and bodies are essential.

Christians hold no common ground on drinking; some feel it is acceptable on social occasions. But I wonder—with the enervating effects of alcohol so obvious, combined with a transportation system that renders even moderate drinking potentially deadly, isn't abstention a better witness from those who claim to be controlled by God's Spirit?

ALTERNATIVES — none good
Numbers 23:6–10; 2 Corinthians 7:5

No Good Choice

General George Washington's army was likely to be destroyed if it attempted to attack the British late that December, 1776. Yet the men would certainly desert if it cowered in encampments west of the Delaware River. In an anguish of indecision the general wrote to his brother Augustine "of the perplexity of my situation. No man . . . ever had a greater choice of difficulties, and less means to extricate himself from them."

Tom Dooley told of an old Vietnamese man climbing aboard the USS Montague from a transporter. He climbed up the steps to the ship and stopped. Looking terrified at the spectacle of boarding an American vessel, he then looked below at the swells—and froze in terror of the sea. There was nothing behind for him and only terror before.

Russians, too, had little choice in the opening months of the German offensive in 1941. If they stayed to defend their homes, Stalin's minions accused them of having German loyalties. If they fled the Wermacht, Stalin's minions considered them cowards and ordered them shot or exiled.

Sometimes we see only distress one way, gloom another, and darkness all around. Questions multiply and answers vanish. When that happens, faith in God provides moral courage that is strong as a steel cable, spiritual intuition that is sensitive as a taut violin string, and spiritual perception that is penetrating as a laser beam. Little by little, possibilities emerge—out of the gloom, glory; out of the misery, the miraculous. We outlive uncertainty, which cannot last, by trusting God's grace, which cannot end.

AMBITION — changing one's lifestyle
Judges 9:1–3, 22–23; James 3:16

Even Changing One's Lifestyle

Hating injustice and greed, Sam Rayburn went to Congress to fight for the rights of the poor and underprivileged. He accepted the challenge of opposing the

Interests—railroads and banks. He made many speeches his first six years, attacking the enemies of those he represented.

Then a strange thing happened. The verbal congressman became a silent representative, making very few speeches in the next twelve years. His first speech had been two hours long, but in the next dozen years he said so little people thought him mute—all because of his zeal to be Speaker of the House of Representatives! Since the Speaker was elected on the basis of popularity, not just seniority, Sam needed friends, not enemies. To avoid making enemies, he stopped making speeches. Waiting in silence almost killed him, his sense of justice being so keen. Greater than his need to speak for the underprivileged was his personal need to be Speaker, where he figured to do more for more people.

The craving to be someone or something can change even our lifestyle and personality. It can motivate us to habits we would not otherwise have and to choices we would otherwise reject. It doesn't have to make us worse, but it definitely makes us different. Christians understand. Their ambition to be Christlike changes their vocabularies, interests, friendships, goals, reactions, and desires. All to become something that makes them like the Someone they love more than life itself.

ANCIENTS — urban society
Isaiah 40:6–8; Acts 17:16–18

Cities Way Back Then

The great cities of the Roman Empire built spectacular public works, including magnificent streets. One in Ephesus was thirty-six feet wide and nearly six hundred yards long, offering ready access to the roofed colonnades on either side; in Alexandria, the Canopic Way was two hundred feet wide and over three miles long; in Antioch of Syria one street was two miles long, complete with street lamps. Persian kings in six century B.C. established a Royal Road, which was useful into the nineteenth century of our own era. Eleven hundred stations guarded the 1,677 miles from Susa to Sardis that royal thoroughbreds raced across in seven days. In meso-America, temples and stepped pyramids soared ten stories high. In Peru, 3,500 years ago, Inca architects built a three-story warehouse bigger than a football field.

In Greece and the Greek-speaking world many libraries contained hundreds of thousands of books. Literacy was widespread. Nearly all townspeople and even slaves could read. Aristophanes left 54 plays, Aeschylus at least 70, and Livy's history ran to 142 volumes. In China, Polo noted that all wealthy or influential citizens had indoor baths and that the Chinese used coal instead of wood to heat their homes.

In great leaps forward one generation builds what the next dismantles. God has warned us of our transience—and encouraged us with his immutability. When will we learn to accept our eventual failure and to trust his ultimate victory?

ANIMALS — man's best friend
Deuteronomy 4:25–26; 1 John 4:1–3

Man's Best Friend

Sensitive-nosed Labrador retrievers, impatiently pulling at the leash, identify pin-hole leaks in underground gas, oil, and chemical pipelines worldwide. If technicians suspect a leak, engineers pump a foul-smelling chemical into the suspect section, then let the dogs track the line. The wet-nosed detectives run until they detect the chemical, even if it is eighteen feet underground. They stop when they smell a leak. Their tails go up, their ears stiffen, and their mouths close. These dogs can detect leaks from lines buried under six feet of water and five feet of earth.

Winston, a yellow Labrador, became famous in Orange County, California, for sniffing out drugs. He found drugs hidden in airtight suitcases, behind bathroom vanities, in car chassis, and in stash houses where dealers had mothballed the place to thwart him. One dealer hoped to outwit Winston by stashing his drugs in suitcases full of garlic. In his brief career, Winston helped confiscate over $52 million in the deadly triad of cocaine, heroin, and marijuana. He also won twelve official commendations.

God orders his people to have a sensitized awareness of false teachers and their doctrines. Since we accept the Bible as God's authoritative Word, we heed God's warning. We don't want to turn into heresy-hunters, always looking for something to condemn, but since everyone has to stand somewhere and since we believe God's Word is true, we stand on it, and we judge all values, teachings, and behavior by it.

ANIMALS — their instinct to save
Judges 16:28; Luke 23:34

More Than a Friend

When Rob and Laurie Roberts took Bo, their nine-month-old Labrador retriever, on a boat ride down the Colorado River, they didn't know he would save Laurie's life. When their sixteen-foot metal boat flipped in swift waters, Rob was swept downstream, but Laurie was caught under the craft. Bo broke free from the under-tow, surfaced, then dived back underwater to grab his mistress by her hair and drag her to the surface.

Sean Callahan and his brother Erin were playing with their poodle, Leo, along the banks of the Guadalupe River in August, 1984. They threw a stick toward the river, and Leo scrambled after it. Suddenly, Sean screamed. Leo heard it and saw a rattlesnake coiled near the boys, ready to strike. The dog instantly leaped between the snake and the boy as the snake uncoiled. Leo took six savage strikes from the six-foot diamondback, standing in place and accepting the punishment until his young master could escape. Undaunted by his ordeal, Leo was later inducted into the Texas Pet Hall of Fame.

God's Son came to save mankind from sin and eternal death. Obsessed with that purpose, he let nothing interfere. He subordinated all his activities to it and devoted himself to whatever expedited it. That purpose prompted him to throw himself between us and God's wrath, taking the punishment we deserved. It caused him to dive into death and plunder Satan of those he claimed could never live again.

APOLOGY — unusual
Ezra 10:2–4; Matthew 5:25–26

Even in Wartime

On April 1, 1945, in the Taiwan Strait, the U.S. submarine *Queenfish* fired multiple torpedoes at what the ship's radar suggested was a Japanese destroyer. When the sub later pulled aboard the only survivor, the captain learned he had sunk the *Awa Maru,* a Japanese cargo ship the U.S. State Department had guaranteed safe passage for a round-trip from Japan to Singapore. With white crosses painted on her hull and two thousand tons of relief supplies for American soldiers in Japanese prison camps in her hold, the *Awa Maru* was to pass unharmed through the gauntlet of submarines swarming the depths in her path. The *Queenfish* never received a clear version of that order.

On April 17, the U.S. State Department and the U.S. Navy issued an official apology to the Japanese government, offering to replace the *Awa Maru* with a similar ship. It didn't have to be done because the war ended four months later.

Most of our apologies will not be so dramatic, but, when we are wrong, they should be as direct. We should assume total responsibility for our mistakes and offer restitution if at all possible. Accepting more than our share of guilt and allowing another more than his share of innocence disarms the egotism that won't and empowers the humility that will . . . apologize.

APPEARANCES — lift our morale
Numbers 17:8–11; John 7:24

Booster for Morale

Agnes Keith gave away most of her cosmetics when she first went into captivity in Borneo, thinking them an irrelevant luxury. For a while it didn't matter. Then, at Kuching, she discovered her mistake. All the women found makeup necessary for their morale. In time, Keith wrote, face powder sold for $10 a teaspoon, lipstick couldn't be found at any price, and cold cream was nearly as scarce and precious. Often, the ruder and simpler life becomes, the less it takes to rehabilitate our confidence. In the internment camps, where every enemy tactic brutalized and simplified life, small, apparently superficial items enabled the women to preserve their self-esteem.

God understands our need to have the basics of clothing, food, and shelter. Deprived of them, we still live, but only marginally and subsistently. God will not deny us the basics. In fact, he promises to provide them for us if we seek his will. He does insist, however, that we avoid making those basics into essentials, thinking that they make us complete. He alone is essential to us. Let us bless any circumstance that develops our awareness of helplessness without him.

AUTHORITY — be careful which you follow
Deuteronomy 18:18; John 8:24

Good or Bad Information

Around 200 B.C. Eratosthenes measured the circumference of the world to within a 5 percent error. Ptolemy, A.D. 120–150, reduced that measurement by one-third. Columbus appropriated Ptolemy's figures when he studied maps for his voyage. As it turned out, God had placed the American land mass the distance from Europe that Columbus thought Cathay would be.

Columbus was fortunate, even though he followed the wrong authority. Not every traveler or pilgrim would be. In 1846, the Donner party accepted the word of Landsford Hastings, who promised a shortcut to California over his Cutoff. Having traveled the Hastings Cutoff himself on his way east, veteran mountain man Jim Clymer urged the Donners to stay on the regular route when they consulted with him at Fort Laramie that summer. Choosing to ignore his advice, they followed Hastings and became casualties of horrendous misdirection in the mountains and massive snows in the Sierra. Half the ninety people in their camp died by following the wrong authority.

How this challenges those who seek a way to heaven but accept the promise of someone other than Jesus to get there. Jesus said that he is the only way anyone can get to heaven. By the mere process of elimination, how many of the other purported ways can be true? If you follow the wrong directions on a trip, you may get lost but you will likely be safe. If you take the wrong direction through life, however, you will be lost forever—you will forfeit heaven.

AUTHORITY — God is absolute
Isaiah 1:18–19; Hebrews 7:22

No Input Allowed

The Golden Hill area of San Diego enjoys a wide divergence of cultures—Asians, Blacks, Hispanics, and Whites. However, the forced intimacy in apartments and ancient houses often irritates personal relationships. The Golden Hill Mediation Center serves as a clearing house between disputants before they reach the police station or courts. Volunteer mediators, carefully screened and selected from numerous applicants, strive to find a middle ground where both parties can accept less than each wanted. Their 89 percent success rate proves that most people would rather solve conflicts than prolong or litigate them.

Mediation works fine when resolving differences in human relationships. Applying this principle where unrepentant humanity has a difference with God, however, has a 100 percent failure rate. We delude ourselves if we think we can discuss the matter of our insubordination with God as though we were his equals; as though we had any input into the agreement; as though God had left open a discussion about it; as if he had suddenly determined not to rule the universe! God makes no deals and strikes no bargains. He makes the rules, and we must abide by them. He establishes the conditions, and we must live with them. He determines truth, and we can take it or leave it—that or nothing!

AWARDS — for what true purpose?
Psalm 2:7–9; Ephesians 1:10

Still Here but Changed

Rhodes scholarships were originally designed by Cecil Rhodes as a means of reestablishing British hegemony over the earth. An unreconstructed imperialist, Rhodes envisioned all the world as British subjects. His will directed that his massive estate be used to expedite his dream, in particular recovering the United States for the Crown. Fortunately, the trustees of the estate revoked his political views and have awarded the scholarship to anyone who is academically qualified.

While Cecil Rhodes had a dream and the resources to fulfill it, he had the wrong intention. God never decreed that the world should be British. He has decreed that not only humanity but the entire universe be brought to renewal through Jesus Christ. Since God has both the resources and the intention, his will shall be accomplished: Through Jesus Christ everything in heaven and on earth will be brought to complete unity.

AWARDS — for outstanding achievement
Malachi 3:17; 1 Corinthians 15:51–57

Different from the Rest of Us

Forty middle-aged men sat on metal chairs on the Capitol steps in Sacramento, California, that January day, 1984. Jimmy Doolittle, Pappy Boyington, and William Stockdale were among them. All forty received the same prestigious award: a reflective automobile license stamped with four distinctive words, Congressional Medal of Honor, and the number of their plate.

The oldest recipient, ninety-six-year-old Philip Katz, received the first plate. He saved a wounded comrade while under machine gun fire in 1918. The youngest, thirty-five-year-old Richard Penry, won his medal in Viet Nam for keeping his badly mauled company in fighting condition.

Massed flags snapped in the chilly breeze as the honored recipients sat and listened to a recitation of their bravery. Only forty men received the coveted license plates in California. Others, their service as redoubtable as a Churchill tank, went unheralded; they received nothing. Serving faithfully from love and duty is pearl enough in their oyster.

Although millions of God's people will never be commended here on earth, they will certainly receive their rewards after the Lord's return. When they stand where no human eye has looked and possess what no human hand has touched, they will be honored beyond human imagination with Christ's sumptuous provisions.

BARGAIN — mutual
Deuteronomy 28:1–6; Ephesians 6:5–8

Both for Failure and Success

In *All's Well That Ends Well*, the king agrees to try Helena's remedy but demands her death if her cure kills him. She agrees. "If I break time, or flinch in property (delay beyond the appointed time or fall short in performance) of what I spoke, unpitied let me die. And well deserv'd. Not helping, death's my fee." What will the king give her if she succeeds? "What do you want?" he asks. "A husband," she replies. Not from royalty, for her humble position would not allow that. "But such a one, thy vassal, whom I know is free for me to ask, thee to bestow."

Sounds like good management-employee relations. If employees cannot deliver, they should be fired. If they can and do, they should be rewarded. The late business guru, W. Edward Deming, suggested a principle to produce both: stress excellence in quality control during manufacturing, not inspection of inferior products after manufacturing.

God always excels human standards. He offers mercy to the frailties of his servants, forgiving their misdeeds, then provides them magnificent and all-out-of-proportion rewards when they succeed. Not only do we not die for our sins (as Helena would have for her mistakes), but we live at an exalted level far beyond our station, in a life we could never deserve, in a place we could never merit. Why would anyone refuse to labor for such a master, in such a kingdom?

BEAUTY — inability to grasp
Joshua 7:1; Matthew 26:14–16

In the Eye of the Beholder

The world values Leonardo da Vinci's *Last Supper* as an art classic. In the refractory where he painted the masterpiece, however, the friars thought less of it. They cut a door through the painting—at the apostles' legs—to make easier access to their kitchen.

Who can grasp the trivialities of the human mind in the presence of uncommon excellence? How could men from the Gadarenes order Jesus to leave their territory when before them sat, lucid, clothed, and self-controlled, a man previously wild with unchainable violence? How could reasonable, religious people demand the death of a righteous man and ask for the release of a murderer? How could men play craps at the foot of the cross while God's Son died on it? How can some Christians not see the value of winning people to Christ for the cost involved in reaching them? We could rail at the friars in the refractory if a taunting voice didn't question our own moral and spiritual anomalies.

BEAUTY — a necessity
Job 40:6–10; Luke 2:9, 13

Beauty Amidst Harshness

The blue poppy grows at 16,000 feet in the Tibetan highlands. It is a beautiful flower growing out of prickly cacti—in the midst of harshness, delicacy. To whiff the aroma one must risk pain. Faithful to the curse of Eden, nature produces thorns, but long after we have forgotten the thorns, the sight and smell of the flower remains.

The soft strength of beauty compensates for the hard homeliness so often seen in a fallen world. Often, stunning beauty exists where only wild brutes live and humans rarely visit. That God could waste wilderness magnificence on unappreciative wild animals proves that he created it to make an unmistakable statement about his resources, wisdom, and genius.

It is native to us, this need to see, enjoy, and create beauty, C. S. Lewis wrote. Composers write symphonies, authors write books, and artists paint pictures to sate their appetite for and need to create beauty. Even here, even now, in this corrupt world, God recognizes our need and allows modest success in fulfilling it, though he steadfastly refuses to satisfy us now. From us, he withholds the conclusion of our search. "But," Lewis wrote, "all the leaves of the New Testament are rustling with the rumor that it will not always be so" (*The Weight of Glory*).

BEGINNINGS — great events from small beginnings
Haggai 2:3–9; Matthew 13:31–32

Small Beginnings

Proofreading W. E. Vine's *Expository Dictionary of New Testament Words* gave F. F. Bruce a profound appreciation of the New Testament text. This single encounter motivated him to a deeper study into the origins of the New Testament, a field in which he became a scholar nonpareil. As an atheist, studying under an atheist, C. S. Lewis bought and read George MacDonald's book *Phantastes*. He hadn't the slightest notion at the time that this single reading would begin his conversion to Christ.

In 1918, Cameron Townsend sold Spanish Bibles in Guatemala. One man, who did not read Spanish, asked him, "If your God is so great, why can't he speak my language?" From that single question evolved the Wycliffe Bible Translators, a mission organization that to this day continues Townsend's work of translating the Bible into every language possible.

While living in immorality, drunkenness, and deception, George Müller and a friend attended an evening service in a layman's home. The group sang, prayed, and read Scripture and a sermon. Insignificant as all this was, it marked the beginning of Müller's new life in Christ and of his orphanage work in Bristol, England to thousands of homeless children.

We should never underestimate small beginnings—we never know when they will grow large. Jesus was born in a stable, unheralded and unrecognized. The morning after, life resumed in Bethlehem as if nothing different had happened. And only one thing had: a baby had been born and in the least auspicious place. But oh the beginning-without-end that occurred in that single birth!

BELIEF — understand clearly
Ezekiel 3:6; 2 Corinthians 1:17

Understanding What We Believe

Before he entered the ministry, and while a practicing attorney, Charles Finney attended services where the minister consistently taught opposing doctrines. In the same sermon he would urge people to repent, then say that repentance came only from the Holy Spirit. Or he would say that sinners could not be saved until they believed, then add that they could not believe until the Holy Spirit changed them.

In private conversations Finney found the pastor mystified by his own sermons. Little wonder he confused others; he confessed he had never resolved the differences in his own mind. He preached only what he had heard others *say*, not what he had *concluded* personally.

Personal acquaintance with Christ necessarily precedes a dynamic witness to others. All those charged with teaching the gospel, in whatever capacity, need to clarify for themselves areas of doctrine still incomplete from neglect or indecision. Sharply-focused messengers communicate sharply-defined messages.

BIBLE — a work of art
Amos 4:4–5; Matthew 15:1–6

More Than a Work of Art

Sotheby's of London auctioned the *Gospels of Henry the Lion* for $11.7 million. Henry founded the cities of Munich and Lubeck, ruled Saxony and Bavaria, and helped create the German nation. A monk in the Benedictine abbey at Helmarshausen created the masterpiece. It contains 226 leaves of golden velum with forty-one full-page miniatures and thousands of brilliant, colorful illustrations. The West Germans who bought the work saw it as a cultural object—representative of twelfth-century German craftsmanship.

Yet the price paid for the Lion's *Gospels* represents only its artistic value. Whether you pay $21.95 or $11.7 million for a Bible, the message is the essence, not the physical appearance. The volume purchased from Sotheby's went on permanent public display at a research library near Brunswick where it could only be seen, not touched by ordinary hands. Those who do have direct access to it are undoubtedly so intrigued by the art that they pay no attention to the script.

What a tragedy, for it will change no lives that way. Better a marked, frayed copy of Scripture than the Lion masterpiece. The torn, worn pages of a Bible are far greater testimony to its true value than the $11.7 million spent on Henry's *Gospels*.

BIBLE — cuts to the bone
Genesis 11:5–9; 1 Timothy 1:8–11

The Heart of the Matter

Harry Hopkins served President Franklin Roosevelt in many capacities before and during World War II, even meeting with Churchill and Stalin as Roosevelt's representative. He also represented the president in meetings with the Chiefs of Staff, participating in strategy sessions. Churchill held him in the highest regard, saying that he played a decisive role in the war. He particularly valued Hopkins' impatience with equivocation and irrelevant detail, a virtue that inspired the great Englishman to call him "Lord root of the matter."

The great value of biblical faith is its instinctive ability to offer permanent, unchanging models of belief and behavior. The Bible always gets to the root of the matter. Forthright, lucid, and unerringly legible, it leaves no doubt about our fallen spiritual condition and God's power to renew it. It leaves no doubt about what sin is and God's threats against it; nor about the mess we are in and exactly how we can get out. Indefinite possibilities and suppositions lie outside the Bible—in it is the clear, the definite, the unmistakable.

BIBLE — evidences of divine origin
Exodus 8:18–19; 2 Corinthians 13:8

No Counterfeit

All currencies need protection from counterfeiting. The United States Treasury employs a variety of safeguards to prevent wily counterfeiters from debasing our currency. While the paper's content is officially secret, it is actually 75 percent cotton and 25 percent linen, with red and blue silk fibers. Our currency also has several hidden security features: a fluorescent quality, a magnetic ink, an almost invisible thread on the left side of the larger notes, and an engraved United States of America around the face of larger bills. The one procedure that makes it nearly impossible to reproduce is the final step of manufacture. A machine using high-pressure rollers sandwiches the sheets of currency between them, providing a uniform thickness that cannot be imitated without the machine.

God's Word is like our currency. Its worth depends on its ability to protect itself from imitation and counterfeiting. God has taken extreme measures to insure that the Bible can never be reproduced by any other power, regardless how clever or beguiling it may be. The Bible has infallible built-in safeguards that protect it against any spiritual counterfeits: its accuracy in comparison to other writings, its fulfilled prophecies, its scientific accuracy, and its historicity.

BIBLE — faith must accompany listening
Numbers 14:29, 31; Hebrews 3:12

Faith in God's Word

In *The Chronicles of Narnia*, Uncle Andrew hears a voice singing during the night. He knows it is a song but does not like the sound because of the feeling it gives him. When the sun rises and he sees that a lion is singing, Uncle Andrew says it is no song at all, but just a roaring—like a lion in the zoo. The more beautifully the Lion sings, the more Andrew convinces himself it is only a louder roaring. Soon, all he hears is roaring. When Aslan calls Narnia awake, Uncle Andrew hears only a snarl, not intelligible words.

People repeat Andrew's mistake when they refuse to unite faith with Christ's message. Like the pillar of fire, God's Word illuminates those who look to it for deliverance and shrouds in darkness those who see it as an obstacle to their goals. The same pillar, the same Word—enlightening some, confounding others. What will it be for us?

BIBLE — history proves it true
Isaiah 51:6, 16; Acts 2:42

No Need to Change

Random House recalled 60,000 copies of a biography of the late heiress Barbara Hutton when errors about a physician who treated her were discovered. The returned copies were destroyed. The author, a respected writer and poet whose other works revealed solid research, misfired with this biography. He claimed that the doctor had been Hutton's private physician from the early 1940s to the 1970s and that he prescribed excessive drugs for Hutton in 1943. This was impossible since the doctor did not graduate from medical school until 1954 and only completed his residency in 1960. So much for the researchers, references, and writings of human authors. Even the best make mistakes—some create disasters.

The Bible never faces this problem. Centuries after its origin, it maintains the integrity of its proclamations, denials, promises, and warnings. It makes no mistakes, misnames no villains, forgets no heroes, mistakes no town or place. It is exactly what God wanted said, so it never has to change, be recalled, reverified, or checked for accuracy even when research uncovers more information. The Bible takes its stand, makes its point, and changes nothing. Time passes, knowledge increases, mores change, fads come and go, political views vary, but God's Word remains unchanged. While all else falters and alters, it remains inflexibly constant.

BIBLE — insists we face reality
2 Samuel 11:27; Galatians 2:11–13

Just as They Are

When the English managed to sabotage the German ship *Bremen,* Joseph Goebbels saw it as a national disgrace. But how were German officials going to explain it to the people? They finally agreed to issue an arrogantly complacent report that politically disarmed the incident.

Changing nomenclature in a disaster or crisis is a favorite gambit of politicians and generals. If you are Japan in the 1930s and you want to invade China but don't want to use that term, you simply refer to the aggression as the China Incident. All the horrors of war will be lost in that harmless word *incident.* Nietzsche is right: When our memory clashes with our conscience over a matter we wish had not occurred, memory often succeeds in silencing conscience.

While this may be true for human judgment, it is not true for the Bible. It forthrightly deals with life, calling it what it is, whether good or bad, ugly or beautiful. Its heroes are no more exempt from stricture than are its villains. It does not gloss over Abraham's lie or David's adultery, making them less serious, because they are so important to the scheme of redemption. The Bible has no problem at all in letting sin be sin and righteousness be righteousness. The purpose of Scripture is not to glorify mankind but to demonstrate the work of the righteous God among mankind.

BIBLE — message never revised
Psalm 119:89; John 14:26

Nothing New at All

Literary scholars in New York were delighted when Herman Melville's personal letters, short story fragments, and the first draft of a novel were found in 1983. They considered it one of the most important literary discoveries in a quarter century. In 1945 novelist Graham Greene wrote a story called "The Tenth Man" about a wealthy Frenchman who escaped execution by having someone shot in his place. The book had been mimeographed and archived by MGM. It resurfaced in 1984 to enthusiastic acclaim.

Some religious people think that discoveries about God are still being made through special revelations or in long-hidden stones, plates, or manuscripts. They want us to believe that the Bible contains part, but not all, of God's message, that he periodically squeezes out more information, uncovering himself in bits and pieces.

Nonsense. Any addition to God's Word as constituted in the Bible is Satan's psychology of fabrication—as mythical as a griffin and just as useless.

BIBLE — most effective in original form
Exodus 20:3; Mark 2:21–22

Let the Word Speak

A team restoring da Vinci's *Last Supper* in 1981 found original details in the masterpiece that had been hidden or altered through the years. The dark windows behind the figures were actually finely detailed tapestry. Orange slices, unseen for centuries, materialized on the plates, as did a golden thread on the rims of the glasses. Even Simon Peter's beard grew longer with the brush of each restorationist.

The same masquerade has been perpetrated on the Bible and Christianity across the centuries. So many books, creeds, and traditions exist that propose to explain the Bible or to be as authoritative as the Bible that many people mistake them for the Bible. So many practices and beliefs exist in Christendom today that were conspicuously absent in the beginning. Whatever the intent, these additions can mask the glory and cloak the blinding luminosity of Scripture and biblical Christianity. God's promise of power comes only through his Word, not through human additions to it.

BIBLE — it remains
Deuteronomy 4:2; John 12:47–48

God's Sole Authority

A disastrous earthquake struck Tokyo and Yokohama in 1923. A quarter of a million people died and over half a million homes and buildings were destroyed. One of the few large buildings left intact was the Imperial Hotel in Tokyo—the creation of Frank Lloyd Wright. An official in the Japanese government cabled congratulations to Wright because his hotel stood, a monument to his genius.

God "does not take back his words," Isaiah wrote (31:2 NIV). In that sentence is the encouragement God offers the world. Whatever else changes or collapses, God's Word remains stalwart and inviolable. Each generation may reassess its tradition and rewrite its opinions, but God's Word remains inflexibly written, unchanging, unchangeable. Other writings may speak only to their time—the Bible speaks to all time.

BIBLE — in plain language
Deuteronomy 30:11–14; 2 Corinthians 4:1–2

No Secret Codes Here

The *Voynich Manuscript* is a 204-page volume in an unknown alphabet. It was purchased in 1912 by a British book dealer, who gave copies to anyone wanting to decipher it. Many tried and as many failed. Finally, in 1921, a professor from the University of Pennsylvania said he had broken the manuscript's code: it was the work of Roger Bacon, the thirteenth-century inventor. Though his findings made him a celebrity among scholars at the time, later evidence discredited his theory. In 1969 the manuscript was given to Yale University, where it remains, an enigma to all who view it.

God revealed himself with unmistakable clarity, so anyone could understand him. No one can complain that we do not know what is true, right, or moral. The Bible has made itself much too plain for anyone to claim ignorance. It speaks powerfully of judgment against sin but just as forcefully promises forgiveness of sin. No, spiritual ignorance cannot be excused, nor can it be explained on the basis of the Bible's difficulty. The problem is that while the Bible remains a yearly best-seller, it goes largely unread! God has purposely written his book to enchant all levels of intelligence and spiritual growth—what he has *written* demands to be *read*.

BIBLE — no alterations to truth
Psalm 119:152; 2 Peter 1:16

The Bible Has Never Been Changed

All speeches on the floor of Congress or in committee meetings become part of the Congressional Record. But you can't always be sure that what was originally spoken or decided will be in the Record. This is due to the exercise of one of the most rigidly guarded privileges of House and Senate members: the right to "revise and extend" their remarks. It was granted originally to allow minor technical corrections in bills and speeches. Congressmen now use it to delete erroneous statements and claims and to add to or subtract from bills that are passed.

The Bible's author wrote and, having written his record, never changed a word. He is never embarrassed by an untimely remark; he never apologizes for anything he said. He never said anything in haste and, consequently, never has to repent in leisure. What is written stands written. We may teach all that God has revealed through Christ in his Word—nothing less and absolutely nothing more.

BIBLE — continual refreshing
Ezra 7:10; Luke 1:46–55

That Endless Stream

The earliest settlers of the West Texas Hill Country inherited a land that grew lush grasses and giant oaks. Their incontinent grazing and farming, however, dried the rivers, denuded the soil of the grasses, and allowed cedars to proliferate. For years the land died under the hard toil imposed on it. Then in 1928, when Hill Country farmers began clearing cedars from the land, they noticed a curious result. The ground in certain areas first grew damp, then soggy, and finally gave birth to springs of water. For two generations the cedars had gulped all that water and deprived the settlers of using the soil. After clearing away the trees, water ran so faithfully in some places that not even a nine-month drought diminished its flow.

The Bible makes a promise to us: If we remove any hindrance to spending time with God's Word, it will pump endless streams of spiritual grace into our souls. It will become, as Jesus said, a spring of water welling up to everlasting life. We may add other sources to develop mental and social graces, or to develop technical or scientific skills, but we should let the Bible alone develop spiritual stamina and illumination for our lives.

BIBLE — endless spiritual insight
Deuteronomy 11:18–22; 2 Timothy 3:14–17

It Never Grows Old

The poet Wallace Stevens was inspired to write thirty-three meditations on *The Man with a Blue Guitar*, each a different interpretation of the painting.

General George Custer spoke in awe of the seemingly endless central plains, echoing the feelings of numerous travelers as far back as Coronado's explorations: The plains were a series of undulating hills, like stationary waves of a vast sea; they rolled in endless procession to infinity.

All who study the Bible experience a similar wonder. The Word seems so simple, but it has the deceptive depth of clear water. Its apparent message to us, while very true, is soon multiplied by other messages, just as true and complementing the first. God gave us a book that has never changed since written, yet it continues to yield new insights as we mature spiritually.

Even if you study all your life through every book of the Bible, when you finish you will say with Joseph Parker (after twenty-five years of preaching from every text of the Bible) that you are essentially at the first chapter, the first verse of Genesis—you have yet to begin.

BIBLE — spiritual engineer
Jeremiah 6:16; Acts 5:41–42

Back to God's Word

In the early American West, mountain men trapped beaver to near extinction. Strip mining, mineral exploration, and overgrazing multiplied the ecosystem's disaster. In southwestern Wyoming, nearly all of the once-thriving trout streams dried up from mismanagement by well-intentioned people. A solution was to put beavers to work along meager waterways. Invariably, meadows began to grow for hundreds of feet along streams surrounding beaver dams, preventing erosion and slowing spring runoff. It was an ingeniously simple idea: Put the original earth engineers to work. Give them the tools—in this case, trees—and let the beavers follow their instincts to build dams.

The same is true spiritually. Humanity casts aside scriptural values to establish their own: living together replaces marriage, military force preempts ethics, and sexual freedom displaces monogamous relationships. All of which leads into a confusing moral wilderness, begetting an eroded self-esteem, a deteriorating public spirit, and a fearful expectation of future calamity. In response, God's people call for a return to his ancient Word. Those who hear and heed God's Word find that amazing things happen. Even in the arid desert of life they find oases. Where useless concepts produced barren results, they find fruitful purpose. In an eroding intellectual ferment they find productive, verdant thought.

God had an outstanding idea when he put the beaver to work conserving the soils of earth—he had a brilliant idea when he gave the Bible as the guide, standard, and touchstone of all morality and behavior.

BIBLE — undiscovered treasure
Deuteronomy 4:6; 1 Timothy 4:13

A Rare Value

Mr. N. Hartas rummaged through an attic in northern England and found *A Hare Among Plants, with a Robin, Lizard, and Insects*—the only existing painting of sixteenth-century German artist Hans Hoffman. Aside from the accumulated grime, the painting was in fine condition and looked exceptional when cleaned. Lying within reach of the homeowners for years, the painting simply gathered dust and went unappreciated. Only when an art expert discovered it did the owners reap the financial advantage they could have enjoyed long before: $610,500.

How often the Bible suffers the same fate in millions of homes around the world. Perhaps it is kept in a safe place as the repository of family history and events, or it is placed carefully on the coffee table or mantle—always closed and unused. If we were to read it, we would find in its message of forgiveness the power to manage life confidently today and the hope to anticipate life tomorrow. We would find the wisdom to imitate the life of Christ rather than the manners of people. We would find the strength to climb to the high ground of committed discipleship and never descend, to embrace spiritual ideals and never compromise.

BLAME — casting blame on others
Psalm 52:1–3; Romans 11:32

Can't Escape It That Way

General Friedreich Fromm retained an active interest in the conspiracy against Hitler in World War II and took part in the July 20, 1944, assassination attempt. When it became clear that the plot had misfired, General Fromm tried to shift attention from himself by arresting and executing the active conspirators in the German War Ministry. Despite his efforts, however, he could not avoid being implicated and was himself arrested on July 21.

Diverting blame by censuring someone, perhaps as guilty as we, is one of the oldest and most graceless maneuvers of human nature. Adam practiced it first in the Garden, and humanity has since refined it to an art. We try to deflect attention from ourselves by implicating another, or at least to reduce our level of guilt by sharing it with another.

Fromm could not escape his guilt and was executed. We cannot escape ours, but we can be forgiven. God knows that we are better at pointing fingers than accepting responsibility, but for our own good he insists that we admit our sins and seek their forgiveness.

BOASTING — mocked by defeat
Deuteronomy 28:45–48; Luke 21:5–6

The Mighty Fall

As the great liner *Titanic* was being loaded at Southampton, England, a lady passenger stopped a deckhand who was carrying luggage aboard and asked if the ship really was unsinkable. Yes, he assured her, it was. God himself couldn't sink the great ship. Yet, an instant's brush against a North Atlantic iceberg buckled the ship's massive steel plates and ripped open her starboard side to tons of ocean water. In just two hours and forty minutes she plunged to the ocean depths with 1,500 people still aboard.

We invariably make mistakes—we certainly fail, and we will surely die. Everything on earth comes to an end: prosperity, health, life. When it all ends, only those whose boast has been in the cross of Christ will have anything to boast about.

BODY — is limited
Psalm 40:6–8; Romans 12:1

Positive Potential in Christ

Meriwether Lewis, celebrating his thirty-first birthday, confided in his diary a disappointment in not using his life to a greater advantage. He had spent too many hours indolently wasting time he should have profitably spent on worthwhile projects. On July 11, 1812, John Quincy Adams also confided in his diary a dissatisfaction with his personal life. He was then forty-five years old and moaned that indolence and infirmity had caused him to misuse and abuse his time. Interestingly, both men were even then engaged in significant careers: Lewis was undertaking his epochal journey to open up the American West; and Adams was serving as American Minister to Russia.

We understand their woes. We, too, order our body, only to have it insolently refuse our summons. We command it to feats of duty, righteousness, and virtue, only to see it buckle to grief, weariness, and temptation. Paul described his life in similar terms (Rom. 7:14–24); still, he marveled that God's creative genius, which fashioned a perfect body from the dust as a fit vessel for his image, could, in a saving grace equal to his genius, refashion and indwell that fallen body through conversion (2 Cor. 4:6–7). Christ's birth as God in the flesh forecast the positive potential for our bodies in him.

BRAIN — capacity of

Psalm 139:14; John 20:22; Luke 24:45

Coincidence or Creation

It weighs about three pounds. It is a collection of one hundred billion nerve cells and a trillion support cells. It endows us with thought, emotion, and reasoning. It is little larger than a grapefruit and in consistency resembles an undercooked custard. It is the brain. Working simultaneously at various levels, it stores facts instantly. It can even heal itself—some doctors and lawyers have been able to return to their occupations after surgery for brain tumors. Soldiers suffering head wounds in World War II scored as highly on IQ tests after their wounds as before. It is estimated that the brain can store more facts, impressions, and information than are contained in the entire nine million volumes of the Library of Congress.

How can such an organ, which faithfully and flawlessly processes millions of ideas, perceptions, and insights, be the product of evolutionary chance? Regularity, dependability, and repetition—each a feature of the human brain—are all antithetical to coincidence. The evolutionists want the benefit of an orderly brain, yet they refuse to honor the God whose great genius created it!

CHANCE — wishing for a second one
Psalm 95:7–11; Luke 9:23

Present Opportunities

Al Simmons, a baseball great of the 1920s and 1930s, fell just short of the 3,000-hit plateau—one of the sporting world's prime fraternities. He deeply regretted his failure but blamed only himself when he thought about it in later life. If only he had known as a youngster what he knew when close to retirement, how differently he would have played! On so many of those earlier days he found excuses to avoid the lineup simply because he did not want to play. Those failures cost him a place among baseball's immortals.

Each day offers to us distinctive chances, challenges, and opportunities. If we make irresolution a policy, indecision a habit, and procrastination a virtue, one day soon we will long for a past that cannot be recovered. In the twenty-four hours that make a day, we build our future. When that future arrives, what will we have built of lasting value in all those yesterdays we thought too far removed from tomorrow to be important today?

CHANGE — some things do
Genesis 3:22–24; Galatians 1:22–24

From One Age to Another

Teddy Roosevelt won a libel suit in 1913 and accepted only the minimum damages of six cents. His priority was to vindicate his reputation, not to gain financially. Apparently, Teddy had never heard of mental anguish as the basis for additional millions of dollars.

In the 1940s, the worst school problems were talking out of turn, chewing gum in class, running in the halls, disobeying the dress code, and littering. In the 1980s, the worst school problems were drug abuse, pregnancy, suicide, rape, robbery, and assault. With society's addiction to violence, the 90s could add guns and knives on campus, drive-by shootings, and stabbings.

Movie censors of the 1950s still honored God's name. Among other changes for the film *Giant*, they suggested that (1) the scene in the railroad car between

Elizabeth Taylor and Rock Hudson had to be less sexually suggestive, and (2) the expressions "good Lord," "damn," and "I wish to God" were unacceptable defamations of deity.

Society's ethical codes have certainly changed! As a major contributor to that change, contemporary media seems determined to abolish traditional values and behavior systems in favor of a galloping prurience—a high-speed elevator to despair. Yet God will never disappear, and Christians who stand solidly with the Bible against immorality will refuse to be silent; they will adhere with a firm commitment to its unchanging integrity.

CHARACTER — necessary
Ruth 3:11; John 1:47

The Essential Factor in Personality

Character and giftedness are two entirely different things. John Lord eloquently described Lord Byron's genius, for which he has been justly famous. Lord added, however, that regardless how great a person's genius, his character would throw either shadow or light on it. Byron, an undisciplined misanthrope in the throes of vicious self-destructive behavior, was no exception.

As Dwight Moody and G. Campbell Morgan drove along the roads at Northfield, Moody asked his friend to define character. After giving his reply Morgan asked Moody, "Well, what do you think it is?" "Character is what a man is in the dark," Moody replied. Indeed. May our private thoughts always be as impressive as our public lives; and whatever our giftedness, may it be excelled by a more excellent character.

CHARACTER — lack of
1 Samuel 2:12, 17, 22; John 12:4–6

The Vacuum of Inner Emptiness

Arthur Walker masterminded Russia's most damaging penetration of American military secrets in the 1970s and 1980s. The judge who sentenced him to life in prison said that he looked in vain for some redeeming feature in the man's character. Jerry Whitworth, sentenced to 365 years in prison, listened in silence as the judge said that he was a zero who believed in nothing. No amount of money received for spying can compensate for such harsh censures of a person's inner emptiness.

Yet wouldn't the same censure be true of those who carefully educate their mind while leaving their soul ignorant of spiritual realities? When God values only the person who admits his spiritual need and kneels at the cross to receive grace, would he say less of those who devote themselves to monetary, scientific, or community gain, while ignoring his existence? If Walker and Whitworth had such moral vacuums in their lives that they welcomed betrayal, what will God find in other hearts that do not know him?

CHARACTER — shows through a disguise
John 3:2; Luke 2:27–32

You Can't Hide What You Are

Joe Pistone, FBI undercover agent, posed as a mob figure for six years while penetrating leading Mafia families. After being pulled from his undercover assignment, a mobster's girlfriend shared a secret with him. She had known for a long time that he wasn't from the mob world. "You carried yourself differently," she said. "You had an air of intelligence, you know? I knew that you were more than just a thief."

When Jesus lived among us, and anyone who wanted to could get up close and personal with him, perceptive observers couldn't help but notice—he was all man, but he was something else too. A divine stateliness lurked beneath his humanity, visible in his eyes but indefinable, obvious in his demeanor but inexplicable.

CHILDREN — blessedness of
Psalm 127:3–5; Mark 9:33–37

Children Bring Joy

John Adams wrote to Thomas Jefferson pitying James Madison's childlessness. As many fathers before and since have said, Adams noted that while children often cost parents grief, anxiety, and even vexation, their very presence lightens and lengthens life.

Agnes Newton Keith would agree. It was horrible to be a mother in the Japanese internment camps—more horrible than even the mothers could say. Yet, in a way, it was heavenly too, she wrote. In the midst of that deprivation there were thirty-four reasons for staying alive—every one a child. Describing how the mothers brought all of thirty-four safely through the tragedy, Agnes added, "I said to begin with that we brought them all through alive. But perhaps they brought us through alive." Indeed, a child is someone worth living for, and the joys they bring more than compensate for the emotional, spiritual, intellectual, and economic costs of raising them.

God, too, experiences both the pain and sometime pleasure of fatherhood. But, truth to tell, if earthly fathers experienced an infinitesimal amount of the frustration and disappointment God experiences with his spiritual children, birth control would never have to be taught anywhere in the world. Governments, like the Romans under Augustus, would be paying parents to have children, not discouraging them from parenthood. Only an infinitely patient Father in Heaven could not only tolerate but love the wayward children his Son's death has acquired for him.

CHOICE — affects destiny
Deuteronomy 30:19–20; Acts 16:6–7

On the Turn of a Mere Choice

On Christmas Day, 1849, a party of twenty-seven wagons broke over a barren ridge and skidded downhill into the desolation southeast of Mt. Whitney. A scorched, tormented land burned before the pioneers. Their caravan decided to split up. One group of bachelors called Jayhawkers went north, and two families and a few single men moved south. In two or three days the Jayhawkers found their way out of the desolate valley. The other group found themselves trapped, trudging through misery day after day only to reach impassable mountains. Two of the men went for help in California. Three hundred miles later, at the nearest store, they acquired supplies and returned for the families. When the survivors finally left the valley, they looked back and muttered, "Good-bye, Death Valley"—an appropriate and lasting name.

We need to make our choices carefully, especially those that affect our moral and spiritual lives. God has determined the limits of acceptable behavior, but he gives us the freedom to accept or defy those limits. He gives us the privilege of accepting him freely or rejecting him. And while wisdom would dictate that we exercise our privilege—not our right—the choice is ours. What will it be for us: escape by grace into life or entanglement by self-will in spiritual death?

CHRIST — among us but separate from us
Isaiah 7:14; Matthew 1:23

He Didn't Forget Who He Was

For six years Joseph Pistone lived among Mafia families as an FBI undercover agent. During that time he had to feign a personal interest in the Mafia's monstrous social schemes: thievery, murder, extortion, and drug dealings. He had to produce funds for his capo (provided by the FBI through unclaimed stolen property) and had to lie for a high moral purpose—to enable the United States government to severely damage organized crime in America. From that horrifying nightmare he emerged unaltered; his personality, values, and attention to physical conditioning were intact. When his superiors finally pulled him off the job, he had no trouble leaving the role of Donnie Brasco.

Jesus came undercover to our fallen world. He stayed plenty long enough to forget why he came—but he didn't. He identified so strongly with us that he could have seen our sins as harmless pranks—but he didn't. He could have become so much a part of us as to forget who he was—but he didn't. Pistone's lifestyle said "I'll become like you." Jesus' lifestyle said "I won't become like you; I'll let everyone of you become like me."

CHRIST — the sure cure
Genesis 3:6–7; Matthew 26:14–16; 27:3–5

A Cure with No Complications

A study by the National Cancer Institute, printed in the *New England Journal of Medicine,* indicated that certain anticancer drugs could actually cause the disease they supposedly cured. In this instance, Semustine was the culprit. While it kills melanomas and malignancies of the brain, lung, and digestive tract, it also brings a high risk of leukemia at a later time. The Food and Drug Administration finally removed it from use because of its dangerous side effects. It offered the potential of a cure worse than the disease it conquered!

Christ's forgiveness—the cure for our sins—will not create worse problems for us later, cropping up in a different form of the malignant sin he first overcame. He rescues us completely from the penalty and presence of sin. When we ask Christ to eradicate the deadly spiritual pestilence, we can be absolutely sure that his cure is initially and ultimately successful.

CHRIST — came, knowing his fate
Leviticus 5:18; Luke 19:10

He Knew When He Came

Three boys were wading illegally in a deserted pond in Monroe, Louisiana. Joe Delaney, all-pro halfback of the Kansas City Chiefs, sat nearby and warned them to stay close to shore. Ignoring his words, they waded out and, moments later, screamed as they plunged from sight.

Instantly on his feet, Delaney rushed to the pond and dove in. His attempts to rescue the boys, however, were futile. One boy drowned, another was rescued in critical condition, and a third made his own way back to shore. Joe Delaney died in the rescue effort; his body was the last to be recovered. He had given his life to help others, without success. Seeing the boys in danger, he placed his own life in jeopardy to help them. But I wonder: If Joe had known he would leave his wife a widow and three small daughters fatherless, would he have jumped into that pond? Would we? Or would we say, "There's no need for more to die"?

Jesus came to the world precisely to die. He would not hang on the cross for a few seconds and then get off, safely. It would not be a matter of a brief agony and intense bravery followed by a cloudburst of adulation. He would be taken off the cross a corpse! He *knew* all that—and yet he came.

CHRIST — is life-changing
Joshua 24:15; Galatians 4:12, 19

Nothing Else Will Do

Bernard Baruch had been a successful Wall Street investor before serving in various national and international capacities during World War I. He went back to Wall Street after the war, but his plunge into international waters made New York's financial affairs seem like a puddle.

As a basketball coach, Digger Phelps felt he had reached his professional zenith when he was chosen to coach at Notre Dame. Yet he altered his perspective after a trip to Europe in 1975. He had not known that a world of culture could be so fabulous. When he returned, paintings replaced trophies in his office, classical music took the place of hard rock, and he started wearing three-piece suits instead of colorful sports jackets.

The apostle Paul had such an experience. At one time he was convinced that Moses personified truth and savagely persecuted anyone who disputed it. Then came the change! Someone, whose blinding incandescence shone through the midday Syrian sun, appeared and opened Paul's heart even as he closed Paul's eyes. From that moment, having met the living Christ, Paul had a new perspective on life. Human pride was replaced by God's grace, pedigree was replaced by faith, and trust in what he could do was replaced by what Christ had already done. Once we see Christ that way, we are all the same—it helps us replace what now matters so greatly with what truly matters ultimately.

CHRIST — only his blood cures sin
Numbers 21:8–9; John 3:14

Only One Blood

An American in Irkutsk, Russia, went to his American doctor complaining of stomach pains and severe vomiting. Surgery revealed a torn artery at the juncture of the stomach and esophagus. Transfusions after surgery should have completed the patient's recovery, but his blood count dropped dangerously despite repeated transfusions. A microscopic examination of the man's blood stunned the physician: the red cells were torn and chewed though the same blood type had been used. The doctor quickly deduced that minor incompatibilities between Russian and American blood were making the transfusions deadly. The man needed American blood, or he would die.

Henry Kissinger, in Moscow at the time, prevailed on the Soviets to allow an Air Force plane to fly the necessary blood in from Germany. Another plane, with the dying American already aboard, would fly him on to Japan. Minutes after the Air Force plane arrived, technicians transferred the patient and began transfusions with the life-giving blood. Within three hours his pulse had returned to near normal. The doctor was right. The man's immunity system had known the difference; it detected even minor inconsistencies in the Russian blood and attacked to kill the intruder.

Many cures have been offered for humanity's spiritual illness—some are foolish and impractical, some are feasible and possible, but none are successful. Only Christ's blood satisfies the requirements of God's justice and human need.

The human soul knows the difference. It will resist any effort at recovery until it is washed in the only blood that cures our sinfulness: the blood of Jesus Christ.

CHRIST — his life challenges us
Genesis 50:19–21; Colossians 1:24

He Also Came

Cabeza de Vaca and three others suffered intolerable afflictions as they walked across what would later become Louisiana and Texas. Often naked, thirsty, hungry, and under forced labor by Indian tribes, these Europeans summoned every ounce of resolve to survive their eight-year odyssey. For de Vaca, his faith in Christ and Christ's example while suffering provided the necessary encouragement to survive. Later he wrote that his only solace in pain was knowing the infinitely magnified torment Christ had endured.

It is often said that Christ came as a human to understand our thoughts and feelings. Yet, having made us, surely he knows us as a watchmaker intuitively understands his timepiece. More precisely, he came to live the model life, so we could know how to live: how to rise above temptation, how to deny self, how to resist the devil, and how to become conquerors! Christ came not so much to learn about us as to teach us to learn from him. He came not only to find out how we felt when facing life but to show us how we should act when facing life.

CHRIST — a never-ending experience
Deuteronomy 32:45–47; 1 Corinthians 15:54–57

No Life Like It

Captain William Stewart spent six years wandering the American West during the mid-nineteenth century. He had lived through tumultuous terror with Wellington at Waterloo where he became a casualty of the war. His war experiences gave him a sense of reality and importance that peace could not. Having lived through such dangerous conditions, he found security boring and senseless. In the uncivilized lawlessness of the American West, he rediscovered adventure.

When famous Western scout Jim Bridger was old and blind, he would stand outside his daughter's home in Missouri and face westward, looking to a world he had known but would never again experience. Visions and memories came of his pioneering explorations; the dangers he had undergone and survived in the West resurrected themselves in his mind. But it was all in the past. His memories couldn't be taken from him, but they could never be made into anything more. Memories they were and memories they would remain.

Like the experiences of Stewart and Bridger, the Christian life ruins its adherents for any other relationship. However, it is very different from the life those men knew, for regardless how exciting earthly experiences may be, they cease. Yet even as we thoroughly explore Christ now, we are just on heaven's frontier. We are heading into a future of reality, not recollections. We will not stand in life's backyard wishing the past could come again, that just once more we could be what we have been before. No, for before us will lie a world with God in person, whose brilliance will obliterate all longings for the past.

CHRIST — the only way to God
Psalm 110:1; Matthew 22:41–46

Nothing Any Better

In September, 1492, Christopher Columbus sailed to the Canary Islands and, bearing westward, reached San Salvador and the New World in thirty-three days. In the centuries since, no better or quicker way to sail the Atlantic has been found. Even modern yachtsmen in sleek, multimillion-dollar crafts equipped with state-of-the-art navigation aids agree that Columbus' charts offer the swiftest and easiest route across the Atlantic.

Would we think modern sailors especially bright if they insisted on a new way of sailing the Atlantic just because Columbus' route was five centuries old? Should we consider contemporary spiritual "sailors" bright who demand a modern way to God just because Christ's way is two thousand years old? What good is it to live by your own light if it is only a dim bulb? Only Christ knows the way to eternal life—and the way never changes.

CHRIST — one died for all
Leviticus 4:3–4; Hebrews 9:26

One Life Lost—Millions Gained

In February, 1943, the transport *Dorchester* sank in the North Atlantic after being torpedoed by a German submarine. In an unforgettable stand of unity and courage, four chaplains sacrificed themselves by giving their life jackets to enlisted men. The chaplains sank with the ship, their arms on each other's shoulders as they sank beneath the waves. Four men died gallantly and selflessly that day, and four others lived in their place. They did all they could do, yet their sacrifice had limited effectiveness.

Outside Jerusalem, on the Place of the Skull, One died—and, as a result, untold millions live again. Just One died that day for sins, yet in every century since, multitudes live forever. The Savior's sacrifice did not replace one life with another; it replenished itself on a prodigious scale of multiplication, reconciling all creation to its Creator. This one sacrifice continues to give a second chance to all who believe.

CHRISTIAN FAITH — demands informed membership
Ezra 7:6; 2 Timothy 2:2

An Informed Membership

The citizens of Parma, Italy, possessed such enthusiastic knowledge of opera that they demanded excellence in anyone who was presented as an operatic star. Once, in the performance of *Lorelei*, a singer could not reach a high note. As she struggled with it repeatedly, vainly trying, the exacting audience grew impatient and began to sing the aria absolutely correctly. The disgraced diva slunk offstage to a barrage of jeers and whistles.

Unfortunately, few churches exist with such an enthusiastic knowledge of the Bible. If church members knew their Bibles the way the citizens of Parma know their opera, preachers would be jeered when they dispensed more milk than Carnation's contented cows, or when they exchanged the robust and eternal Word for a trite and meaningless harangue. Informed parishioners will accept only the truth; the unenlightened will accept as truth whatever they hear, from whomever they hear it. What kind of church do ministers want to preach in? One where they can preach anything, knowing it will be accepted, or one where informed membership will continue to challenge them to excellence and truth?

CHRISTIAN FAITH — nothing hidden
Deuteronomy 31:10–11; Acts 26:26

Out in the Open

Columbus kept two reckonings on his initial voyage of discovery. One showed the ship's true progress, and this he kept secret. Another false record he left open to the crew. In the second, he showed the ship making greater headway than was actually true. Why? In order to make the crossing before supplies were depleted, they needed to cover about seven hundred leagues each day. By claiming they had sailed each day beyond the seven hundred leagues, Columbus hoped to spread enthusiasm and defeat discouragement.

Some religions jealously guard their beliefs, granting access only to a chosen few. Some divulge their doctrines like medicine, a little at a time, as the converts can accept them. They teaspoon out their doctrines, building immunity to shock until their converts will believe anything, no matter how foolish or wrong. Christianity boasts of its availability to all! Jesus revealed God's secrets to everyone. God keeps nothing from us concerning his expectations, demands, promises, and threats. His Word is open for inspection and investigation; it is a floodlight shining into the world so that anyone who wants to can see.

CHRISTIAN FAITH — works positively
Jeremiah 29:11; 3 John 6

The Difference the Church Makes

In 1982, Boulas Goda ministered to people living in the dumps of Cairo, Egypt. Incredibly, the city depended on these people to collect the daily trash and haul it to the dumps. There, they carefully sorted it out, hoping to find something they could sell—a broken toy, a teapot, a tricycle wheel. Sometimes they made as much as fifty cents a day; sometimes they did not.

When Boulas, a converted drug dealer, began preaching to the same people he had formerly victimized, he wanted to prove the positive impact of forgiveness on everyday life. So he helped to establish a social service center that provided literacy programs, child care, family planning, health care, and vocational education. Through these efforts a number of people were able to move from the dumps to build homes elsewhere.

We can always find glaring inconsistencies and failures in the church, but the church also has a thrilling capacity for generating virtue where none is expected. It is time for those who belong to the church to be proud of it and to devote themselves more completely to it. In these vanishing decades of the twentieth century, the church continues to be the only institution that can offer a better life for the lost and downtrodden through salvation in Jesus Christ.

CHRISTIAN LIFE — be consistent
2 Samuel 23:11–12; Acts 17:9

Back to Being Ourselves

The Egyptians scored immense gains in the first few days of the Yom Kippur War in 1973. But on the tenth to twelfth day the initiative shifted to the Israelis when their armor smashed an Egyptian advance and opened the prospect of a swift, punishing Israeli counterattack. The Israeli chief of staff called Premier Golda Meir from the Sinai. His message—simplicity itself—told Golda all she needed to know: "Both the Israelis and the Egyptians are back at being themselves."

God's people sometimes fall from grace in setbacks that humiliate them and disgrace him. Caught by surprise, as the Israelis were in the Sinai, we fall before Satan's sneak attack, our righteousness collapsing before his overwhelming advances. However, we need not worry. The faith that serves as our vanguard serves also as our rearguard. It will stop the panicked chaos of retreat, stabilize our lines, rush reinforcements into the breach, and begin a counterattack! We can be ourselves again, rebounding from sin to righteousness, from defeat to victory. Temporary defeats are expected in any war, even when the enemy is being beaten. What God wants from us is consistent effort and a forward-looking witness.

CHRISTIAN LIFE — a revolutionary life
Deuteronomy 28:2–13; Hebrews 10:35

God Gives Life, Not Tips

The San Diego police department established a We Tip anonymous witness program in September, 1984. By the fall of 1994 the program had helped solve 2,085 crimes in San Diego County. Rewards from $25 to $1,000 were paid to those who informed on drug dealers, homicide suspects, sex perverts, etc. Citizens who participated in the program never had to identify themselves. The tips resulted in the arrest of a thousand suspects and convictions in fifty-seven homicide cases. Through this program, the police department disbursed over $139,000 in rewards, with another $81,000 offered that has never been claimed.

God is not handing out $25 to $500 tips for information. He offers a revolutionary life that cannot be measured, evaluated, or understood just now. He offers a dream of one day being what we can only imagine now, of life at a level that is only a vision now. While our hopes remind us of what we would like to be, our victories remind us of what life sometimes can be—and our defeats remind us of what life often is. We desperately need God's vision of what life can be in him!

CHRISTIAN LIFE — excellence requires time and effort
Nehemiah 49; James 5:11

Meticulous Excellence

Although opinion differs over which is the world's finest luxury car, no doubt exists that the Rolls Royce is certainly one of the most expensive. Meticulous attention is given to producing each Rolls. Handmade by 4,500 workers, each of the 2,500 units produced annually takes months to build. Each of the 85,000 moving parts in every car receives endlessly tedious attention. Specialists stethoscope every engine for eight hours. Painters hand spray and rub ten coats of paint on each vehicle. When a Rolls Royce rolls off the assembly line, it has a million-mile odometer.

It takes time and effort to build excellence in anything. That is why being a Christian demands time, effort, and constancy. However, there are distinct differences between the Christian life and a Rolls: (1) only 630,000 people in America are in a category to even consider buying a rolls, but Christianity is free to all—the price has already been paid; (2) while a Rolls Royce may or may not be the perfect car—or the best car—we know for certain that Jesus Christ is the perfect Savior, and God will one day recreate us all in his exact image; (3) while a Rolls Royce offers a million-mile odometer, God offers eternal life through his Son, Jesus Christ.

CHRISTIAN LIFE — greater effort—greater success

Jeremiah 12:5; 1 Timothy 6:12

Well Worth the Extra Effort

The camera caught them at the instant of total exhaustion—heads back, open mouths gasping for relief, lungs and muscles screaming their distress. The University of Washington Crew had just finished a sub-six-minute victory, only the ninth such in the history of the Crew Classic. They had succeeded, but not easily. Victory had come only after punishing physical, mental, and emotional effort. They won by extending their fit bodies to the limit and then stretching them even more.

Have we ever resisted temptation to the point of screaming at the tempter? Have we ever given such an effort for Christ that it wrings out our energy, drains our reserves, and leaves us flat on our backs, wiped out? Who can calculate what would be the result if we underwent intensive, harrowing spiritual training equal to the training of the members of the Crew when they prepare to compete for the Classic.

CHRISTIAN LIFE — success despite failure

Genesis 12:13; 13:3–4; Hebrews 6:9

Even as We Fail

Internationally renowned cancer investigator Henry Kaplan fell prey to the lung cancer his discoveries had fought for years. Though the disease remains unconquered, baffling researchers and remedies, Kaplan's efforts led to a number of treatments for the dreaded killer, the most famous being the medical linear accelerator. In conjunction with another doctor, Kaplan also pioneered a treatment of Hodgkin's disease, which brought an 80 percent recovery rate to a once-merciless illness. Dr. Kaplan did not reach his goal of conquering lung cancer, but he did achieve many victories as he toiled toward it. The contribution he made to the conquest of lung cancer throughout a spectacular career will certainly be used as the basis of its eventual conquest.

Success in life is almost always partial; it is hardly ever complete. So if nothing we do will be perfect—especially in the Christian life—how should we respond? Why, do the best we can, achieve as much as possible, overcome as much sin as we can at each opportunity, witness as capably as we can (as often as we have the chance), pray often, read God's Word faithfully, resist temptation . . . try, try, try. Success will not come to us all at once, but it will come more fully if we pursue it patiently and unremittingly. The worst thing we can do is *nothing.*

CHRISTIAN LIFE — increasing in worth
Jeremiah 2:13; Ephesians 3:20

Watch Where You Invest

About 650 rabbit ranchers from Alabama to Pennsylvania invested over a million dollars with a fast-talking promoter who promised them large profits. Unfortunately, they didn't get any profits, but they did get a lot of furry creatures. Such results are not unusual in a world where greedy speculators prey on our weakness for the fast buck. Without carefully investigating, investors rise to the lure of an opportunity that might never come again, only to find themselves snared in a swindle.

It happens spiritually, too. People invest their lives in causes that promise great benefits—economics, politics, social action—only to find their input far excelling the values received. Jesus warned us away from such uselessness and warned us to beware temptation. The devil entices us with pleasure for the very essence of temptation is pleasure, not pain. Yet while advertising pleasure is temptation's way, delivering it is not. Temptation's every enticement offers hope, but its every consequence is despair!

CHRISTIAN LIFE — overcoming the past
Genesis 4:7; Romans 2:1

We Must Get Out

In January, 1983, as killer Pacific storms glutted their ferocity against California's shoreline, a San Diego surfer carelessly risked his life in the wild sea. When the youth lost control of his board and suffered serious head injuries, a lifeguard hazarded his life to drag the boy from the surf to the base of steep cliffs. Then firemen ventured their lives to lift him up by a rescue line.

Two months later, more burgeoning tides flung destruction at the coast. Two of three surfers who were about to wade into the turbulence stopped when lifeguards ordered them out. However, the third surfer stubbornly ignored their appeals until one lifeguard repeatedly and adamantly insisted he stay out of the waters. Unbelievably, it was the same youth who had risked so much in January! The same lifeguard who had rescued him then, arrested him now.

We might say, "Fair enough, since he had hazarded human lives twice." But in saying it, we condemn ourselves, for we often return to sinful practices from which Christ has set us free. We pledge never to be so weak and foolish again— only to return to the thing we hate. Grace condemns no one who struggles to overcome sin and, despite the struggle, fails. But grace becomes inoperable when we say that sin is our inevitable condition, when we don't struggle against it. Such defeatism mocks Christ's victory. We must leave the sins for which we beg forgiveness—we must not go back into that dangerous spiritual surf!

CHRISTIAN LIFE — glimpses of what shall be

Genesis 15:6; Hebrews 11:10

A Glimpse of the Coming Life

In the 1800s, three facts about Mexican and Indian life fascinated crewman Richard Henry Dana when his hide ship docked in Monterey, California. First, the Mexican women paid an inordinate amount of attention to their wardrobe, wearing satin shoes, silk gowns, and gold earrings and necklaces. Second, they all shared a common refinement in the use of the Spanish language—even bull drivers and serfs spoke elegantly. Third, while the complexion of the inhabitants varied from fair Castilians to dark Indians, any drop of Spanish blood, no matter how dark the skin, entitled these persons to wear a suit and all its finery, to call themselves Espanól, and to hold property. Even if they were deprived of all physical possessions, they retained their pride, their manners, and their language.

Christians can identify with those Spanish descendants in Monterey. We too feel the loss of a glory once possessed; we seek to regain that pristine joy. Even now God's mark remains in our soul as a reminder of what once was. But being in Christ elevates and inspires us. It opens our lives to the imposing, sublime presence of God. Despite our imperfections, we, like the residents of Monterey, have his blood on us, which foreshadows our repossession of a forfeited stateliness, a departed nobility, and a faded splendor.

CHRISTIAN LIFE — personal relationship with Christ

Psalm 146:5–6; Acts 4:19–20

First, Understand It

Fourteen-year-old Jason Van Boom of Oceanside won the San Diego County Spelling Bee by fortunately guessing the correct answer. He used no technique in getting his last word right. "It was sheer luck, that's all," he confessed. Furthermore, he didn't have the slightest idea what the word meant!

Christianity demands something different. Any attempt to guess at the meaning of the Christian faith, as Jason guessed at the word *tontine*, will render the disciple errant, not successful. For it is not something to be guessed—it involves conscious intent. To say we have a personal relationship with Jesus means that we intentionally acknowledge his leadership in determining our every behavior. The Christian says, "Jesus is my essence!"

CHRISTIAN LIFE — practiced by Christians

Job 31:1; 1 Corinthians 5:1

Taking Our Medicine

The heir to a multimillion-dollar fortune was sentenced to a year in jail for sexually abusing his fourteen-year-old stepdaughter. In a bitterly contested decision, the presiding judge also ordered the man to be treated with a sex-suppressant drug manufactured by his own company. What his company made for others with inordinate sexual compulsions, the man had to take to control his own. In effect, he had to take his own medicine.

The principle applies to Christians also. What we keep prescribing for the ills of others, we need a good dose of ourselves. If we suggest the palliative graces of prayer, we must experience its anointing. Tithing cannot just be something we recommend but a prescription we faithfully ingest. If we dose out resistance to evil, we must purge it from our own life. If we seek to inure others to hatred and division, we, too, should be vaccinated with unity. And if we are going to warn people against carrying contagious tales, we had better follow a gossip-suppression routine ourselves. We must display the behavior we expect from others. Indeed, we, of all people, must take our own medicine!

CHRISTIAN LIFE — successful results
Psalm 119:5–6; Colossians 1:10

Being and Becoming

In *Pygmalion*, Eliza Doolittle overcomes a background of poverty, coarse speech, and backwoods customs to become a sophisticated lady. So well does she play her role that she fools everyone at the garden party where Higgins and Pickering exhibit her. Later, at Higgins' house, Pickering boasts about Eliza's success—which had unsettled him at the party. Eliza had played her part superbly—better in fact than most of the snobs at the party who felt that sophistication belonged only to those born into position or wealth.

Christian converts face a challenge similar to Eliza's, for becoming and being a disciple of Christ are two different procedures. Becoming has a beginning and an end; being, once begun, never ends. Fortunately, while the goal of conversion is excellence and refinement in Christlikeness, God graciously allows us to "practice" while we are being made perfect. He doesn't expect immediate mastery—he will accept efforts marred by failure as long as they are efforts toward mastery.

CHRISTIAN LIFE — unending value
Psalm 23:5; Philippians 4:4

Even Now the Taste

After their ill-fated journey to Florida in 1528, Cabeza de Vaca and three companions sailed around the American gulf coast to Texas and then walked across Texas on their way to Mexico City. They sailed across the mouth of a great river on the last day of October. They did not know they were at the mouth of the Mississippi, but they realized the river had to be massive, for they could dip their buckets into the salt waters of the gulf and bring up fresh water to drink. At that point the mighty river roared into the gulf impetuously and voluminously, overcoming even the salty depths of the ocean.

The Christian life is like that. We live in a polluted world. Yet, even now we can dip our vessels into life and out of guilt find forgiveness, out of aimlessness find direction, out of meaningless find purpose, out of immorality find purity, and out of falsehood find truth. Out of a horribly profaned world we can still draw up all that we hold to be holy and true.

CHURCH — no compromise
Exodus 20:3; Galatians 1:9

Half-Way In Is Out

The Half-Way Covenant Church became popular in seventeenth-century Massachusetts. Where the Mayflower Compact generation had a revolutionary personal faith, the first and second generations that followed cooled in their convictions. This led the to the Half-Way Covenant. Originally, to qualify for membership and privileges in the church, a person had to affirm a conversion experience—a dream, trance, or vision. However, many colonists had been baptized as children and had no such experiences, so they failed to qualify. These were formed into the Half-Way Covenant. They were half-way into the church. They could not vote or receive communion, but they could have their child baptized. They felt that being half a member was better than not being a member at all.

It didn't work—it will never work. Of course, many people want a more convenient, less demanding, more fashionable, less harrowing faith. They prefer scraps to a feast of truth. They like it by the teaspoon, not the gallon. But any agreement to accommodate our fallen nature stifles spiritual development and hastens rebellion.

CHURCH — the body of Christ
2 Samuel 7:1–7; Acts 5:12

The Church Survives Without the Building

On Christmas day, 1983, an uncontrollable blaze destroyed a majestic, old German church. It was built in A.D. 1140, when Florence and northern Italy flourished under the Medicis; when humanists reaped a renaissance in ancient manuscripts from Constantinople; twelve years before da Vinci was born; 35 years before Michelangelo; and 52 before Savanorola. Authorities determined that a Christmas tree, traditionally lighted with candles, must have started the blaze. Hundreds of worshipers had attended services there just hours before the destruction.

Though the church building perished, God's church survived. After all, a church building provides a meeting place—not meaning—for Christians. Their relationship with Christ, not with a structure, gives them identity and defines their mission. That is why the trappings of Christianity may perish: by fire, theft, flood, or old age, but the Church survives. All outward signs of God's kingdom can fail—buildings, hospitals, schools, mission stations—but Christianity goes on going on. The Holy Spirit within empowers God's people, and that can never be destroyed!

CONFIDENCE — self-confidence is necessary
Psalm 27:1; 2 Corinthians 5:6–8

To Have It Within

Nicolas I ruled Russia with unopposed sovereignty for thirty years. All his people, and all the world's rulers, recognized his dominion. Yet he never felt secure. While he shouldn't have cared what any citizen or foreigner thought, he craved obedience by all, even those over whom he held no power. The constant repetition of his authority demeaned rather than enhanced his reputation.

Confidence starts within us, providing a solid basis for relating to others. For Christians, God's presence within should be sufficient to build that confidence. Our importance is based on what God has done for us in Christ! We are God's children. However unsure of ourselves we become, we can always have confidence in our relationship with Christ. That awareness should make us masters of all we face—and it eliminates the need to look to others, to sexual conquests, to riches, to fame, or to any other source for self-esteem.

CONSCIENCE — listen and obey
1 Samuel 25:31; 1 Peter 3:16

Our Inner Sentinel

Scientists have long known that the body's immune system relies on the intimately choreographed work of B and T cells. B cells from the bone marrow and T cells produced in the thymus gland work together to destroy viral and bacterial enemies within our bodies. The T cells, like cops on patrol, monitor the blood and trigger an alarm when they spot something suspicious. The B cells burst into action, dividing into a host of cells that attack the invader. Science cannot explain what sensitivity enables the T cells to recognize danger or how a proliferation of receptors in the B cells allows them to respond to the multitude of germs that assault the body.

God gave our bodies the capability to protect us from the common cold, a tiny scratch, or a deadly disease. He has structured that same protection inside our minds, building an inner sentinel to warn us when we are heeding false, immoral, and dangerous ideas. To sin, to use self unwisely and destructively, we have to ignore the sentinel's warnings. It can save us if we listen to it and obey. But the sentinel—call it conscience—cannot overcome our will. All it can do is warn us away from the path we have taken, the idea we are embracing, or the behavior we are practicing. Unlike the immune system, which works even without our awareness of its complexity, the inner sentinel will work only in subjection to our will.

CONSISTENCY — in relationships
Psalm 26:4–7; Luke 12:1

The Inconsistency of It All

Defense Secretary Caspar Weinberger once noted that a Soviet listening device had washed up on a beach south of the Strait of Juan de Fuca, Washington, near a Trident submarine base. Interestingly, the electronics in the device paralleled those manufactured in this country. We found ourselves competing not only against Russians but against our own technology. We had created advanced systems that they stole and put into their systems. Then we had to develop even more advanced concepts as countermeasures. We were essentially fighting ourselves.

How often do we find ourselves at odds, not only in our evaluation of others but also in struggles against our own subjectivity. We demand of others good behavior that we ourselves don't exhibit. We want people prosecuted for misbehavior from which we expect to be exempt. Virtues we want praised in ourselves, we overlook in others. Vices we want minimized in ourselves, we magnify in others. But Jesus has another idea. He expects us to give grace in the same measure we have received it—grace that enables us to shine, not tarnish, our brother's halo.

CONVERSION — advantageous
Psalm 31:19; Romans 6:20–22

Harnessed!

When Lewis and Clark floated down the Columbia River to the Pacific, it was known as the Great River. Its current boiled furiously through steep gorges, then flowed placidly but swiftly in broad stretches. Ever undisciplined, and sometimes consummately violent, it moved everything as it chose—giant trees as well as saplings, huge boulders and pebbles. Into the Pacific swells it charged with such fury that the resulting breakers defied passage without the threat of instant death. Far out into the briny ocean it discharged it fresh water flows.

Today, a sluggish whisper of its former thunderous mayhem, the Columbia is restrained by nine major dams. Grand Coulee, the greatest power dam on earth, harvests the river to develop millions of watts of electricity, its huge turbines charging longdistance lines with power to industries and homes.

Before we knew Christ, we were like the Great River—untamed, unrestrained, passionate. With little regard for control and discipline, we did what we pleased, said what we wanted, and went where we chose. Then Jesus came into our lives and harnessed our undirected energies into useful and productive habits, relationships, and purposes. He turned our chaos of complexities into disciplined harmony, our unregulated passions into exercised resolves.

CONVERSION — miraculous transformation
Joshua 1:8; Galatians 1:23

Always the Danger

Robin appeared before applauding crowds, wearing a fur coat worthy of any actress. She waved at fans, who gawked at her incredibly long nails and big brown eyes. But she had grown accustomed to such attention, starring in the movie *Hotel New Hampshire* and appearing regularly in the Circus Vargas. She was a 250-pound bear and the prized possession of her trainer, Wally Nagtine. He had raised Robin from a cub. However, he warned, you can't make a bear do anything it would rather not. Threats of retaliation were useless in training the bear; instead, Wally used rewards like honey and words of praise when she did well. She lived with people and existed peacefully with Wally, who controlled her ferocity, but she was not domesticated, for all that. Without constant restraint, she would quickly revert to her natural self.

Conversion gives us what the trainer gave his bear: control and direction. We might say it spiritually domesticates us—it makes us something altogether different. Yet this also is true: If we slip the leash from our conversion, we will rush right back to being a wild, rebellious sinner, hating grace and living unworthy of divine companionship. Only as we allow conversion to keep applying its grip on us will we be fit to serve God. Only as the Holy Spirit leads us do we find ourselves less like the sinners we naturally are and more like the saints he is pleased to make us.

CONVERSION — speaking God's words
Jeremiah 35:13; Hebrews 12:28–29

To Speak a New Language

Hoover came to the Swallow home in new England as an orphaned, silver-furred seal. When Mr. Swallow forced some ground mackerel down his throat, the baby found his appetite—and his name.

When Swallow went to the family pond, he often found Hoover among the cattails. "Hey, get outa thay ah," Mr. Swallow would shout to him. Hoover would ignore the man and slowly submerge, playing a game. That was only a small amount of the talking the man did to the seal. Then one afternoon Swallow met Hoover on the path to the pond and said, "Hello thay ah,"—and, to his astonishment, thought he heard the seal repeating the words. When the Swallows eventually took Hoover to the New England Aquarium in Boston, they mentioned his speech, but no one was impressed.

However, Hoover began making news at the aquarium by his sounds. Seven years after his arrival, he could say his own name, "Hello thay ah," "Get outa thay ah," and "How ay yuh?"—all in a New England accent.

Christians understand how something of one kind can assume the thoughts, language, and behavior of another kind. Renewed souls do it all the time in becoming Christlike. Why would we think it incredible for Hoover to repeat human words when sinful humans learn to speak God's? The difference between Hoover and us is awareness. He merely repeated words; we express convictions.

CONVICTION — develops behavior
Daniel 3:16–18; Acts 5:29

Power to Do Right

Captain John Dramesi suffered imprisonment in North Vietnam from 1967 to 1973. From the first to the last, he resisted as much as possible in as many ways as possible. He had a choice to make, he wrote: Do it right by resisting at first, when he had the mental and physical stamina to reinforce his values; or surrender at first, and only when he had grown weary of compromise, try opposition later. Since imprisonment would by then have sapped the initiative and vitality from his values, he decided to build his resistance at first and let that dictate his later behavior.

Each of us faces a similar challenge. None of us has a choice about whether we will build a life—each day we are building it and living in what we build, now and forever. However, we do have a choice about how we build our lives—and what we construct will be either an eternal benefit or a bane to us. God's fervent wish is to have us do it right at first, so we don't have to go back later and redo it. He knows it is always easier to build it right the first time than to tear it down and rebuild it later.

COUNTERFEITERS — always imitating reality
Jeremiah 2:13; Galatians 4:9

Only the Real Thing

Counterfeiting is epidemic in the business world. Imitations are made of almost anything Americans use—pills, jeans, spark plugs, aircraft parts, pacemakers, car brakes. Bogus transistors were even pawned off on Rockwell International for use in the 1976 Enterprise, a prototype of the space shuttle. Whether through an international consortium or privately, businesses tenaciously pursue counterfeiters, trying to protect their name brands and assure their customers of quality and value. Consumers like to know they are getting the full value for their money.

Impostors all have two factors in common: (1) they claim to be as good as the real thing, and (2) they're cheaper. Such an appeal is difficult to resist for the hard-pressed shopper looking for a bargain. And most people cannot make the distinction—the sham looks as good as the prototype.

Satan is a counterfeiter. When he whispers "I can give you the same thing Jesus offers, and you can practice self-fulfillment instead of self-denial to get it," people listen. They want both the good life and heaven. Many seekers accept a cheap salvation, thinking it is equal to the real thing, only to find it is worthless! We need to remember: Nothing is real but the real thing.

COURAGE — how it develops
Joshua 1:2, 9; John 18:15–18

Returning to Face the Terror

Ernest Hemingway's *The Short Happy Life of Francis Macomber* centers on an American on safari who shoots a lion but does not kill it. Losing his nerve, the hunter refuses to go into the bush to stalk and kill the beast. After struggling with his conscience all night, he asks at breakfast to be allowed to hunt again. This time he finds a buffalo, stalks it, and successfully shoots it. The hunter, Wilson, "had seen men come of age before and it always moved him. It was not a matter of their twenty-first birthday," Hemingway wrote.

The best way to recover a loss of courage is to quickly reengage what brought the loss, whether it is a problem we cannot solve, a temptation we cannot overcome, or a virtue we cannot acquire. Whatever causes our loss of courage and brings our surrender, we must confront it again and work to master it. Otherwise, we will be gored on the horns of the fear and failure that snagged us. Admitting our fear but refusing to flee from it, choosing instead to run directly at it, builds confidence.

CREATION — enormous energy in
Psalm 8:3–4; John 9:5

An Undimmed Brilliance

In May 1982, a solar flare, so huge that scientific instruments could not measure it, exploded from the sun's surface and scattered into the universe. In less than twenty minutes that single flare released more energy than all the natural and manufactured energy the earth uses in an entire year.

Like that solar flare, Jesus issues more light on life than we will ever use. Not all humanity in all its years on earth has used even a trace of the illumination he has given the human race. As the solar flare travels through space it loses its brilliance, finally disappearing. Christ's brightness, conversely, loses no strength as it blazes though time. Our age lives in his illumination as fully as all before us and any to come after—he shines forever with an undimmed brilliance. His light will be the source of light for the new world.

CREATION — no answers to our questions
Malachi 3:16–17; 1 John 3:1–3

Look in the Right Place

The last forty years have seen an accelerated effort to contact beings of higher intelligence in outer space. In 1982, Congress funded a computerized radio system that gave scientists access to seventy-four thousand radio channels as they tried to extract meaningful, repetitive signals from the flood of radio waves emitting from human activity in space and on earth. These speculative efforts indicate that, however poorly we understand the meaning of the search, everyone wants a relationship with superior beings. The motivation behind the entire space project rests on the assumption that a higher life form than ours exists and that we would profit from making contact with it.

Christians certainly agree with the scientists. An infinitely advanced Life does exist beyond this one, in a dimension not even the most powerful telescope or radio can ever reach. And we certainly agree that we profit by contact with that infinite Life: Jesus Christ. In fact, we do not merely profit, we become someone altogether different from what we have been before—part of God's royal household.

CRISIS — can cause incredible achievement
1 Samuel 17:45–47; John 17:3

In Times of Danger

During the battle of Midway in World War II, a gunner on an American plane saw his gun tear loose from its rack. Without thinking, the slightly built youth grabbed the 175-pound weapon, steadied it against the fuselage, and fired at the attacking Zeroes, downing one. Back aboard the carrier *Enterprise,* he tried just to lift the gun but could not budge it.

A couple hiking in Glacier National Park unwittingly enraged a grizzly sow by getting between her and her cubs. The sow grabbed and mauled the man. Without thinking, his five-foot three-inch wife waded into the five-hundred-pound behemoth with nothing but a pair of binoculars, swinging them angrily and repeatedly bouncing them off the bear's head. Taken by surprise, the bear dropped the man and scurried away.

The release of endorphins by the brain—hormones that affect the emotions—may explain such sudden bursts of incredible energy, strength, or bravery in the face of danger or crisis. If short-term eruptions of energy or skill can be ascribed to endorphins, to what can we ascribe Christ's expression of sovereign powers over all the crises he confronted: demon possession, leprosy, blindness, paralysis, death? Even the fringe of his cloak possessed life-giving energy. To what shall we ascribe the continued sovereign power of Jesus if not to that mysterious unity of flesh and deity in the God who became man?

CRISIS — response to
Job 12:5; 2 Corinthians 2:12–13

Who Knows in a Crisis?

The highway patrolman drove his unmarked van down the freeway, calmly watching traffic, listening to his police band, and keeping an eye out for stolen vehicles. His serenity vanished instantly, however, when a two-tone pickup passed him—it was his truck! He called for assistance, then pulled over and arrested the illegal aliens who had stolen the pickup off the street in front of his house. Afterward, he puzzled over his emotional response to the incident. When investigating robberies or break-ins, he had always been carefully detached, but all that objectivity disappeared when his own property was jeopardized. "I was yelling and cussing," he said. "The other cops thought I was nuts." In spite of strict academy training against heated responses to crises, he could not prevent it in this crisis. In an instant, instinct obliterated training, and the cop in uniform became a common citizen enraged by the theft of his possession.

We can never know how we will behave in a crisis. We can make plans, establish intentions, and indicate resolutions, but we will never know until that instant. Training can help us react correctly, but it is not foolproof. Experience can make us invulnerable to drastic mistakes, but the policeman's reaction cautions us against overconfidence. It also shows us why humility should characterize our anticipations and forbearance our reactions to those who fail. Cowardice can envelope anyone as suddenly as darkness in the southern latitudes. And when it does, those who act bravely should throw rose petals at those who fail, not cast stones.

DANGER — lurking close by
2 Samuel 11:2; 1 Corinthians 10:12

Closer Than We Think

On April 14, 1912, when the *Titanic* sank, 1,500 people died. On July 24, 1915, when the excursion ship *Eastland* turned over and sank, 812 of the 2,500 aboard died. While the *Titanic* sank in the great depths of the Atlantic, with a few pitiful survivors in sight, the *Eastland* capsized while tied to her pier on the river in downtown Chicago as thousands watched in horror.

How often we take safety for granted when danger lurks nearby. We would think using a painted intersection the safest way to cross the street. Yet a three-year study in Long Beach, California showed that eight times as many people were hurt in intersections with painted crosswalks as those without them. A five-year study of 400 intersections in San Diego showed six times as many accidents in marked as in unmarked crosswalks.

Sometimes, Christians steadily scale spiritual challenges, only to fall into disgrace afterwards. Just a few days separated Peter from being a rock of support and a sorrow to Christ, because Peter felt that his confession of Christ's deity allowed him the right to interpret its meaning. We are never so close to spiritual disaster as when we think ourselves impervious to it. Satan loves to humiliate those who proudly feel themselves above it.

DEATH — close calls
Genesis 2:16–17; Hebrews 9:27

A Lurking Foe

Throughout history people have experienced close calls with death. General Ulysses S. Grant had several in the Civil War. He had a horse shot from under him, a shell blasted a couch aboard a steamer he had vacated only minutes before, and Rebel cavalry saw him, but did not fire on him.

The brilliant Charles Fox once fought a duel and was hit in the middle of his stomach—or more accurately, in the buckle of his waistband; the bullet fell harmlessly away. Art Sala stood in his Seattle yard, moved to one side, and gaped in astonishment as the door of a Rainier National Bank plane fell from the sky, hitting the very spot he had vacated moments before.

John Wesley nearly died at six years of age when fire burned the family rectory. Left for dead amid the flames, he suddenly appeared at a second story window. A neighbor, by standing on the shoulders of a friend, lowered him to safety. He thereafter called himself "a brand plucked from the burning."

Death can be momentarily eluded but never indefinitely escaped. From emergence to extinction, this is our inescapable fate. Each one must pay for Adam's sin with his own bodily death. Thanks be to God, we can escape paying for our own sins with our spiritual death. For while God hurries the day of evil to its eternal night, he rushes the night of the righteous to its eternal day.

DEATH — final words
1 Kings 2:1; John 13:1–2

Before Life Goes

John Adam's last words, uttered about 5:30 A.M. on July 4, 1826, were, "Thomas Jefferson survives." In truth, Jefferson had preceded his friend in death earlier that same day. Jefferson's last discernible words, spoken the night of July 3, 1826, were, "Is it the Fourth?"

Chicago murderer George Appel, after being strapped into the electric chair, announced blithely: "Well folks, you'll soon see a baked Appel." President James Polk whispered his love to his wife, Sarah; Napoleon thought at last on what he had pursued from the first . . . his nation, his army, his Josephine; Henry Ward Beecher anticipated the mystery ahead; and Christian missionary Jim MacKinnon died murmuring, "Jesus, Jesus, Jesus, Hallelujah!"

The seven last words of Jesus offer a recapitulation of his entire ministry:

- *I thirst*—is proof that he lived among mankind as a complete human being
- *forgive them*—encapsulates the entire purpose of his incarnation
- *here is your son/mother*—reflects the concern he had always shown for others
- *today you will be with me*—represents an earnest of the multitudes to go with him into heaven
- *my God, my God*—foreshadows his separation from God when he paid the supreme penalty for sin
- *it is finished*—assures that the forgiveness he came to offer was perfectly effected
- *into your hands*—tells of his return to God, with whom he had pre-existence

DEATH — means of reconciliation
Deuteronomy 21:23; Luke 23:34

Together in the Grave

Franklin and Eleanor Roosevelt nearly divorced in 1918 when Eleanor discovered his affair with Lucy Mercer. Eleanor remained in the relationship on two conditions: They would have a marriage of convenience only, and FDR would immediately sever his relationship with Miss Mercer.

Eleanor wasn't present when FDR died in Warm Springs, Georgia in April, 1945. When she learned that Lucy Mercer Rutherford had seen FDR before he died, she was incensed. When she further learned that FDR's closest associates, and even her own daughter, had been aware of the president's continued relationship with Mrs. Rutherford, Eleanor was stunned and enraged.

Yet, at the graveside in Hyde Park as her husband was being buried, Eleanor radiated a peace her son Elliott could not understand. She later explained it. When she stood at the grave, she saw the inscription FDR had designed—just their two names together. She concluded that he did love her after all and wanted to be buried beside her.

While Jesus lived, he urged us to take on his yoke and learn of him. When he died, he took our sins upon himself and forgave them. Knowing the inimitable uniqueness of his Son, God took out a patent on the death of Jesus, commemorating it as the only death ever to reconcile lost humanity to divinity. "The Old Rugged Cross" has become the most popular hymn ever written, because the resurrection of Jesus interpreted the cross as love, not wrath. It was the means by which God cursed his son with our sins and blessed us with his holiness.

DEEDS — good returned
Ecclesiastes 11:1; Matthew 26:40

Cast Your Bread . . . After Many Days

While walking outside his Vienna hotel in 1938, a Polish pilot was nearly upended when a man fleeing his pursuers rushed headlong into him. About to lecture the miscreant, the officer noticed he was ashen with terror. Panting heavily, he kept repeating "Gestapo! Gestapo!" The Pole quickly secreted him in his hotel room. Unaware of his guest's identity, but anxious to help him elude the Nazis, he flew the fugitive to Poland, landing in a meadow outside Cracow to protect him from arrest.

The Polish pilot went on to fly in the Polish, French, and British Air Force. In June 1940, after being wounded in a dogfight over the English Channel, he nearly died when he suffered a severe skull fracture while landing his plane. Initially, the hospital authorities considered surgery useless. Only when a respected brain surgeon arrived by plane and doggedly insisted did they allow him to operate.

When the pilot regained consciousness, the first face he focused on was the white-smocked Jew he had saved from the Gestapo two years before. When the officer weakly asked what he was doing there, the man told him his story. He had slipped into Cracow and, though pursued by the Nazis, had fled to Warsaw and then to Scotland. Appreciating the officer's kindness in flying him out of Austria in 1938, he noticed the officer's name on the plane's map and committed it to memory, vowing to repay the debt if an opportunity came.

When he heard that a Polish squadron had distinguished itself in the Battle of Britain, he found that his friend was involved. When he discovered that his friend had been critically wounded in combat and nearly killed in a crash landing, he asked to be flown to him.

"But why?" the pilot whispered.

"I thought that at last I could show my gratitude. You see, I am a brain surgeon—I operated on you this morning."

How many will rise at judgment and call us blessed because in Christ's name we did what we could for that one in need?

DIET — of almost anything
Numbers 21:4–5; Mark 1:6

If You Get Hungry Enough

Prisoners of war in Japan often found worms boiled with their rice rations. Though at first they refused to eat them, they soon realized that the worms could provide nourishment to help them survive. The worms became the meat ration. In fact, some of the men picked them out of the rice and set them aside to be enjoyed separately.

A plump moth larva might turn Western stomachs, but other cultures consider it a delicacy in their daily diet. While American Indians ate a large variety of crawling and flying insects, the locust was an American pioneer staple. Ants are a favorite in Asia, Africa, and Latin America. Indeed, honey ants, which store nectar in their abdomens, are obligatory fare in rural Mexican weddings. Natives in Zanzibar, Tanzania, serve a mixture of sugar, banana flour, and ground up termites in a delicacy called "white ant pie." Locusts—up to four inches long—are a particular favorite in Asia, Africa, and the Middle East.

Scriptural teachings resemble diets. What some think unimportant others consider essential to belief. For example, the lists of genealogies may seem irrelevant to most, but a Bible translator found them a key to unlocking faith in the hearts of the villagers to whom he ministered. God expects us to teach the entire message of Christ. If genealogies can powerfully impact some people, what invincible conviction lurks in Scripture's profound doctrinal and practical sections? Or in its narrative, historical, and poetic sections?

DISASTER — immense
Psalm 51:11–12; Matthew 16:26

Incalculable Loss

Philip II of Spain sent 130 ships to invade England as the Spanish Armada sailed to avenge the death of Mary Queen of Scots. Up to half of the ships failed to return, and most that did had to be scrapped. Of the thirty thousand men aboard the Armada, almost twenty thousand died—in battle, in shipwrecks, by murder in Scotland and Ireland when they straggled ashore, and many from starvation and disease. Philip II enjoyed no offsetting compensation for this debacle. It permanently reduced his importance in European history.

The Christian, conversely, willingly accepts self-denial—what the unsaved call a tragedy—to enjoy the victory Christ shares. In what many call our defeat, we find victory; in our surrender, conquest. Our very self—the personality, creativity, and perceptivity that make us truly human and truly God's child—finds its fulfillment only in the loss of itself to God's will.

DISCIPLESHIP — centered in self-denial
Micah 6:6–8; Galatians 2:20–21

To Prove It

Niccolò Machiavelli, sixteenth-century Italian political theorist, wrote *The Prince*, a book about a ruler who lets no scruples deter him in his ascent to power. The very term *Machiavellian* has since been synonymous with treachery, deceit, and expediency. As an example of that concept, Machiavelli said that an ambassador was a good man sent abroad to lie for his country. He dedicated *The Prince* to Lorenzo De' Medici, Florentine statesman, ruler, and patron. It behooved any supplicant to offer something precious to his benefactor, the author said, and his gift was *The Prince*, valuable to him and, he hoped, to his patron.

When we come to God, we too must bring something of great value. However, we possess but one commodity that both we and he treasure above all: self. We cannot offer him gold or riches, for they are of no value to him. Nor can we bring fame or success or any of the thousand trinkets and toys we value, for he treasures nothing of the kind. Only one possession can satisfy our need to give the inestimable: self. We come to God just as we are, knowing he will never demand more. But we come with self crucified, because he will never accept less.

DISCIPLESHIP — challenges the best of us
Proverbs 18:9; Colossians 3:23–24

Have We Even One Day?

The work ethic faces a drastic challenge, not only in America but in formerly work-conscious Germany and Japan. Less than one-fourth of Americans work at full capacity. In fact, a survey of four thousand people has shown that the average worker spends a third of his day goofing off. That translates into four months paid vacation every year. Commitment to work ranked highest among the Israelis, at 57 percent, and lowest among the British, at 17 percent. One reason given for these miserable statistics is a discrepancy between employee potential and position. Only 6 percent of the workers in Israel felt themselves in dead-end or inferior jobs contrasted with 22 percent in Britain.

Obviously, some new strategy is in order for businesses and corporations. The unused talent offers a potentially devastating pool of discontent for any nation, to say nothing of the victories and successes lost by this failure to excel. All of which has significant spiritual implications. If laziness characterizes the average worker in his or her job, how lazy is the average Christian? How much time do we actually devote to the development of spiritual excellence? And we have this further challenge. While many workers fail to offer more to tasks they feel beneath their skills, Christians have no such excuse. Our Lord's ideals stretch infinitely ahead of us; his excellence always challenges us to grow beyond ourselves, to produce more than we have given, to develop our abilities so we can become more like him.

DISCIPLESHIP — growth is necessary
Psalm 19:14; Philippians 3:12–14

Always Keep Growing

Favored to win the gold medal in women's figure skating in the Winter Olympics, 1984, Rosalyn Sumners returned to America with a silver instead. A performance marked by her accustomed skill in the long program would have won the gold. Rosalyn explained the failure by saying that while she had wanted to be the best, she had not been willing to practice until she proved it. Perhaps her coach was partly to blame. Having detected Rosalyn's lethargy, she should have reminded her that she would be good enough only *after* the competition.

Christians often follow Rosalyn's example in their discipleship. They grow so far in faith and then, thinking they have gone far enough, stop. They improve their skills to a certain level, but no further. Yet Christians have a Savior whose personal example destroys self-satisfaction. Even when he was persecuted, questioned, tested, rejected, blasphemed, arrested, beaten, and crucified, he remained faithful to his task. God intends for us to become more and more like Christ. And since we are much farther from that goal than Rosalyn was from hers, we had better bear down and practice . . . practice . . . practice!

DISCIPLESHIP — investigated firsthand
Joshua 22:10, 24–25; Acts 17:11

That Personal Experience

When the Wright brothers first began experimenting with flying machines, they

accepted as fact the data and conclusions that were available in the theory of aviation. As they experimented, however, their own experience provided different
conclusions. They began by doubting nothing, yet grew to disbelieve everything
about accepted aviation theory. Finally, disregarding all they had learned, they
relearned through personal investigation. This led them to build man-carrying
gliders in which they spent hundreds of hours over Kill Devil Hills, North
Carolina. In their Dayton bike shop they built a custom wind tunnel and tested
over two hundred different wing surfaces. With minor refinements, their wind
tunnel became the prototype of the one used today, and the control system they
devised is still used on fixed-wing aircraft.

So many people accept the word of another for the reality of Christ, or for
a teaching that is supposed to be in the Bible. In reality, they base their faith on
the faith of another—which might be real and true; but again, it might not. The
only way to know that you are seeing Jesus personally, Jesus really, and Jesus
alone, is to have a personally investigated faith. Study his word—let God speak
for himself. His Word deals with the intellect and with morality, with the brains
and the emotions, with thoughts and behavior.

DISCIPLESHIP — commitment
Psalm 50:9–12; Acts 5:1–11

Not as Expected

General Washington labored under the twin shortages of men and supplies as he
contested British power in the Revolutionary War. He never commanded more
than twenty thousand men. His troops often went unpaid, unshod, under-
clothed, and hungry. We might conclude that the meager numbers reflected the
country's population. But, no. The colonial population could have fielded over
one hundred thousand men for its military. We might also surmise that the
country was simply too poor to feed Washington's troops. Again, this was not so.
In reality, the reluctance of farmers to accept Continental currency, not the lack
of grown and manufactured goods, precipitated the continual supply crisis for
Washington's troops. Obviously, many Americans did not concern themselves in
the struggle for independence. Others, who claimed to, didn't care to fight or
even risk financial loss for it.

The kingdom of God often resembles our colonial army. To witness the
inadequate support received by worthy mission fields, colleges, and church programs, you would think the kingdom of God just did not have enough people to
staff its mission. Not so. Half the people in America—almost 125 million—claim
membership in some church. Or we might think that those millions must be
intolerably poor to so meagerly support a work they claim to love and honor.
Again not so. Rich in this world's goods, those millions are simply poor in faith
and spiritual grace. That they give so little to God proves their small interest in
his work, however large an interest they claim.

DISCIPLESHIP — lived daily
Jeremiah 17:9; Luke 9:23

One Day at a Time

Fritz represents the Air Force Academy football team, making remarkable catches. But he doesn't play wide receiver or running back. A prairie falcon, Fritz regularly accompanies the team as a mascot, staging halftime shows that delight the crowd. Plunging from the top of a stadium at speeds up to 100 miles per hour, Fritz can pluck a leather pouch out of midair. A group of cadets raise, train, and show the falcons. While a number of necessary factors enter into the training, there is one that guarantees success: daily discipline for the birds. Should the trainers relax the regimen for even a week, the birds would return to their wild state.

    With good reason Jesus taught the need of daily self-denial in our Christian life. Without it, we run the risk of returning to a more familiar, less demanding lifestyle. While we live in the flesh, the danger of reverting to our undisciplined, unspiritual state demands daily self-denial. As in the falcons, our past always lurks closer than we think. Only as we train daily do we keep it at bay.

DISCIPLESHIP — needs forbidden zones
Numbers 33:55–56; 1 Corinthians 9:24–27

The Forbidden Zones

Donald Kennedy served as one of the most able coastwatchers in the Solomon Islands during the early months of World War II. Based at Segi, on the southern tip of New Georgia, he provided valuable intelligence on Japanese traffic up and down the Slot and Blanche Channel. Only a few miles from a Japanese headquarters, he remained isolated enough to continue his work. To protect himself from accidental discovery, Kennedy established a forbidden zone into which no Japanese could come without being destroyed. As long as they stayed outside that invisible perimeter, he left them alone. Should any enemy force cross that line, however, they would be attacked and annihilated.

    On one occasion Kennedy and his men hurried to a lagoon where two enemy barges had temporarily anchored. Although the barges were not looking for Kennedy, they had passed into his forbidden zone. Kennedy's men ambushed the Japanese, towed the barges to deep water, and sank them without a trace.

    Christians need forbidden zones in their lives, too; areas where they will allow no temptation to come without destroying it. There may be some things we can do and not be in danger, but there must be a forbidden zone where temptation will be abolished. The farther from our essential interests we draw those lines, the better. The secret to spiritual safety is to keep the enemy as far removed as possible, not to let him get as close as possible where a slight misstep could bring disaster.

DISCIPLESHIP — no limitations
Ecclesiastes 12:13; Luke 17:10

Not Just What's Expected

The mule is a genuinely intelligent animal that has proved its superiority to the horse in durability, memory, and dietary control. Pack mules have been used for years to lug gear for exploratory and recreational expeditions. They will carry seventy-five pounds on each side—but only seventy-five pounds. According to one veteran packer, if you put additional weight on a mule, it will buck the load off, refuse to move, or head for a tree to scrape the load off. These animals have sensitized their inner scales to the ounce and will haul nothing more.

Jesus warned about the mule in each of us: the spirit of mere duty that produces only what is expected and nothing more. He encourages us to go beyond that, to love him with the same unqualified depths that he loves us. The mule has an excuse—it's only a mule. What possible excuse could we have who are made in the image of God, redeemed in the likeness of Christ, and possessed even now of the Holy Spirit?

DISCIPLESHIP — a personal experience
Deuteronomy 5:1–2; 1 Corinthians 9:1

We Must Experience It

When Amerigo Vespucci sailed south along the east coast of South America, he went into and beyond the torrid zone, an imaginary line that Europeans thought divided habitable lands from hostile areas. By sailing farther south than anyone had previously—and returning—he proved the nonsense of the torrid-zone theory. Wherever he went, he found the air agreeable. Wherever he landed, he found people. In his journal he recorded: "Rationally, let it be said in a whisper, experience is certainly worth more than theory."

This is especially true in discipleship. Abraham lived as a nomadic merchant because God called him to the desert, not because he couldn't afford city life. We might think that Abraham could have hired a steward to serve his desert interests while he occupied his riverside villa. But, no; faith doesn't allow substitutes. If God says, "go here," the faithful disciple doesn't respond, "I'd rather go there." Another person's testimony can encourage our faith, but only our own experience can empower it. As we consciously acknowledge Christ's leadership in our behavior, we sanction the talk of our walk.

DISCIPLESHIP — service
Jeremiah 1:6–8; Luke 1:38; Matthew 1:24

Unchosen Places

The whooping crane named Tex thought it was a person, since it had been raised with humans from a chick. Consequently, when zoo officials tried to replenish the breed by placing a male crane with her, Tex resolutely refused to mate-dance and develop the egg. Then her handler had an idea. Noting Tex's strange penchant for male humans, he offered to be her "beau." He danced with her, flapping his arms grotesquely, ducking his head, then throwing it back in the best crane fashion. He even "moved in" with the bird, taking walks with her and helping her build a nest. Tex couldn't believe all her good luck and soared into such ecstasy that she laid an egg, which other cranes hatched.

Strange behavior for a man, we might say. And the keeper was the first to admit it. It wasn't his choice, he said, but it had to be done. Christians understand that. We begrudge no inconvenience to serve, though God sometimes calls us to a part we would never choose for ourselves. "Bred," in Plutarch's words, "to the art of obedience," we willingly help in ways we would not ordinarily choose, in tasks that are not publicly rewarding or highly successful. We feel that being called to any ministry indicates God's high regard for us.

DISCRIMINATION — in things seen
Genesis 3:6; Matthew 6:22–23

Watch Your Eye

Dr. Judith Rodin, a professor of psychiatry at Yale University, offers news to those with weight problems: though other factors affect weight gain, just looking at the wrong foods can add pounds. The insulin that directs sugar and fat into cells is the culprit. High levels of insulin in the bloodstream increase the likelihood that more calories will be consumed. And simply looking at certain foods will boost insulin levels, thus encouraging people to eat more. Cornflakes boost the level more than oatmeal, pastries more than peanuts, and raisins more than apples.

It reminds us of the principle Jesus taught: Our eyes are the lamps of our bodies. Indeed, what we look at, fix our eyes on, and gaze at, is often the very thing we find ourselves craving and wanting to do. Imagine three pictures: a scantily-clad person, a starving child in Africa, and a family reading the Bible around a table. Each picture affects us differently, evoking its particular emotion: prurience, pity, and piety. If we look wholeheartedly at one, the particular emotion it evokes will grow in us, dwarfing the others. How carefully we need to look! How discriminately we need to consider all the sights in the world clamoring for our gaze.

DISCRIMINATION — practice it
Psalm 15:1–5; Matthew 13:47–48

Give Me Discrimination

Although William Randolph Hearst's income ran as high as $15 million a year, friends found him constantly broke, unable to pay a bill of $50 or $100. James

Gordon Bennett, one-time publisher of the *New York Herald*, spent $30 to $40 million on any whim and impulse that struck him—business, pleasure, relationships. Obviously, if these men ever possessed financial discrimination, they silenced it long before adulthood.

We need to discriminate, to develop a filtration system in our lives that separates virtue from vice, the unnecessary from the needed, the possible from the unlikely, good ideas from bad, and best ideas from the better. Without that system, a chaos of ideas, hopes, and dreams will glut our mind and soul—leaving us at the mercy of our urges.

DISEASE — deadlier than war
Leviticus 26:14–16; Matthew 4:23–24

Far Worse than These

Disease proves far more effective than war in obliterating vast populations. The black plague emigrated from the Orient in the fourteenth century, spread westward and wiped out one-third to one-half of Europe's population. Cholera that began in India in 1816 reached Russia and the Near East by 1830. By 1832, it had swept through Europe and England. Irishmen brought it to Canada, and from there it was brought into the United States via Lake Champlain. From the East Coast, down the Ohio and up the Missouri it raged, killing thousands in the most savage plague since the Black Death.

Over twenty-one million died from war-related deaths between 1914 to 1918. Yet nearly as many died around the world from swine flu in just four months—between July and October 1918. Had it continued unabated, humanity would have been eradicated in weeks. It mysteriously appeared, violently afflicted millions, and mercifully passed in four months.

However rabid the bite of plague, cholera, or swine flu, resistance against it occurs even as it devastates human populations, for many who are healthy can acquire an immunity. Unfortunately, we have no comparable success rate against sin. No one develops immunity to sin, not even the saved. The Master's intercession at God's throne is perpetual, because our sins are continuous and are far deadlier than black plague or swine flu; for sin destroys our self. The only remedy to sin is forgiveness at the Cross.

DISTANCE — relative
Isaiah 30:15; Acts 3:19

Not Always in Physical Terms

Distance may not be a matter of feet or miles, but of perceptions. Before the Erie Canal relieved the problem, settlers across the Appalachian Mountains found it easier to ship their goods for the East Coast down south to New Orleans, then up the Atlantic seaboard (some three thousand miles) rather than shipping them directly east, only two to three hundred miles. The mountain barrier stood in the way.

Before 1815, businessmen paid as much to transport a ton of goods thirty miles inland from an American port as to ship the same ton from Europe. Lack of suitable vehicles and roads kept the infant nation's economy slow, its investments limited, and trade nearly impossible.

What stratospheric distances exist in spiritual perception between God and us! How far has our sin removed us from the Creator's original and continued purpose for us! God has made it clear that the only way to remove the distance of separation is by believing in Jesus Christ. God has not moved—we have, and we must return.

DIVISION — natural
Deuteronomy 15:10–11, 18; Romans 12:4–8

We Naturally Do It

In sixteenth-century Italy, once partisans of the pope (known as the Guelfs) and those of the emperor (the Ghibellines) took sides, nothing proved too small for a conflict. The "lava of hate flowed into all the avenues of life," Durant wrote. The customs one group embraced, the other shunned as heretical. The traditions one fellowship practiced, the other intentionally and flagrantly violated. Unable to wear different clothes, each group wore its clothes differently. If one side wore feathers on the right side of their caps, the other moved theirs to the left. Unable to eat different foods, each sect ate its food differently. Neither group hesitated to kill anyone foolish enough to act as if the dispute were trivial.

That may seem to be extreme nonsense, but modern church members have been known to divide their congregations over the color of a carpet, the size of a building program, or procedures in worship. Mankind needs no instruction in the differences that divide. That comes with birth. What we desperately need is instruction in the similarities we all share. God teaches us to love those who reject us and to do good to those who hate and persecute us. He reminds us repeatedly that we are all one body.

DIVORCE — children hurt
Job 1:4–5; I Peter 3:1–7

In Ways Not Immediately Seen

In her book *The Case Against Divorce*, Diane Medved details some interesting facts about how children of divorce are adversely affected. Referring to a University of Nebraska sociologist who conducted research in 1986, she states that the very young have immediate symptoms, but five years later seem to adapt. Older children appear to have less difficulty at first but generally have more severe problems in the long run. A *Psychology Today* article in April 1987, emphasized that boys at every age suffer more from divorce than girls; adolescent girls, with little fatherly contact, are more likely to become sexually promiscuous than girls with an available father. All this says nothing of the financial hardships inflicted on children when divorce comes. The 1990 census showed that children can expect to become 37 percent poorer almost immediately after divorce occurs. The percentage of children living in poverty increased from 19 percent to 36 percent immediately after a family breakup.

God formed the nuclear family as a male and female with children. This is the biblical model, and anything different proves inadequate and harmful. While government billions have not eliminated poverty, a return to God's model of family will send it reeling, as even government statistics show. And that doesn't even consider the greater values of security, self-esteem, discipline, and example that the biblical model provides for society. Why will we not humbly return our families to the model that really works?

DIVORCE — costly
Proverbs 5:18–20; Matthew 19:1–9

It Isn't Cheap

The divorce between movie mogul George Lucas and his wife cost him as much as $25 million. When Johnny Carson divorced his wife, she requested $220,000 a month to continue the lavish lifestyle she had enjoyed as the superstar's wife. Fred Couples, a premier golfer, thought his estranged wife could live on $17,500 a month. She wanted at least $168,000 a month until polo season was over, then $55,000 a month. The judge considered all the economics involved and decided that $52,000 monthly would be sufficient until the divorce proceedings were finished.

Expensive! The national average cost of getting a divorce in 1989 was over $10,000—just to process the papers, pay the court costs, and the lawyer's fees. Then comes the whopping settlement costs! One must certainly be miserable in the marriage to pay such astronomical costs to be free of it. Why not try reconciliation? Instead of beating a path to a divorce lawyer's office—who is glad you are splitting—why not seek counseling from someone who wants you to stay married? Given our fallen nature, marriage may not be easy, but will it be harder than going through a divorce?

DREAMS — coming true
Genesis 40:4–8; Matthew 1:20

Strange Events We Cannot Explain

Food market owner Rafael Gonzalez dreamed that an ex-employee robbed and killed him. Six days later he bled to death after being shot during a robbery. Having learned of the dream from family members, detectives began their investigation. When prints from the cash box matched those of a store employee, police told him about the dream and he confessed.

A few days before his assassination, Abraham Lincoln dreamed that he awoke and heard sobbing in the White House. Walking downstairs, he saw a catafalque and coffin in the East Room. Approaching the mourners, he asked who was dead. "The President," they replied, "felled by an assassin."

Mark Twain once dreamed that his brother died. Twain saw him in a metal coffin, a bouquet of white flowers with a red blossom in the center on his chest. A month later the brother died in a Mississippi steamboat explosion. At the funeral Twain stared in astonishment—there lay his brother exactly as in the dream, the single red blossom resting among the white flowers.

God often used dreams to communicate with people in ancient times. Genesis alone details how Abraham, Abimelech, Jacob, Laban, Pharaoh, a baker, a cupbearer, and Joseph received dream messages from God. In Matthew, Joseph received one dream guaranteeing Mary's virtue and had others that related to Christ's safety. Today we do not need to wait for a dream to be guided by God because he has given us guidance in his Word.

DREAMS — energy used
Daniel 2:1, 24; Acts 2:17

It Can Get Wild

He found himself roller-skating on the main floor at Neiman-Marcus, a bare-fanged tiger in hot pursuit. She heard her boss demanding that the floor be painted in multicolors immediately. Riding a horse in the country, another fellow suddenly found it galloping out of control despite his commands to halt. A woman found herself pursued by a robber and began running away, but the harder she pumped her legs the heavier they became until she couldn't lift them at all.

This would be stressful work for anyone who was awake and alert; yet it is just as tough on the brain when someone is asleep. Sleep without dreams allows brain activity to drop by an average of 23 percent. The brain needs to rest just like our bodies, but researchers say that during dream time the brain lights up with activity.

How wonderfully and mysteriously God has made us—wonderfully, in that the body and mind have immense skills; mysteriously, in that we hardly understand even their most basic functions. It causes us to reflect in amazement at the infinitely greater wonder and mystery of the Creator.

DREAMS — giving insight
Genesis 41:25–32; Matthew 2:13, 19

Good for Life's Work

Elias Howe once dreamed that a hostile tribe threatened to kill him if he didn't produce a sewing machine: he would die by spear thrust. The images of spear tips being hurled at him inspired the concept of a needle carrying thread in its tip. Struggling to understand the structure of benzene, German chemist Friedreich Kekule dreamed about six snakes in a circle, biting each other's tails. On awaking he realized that the hexagon represented benzene's molecular structure.

Samuel Coleridge wrote *Kubla-Khan* after a dream, Frankenstein came from Mary Wallstoncraft's nightmares, and *The Strange Case of Dr. Jekyll and Mr. Hyde* came from Robert Louis Stevenson's dreams. Beethoven and Donizetti based some of their most famous symphonies on their dreams, and Albert Einstein saw his famous formula $E=Mc2$ in a dream.

George Washington Carver believed that God spoke to him in dreams, giving him information for such inventions as sandpaper. Directions for life came to Jeremiah, Daniel, Solomon, and Joseph in dreams. Christian workers can testify that insights and ideas come to them as they dream, or at the instant of wakefulness, perhaps from a dream. We also know that the creative effort of study and application during the day can return to us at night in the form of answers and ideas.

EARTH — leave it intact
Genesis 1:26; Romans 8:19

Must Remain Undisturbed

The Brazilian rain forest supports a vast and diverse ecosystem of a million species of flora and fauna—if left intact. Once disturbed and burned, its truly fragile constitution expresses itself. Four-inch soil, powerful enough to secure shallow-rooted trees, holds so few nutrients that farmers can only cultivate it for a short time. Once its brilliantly synchronized system is disturbed by slash and burn practices, the rain forest can quickly resemble a barren wasteland.

It is a parable of humanity. If we had remained true to God's intended purpose for us, we would have flourished undiminished. When Adam removed us from that purpose, our vulnerability became obvious. Death appeared, accompanied by disease, war, famine, and catastrophes.

Once the rain forest is destroyed, little can be done to reclaim it. However humanity fares better. Though completely lost to God's original purpose, he acted to reclaim us by offering new life through salvation in his Son, Jesus Christ.

ECONOMY — of Rome
Genesis 4:1–4; Matthew 25:14–30

Working while the Master Relaxed

The paterfamilias of the Roman family allowed his slaves and freedmen to control his affairs, sell his produce, and to make financial decisions for the family. Their business acuity made them indispensable to the economy of the Roman Empire. Most were scrupulously honest; they kept accurate records of all income and expenses, and sometimes went years before being called to an accounting. But, as Jesus stressed in the parable of the unjust steward, any dishonesty brought immediate dismissal and worse, for penalties were severe.

God has given us the freedom to choose and to make decisions. He holds us accountable for our stewardship of all he has given us. It is a challenging responsibility. Human stewardship of the earth demands reevaluation, less exploitation, and more cooperation. The spiritual root of environmental abuse must be recognized—we have treated the earth badly because we have left God's original intention for our personal lives.

EDUCATION — answers from college
Exodus 2:1–10; Acts 7:20–22

I Can't Believe They Said That

Apparently, not all of the students who take exams are thinking in the process. A professor in Bible College shared these answers from an exam on the book of Hebrews: (1) Question—Give what you feel is the best date of writing and why. Answer—60 A.D. It gives Paul time enough to be grown enough to write this letter. (2) Question—In what way was Melchizedek without father or mother? Answer—By the tithes Abraham gave him, and by his name. (3) Question—What is an encumbrance or weight? Answer—The cloud of witnesses. (4) Question—Who is the likely author of Hebrews? Answer—Agrippa. (5) Question—What does it mean to enter one's rest? Answer—This is where Jesus rested after praying. The word *rested* means that Jesus sat down and thought about everything. (6) Question—Why couldn't David build the Temple? Answer—God didn't live behind any door.

It makes you wonder. Isn't the purpose of all education, even at the most elementary level, to create the ability and arouse the energy to think? Because we live in a ten-minute-attention-span culture is no excuse for anesthetizing our brains. The greatest of all commandments still challenges us to love God with all of our mind!

EDUCATION — the things they learn at school
Genesis 11:7–9; Acts 2:4, 6–8

Could You Repeat That?

Students from grade school through college wrote the following gems of disinformation: (1) The pyramids are a range of mountains between France and Spain. (2) In Guinessis, the first book of the Bible, Adam and Eve were created from an apple tree. (3) Moses went up on Mount Cyanide to get the ten commandments; he died before he ever reached Canada. (4) Socrates died from an overdose of wedlock. (5) History calls people Romans because they never stayed in one place for very long. (6) Rome was invaded by ball bearings and is full of fallen arches today. (7) Victims of the bluebonnet plague grew boobs on their necks. (8) Johann Bach wrote a great many musical compositions and had a large number of children. In between, he practiced on an old spinster which he kept up in his attic.

Honestly, some of these sound too creative to arise from ignorance, but others do have an authentic ring to them! Communication often gets garbled somewhere between the teacher's tongue and the student's ears; or somewhere in the student's brain, from lack of study or comprehension. In desperation, the student fishes for something that sounds similar to what the teacher has requested—and lands a whale where minnows were expected. Sometimes what God asks, commands, and expects in his Word fails to reach into our minds also. Filtered through our prejudices, predilections, and spiritual innocence, it gets turned and twisted, producing an uneven impact that, more often than not, produces a skewed response.

EFFORT — what purpose
2 Samuel 15:61, 18:14–15; Matthew 26:14–16, 27:3–4

To No Useful End

During an overhaul in February, 1942, fire jeopardized the *Lafayette,* the former French liner *Normandie.* The water that was pumped in to save her capsized the ship at dockside. After eighteen months of intense salvage she was raised and placed in dry-dock—but to no avail. Her hull was so deteriorated and her machinery in such poor condition that further work was impractical. Although the allies thought the ship was worth the time, effort, and money necessary to raise it from death, it wasn't. Too many months spent buried in the water had ruined it for any useful purpose.

Life without God is like the raising of the *Lafayette.* You spend enormous amounts of time, money, and energy, only to find it useless. It is so sin-stained and corrupted that it hardly serves any purpose in this life, let alone in the life beyond.

EMOTIONS — hidden at critical time
Deuteronomy 3:25; Luke 22:15

All for Show

For eight days Major Sandy Forsyth and his men were surrounded by Cheyenne and Sioux Indians on an island in the Arickaree River. On the ninth day a relief column from Fort Wallace appeared. Wounded three times, Forsyth knew he couldn't trust his emotions as the relief force descended the hill and raced across the water. To act disaffected by the merciless ordeal and the elation of being safe, he quickly reached into his saddlebags for a little novel. When Captain Carpenter rode up and dismounted, saluting, there was the major pretending to read *Oliver Twist.*

American soldiers and their generals visibly recoiled in tears and rage when they liberated concentration camps in 1945. Even hard-bitten General Patton wept and vomited. General Gavin and his paratroopers cried at the unbelievable depravity, and an enraged Eisenhower ordered wide media coverage of the horrors to prevent later denials by revisionist historians.

Of all Scripture writers, Paul especially shared himself freely in his writings. Often a volcano of controlled emotion, he shared his sorrows, confidences, struggles, joys, fears, and occasional rages. That may explain why, at Miletus, after his farewell address, the elders all wept as they embraced and kissed him—and why afterwards Paul and his companions had to tear themselves away from the Christians. When those who serve God commit their humanity to Jesus, only the good they do will be remembered by those they serve. The law of the echo remains.

EMOTIONS — overcoming
Psalm 126:1–2; Romans 8:18

Left without Words

Columbus suffered intolerable indignities after returning to the new world in 1498. His own people and trusted commanders had mutinied, and his enemies shamelessly lied about him. In 1500 he was sent back to Spain in chains. All this he bore with no outward emotion. But when he arrived in Cadiz, the sovereigns ordered him freed and brought before them in kingly fashion. When he approached the throne and saw tears in Queen Isabella's eyes, his own long-suppressed feelings burst. He threw himself on his knees "and for some time could not utter a word for the violence of his tears and sobbings."

We have had enough plowmen ploughing our backs to become discouraged. We have known enough treachery to become paranoid. We have been to enough graveyards to become bitter. We have known enough opposition to become reactionary. But when Jesus welcomes us into his presence, we will be free—not in chains—filled with expectation, not dread. And the look on Jesus' face will bring the deepest joy ever. There will be no weeping. We will have come out of desperation into hope; out of trials into triumph.

ENEMIES — admitted
Esther 3:5–6; 2 Corinthians 11:12

It Is Better to Know

In World War II Britain and America had a radio detection finder called Huff-Duff. It intercepted transmissions between German U-boats and gave anti-submarine forces time to concentrate their strength for the kill. Used from the fall of 1941, the device offered a margin for victory in the Atlantic antisubmarine warfare. Blissfully unaware that it existed, German headquarters transmitted top secret orders to their submarine commanders. Ignorant of how completely the Allies had breached their security, the commanders found themselves to be targets instead of marksmen.

No one likes having enemies. But if you have them, pray they will be out in the open with it. Then at least you can attempt a reconciliation. But how can you counter a threat you don't know exists or reconcile with a person you did not know you had alienated?

EVANGELISM — incumbent on Christians
Esther 8:17; Luke 19:3–4

While They Cry for Help

On September 24, 1983, three sports fishermen motored to an island off the west coast of Florida. Sudden squalls whipped five-foot waves into their boat, drowning the engine. Helpless before the tide, they drifted into the Gulf of Mexico. There was no need to worry, they thought. The sea lanes hummed with activity, and early rescue seemed likely. When, finally, on the third day a Coast Guard jet flew overhead, they felt they had been seen and celebrated by eating nearly all the food left aboard.

No deliverance came. In desperation, they watched thirty ships pass close by and move on, despite their frantic gestures for help. They ate fish to survive and drank water by the sip morning and night to prevent dehydration. Finally, on their tenth day adrift, a freighter spotted and rescued them. Later the men asked angrily how they could be so close to so many potential rescuers, yet never be seen.

People show their desperation for God in strange ways. Sometimes they argue against him, wanting someone to prove them wrong; or they express doubts about him, hoping someone will take time to talk with them, to care. Their need of God can come as a whimper or a shout, a curse or a prayer. As Christians, we must stop and attempt a rescue under any situation. The sinner will have to reach for the life preserver—but we must throw it.

EVANGELISM — limited
Isaiah 42:1–4; Matthew 8:10–12

Why So Long?

Columbus wrote an eight-page pamphlet describing his discovery of America. It sold briskly, reaching major continental cities by 1493–1494. The wonder is that no one thought to broadcast it everywhere in Europe. The Nuremberg *Chronicle*, printed July 12, 1493, made no reference to it at all. Not until March 1496, did word of it reach England. The first German translation of Columbus' report came from the presses in Strasbourg in 1497. Here was information the like of which had never been received in Europe, and some major centers did not get the message for months, even years.

Expectation overwhelmed those who read the report. Letters among the literati flowed back and forth, congratulating each other for having been alive at such a historic time. Still, the knowledgeable seemed in no hurry to educate the uninformed!

If that is a mystery, it is even more perplexing that Christ's redemptive message is still unheard by so many in the world today. Two thousand years after the fact—with unrivaled communication skills at our disposal and Christians everywhere in the world—millions still have not heard of Christ's sacrifice! How strange that every person in all the world should not have heard by now that Jesus died and lives—for them!

EVANGELISM — public witness
Joshua 2:12–13; John 3:1; 7:50–51

It Must Be Public

Stanislav Levchenko served in the KGB and ultimately became a member of the First Chief Directorate of the Soviet Union, an organization that conducted all foreign intelligence operations for the Soviets. Throughout his many years of service, Levchenko underwent and survived three separate investigations by the KGB as he climbed higher into the Soviet hierarchy. But not all of their investigations uncovered his Christian faith.

He kept his faith so secret that no one but he knew of it. Yet when he learned of his transfer to Japan, Levchenko openly went to a church in Moscow and prayed. Openly that time, though he had carefully hidden it before. Openly, so all could see, though previously he had wanted no one to see. He decided he could no longer desecrate God's name by hiding his faith in secret. He let God decide whether worship should be punished.

Faith in God may begin in secret, but it cannot remain there. It must become an open confession, not a hidden resolve. It must he demonstrated visibly, despite fear of retribution, rebuke, persecution, and loss. It perishes in secret, but thrives by being lived and tested. If that Russian Christian, who had his job, his security, and, possibly, his life to forfeit for a public confession, made it anyway, could we possibly think of any excuse to keep our faith secret?

EVENTS — symbolic of a movement
Exodus 14:5; 1 Corinthians 1:26–28

Just Like the Entire Cause

Benedict Arnold's traitorous betrayal of West Point was thwarted by the two farmers who had been hoodwinked into rowing a boat down the Hudson River to get Captain John Andre and rowing back to the American lines. After waiting through the night for Andre, they staunchly refused to row him back to the *Vulture.* These two farmers, who refused to be bribed by Andre, dynamited the whole dangerous expedition in the faces of the conspirators. In a strange way, they symbolized the entire Revolution, made up of stubborn individuals who did as their consciences or desires directed.

New Testament Christianity drew its volatile energy from common people who were won to the egalitarian Christ. Denied personal participation in heathen and Jewish religions, they found acceptance in the emerging Christian church. The gospel would exempt no one, not even the rich and famous. It included everyone, especially those the patricians thought fit only for servitude. Those simple folk became leaders in their congregations, guiding into spiritual maturity many who lived above them socially. The church offered everyone access to membership and leadership.

EVIDENCE — essential
Numbers 9:8; John 19:35–37

But Not in Exact Detail

A friend asked Frederick Renner, a Charles Russell scholar, to determine whether a portfolio of drawings with CMR scribbled on them were genuine or forgeries. The sketches were consonant with Russell's western themes and the titles seemed authentic, but Renner was baffled by significant inconsistencies. The compositions betrayed a distinctive immaturity, an ignorance of Indian culture, and contradictions of Russell's famous signature and symbols.

Renner investigated the sketches more closely and, despite the evident paradoxes, sensed the hand of the master artist—not when he was mature, but in his youth. The word *Burlington* on one of the pages provided the decisive clue: it was the military academy Russell had attended. Even at age fifteen he loved to paint and hated to study. The portfolio represented the apprentice's first efforts in the craft in which he would one day be a master.

Renner found agreement in the essentials, though not in details. It is a principle that should guide our study of biblical teachings in both the Old and New Testaments. Like witnesses in a courtroom, the Bible's many writers offer essential agreement in all their personal perspectives. This unity in diversity stamps the imprimatur of authenticity on Scripture. Without saying exactly the same thing in exactly the same words (which would make us suspicious of collusion), each writer revealed truth as the Spirit moved him to express it.

EVIDENCE — compelling
Exodus 10:7; Matthew 12:38

When Enough Has Been Offered

In *The Red Badge of Courage,* Jim runs to his unit, excited with news of their movement to battle. The men have heard similar rumors before, so they argue with him. One even comes close to blows with him over the news. Another asks how Jim knows that it is true. Jim simply answers that they can believe or doubt as they please; he doesn't care. There is food for thought in his manner of reply, the author says—"He came near to convincing them by disdaining to produce proofs." Perhaps Jim thought his affirmation offered enough proof, and being firmly convinced himself, thought others would also believe.

The Bible is firm in its position that further proofs of God's existence, or our need to be saved, or the means he has provided to save us would not be in anyone's best interest. Therefore, it refuses to offer additional evidence when we refuse to believe and act on the reams of proof already given. Jesus would not perform miracles just to convince the leadership of his messianic character. He would not answer when Pilate asked where he came from, because Pilate had already had more than sufficient evidence at his disposal. Jesus would not respond to Herod's appeal for miracles when arraigned before him. Jesus didn't care about their clamorings. He claimed to be the Messiah and offered indisputable proofs of that claim. Scoffers who continue to demand more proof from God should ask themselves whether they really want to be convinced, or merely entertained.

EXAMPLE — powerful
Esther 1:16–18; John 13:15

To Show the Way

No one had climbed Mount Everest until Sir Edmund Hillary achieved the feat in 1953. Since then hundreds have ascended the world's highest, most forbidding peak. In 1864, General William Sherman marched fifty thousand troops through four states of the Confederacy, living off the land. Without a previous expedition set in motion by General Grant, however, Sherman might not have made such a foolhardy effort. When Grant marched from Grand Gulf on the Mississippi into the interior of the state to battle Pemberton's troops, he supplied his men with only hardtack, salt, and coffee. The rest of their food had to be gleaned from the countryside. Sherman didn't originate the idea behind his bold scheme, but having seen it demonstrated by Grant, he never forgot the lesson.

The greatest value of leadership is to show those who follow that a problem can be solved, a hurdle overcome, a victory gained. Once someone shows the way, others will follow. Leaders must lead—and stop thinking of themselves as followers.

EXPECTATIONS — unfulfilled
Judges 2:7, 10; Romans 2:17–23

Not Much Returned

Sohio, the Alaskan subsidiary of Standard Oil of Ohio, drilled a well in the Beaufort Sea in 1983, hoping to tap a geological formation holding several billion barrels of oil. Instead, they hit water, and $120 million went a glimmering. The oil companies know the risk. They drill only after extensive soil samples and aerial photos offer substantial possibilities of success. Yet despite the precautions, geological formations that promise to break all records for oil or gas deposits break the bank instead. Such risks are considered acceptable, however, as a strike like the one contemplated would have repaid the investment many times over.

God understands the problem of bad investments, dry holes, wasted millions, and unrequited love. How often have our lives turned out to be water where oil was expected; wild grapes instead of pruned vines; rebels instead of allies. And we have no excuse. God has built energies, talents, and giftedness into every generation of Christians, in order that Christ's mission can successfully be implemented. But does the will and personal commitment exist to do it? If we would invest energy, time, and expertise equivalent to a modicum of the money spent by the oil companies, what miracles the Holy Spirit would perform in society!

EXPERIENCE — sets you apart
Exodus 1:11–14; Mark 15:34

Only He Knows

In December, 1960, Fidel Castro proscribed religion as a counter-revolutionary dogma no longer tolerated in Cuba. Twenty-three-year-old Armando Valladares couldn't believe the decree. On Christmas Day he went as usual to pray in a nearby church. Three days later the government arrested him for "offenses against state authorities." Thus began a twenty-two year horror, while he endured the shocking cruelties and tortures of Castro's prison system.

Valladares survived the nightmare through his faith in God and his love for a girl who befriended him while in prison. The chastisements inflicted to break him deepened him instead. Poetry and paintings that anti-Castro accomplices smuggled from the prison revealed an unconquered soul within a beleaguered body. Finally, after intensive lobbying in world capitals for Valladares' freedom, the Cuban government released him.

The personal affliction of that Cuban hero sets him apart from us. Only he knows what it cost him. Likewise, no one ever can understand our Lord's ordeal. Only he assumed the burden of a fallen race, whose swollen egotism had inflicted horrendous plagues on itself. Only he accepted the penalty for those iniquities, as he absorbed God's belligerence towards sin. The sufferings of Jesus place him in a category all alone. He endured more than anyone in all of history. No one else has any idea!

EXPERIENCE — value of personal
Exodus 19:9; Acts 9:3

The Value of Firsthand Experience

In the 1960s Albert Sabin developed the live-virus polio vaccine that gave a life-time protection against the dreaded crippler and killer. Dr. Sabin and Dr. Jonas Salk pioneered the vaccines that have virtually eliminated the worldwide menace. Dr. Sabin himself later suffered paralysis due to risky surgery on his spinal cord. After surgery, when he seemed to be recovering, an excruciating pain hit him like a lightning bolt, affecting his legs, chest, and arms. It was stifling, teeth-clenching pain! Yet the doctors hesitated to kill the horrifying pain for fear that the sedatives would interfere with his respiration. Sabin said that if he ever cursed at doctors, it was then. For, as a patient, he felt that the first responsibility of a physician was to stop the pain that consumed him. Oh, the value of first-hand experience! Never again would he speak casually of pain.

No minister or lawyer could have written *Common Sense*. Only Tom Paine could—from the depths of his own agony, sorrow, and rejection. Again, the value of personal experience! Yet we need not fall prey to every infirmity to sympathize with the infirmities of others. After all, Jesus never sinned, yet he perfectly understands sinners. When we do experience infirmity, we should let it equip us to more adequately witness for Christ.

EXPLORATION — success even in failure
Genesis 3:21; 1 Peter 1:7

Initial Failure Can Be Ultimate Success

Following the Green River Rendezvous in 1833, Captain Benjamin Bonneville ordered Joseph Walker and forty mountain men to trap the streams of California. Towards Salt Lake they rode, killing buffalo and drying sixty pounds of meat each. Westward to the Humboldt they traveled. After three weeks of shocking hardships they descended from the Sierra Nevada into the lush San Joaquin and Sacramento valleys. The mountain men had found the paradise that rumors had fashioned: a land of game, cattle, orchards, farms, vineyards, and Missions. Walker traveled east the next spring, discovering the pass along the Kern River that now bears his name. In spite of all this, Captain Bonneville never forgave Walker for his failure to bring back furs—the object of the entire mission. In Bonneville's mind, the whole enterprise had been a failure.

In reality, Joseph Walker had achieved an unparalleled success; first, by leading so many men across so many miles of unknown wilderness; second, by planting in the American conscience the notion of empire, later called Manifest Destiny.

The kingdom of God originated in his desire to love us, not to swell our bank accounts. Love, not the prospect of wealth, brought Jesus here and led him to the cross. The greatest idea of all time exists outside the profit motive: All sinners can be reconciled to God through Jesus Christ. So here we are, children in a kingdom whose King rules the universe and owns the resources of all world corporations, governments, and individuals. We can't cash a five dollar check on it, but we are rich beyond measure with a wealth King Midas couldn't touch.

EXTREMISM — get their attention
Jeremiah 44:28; John 8:24

The Radical Thought

William Lloyd Garrison intemperately advocated the abolitionist's cause prior to the Civil War. Violently opposed to slavery, he shocked slave owners and moderates alike with his fire-eating detestation of the system. Garrison couldn't approach the subject quietly. Slavery had been embedded in the South and tolerated by the North for too long. The voice raised against it had to shout in outrage. How often the first voice raised against injustice must shock and traumatize to gain attention. It requires the brute force of extremist, uncompromising dogmatism.

In many ways, Jesus was an extremist. Since he alone possessed truth and the way to heaven, he first had to disassociate himself from all others who claimed to have found the true way to God. His teaching sounded radical then, especially to the devout Jews. It sounds just as radical now, for the modern mind thinks it incredible that there is only one way to heaven. But it is simple, really. If Jesus is what he claimed to be, he is the only way to God—no other way exists. Once he is accepted as God, all his claims and demands are simply *expected.*

FAILURE — but still competitive
Genesis 31:38–42; Luke 22:55–62; Acts 1:15

To the Loser

For all the pack's killer instinct, only one of every fourteen wolf hunts succeeds. For all its cunning, speed, and strength, the polar bear succeeds in the kill but once in every five attempts. And an adult tiger can miss nineteen out of the twenty times it hunts. But you won't hear the wolf, bear, or tiger griping about bad referees, sore ribs, or incompetent teammates. They all fail with style, trailing off when the prey is too swift or too far away, waiting for a better opportunity. The animals instinctively know that the one successful kill keeps them alive.

To lose with style and tact, to accept failure with grace, offers proof of a mature disposition and character. Here's to the loser: to the runner who failed to win, but finished the race; to the team that was beaten, but fought to the last; to the teacher who wishes to teach a thousand, but patiently teaches a few; to preachers who preach in small congregations, unheralded and undervalued, but who treat their ministries with loving care; to the Christian who tries to be righteous, but fails and repents and tries again.

FAILURE — career from correcting others
Deuteronomy 18:15; Matthew 17:5–8

Fixing What Others Break

When the Kansas City Hyatt Regency walkway collapsed in 1981, Failure Analysis Associates linked the tragedy to an improperly placed bolt that was unable to support the weight imposed on it. When the Space Shuttle Challenger exploded in 1986, Failure Analysis Associates helped trace the failure to O-rings that cracked in cold Florida weather. When fumes at the rocket-fuel plant in Henderson, Nevada, overcame fifty-five people in 1992, Failure Analysis Associates found a leaking chlorine gas line responsible.

Naturally, then, when San Diego's undersea sewage line burst in early 1992, the city called the "master of disaster"—Failure Analysis Associates. Nine months and $352,000 later, after poring over data, creating computer models, consulting engineers in various disciplines, and scrutinizing the broken pipe sections, they determined that trapped air had caused the eruption. Not even in existence twenty years ago, this company has become a necessity today because of present labor rates and escalating litigation.

God has a single spiritual engineer—his Son—and a single organization—his church. His son unerringly diagnoses our failures; he understands their bases and unfailingly prescribes their cure. The church holds safely in forgiveness those who "hire" God's engineer through faith in his redemption of sins. If an earthly company is worth its fee for telling us how we fail, isn't Christ more than worth his for guaranteeing how we can succeed?

FAILURE — chance one takes for trying
Psalm 42:1; Philippians 3:10

Willing to Fail for the Chance to Succeed

The best Major League teams lose one of every three games. The best batters fail to get hits six to seven times out of ten. One minor league player in fourteen makes it to the big leagues. Still, they consider the chance to succeed well worth the possibility of failing. They say you can't stop swinging for fear of striking out.

Only those who try have the right to fail. You can't fail if you don't try, and that's one way to escape the frustration of trying and not succeeding. Think nothing, try nothing, expect nothing—you can hardly be disappointed. But God made us for something else: to be a roaring success!

FAILURE — a motivation
1 Samuel 12:23; Luke 22:32

Something Positive from Fear

Fear of failure can be a positive motivation, Mark McCormack wrote. "If you aren't afraid to fail, then you probably don't care enough about success." Bjorn Borg, McCormack said, had to summon all of his courage just to put the ball in play on key points. Arnold Palmer often succeeded because of his fear of failure, and when he did fail, you could see it in his face; it said he cared.

We might argue that talent helped both Borg and Palmer to succeed. That while others might have had a similar fear of failing, they didn't have their splendid giftedness. Still, the desire not to fail has motivated many to excellence in hard work and play. When someone asked Joe DiMaggio why he always played so hard, he said it was because someone might be in the stands who hadn't seen him play before. He had a fear of having anyone think him a slacker. Cliff Livingstone, who played with Michael Jordan on three Chicago Bulls NBA championship teams, said that Jordan's practice intensity equaled his game intensity. Without practice, he knew he would never be able to perform those magnificent slam dunks at game time.

Christians can accept that definition of fear: something that motivates you to succeed because you don't want to disappoint by failure. Fear of failing God encourages us to resist temptation longer, to reach for excellence instead of mediocrity, and to live by faith even when it seems useless.

FAILURE — a lesson
Exodus 17:14; Deuteronomy 31:3; Acts 15:37–81; 2 Timothy 4:11

Even It Can Teach Us

Publishers refused George Bernard Shaw's first five novels. Far from being wasted, however, the effort taught him valuable writing skills. Once he became famous, one of those novels was published and became a bestseller.

Claire Trevor began her acting career in the Depression to provide financial help for her family. She found herself stuck in B pictures, working six days a week and completing eight films. At the time she thought it a waste, but in retrospect, she understood its value to her career. When she won the Academy Award for Best Actress in 1948 she expressed gratitude for the invaluable education the B pictures had given her.

What we consider failure, then, may be vital education without the degree. It is training in the trenches that teaches us about ourselves and our intentions. Failure can also provide a spiritual silence, too often buried under life's distractions—a silence in which to rethink and refit, to consider previously unwelcomed or overlooked alternatives, to interrogate our motives, and to question our procedures. Failure can be useful if we see it as potentially good, if we react courageously, if we mentally compensate for it with a corresponding success, and if we trust in God as our unfailing friend.

FAILURE — means of success
Exodus 10:7; Acts 8:1, 4; 11:19

Not Final

It helped to build the atom bomb and made nonstick frying possible: teflon. It was inadvertently discovered in April 1938 from a failed experiment with refrigerator gases.

It took an accident on September 17, 1908, when Orville Wright's passenger was killed and he suffered massive breaks in legs, ribs, and hips, to awaken people to the airplane. All of Wright's previous successes had failed to stir any interest—news editors relegated them to back pages. Then came the accident, and the Wrights became household names overnight.

The persecution by Saul of Tarsus threatened the existence of the Greek church. Stephen, as a representative of the Greeks, so brilliantly withstood Saul and his cohorts that they determined to eliminate the entire Christian movement among Grecian Jews. Severe persecution scattered the Grecians out of harm's way, yet those who left Jerusalem carried their faith with them like hot coals. Wherever they visited, new fires of faith were ignited, until spiritual flames consumed whole populations, including Gentiles in Antioch of Syria. What a powerful encouragement to Christians who sometimes feel the weight only of their failures, not of God's glory within them. Satan can hurt God's people, but he cannot overcome God's cause.

FAILURE — one generation affects the next
Deuteronomy 5:9; Matthew 27:25; Acts 5:28

By Just One Vote

In Congress, 1783, Jefferson proposed that after 1800 no slavery could exist in any new state. Every delegate from Pennsylvania north voted aye, joined by Jefferson and Williamson of North Carolina. All other Southerners voted no. New Jersey, which would have voted aye, lost its vote because its single delegate was ill. Jefferson got six of the seven states necessary to pass the bill. By the failure of one vote the horrors of the Civil War, Reconstruction, and civil rights abuses we have yet to solve visited our nation.

Churches have bequeathed similar disasters on succeeding generations of believers. Consider some of the ways we have brought disgrace to Christ's name: we have waged wars to regain religious sites, we have politicized the church by allying it with governments and political parties, we have begotten or tolerated racism, we have foolishly assumed that a weakly held commitment to discipleship can motivate sinners to repentance, and we have supported colleges and seminaries whose professors denigrate the Christian faith that pays their salaries. God can always count on Satan to be his enemy—can he count on Christians to be his friends?

FAILURE — without knowing it
Numbers 14:40–41; Luke 23:28–29

A Meridian Too Far

The ninety-eighth meridian in Texas divides the wet land from the arid land of the state. East of the meridian, crops can be grown in ordinary ways—west, they cannot. When the earliest settlers came to Texas, they passed that meridian without realizing they had gone into a country unable to support them, their cattle, and their crops. They didn't know it, but they had sentenced themselves to failure by going past the line that divides fertile from marginal agricultural lands.

Working for lasting peace without Christ is like that. Brief armistices interrupt the monotony of war, only to be buried under more conflict. We regret the animosities, plead for understanding, grieve over the savagery, but cannot say how to eliminate the war. Good people will continue to exhaust themselves, breaking their hearts trying to iron patches on shredded garments, but only when the

Prince of Peace dictates the conditions will peace come. Only when the Bread of Life feeds us will we eat. Only when the Light of the World illuminates will we see. Only when the Good Shepherd leads us will we find pasture.

FAME — evanescent
Genesis 13:10; 19:29; Colossians 4:14; Philemon 24; 2 Timothy 4:10

It Won't Last

In early February, 1987, the United States toasted the twelve meter sloop *Stars and Stripes.* Dennis Conner had just sailed the sixty-five-foot beauty to victory in the America's Cup. Seen nightly on news programs, she also occupied magazine and newspaper space around the world. However, instead of becoming a national treasure, she was simply auctioned to the highest bidder in May, 1993.

A generation earlier, Gregory "Pappy" Boyington would be warned of fame's temporary nature. As his Cadillac rolled along New York's Fifth Avenue and he absorbed the cheers of the crowd, a ragged, middle-aged man broke through the police lines, ran up, and grabbed Boyington's arm. The American Ace listened intently to the man. "Enjoy it today my boy, because they won't give you a job cleaning up the streets tomorrow."

God will take from us what we cannot keep only to give us what we cannot lose. Are we wise enough to let him?

FAME — not equal to faithfulness
Jeremiah 26:20–23; Revelation 2:9

Not Getting Their Fair Share

The battles of Forts Mercer and Mifflin produced some of the most dramatic action of the Revolutionary War. Four hundred Continental troops in each fort successfully withstood powerful attacks by Hessian troops and British cannon. Fort Mercer, on the Jersey shore, viciously contested two assaults by Von Donop's Hessians and wiped out a third of his command. Fort Mifflin's defenders, on Mud Island in the Delaware, resisted four days of savage bombardment from British ships of the line.

Why these battles haven't received more attention is a mystery. Perhaps Private Joseph Martin, of the Connecticut line, accurately appraised it. "There was no Washington, Putnam, or Wayne there. Had there been, the affair . . . would have been extolled to the skies. No, it was only a few officers and soldiers who accomplished it in a remote quarter of the army. . . . Great men get great praise; little men, nothing."

This is often true spiritually. Big churches get the press coverage, well-known preachers the renown, and visibly productive mission fields the lion's share of support. But workers in smaller churches and in less fertile fields work just as hard, expend just as much energy, and continue to pray in just as much hope.

They are God's Joseph Martins—the unknowns who faithfully serve, but without bumper harvests or fame. There may be no earthly honor for the obscure, but God sees the value of his servant in the honesty, intensity, and sincerity of the labor.

FAME — missing it
Jeremiah 45:1–5; Revelation 3:8

Fated to Be Unknown

Superb composer Harold Arlen teamed up with equally superb lyricist Johnny Mercer to write the music for the 1940s movie *Blues in the Night*. Although Arlen wrote other songs that soared in popularity—"Last Night When We Were Young," "Somewhere Over the Rainbow," "It's Only a Paper Moon," "I've Got the World on a String"—fame never tapped him on the shoulder. He delighted in telling a story illustrating his anonymity.

While in a New York cab zipping along the avenues, he heard the cabby whistling "Stormy Weather," an Arlen song. Arlen asked the driver to identify the author. After a moment's reflection, the man suggested Irving Berlin. Arlen playfully denied it and offered the cabby two more guesses, himself suggesting both Cole Porter and Richard Rogers. The man answered in the affirmative on each one, only to be corrected.

Finally, Arlen broke the news. "I wrote 'Stormy Weather.'"

"No kiddin'?" the cabby said. "And who are you?"

"I'm Harold Arlen."

The cabby turned to look closer at his passenger. "Who?"

The essence of personal maturity is the ability to give yourself to your work because you love it, unmindful of fame or anonymity. It is also the grace to ignore paltry praise for your efforts while delighting without jealousy in another's success. Serve, Jesus urges us, because service is essential to discipleship, not because someone sees, knows, and will applaud or praise. He trusts us to serve him; we can trust him to reward us.

FAME — not desiring it
Numbers 11:10–15; Galatians 1:11–12

He'd Just Say No

When Congress tried to vote Sherman a rank equal to Grant, Sherman angrily rejected the nomination. He would accept no such commission, he said. Having successfully commanded one hundred thousand men was enough of an honor for him. Regard for Grant may have colored Sherman's view of Congress' actions, but he also saw it as gilding a lily—he had reached the zenith of his profession in the Civil War. He was really saying that the honor his men had given him by following his leadership meant more than the highest rank. He rated the respect of his troops above military titles.

The Lord Jesus is called Savior, Lord, Redeemer, Master, Teacher, King, God, Word, Son, and Messiah. We would think those titles exhaustive. That, having said all that about Jesus, little would remain unsaid. Not true. In Heaven, after we ascribe to him all the adulation possible, in all the terms and titles we can give, even then there will be more about Jesus than can ever be ascribed or told.

FAME — with preferential treatment
1 Kings 10:14–25; 2 Corinthians 6:3–10

Titles Make a Difference

While marching with English Suffragettes to win the vote, Lady Constance Lytton was arrested and jailed. Where all other suffragettes were force fed when they refused to eat, she was examined and released due to "a bad heart." Suspicious that her title, not her heart, had caused the special concern, she went to Liverpool and demonstrated, getting arrested. There, she gave her name as Jane Warton, and when she refused food, they force fed her—with no examination of her heart.

Because she was known as a Lady, Constance wouldn't be abused. It is different for Christians. We should suffer precisely because we are Christians. Each generation of disciples shoulders the burden of reconciliation that Jesus assumed at Calvary. He died to forgive all generations, and we must pay the price of proclaiming that appeal to ours.

FAME — you want to miss
Ezekiel 26:19–21; Matthew 11:20–24

On Small Matters

Kokura, a city on the North coast of Kyushu, Japan, was the primary target of the second atomic bomb drop on August 9, 1945. Smoke and haze obscured the city, however, and after three bombing runs, the crew diverted to Nagasaki. By that small margin Kokura escaped the devastation visited upon Nagasaki. No one in Kokura objected to being overlooked that fateful day.

There are certain kinds of fame you don't care for. John Dillinger lived by his wits, escaped from jail, and enjoyed a grudging admiration among many people. But would anyone care to be an infamous criminal, living by fraud, deceit, disloyalty, and treachery?

If we can assure our success only in unacceptable ways, it is better to fail. If to succeed we must silence or betray our conscience, what success could possibly cancel such a stupendous error? If, just to prove we are free to choose, we elude or harden, ignore or bribe our conscience, is personal freedom worth it? Better flagrant slavery than slavery disguised as liberty. The former at least offers the opportunity to revolt; the latter makes us willing conspirators in repression.

FAMILY — fathers in leadership
Ruth 4:17; Luke 2:21–24, 41–50

Three Fathers

When Sam Rayburn's father died, someone commented that it was too bad he hadn't left him much of an inheritance. Sam instantly reproved the man, saying that his father had left him an unrivaled inheritance—an untarnished name. No one knows for sure about Columbus' origins. He could be linked to a number of noble families in Italy. That made no difference to his son Hernando. Defying the class conscious values of his society, he claimed that his father expressed a personal nobility that excelled any honor derived from an inherited title. Pierre Beaumarchais, who played such a strategic role in providing French help for the American Revolution, had lowly parentage. But he never undervalued it. "I can only reply that I never saw the man with whom I would exchange fathers."

God's Word has established the dominance of male leadership in the home. Children need fathers who consider familiarity with God superior to handling a bat or fixing a doll house; who freely talk to their children about God and to God about their children; and who zealously strive for the Christlikeness that assures the willing submission of all family members to their leadership. God wisely provided complementary roles for fathers and mothers, choosing to trust primary responsibility to fathers.

FAMILY — why risk failure
Genesis 22:1–14; Titus 2:4

Mistakes to Avoid

A man wrote Dear Abby saying he told the mother of a seven-year-old boy that he wanted to marry her but didn't want to rear her child. Not to worry, his intended replied. She would send the boy to summer camp, to his father's or grandmother's for weekends and holidays, and to boarding school during the year.

An attorney in San Diego spotted five preteens ripping down Christmas tree lights one December evening. He caught the pranksters and took them home. To his dismay, at the three homes, not one father was home (at ten o'clock) and not one mother knew her child was out of the house.

In San Diego, a sailor taking his girlfriend home late one night saw fire in a garage. He rushed into the house and found three sleeping children in the bedrooms. He led them to safety, wondering where the parents were at such an hour. It was later discovered that the single-parent mother had left the house unlocked, the garage open, and the children alone at 2:00 A.M. while she took a friend home.

Mistakes can destroy any family—not even the best efforts will guarantee success. But to boldly and wildly risk failure by foolish, senseless actions invites disaster. Parents must determine that if failure comes to them, it will be despite their best efforts, not because of inexcusable mistakes.

FEAR — of one thing
Lamentations 1:12; Luke 12:50

Fear Stared Down

Oliver Hazard Perry suffered a psychopathic fear of cows. He would even cross the road to avoid passing a cow. Yet that same man audaciously and fearlessly directed the American fleet against the British on the Great Lakes in the War of 1812. In the midst of battle, with his ship disabled, he rowed from it to another to keep his command afloat. Petrified of cows, he had no fear of guns, swords, or death. Fear of a single thing did not mean cowardice in all things.

Christians struggle with multiple acts of obedience, and we may think we are not Christians because of that struggle. This is not true. The outcome, not the conflict, determines our place with God. We can have every intention of obeying, yet have to fight ourselves to obey. Jesus sympathizes, for he experienced the same struggle when he confronted the cross. His sympathy goes beyond even that. He also understands what it means to accept a burden we don't want to bear, but cannot escape.

FELLOWSHIP — valuable
1 Samuel 10:1; John 21:9–10

Our Need for Each Other

The symbiotic relationship between vain, ambitious Charles Fremont and modest, self-effacing Kit Carson offered both men advantages they couldn't have enjoyed separately. Carson became pathfinder of *The Pathfinder*, while Fremont's appreciation of Carson on the Senate floor and in the press gave Kit the fame he could never have achieved on his own. He was so anonymous in 1842, in fact, that when he offered to guide Fremont, the explorer had to investigate Carson's references.

We need the emotional and intellectual nourishment cross-fertilization brings. We need to associate with those different from us, as Carson associated with Fremont. Relating to people of dissimilar personalities, traits, and levels of maturity builds the whole human fellowship and spiritual body. It leads to synergism, with the combined efforts of all achieving significantly more than any could achieve working alone.

FORGIVENESS — available for asking
Hosea 14:1–2; Acts 8:36

It Comes Right Now

Ted Tinling spent twenty years as master of ceremonies of the prestigious Wimbledon tennis championships. Then, in 1949, he committed an unpardonable breach of etiquette by outfitting Gussie Moran in lace-trimmed panties. Fired for his mistake, he lingered as an outcast for the next thirty-three years.

Only in 1982 was he forgiven and once again received into their ranks.

When people repent of their sins, they find God eager to forgive and have them back. The acknowledgment of their sin, their sorrow for having so grievously offended him, and their request for cleansing will bring a complete pardon. God won't put them on probation, but automatically grants his love and acceptance. We cannot overvalue the hope, optimism, and joy that God's readiness to forgive offers us. He never says, "I'll have to think about it," or "maybe next year I'll forgive," or "prove your penitence first."

Wimbledon officials felt they had to protect the sanctity of their name and tournament when they fired Tingling in 1949. They also felt that a thirty-three year exile from the club would be a good dose of punishment. But then, it's a proud club, with the fear of being tainted. God has no such fears. He is anxious that we receive his Son's instant, full, refreshing forgiveness. His grace is greater than all our shame.

FORMALITY — important, if costly
Genesis 17:10; Mark 1:4

It Has a Place

In June 1987, *Working Woman Magazine* explored the financial costs women paid as they climbed the corporate ladder. The women felt they needed to project an image that matched their position, especially when they ascended from mid- to upper-level management. The necessary power wardrobe—including executive accessories, personal beauty treatments, health club membership, and speech lessons—cost a total of $9,451.

Intricate and extravagant protocol vexed social life in seventeenth-century England. Meticulous etiquette governed gatherings of the upper class, and none dared to defy it. Guests learned to determine their importance to the host by the room they were received in, by the host's willingness to greet them personally, and even by the kind of chair offered for their repose.

Good manners are essential to social life, but etiquette often becomes absurd, however reasonable its origins. Yet social forms provide an important visible expression of an invisible relationship, authority, or commitment. They are valuable as the form of a shadow. God often hides spiritual realities that are difficult to decipher in earthly figures we can clearly understand. For example, the death of Jesus was offered to us in terms of bread and wine—which give life and offer enjoyment to the partaker.

FORMALITY — dismissed in crisis
Joshua 2:8–11; Acts 17:6

More Important Things

In the early 1900s, the Wickford, Rhode Island volunteer fire department raced to extinguish a fire at the town depot. Sam Brown, the new fire chief, got to the fire before he remembered his helmet. "Wait, boys, I forgot my chief's helmet!" he shouted. He dashed home, put it on, and dashed back to the depot, only to find it in ruins. The boys had taken him literally.

Is the church in a similar crisis today? While we fanatically defend our customs, society deteriorates and lives depart into eternity without Christ. Wouldn't it be worthwhile if we thought less of maintaining traditions and more of creatively changing our worship and educational programs to reach the spiritually untouched? Are we going to keep stressing our comfort or start asking how we can make an irresistible appeal to those still lost?

FORMALITY — without content
1 Samuel 4:3; Luke 3:7–8

All for Show

Milli Vanilli sold twelve million records and won a Grammy for best new artist in 1989. All the while Vanilli was merely lip synching—not singing—the lyrics.

When Buffalo Bill Cody was an old man, forced to work in Wild West shows by economic necessity, his helpers would take him into an alcove of the show tent and help him on his horse. He would sit there, slumped over, the victim of arthritis, rheumatism, and kidney failure. When his cue came, however, he pulled himself to full height and dashed out, strong, and able, tearing around the arena like a youth. Then, he rode back into the alcove, the flap closed—and once again he slumped over his horse, waiting to be helped down.

How often true it is, as historian Merle D'Aubigne wrote, that humans carelessly allow the perfume of faith to escape while they bow before its empty vase. Formalities are essential to faith only when personal faith in God is intact. Look at the Israelites fighting Philistia. Without the ark they lost four thousand men. Yet with the ark in their camp, leading them in battle, they lost thirty thousand men. What good was the ark when God's glory had departed? Any spiritual form can become a religious tradition unless the Origin of the form, not the form itself, is worshiped.

FORTUNE — from good to bad
Psalm 119:14, 24; Matthew 6:21

Some Are Unfortunate

Gary Jenkins bought a winning Lotto ticket, hitting on five of six numbers for a jackpot of $581,732. A week later his wife was found slain in their home. Suddenly, a horror money couldn't banish overwhelmed five children and a grief-stricken husband.

In 1860, Mary Chestnut lived in a world of plenty, attended by faithful slaves, her husband a high-ranking Confederate government official. By 1885 she had one piece of property and an annual income of $100—between the two extremes stood the Civil War.

Within twenty-four hours of the San Francisco earthquake author Jack London spoke with two men whose fortunes had vanished in the disaster. One, who had been worth $30,000 the night before, had only a pair of crutches. The other owned a Nob Hill mansion worth $600,000. It was all he had left, and flames were burning inexorably towards it.

If we have our wealth—our life's deepest interest—in friendships, family, career, investments, and they are taken from us, what have we gained? How wisely Jesus urged us to have our treasure in heaven, for he knew that our heart follows our deepest interest. In pursuing spiritual goals, these jars of clay contain God's golden treasure.

FRAUD — based on greed
Joshua 7:1, 20–21; Acts 5:1–2

A Sin Not Often Condemned

L. William Seidman, chairman of the Resolution Trust Corporation that supervised the sales of failed Savings and Loans in the 1980s and 1990s, estimated that serious criminal activity had occurred in about 60 percent of the failed Savings and Loans. Think of almost any kind of fraud, he said, and the RTC could find an example of it. Bad management and greed, not a downturn in the economy, had caused the bankruptcies.

Thomas McKernan, president and CEO of California's AAA Auto Club, stated that 33 percent of all accident claims are staged or manipulated. Policyholders pay 30 percent more in premiums to underwrite and combat this fraud. Add to these the millions stolen yearly from the government in welfare fraud, the millions that ruthless investment firms filch from undiscerning investors, and other millions raised by fraudulent charities, and, as the late senator Everett Dirksen quipped, "You're talking serious money."

Greed is a sin sometimes condemned, but most often overlooked by us—and seldom denounced in the pulpit. But God has a different standard: his Word unsparingly and frequently denounces it. Scripture excoriates greed as idolatry because it replaces God with an earthly commodity. The greedy never have or get enough. The love of money makes one anxious about keeping it, ruthless in pursuing it, and devastated by losing it. When dollar signs begin to dance in our eyes, it is time for a spiritual eye exam.

FRAUD — perpetrators caught
Jeremiah 28:1–4, 15–17; Acts 13:8–11

The Good Guys Win One

The pigeon-drop scheme perpetrators picked the wrong lady that day. Sitting at a bus stop, the seventy-one-year-old was approached by three women and a man claiming they had found $84,000. They offered to share the money with her if she would put up $3,000 in "good faith" money. Instinctively suspicious, she pretended to agree, then called the police. The next day she rendezvoused with the criminals, put $10 on a stack of paper money the detectives had given her, and handed the suspects what appeared to be $3,000. Then, from out of nowhere swooped the cops.

What a challenge for Christians! Confidence men may not be able to cheat an honest person, but Satan has an infinite number of ways to deceive people, especially those whose grip on the material life is stronger than their grip on the spiritual. Jesus withstood Satan for forty days and nights, and then deflected his rages in the three great temptations. Our Savior's refusal to collapse holds out hope for us—if Jesus could overcome Satan, we can. In Christ's victory rests our own!

FUTURE — present habits determine
1 Samuel 18:8; John 20:25, 29

The Future of It Must Be Considered

The American colonies revolted against the British crown in 1776 with the Declaration of Independence. The French Revolution began in 1789 when the citizens of Paris stormed the Bastille, the despised symbol of absolutist rule. These respective revolutions soon soared into different orbits, however. The American colonies established constitutional law that guaranteed peaceful change and security for all citizens; the French established the guillotine as arbiter, bludgeoning all hopes of a peaceful settlement of disputes. The collapse of an accepted central government in France degenerated into warring factions, each claiming absolute authority. The outcome could only be the colossal calamity of the Reign of Terror.

We should always evaluate our present habits in the light of their future possibilities: what will we be in a year, or ten years, if we keep doing these things? One drink might not hurt us, but what if we become addicted to alcohol? The marijuana joint may seem harmless, but what if it leads to doses of stronger, deadlier drug? The harmless vice today can become a ravenous depravity tomorrow. We all share a common susceptibility to temptation's pleasant allure and hideous influence.

GENERATION — building from previous
Genesis 15:16; Matthew 23:35–36

Providing a Model

A Connecticut farmer lives on the same farm his ancestors have worked for almost 350 years. They provided provisions for Washington's army, the marsh feeding the cows and pigs that provided salt pork, salt beef, butter, and cheese. "And we've been haying and pasturing this marsh . . . ever since," the man says proudly.

The U.S. Navy made a Pacific cruise from 1838 to 1842 with surveyors, botanists, and geologists. The ships sailed as far north as Alaska and as far south as Antarctica, making charts of Polynesia and Micronesia. In 1943 those same charts were used by the Navy when invading Tarawa.

We inherit from the past; we bequeath to the future. We can't control our endowment, but we can control our bequest. What does the contemporary scene suggest? A worthwhile morality inherited from our fathers has been passed to our children as an undisciplined hedonism. Rigidly enforced standards of behavior have degenerated into an indulgent permissiveness of misbehavior. So out of control are our moral standards that it took a recent secular survey to assure us that we are not a nation of sex-starved maniacs! Media indulgence in sex, violence, nudity, and profanity is not an *expression* of our private values but a *reflection* of the godless profligacy of the entertainment industry.

GENEROSITY — God's gauge
Genesis 14:20; Mark 12:43–44

Not as Thought

Americans give so generously to nonprofit causes that foreigners gape in astonishment. The $79.8 billion given to charities in 1985 exceeded the gross domestic products of Israel, Egypt, Lebanon, Syria and Jordan combined. One hundred and eighty six individuals have given from $5 million to more than $300 million during their lifetime. Hundreds have given $5 million to $100 million over their lifetime. In 1986, real estate magnates Harry and Leona Helmsley gave $33 million to New York Hospital. People such as these are called the "most generous living Americans," Leona's prison sentence notwithstanding.

Didn't Jesus say something about a different gauge to measure true generosity? Past the trumpet-mouthed boxes in the treasury the rich people moved, putting in much. Then, all alone and unnoticed, an old woman moved to put in two pennies. Jesus ignored the wealthy and their gifts while lauding her small offering. The reason was simple: the rich gave out of their excess, while she gave from her penury.

How many of the million-dollar benefactors do without any luxury, let alone any necessity, to give their millions? Make no mistake, generosity is preferable to parsimony, but Christ's emphasis has to be appreciated. Generosity should be based as much on what we keep for ourselves as what we give to others.

GOALS — falling just short of
Deuteronomy 32:52; Hebrews 10:13–14

Not Quite Enough

In June 1983, thirty miles short of his goal, British adventurer Peter Bird had to abandon his nine-month, ten-thousand-mile solo rowboat journey across the Pacific. Treacherous seas on Australia's Great Barrier Reef forced him to call for help after rowing from San Francisco to Grenville, Australia. Reaching goals is not always necessary to make them worthwhile—but try to convince Peter Bird. To have prepared, saved, disciplined himself, and expended energy as he had, only to fail thirty miles short of the goal renders weak and useless any sympathy or excuse.

Succeeding is always better than simply trying, only to fail. God has enabled his people to successfully reach their goal: to get heaven in sight and to enter it, having overcome, not succumbed to Satan. Each one will be there because of trust in the one historical person who settled for nothing less than absolute perfection in every endeavor he undertook—Jesus Christ!

GOALS — necessary
Psalm 27:4; Galatians 2:20

In Pursuit of a Goal

Donald Thornton worked as ditch digger, and his wife, Tass, worked as a domestic. But Donald had other plans for their five daughters: they would be doctors and escape the hardships he and Tass had experienced. The girls' early discovery of music proved to be the means to accomplish these goals. They practiced to become excellent musicians and won a talent contest in the Harlem Apollo Theater. Donald wouldn't hear of his daughters pursuing a musical career, however. Doctors he planned for them to be, and nothing else would suffice. He encouraged them to use their musical skills to earn money by playing weekends at eastern universities. Their concentrated study opened college doors to them, and every girl graduated—two became doctors, one a psychiatrist, another a dentist, and another a professor working on a doctorate. What intense energy flowed in that family to envision, pursue, and achieve the goal of a college education for each girl!

Sometimes, having a goal is the only way we can keep ourselves committed to a course of action. The goal develops resources, skill, and application. Having Christlikeness as our goal fills us with a fiery enthusiasm to study God's Word, to pray, to witness, to serve, to overcome, to sing, to acquire virtue. Those who are committed to that single purpose explicably find the power to achieve it.

GOD — as creator
Isaiah 40:26, 28; Romans 1:18–20

But ... for Realities

The late Theodor Geisel attempted to write a serious novel, and failed. He whittled it down to a novelette, and failed; then to a short story, and failed; and finally to a joke, which sold for $15. Undaunted, as Dr. Seuss, Theodor Geisel outsold all other children's writers in the world. Asked where he received his inspirations, Seuss replied tongue-in-cheek, "From a small town in Austria, high in the Alps, called Gletch. Thousands of feet above it is a still smaller town called Uber Gletch. Once a year, on August 4, I go to Uber Gletch to get my cuckoo clock repaired. And it is there that I get my ideas." On another occasion he explained that his ideas came from picking the brain of a retired Thunderbird.

Imaginations should soar when creating a nonsense tale designed for children. For reality, however, another source is needed. The foundations of the world must stand on the immovable and immutable. Imagination must surrender to truth when dealing with historic souls and their eternal salvation or damnation. To get a perspective on these issues, one must drink at the deepest, surest fountains of knowledge. Prehistory, creation, and the nature of humanity all derive their true explanations from the Someone who was there at the beginning, conceiving and creating them. The Bible points us clearly to that One—to him we owe everything.

GOD — let him prescribe
Psalm 2:4–6; John 6:61–62

Let God Speak

Otto Von Bismarck, the Iron Chancellor of Germany, hated going to doctors, but one time he was seriously ill and had no choice. When the doctor said he could help him, Bismarck replied, "O.K., but don't ask me a lot of questions." The doctor shot back, "Then you'd better go to a vet."

People treat God like Bismarck treated the doctor; they don't want him to interject his thoughts into the conversation. They feel free to express their views, but why does God have to express his? God must have the opportunity to have his say and to explain himself. Listening to God precedes understanding him. Really listening! That's why Jesus often began or ended a teaching by declaring "Hear this, all of you."

GOD — listen to him
Isaiah 8:19; 1 Corinthians 1:22–25

Everyone with an Opinion

Tipsters! They travel the Southern California racing circuit, handicapping races from Del Mar to Pomona, from Santa Anita to Hollywood Park. For $2, betters can buy their tips on the races of the day at any of the tracks. They follow the circuit each year, scrutinizing horses, trainers, jockeys, and track conditions. They've been in business many years, some as far back as 1943, and cater to an established clientele who patronize them annually. If there is anything to know about horse racing—jockey, track, training speeds—they know it. Yet, to a man, they admit to being right only 38 to 45 percent of the time.

Everyone has an opinion about life and its vagaries. There's always a "tipster" who's studied the problem, figured the odds, and devised a·plan to outwit and outfox it. But while opinions abound and self-appointed experts pontificate, who knows for sure but life's Author? Of all the experts poking around in the human body, brain, and psyche, trying to explain, calculate, and predict behavior, who knows but the One who created us in his likeness? Who alone knows the future, as the past?

GOD — love, enjoy
Genesis 3:22; Acts 17:29–31

Not to Be Confused

Sisquoc pecked his long beak from the shell to become the first condor ever born in captivity. In two hours he ate a meal of water and minced meat. The keeper used a mother condor puppet when feeding the chick to keep it from confusing human keepers with its own species. That would never do, of course. A vulture might weigh in as an eight ounce cutie and grow into a sixteen to twenty-two pound monstrosity with a wing span of nine feet, but its identity with its own kind must be preserved. For his own sake, Sisquoc ate from a human hand disguised as a mama vulture.

The keepers wanted to prevent an identity crisis for Sisquoc, and God seeks to prevent an identity crisis in us. He wants us to love only Him, even as we enjoy his gifts. He wants us to delight in him as the God of peace, not just in the peace he gives. To possess him as the "God of consolation," as Madame Guyon wrote, not just the consolation he provides; to delight in him as the God of creation, not just in the creation he made.

GOD — tragedy without
Deuteronomy 32:39; John 15:4–5

The Greatest Tragedies

In his middle twenties, doctors removed a growth from a young man's groin and found it malignant. He underwent chemotherapy, but that failed and the cancer spread to his vital organs. Yet, when he discussed it with a former professor, he said it could be worse. There he was, in his twenties, with only a few weeks to live, yet he said it could be worse. How? Well, he said, he could be fifty and have no values or faith in God. He could still think that life consisted of seducing women, drinking booze, popping pills, and making money.

Life's greatest tragedies *are* of the spirit. We curse the lesser tragedies and want them removed, little realizing that if they were, others would rise in their place, because we haven't solved the reason they exist—our misunderstanding of almighty God and his Son, Jesus Christ.

GOD'S IMAGE — on our soul
Genesis 1:26; Deuteronomy 4:32; Acts 17:26

That Ancient Call

Buck, the great dog in Jack London's *Call of the Wild,* felt an urging more ancient and natural than the one he found in domestication. Within his genes resided generations of wild creatures whose call sounded across the breeding lines and beckoned him back to the untamed state.

In unexpected ways Buck represents the Christian. In us, too, a call resides: in some bright, in others dim; in some clamorous, in others subdued; it comes from a source more ancient than our generations—a call to the Source of our being. To be something better than we were, to be someone better that we are going to be, that persistent call sounds.

Buck's call beckoned him downward, to something lesser, lower, to a savagery he had escaped. Our call beckons us upward, to something greater, higher, and nobler—to oneness with the One who made us in his image.

GOD'S WILL — his aims, our interest
Genesis 32:12; 2 Peter 1:3

In the Best Interest of Both

Henry Higgins teaches phonetics in *Pygmalion.* On a wager he accepts the task of remaking Eliza Doolittle from a poor street vendor into a sophisticated lady. Higgins sees Liza merely as an object of his workmanship, not as a person with feelings. She offers a means to prove his skill, whatever her individual dreams and fears may be. When the project is finished, he shows no concern for her future. He has proved his point, regardless how it affects Liza forever after.

When God calls us into his will, it automatically accomplishes two goals: it brings the kingdom of God to earth and it gives us every advantage of his presence. What makes us obedient to him also prepares us for life's challenges, problems, and possibilities. What is advantageous for God's work—redeeming lost souls—automatically becomes advantageous for anyone enlisting in his work. As God accomplishes Christ's cosmic ministry, he enriches the personal life of his people.

GOSPEL — communicate clearly
Judges 7:13–14; Colossians 4:4

First It Must Be Clear

On July 28, 1945, the heavy cruiser *Indianapolis* left Guam for Leyte Gulf, in the Philippine Islands. She radioed the standard message to Leyte that she was on her way, but due to atmospheric interference the signal was scrambled, and Leyte received nothing intelligible.

This lack of communication proved disastrous, for at 12:15 A.M. on July 29, the Indianapolis received two torpedoes from a Japanese submarine and sank in twelve minutes. More disastrously, the first torpedo knocked out her electrical system, preventing an SOS call. Nine hundred of the 1,200 men aboard survived the sinking, taking refuge in the few lifeboats afloat or clinging to debris, hoping for a quick rescue. However, since no one in Leyte Gulf knew when the ship was expected in port, the sailors waited in vain. Over three days passed before search planes finally spotted the survivors—only 316 of the original 900 left after the sinking. It was a tragic loss caused by poor communication.

We face the same problem in teaching the Bible. God sends out his message plainly, intelligibly, and precisely—until we begin to communicate it. So often our poor efforts mask its glory and cloud its clarity; the message is garbled and unclear. Yet eternal destinies depend on this message. We must convey correctly the clear, intelligible message of God's Word. Would we have them any less clearly informed than we?

GOVERNMENT — excessive costs
Malachi 3:8–10; 1 Corinthians 9:14

How Exorbitant Can It Get?

In its December issue, 1888, *Harper's Weekly* noted that the U.S. Treasury projected a surplus of $203 million for 1890. The editors concluded: "This prefigures a situation demanding imperatively enormous reduction of revenue or utterly reckless expenditure." Shades of another age—when government officials had to be goaded into spending money! The cost just to run Congress increased from $343 million in 1970 to an estimated $2.8 billion in 1992, more than double the

280 percent rise in prices over the same period. The House and Senate have legislated themselves into the most expensive governing body on earth. Salaries have skyrocketed from $22,000 in 1960 to $129,000 in 1995. Then, of course, taxpayers spend $642,000 yearly to provide free parking for our representatives. In addition, our taxes provide them with franking privileges and bloated staffs—which the 1995 Republican Congress vowed to trim. "Enormous reduction in expenditure," not "utterly reckless rises in revenue" is certainly the need of our time.

To keep the gospel at work in our communities also costs. If political leaders deserve support, so do pastors. If governmental workers need buildings, so do congregations. If taxes need to be raised to repair, restore, and build infrastructure in the community, offerings need to be raised to support local and foreign missions, seminaries, and children's homes. As for value received for money spent, don't church leaders consistently spend little to achieve much while Congress invariably spends much to achieve little?

GRACE — helps though we offend
2 Chronicles 30:8; Titus 2:11

By Grace Alone

A Hispanic worker crossed illegally into the United States from Mexico late in 1983. He went to work at a local ranch for $3.35 an hour. After several months of being paid half that, he got fed up and sought help from the local authorities. When the Department of Labor Relations in Los Angeles discovered his grievances, it extended protection to him. Rightly or wrongly, the department feels that undocumented workers enjoy the same protection as legal citizens in wage and hour laws.

It's a bit like lost souls and God's grace. Born rebels against spiritual discipline, we have no claim on God's mercy, anymore than an illegal can claim protection from our laws. Yet, at the first appeal for mercy, God moves to help; at the first request for forgiveness, he grants it. It is all due to his grace. He sought us, and we are found. He took the initiative—we simply responded.

GRACE — saved by
Isaiah 41:14; Galatians 5:4–5

God's Complete Answer

The flashblaster is a xenon lamp capable of generating four million watts of light, each burst roughly a thousand times more powerful than the brightest headlight. Many uses have been discovered for the laser, from delicate surgery to massive explosions against the pesticide malathion. The brainchild of physicist John Asmus, the high-powered laser has been used to restore ancient art masterpieces and buildings to their pristine state. The flashblaster was used at the Capitol rotunda in

Sacramento, California, to peel away multiple layers of paint that covered treasured murals and frescoes. Other attempts to do so had failed. The procedure also saved Indian paintings in Texas threatened by limestone growth. The flashblaster has vaporized animal fat in the cracks of European statues and removed overprint from medieval frescoes in Italy. Radiation therapy, eye surgery, and military applications of the instrument have all proved its usefulness.

God's forgiving grace is as sovereign over human sin as the flashblaster over numerous coats of paint. It alone can do the job. Mankind tries conventional methods of eliminating sin and relieving guilt—stiff laws, long prison sentences, capital punishment, psychiatry, and a revised morality—but all fail to solve the basic problem because they all leave in place the basic corruption. What human efforts cannot accomplish, God's forgiving grace can. Christ's sacrifice obliterates sin's power.

GRACE — value of
Hosea 2:19–20, 23; Galatians 6:1–2

But Not with Grace

On New Year's Day, 1983, the Louisiana State Tigers played Nebraska in the Orange Bowl. Jerry Stovall, Louisiana State coach, had been chosen Southeast Conference Coach of the Year in guiding his Tigers to an 8-3-1 record in 1982. In December, 1983, the LSU Board of Supervisors ignored widespread fan and alumni protest and fired him. Just twelve months earlier they had given him a bonus—now they gave him the sack. So much for collegiate sports being merely for the thrill of competition! It's win, tie, or be canned. This win complex subordinates the worth of individuals to the team's record.

Christians can be grateful their Master treats them differently. He doesn't order us out of the kingdom if we have a bad day. God won't fire us if we have a record of ten wins over temptations but three defeats. He won't thumb us to the sidelines and out of the church when we run into a spiritual dry spell. And he will never disgustedly call for our resignation if we just can't get a handle on a temptation, however zealously we try. With grace at work in our lives, Christ's unique life compensates for our failures. He pays the difference between the little we can afford to pay and what heaven costs to enter.

GROWTH — doing what hasn't been done
Psalm 92:12–14; 1 Thessalonians 4:1

Only by Pushing the Envelope

General Jimmy Doolittle knew the qualifications needed in pilots. He said he looked for balance, fast reactions, and a love of flying. In addition, he sought a pilot who could learn his limitations. A poor pilot wasn't necessarily a dangerous pilot if he lived within his limitations, Doolittle affirmed. A pilot finds his limits in the air by getting closer and closer to the edge, and sometimes going beyond, and still surviving.

Our Christian life grows when we extend ourselves beyond our personal comfort zone into unfamiliar territory. Christians fearlessly face the unknown. Out there, where we have never been before, the Savior awaits, urging us forward. Since our soul shrinks or expands to the degree it is unused or challenged, we boldly push at our spiritual boundaries, testing their limits, only to discover that none exist. Ever onward we go in our spiritual journey to the point of no return, where it is farther to go back than to go on—where we are so much closer to where we want to go than to where we have been.

GUILT — haunts
2 Samuel 12:7; Psalm 51:7; 1 Timothy 1:12–14

To Free, Not to Condemn

In the closing days of World War II, German headquarters in Denmark dumped a number of waterproof ammunition boxes into nearby Lake Ornso. They lay there undisturbed until late 1982 when two Danish divers dug the boxes from the lake's mud and found that they contained material, uniforms, and weapons from the war. While engaged in the initial dive, the divers had come under sniper fire, narrowly missing a hail of bullets. Investigation pointed to a man who was known as a Nazi informer during the war. Apparently, he wanted to keep those boxes— and the information they contained—safely on the bottom of the lake. What guilt he must have carried all those years, to say nothing of the fear of being discovered and incriminated in activities he wanted to forget. How many days and nights had he gone to the lake, looking to see if anyone was there, searching?

Sin isn't a thorn in the flesh, but the contamination of the soul. A thorn can be pulled; sin must be forgiven. We can't just say "I'm finished with sin." That is beyond our power. Christ's grace must be effected in us before we can finish with sin. Surely his sacrifice banishes sin's power and penalty, along with the guilt, fear, and doubt it inflicts.

HABIT — changing
Exodus 13:9; 1 Corinthians 15:31

A Little at a Time

William James suggested three keys to acquiring new habits and losing old ones: (1) start the desired behavior immediately; (2) consistently repeat the behavior until it seems a natural, not an acquired, trait; (3) express the new behavior as soon and as often as possible.

Exchanging bad behavior with good offers formidable, sometimes insuperable, challenges. Since the brain merely overrides old patterns with new, an occasional reversion to more established deportment isn't surprising. Yet the greater the distance between an original impulse and its last repetition, the less distinct it becomes in us; we more readily forget what has not been recently reinforced.

Given these factors, and the fact that life follows belief, Christians must concentrate on material, relationships, and attitudes that reinforce Christ's likeness. By conscientiously and persistently refueling with such resources, we will find ourselves transformed gradually to be more like the Christ we admire and less like the self we despise.

HABIT — force of
Genesis 39:10; 40:6–7; Acts 12:6–7

It's Natural After a While

The people of Thailand break wild elephants to domestic use by chaining them to banyan trees. The pain the elephants experience by pulling against the restraint gradually breaks their will to resist. When an elephant finally refuses to lift its massive leg in an effort to free itself, the workers release it from the tree and secure it to a circus stake. The beast could pull the stake from the ground like a toothpick, but it remembers the pain and isn't smart enough to realize that circumstances have changed.

Although Christians are freed from Satan's power, we sometimes act as if we are still imprisoned by it. He lies, telling us we cannot escape. But we are not elephants; we are intelligent enough to see the shackles laid aside, to feel the freedom Christ brings us. He has entered our dungeon and set us free! Why continue to be chained to a spiritual stake when Jesus has freed us to soar?

HABIT — need daily
Daniel 6:10; Acts 3:2

The Habit of Overcoming

When James La Fleur left Maine to sail solo to Ireland, he understood that the psychological and mental pressures of twenty to thirty days at sea might disorganize his behavior. So he made an intentional effort each day to maintain his normal, daily habit. He washed and shaved, dressed in clean clothes, and set his table for three formal meals. These persistent regulations motivated him psychologically, kept him alert, and swiftly passed the time at sea. He made the twenty-one day crossing with no major problems.

To consolidate our faith into manageable units, Jesus has established a day-by-day rule: Die to yourself daily. Anyone can live for Jesus one day—day after day. The result? Sooner than we think we have lived a lifetime of discipleship—any number of yesterdays piled together, day after day, twenty-four hour increments lived faithfully for him.

HATRED — indiscriminate
Genesis 4:5; Colossians 3:13

Even Those We Wanted Spared

A nerve poison, 1080 was developed in the 1940s to control predators. Theoretically it would kill only prairie dogs and coyotes. But the powerful toxin remained stable in rodent bodies, and the secondary poisoning of scavengers and predators rose alarmingly. Coyotes died, but so did the eagles, foxes, ferrets, and condors that consumed the carrion. The poison killed indiscriminately, eliminating pests but victimizing desirable and rare wildlife.

Hatred is like nerve poison 1080. Once loosed, it's virulence spreads through a long line of people. Perhaps those we wanted to hurt felt the sting of our wrath; we repaid them for their harm to us. But something else happened. It began to affect our relationship with friends—they suddenly had other plans when we invited them over. It began to affect our family life—spouse and children suddenly seemed uneasy around us, as if afraid to offend us. It began to affect our own thinking—suddenly, any offense by anyone roused our anger. Yes, we felt avenged for the slight, the insult, the oversight, but too late we discovered that hate, once released, doesn't spare anyone. Indeed, those to whom we wish no harm at all, including ourselves, can become the first, and worst, casualties.

HEART — physical and emotional
Proverbs 4:23; Luke 6:45

Our Own Pump

The human heart, less than a pound when fully grown and only a little larger than our fist, beats seventy-two times a minute, one hundred thousand times a day, forty million times a year. Each day it pumps the equivalent of 1,800 gallons of blood weighing six tons through more than sixty thousand miles of our circulation system.

Sometimes when people have negative experiences, especially in their early years, they veneer their soul with repeated layers of hardness to keep from being hurt. This only prolongs their problem. They become irascible, isolationist, and difficult. Their reactions are brittle, not pliable. Everything they experience hits and bounces away, because the toughness they have painted on keeps them from being healed. All those layers of hardness have to be peeled away. God's forgiveness will give us an inner strength and toughness, but not until we eliminate the hardness we have painted on. God would have us tough inside our hearts, not outside. That inner toughness keeps us cheerful in adversity, peaceful in turmoil, and optimistic in discipleship. It accepts even the harm that life offers and transforms it into benefactions.

HEAVEN — disproportionate to now
Ezekiel 1:26–28; 2 Corinthians 12:3

All Out of Proportion

The late Yul Brynner played the king in *The King and I*. Starting in 1951, he gave an incredible four thousand performances—the last performance on Broadway where he had first played the part. His last tour with the play grossed between forty and fifty million dollars. To express his appreciation, the producer gave his star a new limousine: a $160,000 Mercedes. "There's very little I wouldn't do for him," the grateful producer added. Not bad for a "little" Christmas gift. But then, in three years, Brynner's sparkling efforts had grossed three hundred times that.

When God comes to reward his servants, not one of them will receive less than he or she has invested. Even now, the rewards of discipleship incomparably exceed our efforts. But the promise of rewards incomparably exceeds our imagination.

HEAVEN — God's endowment
Psalm 16:9–11; 1 Corinthians 15:4, 12

Why Is That Thought Incredible?

A sixty-five-pound, nine-year-old boy saw the family car fall off its jack onto his father's chest. The boy rushed over and, without thinking, lifted the 4,100 pound car so his father could breathe. Another jack lifted the car so the man could be pulled out. A sixty-five-pound boy lifting a two-ton car? Impossible—except that it happened!

God's enormous endowment at creation has been severely curtailed by our fall from grace. The mind, built and equipped to love and serve God but now retarded by sin, falls short of its original potential. But one day, restored to that purpose, we will repossess powers now alien to us. When that happens, the incredible will be commonplace, the unthinkable ordinary.

HEAVEN — not everyone belongs
Jeremiah 31:29; 2 Corinthians 5:10

No Gate-Crashers

Minutes after Debbie Armstrong and Cristin Cooper placed first and second in the women's giant slalom at Sarajevo in the 1984 Winter Olympics, a tall stranger stood by them in the Mt. Jahorina pressroom, congratulating them. He even got Armstrong's autograph.

Trouble was, he had no business being there. He wasn't a press agent, a reporter, or an official—or anyone else important. He was simply a gate-crasher who had slipped past security guards to mingle among the famous. Two days later he breached even tighter security to enter the main press center. Later that day he worked his way into the media center at the speed-skating oval.

It's a hobby with him. He has successfully crashed World Series press conferences and at least seventeen Super Bowls. Once he even sat next to Farrah Fawcett at a heavyweight boxing match. He fakes credentials, outwits rigid security, bluffs his way where he isn't welcome, and makes himself so comfortable that everyone thinks he belongs.

There is one place he will never enter if he doesn't belong, however, and that is heaven. No one slips in there unnoticed, unwelcomed, or uncalled. Nor is there any masking one's self in a clever disguise to outwit security, or flashing a fake ID card to scoot past a harried angel. Only those with their credentials intact will walk into the new Jerusalem.

HEAVEN — resplendent grandeur
Genesis 2:1; Ephesians 2:7

All Eternity

In January 1983, a three-nation infrared astronomy satellite soared into a 560-mile orbit above the earth and pointed its tracking antennae toward deep space. Almost at once, an avalanche of information poured into the computers at an English ground station. More than two hundred thousand new objects were soon spotted in the heavens, including twenty thousand galaxies in interstellar space. Astronomers couldn't believe their good fortune. Having convinced themselves of the universe's emptiness, the new treasures stunned them.

Christians are delighted, but not surprised. The God of Scripture created more in this world than can ever be investigated, studied, or understood. As a dim reflection of God's incomparably resplendent grandeur we expect what the satellite revealed. Yet, all we have experienced here, or ever shall, reads like an empty page compared to the fullness of life to come in his presence.

HELP — arriving too late
Genesis 17:5–6; Matthew 28:18–20

After the Crash

The Genessee County Sheriff's Department received a call reporting a car being driven erratically. Within three minutes a trooper received the alert and rushed to intercept the offender. The deputy stopped at an intersection and gasped in astonishment. Twenty seconds before, the speeding car had crossed that intersection and down the street he saw the results: the wreckage of a driver education car nearly demolished from the head-on collision. Three students and their driving instructor were dead inside. The guilty party and his friend had been drinking while driving.

Only three minutes elapsed between the time the call came into the Sheriff's office and deputies began seeking the car. By only twenty seconds the car beat the deputy to the intersection. For the families of the deceased, it might as well have been aeons. Help coming too late is like a pardon after the execution.

Knowing that Jesus met us at our point of greatest need, will we, while time allows, meet the lost at theirs? God sent good news of great joy in Bethlehem. Never voiced before that night, it has never since been stilled. It is the message Christians must continue to tell—while there is time.

HELP — from unexpected source
Ezra 9:5–7; 1 John 1:9

Not from Them

CIA hearings held in 1982 revealed that the Abwehr, Germany's Intelligence service in World War II, had been seriously compromised by Allied agents. Allen Dulles, then chief of OSS, reported that 10 percent of the Abwehr was involved in passing information to the Allies. He even had direct communication with Admiral Wilhelm Canaris, the Abwehr chief. Included was some of the first information about the guided missiles Germany would deploy as the V1 and V2 rockets. Irreplaceable intelligence came to America and her allies from the very heart of the enemy. News of German decisions at the highest level were passed to Moscow, Washington, and London.

Sadly, Satan has such operatives at every level in a kingdom where the privilege of belonging should make treason unthinkable. But Christians find themselves, against their wishes, betraying the Master they love and benefiting the enemy they loath. One difference exists. Germans helped the Allies from their outrage against Hitler. Christians help Satan purely out of their frailty as fallen creatures. And one blessing distinguishes the two groups: if caught, members of the Abwehr would have been hanged or shot by an incensed government. Christians, by repenting and praying, have their sins forgiven by an offended but merciful God.

HEROES — curious about
Deuteronomy 34:10–12; Hebrews 12:1

How Did They Live

Scholars beamed as they examined the faded pen strokes on the ledgers before them. The invaluable books belonged to George Washington and came to light when other Washington family treasures were found in a Washington and Lee University vault. The find, which vastly enriched the already bulging store of Washington memorabilia, proved that Martha Custis brought enormous wealth to the marriage: 26,650 pounds, or nearly six million dollars. The thirty-six page document from the General's account book details both his settlement of the Custis estate and his guardianship of the stepchildren.

The ordinary person has an inveterate curiosity about the everyday life of the famous. Perhaps we wish to share vicariously in the riches and influence that are beyond us personally. Christians elevate this curiosity to a higher level. Living in a secular world and seeing unacceptable models of behavior, we seek a spiritual model. In Scripture famous spiritual heroes march in unbroken ranks before us. Desiring most intensely to please God, we search his Word to see how people have pleased him in the past. Their example helps us to please him now.

HEROES — kids need
2 Kings 2:23–24; Matthew 18:5–6

It's Natural in the Young

Kids in America buy baseball trading cards, swap them among themselves, and attend conventions where they ponder the value of advertised collectibles. Kids in Jerusalem's ultraorthodox neighborhoods can't indulge in secular heroes, so they have developed a flourishing enterprise in collecting and trading rabbi cards. Keenly aware of the fame and influence of individual rabbis, they haggle freely with each other to get the advantage in any trade.

Children need authentic heroes, whatever their culture or age. Youngsters nearly always look to adults as models; they need to see men and women of courage and perseverance. They need to see mothers, fathers, and teachers who freely admit their guilt when wrong and who apologize. Young people need to see adults whose uncompromising faith in God inspires them to high values and morals. These adults attract youth by character, not glitter. If adults will summon their strength to lead, multitudes of youth will summon theirs to obey!

HISTORY — renewal needed
2 Kings 22:10–11; Acts 19:9–10

The Need of Renewal

She stood in New York Harbor for ninety-seven years, welcoming seventeen million immigrants to her shores. As her century birthday approached, it was obvious that the Statue of Liberty needed restoration. Two thousand iron bars within her superstructure had deteriorated to less than half their original thickness. The skin had been thinned by acid rain and air pollution, and pieces of her torch had fallen off. Americans gave millions of dollars to restore the lady in time for the nation's 112th birthday, July 4, 1986.

Human monuments, history, life, and morals must be constantly reinforced and resupplied, fixed and repaired. Everything in creation suffers constant deterioration. Likewise, our Christian lives demand constant reinforcement to serve at optimum strength. Always subject to influences that bear us away from God, we cast an anchor into his Word to hold us steady. Knowing that spiritual fervor is lost from slow leaks, not blowouts, we must constantly check our spiritual pressure by feeding daily on God's Word and renewing our life through prayer. Revivals aren't just convenient intervals in otherwise normal lives; they are essential reclamation projects for our souls.

HOLY SPIRIT — always at our side
2 Kings 3:14; 1 John 2:1

Faithful to Himself

In 1951, Representative Richard Bolling of Missouri proposed a dam for his district but saw it defeated in committee. He brought it up before the entire House, knowing he lacked enough votes for its passage. But Bolling had befriended Sam Rayburn, Speaker of the House. When Bolling rose to present his cause, Sam Rayburn, who had sat down beside him beforehand, rose to stand at his side. Rayburn said nothing at all. He didn't have to. By simply standing with the Representative from Missouri, Rayburn meant he wanted the bill passed—and it was.

In whom, or in what, will we have ultimate confidence? Our mortality forces the choice upon us: we need someone to stand by us and for us. We must choose carefully, for we will live with the results forever! Who is better qualified to be that one than Jesus Christ?

HOMOSEXUALITY — not as many as claimed
Leviticus 18:22; Romans 1:26–27

A Skewed Statistic

Studies of homosexual behavior in the early 1990s put to rest a long-standing myth homosexuals had used to trumpet their cause. Using figures from Professor Alfred Kinsey, the homosexual/lesbian lobby had claimed at least 10 percent of the population. However, the latest studies, the most thorough on sexuality since the Kinsey report, dramatically reduce the number to about 2 percent who engage in homosexual sex and 1 percent who consider themselves exclusively homosexual. The new figures are in agreement with other studies by researchers in France, Denmark, Britain, and at the University of Chicago.

The reply of strident homosexuals, after having the 10 percent ground eroded, now becomes "the issue isn't numbers, but civil rights." How interesting! They trumpeted the 10 percent like it was a tithe to God. Now, with 9 percent obliterated, they rely on the oldest canard: "We have our rights." Rights? How can wrong have its rights, even civil rights? Wrong is censured in Scripture, denounced and condemned without appeal, whatever rights governments grant.

Margarine offers an alternative to butter. Junior Colleges offer an alternative to State Universities. Poultry and fish offer an alternative to red meat. However, homosexuality does not offer an alternative to heterosexuality. The Bible declares homosexuality a deviant, not an alternate, lifestyle.

HONESTY — absence of
Proverbs 11:18; Romans 1:14

A Regrettable Loss

A 1991 survey of American retailers revealed a dishonest streak as broad as Kansas. Twenty percent of job applicants admitted they would steal from their employers; 21 percent of all applicants flunked preemployment honesty tests and were rated as high risk. "Employee dishonesty is one of the major problems retailers face," an industry specialist said. Retailers who participated in the annual Survey of Retail Loss Prevention Trends reported losses of $1.4 billion to employee theft in 1990—about two cents to every dollar of sales.

A Christian employee, obeying Paul's instructions in Ephesians 6:5–8, would be revolted by the very idea of theft, let alone the practice. The gospel engenders integrity in our personal relationships, honesty in all transactions, and responsible effort in any task. We obey human authority as an example of our obedience to Christ. We serve wholeheartedly in any endeavor as an extension of our spiritual commitment. We live without pretense, we behave with propriety, and we act responsibly. We want to please God in the highest cause, so we work hard and honestly in any lesser cause.

HONESTY — subject to conditions
Proverbs 19:9; John 8:44

To Harm for Gain

The 1828 presidential election campaign seethed with heated, hateful innuendoes.

President John Quincy Adams was the bull's-eye. After the election, which Martin van Buren won, the new president admitted Adams' absolute integrity. "Adams was an honest man," he wrote, "not only incorruptible himself, but an enemy to venality in every department of the public service."

For political gain, Van Buren had taken the lead in smearing Adams. He was the first to unleash charges of outrageous corruption. Apparently, honesty to Van Buren was relative. If being honest about Adams would lose the election, Van Buren preferred to lie. Later, in his autobiography, he declared Adams scrupulous honesty, perhaps as a means of apologizing for the scurrilous tactics he had employed to defeat him in 1828. However, a later apology is a poor substitute for original honesty.

Situational ethics offers nothing substantial to competition or personal relationships. It's as fluid as mercury and as impossible to grasp. Moral ethics result from faith in God; situational ethics occur in the absence of faith. Obviously, when 90 percent of Americans affirm belief in God to a Gallup Poll, yet situational ethics have never been more pronounced in our culture, either we have lied about our faith or we haven't taken seriously its demand for moral rectitude.

HONOR — coming late
Esther 6:1–3, 6, 10; 1 Peter 1:7

Better Late than . . .

Captain Joseph Rochefort and his merry musicians performed prodigies of excellence in breaking the Japanese codes during World War II. They provided the Navy with their greatest coup—the information that led to the incredible victory at Midway. Nominated for the Distinguished Service Medal by Fleet Admiral Chester Nimitz, he never received it. The victim of military bickering, he was transferred in 1942 and spent the war in Tiburon, California. He died in 1976, embittered by his mistreatment. In 1983, as an apology, the Navy honored Rochefort with a plaque at the old Pearl Harbor offices, a tardy acknowledgment of the man who led a corps of code breakers to give the U. S. Navy the advantage it needed to blunt Japan's surging conquests in 1942.

God won't overlook any servant who deserves special rewards. No rival exists to challenge the bequests as he chooses to grant them. God rewards his servants daily by making them coheirs with Christ of an immense, eternal inheritance. Since it is presently ours, we borrow against it for the daily grace needed to overcome the world. Aspiring to an exalted place we don't yet have doesn't daunt us, for we presently possess an exalted position we don't deserve. It is all our birthright through Jesus Christ. And anyone can share in it who accepts him as Savior and Lord. Not one of us in the world is enriched with all of God's grace; it just seems that way!

HONOR — ultimate German military
Genesis 15:1; 2 Corinthians 12:10

No Better Available

General Irwin Rommel figured prominently in Germany's six-week conquest of France in 1941. Sent to North Africa, he became the legendary commander of the Africa Corps. His brilliant capture of what the British considered an unassailable Tobruk made him a field marshal: the most honored rank in many armies and the ultimate honor for a German soldier, exalting him to a military immortal. In Prussia, a field marshal enjoyed lifetime perks and benefits. Wherever he went, for as long as he lived, his embossed baton accompanied him, and his fame followed after.

The Christian understands the concept, but finds ultimate honor in being conquered by Christ, not in conquering others. Christians count as strength temptations resisted and sin overcome. They pin on their chests the satisfaction gained from reaching people for Christ, not medals for military campaigns.

HOPE — absolute need
Proverbs 13:12, 19; Romans 5:2, 5

You Gotta Have Hope

College football fans knew the late Woody Hayes as a fierce competitor whose passion for winning once led him to slug an opposing player who intercepted an Ohio State pass. But when columnist Bob Greene interviewed him just before his final illness and asked if anything was as important as winning, Woody said yes. "The important thing is not always to win. The important thing is always to hope."

Hope kept Red McDaniel going in his Vietnamese imprisonment. For him to abandon hope, he wrote, was to abandon survival itself and with it his sense of self and all his personhood. The Jews at Auschwitz and Treblinka lived in daily horror and fear of dying, even as they saw other Jews die. Still, they never lost hope that they personally would survive. "Where there is life, hope must never be relinquished," one said.

Faith in the eternal God offers a hope that despair cannot diminish. It brings an optimism that pessimism cannot eclipse. It builds a confidence that adversities cannot weaken. It instills a pleasure that pain cannot destroy—faith in the eternal God!

HUMANITY — always the same
Ezra 10:2; Matthew 23:29–32

For the Answers

On February 8, 1496, four caravels sailing to America with supplies for Christopher Columbus sank in a storm in the Bay of Cadiz, Spain. They joined what is perhaps the world's richest marine archaeological graveyard, especially for so small an area. Over three hundred vessels from Phoenician, Greek, Roman, Viking, and present times have sunk in the bay.

Archaeologists find many of the wrecks in pristine condition. The bay's deep, oxygen-free mud has engulfed the hulls and kept worms from boring through. The ships are actually time capsules, offering insights into ancient construction methods and life for sailors aboard the vessels. Divers also find coins, statues, and amphorae.

If you want to know about the daily life, habits, and beliefs of people in any age, look in the Bible. The history of the race is encapsulated there. Did people have faith then as we do now? Did people make the same mistakes then that we make now? Did any disbelieve then, as so many seem to now? We need to ask the right questions about humanity and life, and we need to get the right answers to those questions. Let's ask; the Bible is ready with the right answers. Mankind at any particular time is mankind in every period of history. The Bible seizes the instant and records it for everyone in every age to view and contemplate.

HUMILIATION — abject
Exodus 34:29; John 12:28

To Be So Abashed

Congress voted the Marquis de Lafayette land and $200,000 for his service in the Revolution. They voted nothing for Thomas Jefferson after his retirement from public office, despite his service as ambassador to France, vice president, and president. Jefferson, who carefully managed the nation's finances as president, as badly mismanaged his private affairs. He finally became so impoverished that he authorized a lottery for the sale of his land, hoping to raise enough money to support his daughter and her family after his death. In applying for the lottery he suffered the humiliation of having to enumerate his services to the nation.

When Jesus died on the cross he took upon himself our sickness and disease, our blindness and lameness, our leprosy, death, and our sins. His sacrifice has been recognized and rewarded by God and humanity!

HUMILITY — example of
1 Samuel 18:4; Acts 11:25

Just a Sinner Saved by Grace

Franklin Roosevelt once praised Robert E. Lee as one of America's greatest Christians and gentlemen. Lee, however, described himself differently, seeing himself as "nothing but a poor sinner, trusting in Christ alone for salvation." That humility accounts for Roosevelt's evaluation.

Percy Johnston, a San Diego investment banker, attended Oxford University. He and two friends were lawn bowling there one day when a distinguished elderly gentleman came by and stood watching them. Percy went over and asked if the gentleman would make a fourth. He agreed and extended an introductory hand. "Albert Einstein," he said. "Relativity?" Johnston asked. Einstein smiled and nodded. That began a lasting friendship. Percy later said Dr. Einstein's humility had deeply impressed him. During a conversation at an afternoon tea, Einstein was explaining an experiment, and volunteered that he had "so much to learn."

God looks for servants whose sense of their humanity engenders humility, even as their awareness of his grace develops confidence—women like Hannah and Mary; men like Moses and Paul.

HUMILITY — forced on one
1 Samuel 19:23–24; John 17:24; Philippians 2:5–7

Hard Lessons to Learn

Although he lived in the splendor of the magnificent Russian Winter Palace, gilded in gold and furnished with all extravagance, Czar Nicolas I slept in a narrow, hard bed. He also insisted that his son Alexander learn humility by sleeping in a similar bed. Perhaps Alexander would have learned more sufficient humility had he gone to the peasants, eaten their potato soup, and slept on their straw mats on cold, drafty floors. As Alexander II, he did express enough humility to free the serfs in 1861. But there was only so much humility he could learn from sleeping on a hard, narrow bed, while surrounded by ostentation that would one day be his.

To assume the lowliest humiliation, God sent the Person who had, with him, been the object of the greatest glory. Christ emptied himself of all the prerogatives of godhood and humbled himself to servanthood. Jesus proved that far from being a condition imposed from outside, humility arises from within in response to God's call for service. For the highest possible responsibility, God chose the only One who could truly proclaim himself "humble in heart."

HUMOR — part of good health
Genesis 21:6; John 15:11

Only for the Short Term

The late Norman Cousins, formerly editor of Saturday Review, had so serious a disease in the 1960's that doctors gave him only one in five hundred chances of surviving. That gaunt prediction notwithstanding, he beat the odds by rejecting hospital treatment and formulating his own plan. He took massive doses of vitamin C, watched Marx Brothers films and Candid Camera reruns, and read exhaustively from humor books. He found that laughter banished negative feelings and relieved his pain. Previously, pain led to tension and tension to more pain. He discovered that ten minutes of "genuine belly laughter" gave him at least two hours of pain-free sleep.

Gelotology—the science of humor—is in its infancy and cannot explain all the reasons laughter is so valuable to us. Perhaps it relieves pain by releasing endorphins, the body's natural opiates, into the bloodstream. It certainly protects us from negative emotions and attitudes. It encourages us to develop self-enhancing behavior patterns.

While humor encouraged better health for Mr. Cousins, it was still a limited benefit. Christ offers an eternal benefit. He removes sin from our lives altogether, absolutely, completely, and forever. In Christ, God claims complete amnesia over the sins we have committed and confessed. For good reason. Jesus had the perfect sacrifice to offer: himself. He had the place to offer it: the cross. He had a compelling reason to offer it: forgiveness. He had a place to take it once offered: into heaven. He had a purpose in taking it there: to represent us eternally before the throne of God.

HUNGER — obliterating other feelings
Psalm 40:4–5; 1 Peter 2:2–3

A Basic Need

During their attempt to reach the South Pole, Ernest Henry Shackleton and his men were reduced to twenty ounces of food per man each day. This left them constantly hungry and continually craving food. They imagined meals of plenty and dreamed of giving banquets to each other. Neither the glory of great mountains towering around them nor the majesty of the glacier up which they moved had any appeal. "Man becomes very primitive when he is hungry and short of food," Shackleton wrote, "and we learned to know what it is to be desperately hungry."

Jesus offers special blessing to those who, through knowledge of their spiritual poverty, passionately seek God. They will be filled with the God for whom they hunger, he promises. And what a difference. When physically starved, we indeed become primitive, seeking only to save ourselves. Yet when spiritually starved, we reach our highest level of development. We are at our best, not our worst, for we become like the God we seek.

HUNGER — visceral
Deuteronomy 8:3; Mark 22:1–14; John 6:27

The Need to Eat

With Biosphere II sealed against outside influences, the crew members discovered the time and difficulty involved in preparing meals. When they ate a particularly delicious meal, they would often reflect on the time and energy it demanded, from planting to harvesting then processing and cooking. They calculated that the preparation of biospherian pizza—their favorite dish—took at least four months from start to finish.

They all developed a renewed awareness of the essential nature of food. Having constant access to it before entering the enclosure, they thought little of its visceral relevance. The Biosphere accentuated their awareness. Nowhere was the importance of food more obvious than in their inordinate celebrations of every special day: birthday, holiday, solstice became an excuse to eat!

How essential food is, and what joy we experience in sharing it with loved ones. With good reason Jesus described the kingdom of God as a feast in which the redeemed will eat at leisure and to their fill. Our hearts hunger as much for God as our bodies for food. And those who continue their growth in Christ appreciate the time-consuming expense of the effort. That very awareness exalts their appreciation of it. They have this added blessed assurance: they will sit one day at God's table and have opened to them all the divine mysteries they cannot fathom now.

HYGIENE — varies in cultures
Psalm 51:7; Mark 7:3–4

The Need to Stay Clean

The houses of Tudor England were filthy, germ-infested disease traps, with fleas and lice everywhere. People seldom took baths and clothing was truly clean only when it was new—washer women "cleaned" with cow dung, hemlock, and remnants of soap. The streets were worse. Unpaved and rutted, they were either muddy or dusty. Household garbage was deposited there every day, as were the contents of chamber pots. Refuse piled up in putrid heaps until it was finally scraped away, the stench overwhelming. Cardinal Wolsey solved the problem of horrible odors by holding a scented rose under his nose when in public. Those who could afford it sloshed heavy perfume on themselves.

Cleanliness may not be next to godliness in social success, but it far excels beauty and adornment as we witness of a Christ who cleanses!

HYPOCRISY — flagrant
Amos 5:21–23; Acts 23:3

What Inconsistency

Born to royalty in Africa, Cinque led the revolt of fifty slaves aboard the ship bound for America. They killed all but two of the crew, manacled them to the bridge, and demanded a return to Africa. The Spanish ship's mate deceived them, however, and took them to Connecticut. There the slaves were indicted for murder and piracy. The case became a national sensation. Former President John Quincy Adams represented the slaves and won them an acquittal. Released to freedom, Cinque returned to Africa to become a slave trader!

Hypocrisy denies the essence of religious faith. It expresses itself in many forms, some of which surprise us. One in particular Jesus harshly pilloried—the unforgiving servant. For the forgiven debtor to become the unforgiving creditor reeks of insincerity. The man demanded of others the payment of debt from which he had been exempted. Once begun, hypocrisy assumes a life of its own, sometimes against our will. It often begins when we want to save face in some way, so we play a part to gain an advantage. Once welcomed as a means of self-protection, however, hypocrisy contests our later efforts to take off our masks, for it whispers that we cannot be honest now without admitting we had lied before!

I

IDEAS — more attractive than reality
Judges 10:6–14; Matthew 2:3, 7–8, 16

A Fine Idea . . . But

In 1983, touring American editors found a time warp in Communist Russia—the streets, buildings, and public works systems were unbelievably dated. Social progress had simply stopped dead in its tracks. Hospitals had nothing but cast-iron beds in the rooms. In major food stores butchers cut meat manually, while people waited patiently in interminable lines. Narrow, poorly maintained roads constantly threatened danger, and decrepit vehicles rumbled along them. With the fall of communism, western travelers discovered even bleaker truths: 20 percent of the people lived in abject poverty, and there was little welfare to care for the unfortunate.

Many people have an idealized view of life without God, even to considering the advantages such a life might offer. The attraction is only an idea, however; it is far from reality. Without God life is barren, not decorated; it is drab and empty, not full. All that awaits those who refuse God are unsatisfied cravings, ignored needs, unassuaged pains, and unhealed wounds.

IGNORANCE — of the impossible
Numbers 15:26; Acts 17:30

An Ignorant Innocence

Pascal said there are two kinds of ignorance. One comes as our birthright. The other comes as we grow in knowledge, only to realize how little we know of all that is available. When he felt boastful of his knowledge, Churchill once said, he walked into a library. The very sight of all those books reduced his hat size.

Christians need a third "ignorance"—the ignorance that something "can't be done." We need to teach, with the ignorance that "it can't be done." We need to evangelize, with the ignorance that "it can't be done." We need to start new churches and rebuild wounded ones, with the ignorance that "it can't be done." Not knowing it can't be done, with God's empowerment, we will do it! Even mountainous challenges, even insoluble spiritual defiance, yield to God's "everything is possible" promise.

ILLUSIONS — exist in what seems
Ecclesiastes 2:4–10; Galatians 6:7

It Only Seems to Be

A Wall Street clerk went for a tuna sandwich one snowy noon and returned to work with $37.1 million in negotiable certificates of deposit found in a pouch dropped by a courier. The clerk turned them over to his supervisor, who notified the securities company. The man received a $250 reward for his honesty. As it turned out, that was more than the certificates were worth to him—they could only be converted with special clearance.

People give themselves to goals that are like those certificates. They seem real, but they aren't. They seem so worthwhile, but are terribly disappointing. They promise millions, but return pennies. They are shameless—wealth, fame, career—tantalizing, alluring, then betraying. They leave us bitter, heartsick, and spiritually bankrupt. Only the goal of God's unshakable kingdom can offer opulent wealth and sure and splendid promises. It guarantees an enhancement to perfection of all present benefits now possessed by those within its embrace: an undisturbed inner peace, an unmarred victory, an unsullied righteousness, an unbroken life.

ILLUSIONS — many build on
Jeremiah 7:4; Matthew 15:13

Facing Reality a Must

Japan entered World War II with specific objectives: (1) cripple the naval power of America and Britain, (2) seize territory essential to postwar development, and (3) withdraw behind an unassailable defense perimeter. Japan presumed that the United States and Britain would negotiate peace, leaving Japan in possession of its conquests.

The Japanese deluded themselves. Had they faced the reality of the Allied response, they would never have attacked Pearl Harbor. They had to imagine how they wanted the Allies to respond and plan their strategy accordingly. It was foolish, but was all Japan could do since it wanted both its conquests and peace.

Yes, we all refuse to face facts sometimes. We postulate certain actualities and build our future, our relationships, and our decisions on them. Reality becomes what our imaginations devise. That is why the doctrines some people hold reflect their illusions instead of God's Word. Their beliefs originate everywhere but the Bible. Without confirming them in the Bible, they just imagine that God will accept them. The Japanese were tragically wrong in 1941. And what about us? Can we expect God to casually honor all our beliefs and convictions just because we feel he should?

IMMORTALITY — exceeds all our anticipation
Isaiah 65:17; Revelation 21:1–5

The Half Has Not Been Told

With his ship at anchor in Boston harbor after a two-year absence, Richard Henry Dana should have been elated. A year before, the thought of being home drove him wild with excitement. He couldn't account for the change. "But now that I was actually there, and in sight of home, the emotions which I had so long anticipated feeling I did not find, and in their place was a state of very nearly entire apathy."

In this life realization often fails to deliver what expectation advertises. In the next, God guarantees an experience whose meaning deepens with each new discovery, whose significance grows with each new revelation, whose dimensions expand with every explanation. He promises an immortality as superior to forgiven mortality as grains of gold to sand.

INCONSISTENCY — in behavior
2 Samuel 12:14; Galatians 2:11

Incredible Double Life

One night a small-town family hosted a neighborhood-watch meeting. One lady came and was shocked to see her television and other possessions in the house. The hostess even had on one of her dresses! When detectives searched the house and a locker the family had rented, they found $9,000 worth of stolen property belonging to their neighbors and area residents. The hostess had to be either blissfully innocent or supremely arrogant to furnish her home with stolen goods, then invite into it the very people she had robbed, confident they wouldn't recognize their own possessions.

How often we betray our Master with our spiritual inconsistency. Like John Bunyan before he committed himself to Christ, we attend church, sing vigorously, repeat the sacred words, yet retain our wicked life. We are foolish to think we can invite people to Christ and they will hear our words but not see in our lives the same disharmony, anxiety, and profanity they have in theirs. Why would they be interested in more of the same misbehavior?

INCONSISTENCY — in the religious
Isaiah 58:3–5; Matthew 23:23–24

Not Relating Faith to Life

A businessman in a western city owns six adult bookstores, an X-rated theater, and a Condoms Plus store. He faithfully attends his cultural church, contributes generously to it, and vigorously promotes law enforcement. Titian, the great Venetian painter, painted the most flagrant Bacchanalistic scenes—naked people in sexual orgies; drunkards sprawling, gorging themselves—then used the same talent and brush to paint *The Tribute Money*. He could pass from Bacchus to Christ, Durant said, "with no apparent loss to his peace of mind."

Peter the Great of Russia would regularly sing in the church choir, take communion, discuss theology expertly, and fine anyone who talked or dozed during Mass. A few hours later he would abandon himself to immoral, sadistic orgies. He severely punished anyone who insulted the Church, but amused himself by ridiculing the objects of the faith.

Given the certainty that little "clean" money exists in a fallen world, can Christians own or work for businesses that intentionally corrupt spiritual values? Given the certainty that honey bees die out in our hearts while roaches thrive, we must restrain ourselves from moving casually from the most sacred thoughts to the most profane.

INCONSISTENCY — of skeptics leading one to faith
Habakkuk 2:18–19; 1 Thessalonians 1:8–9

Those Who Doubt Have No Answers

Chesterton and Augustine had similar experiences in their long journey to faith. After exhausting himself looking for answers among philosophers, Augustine found satisfaction by reading the Bible. Only by having the inconsistencies of philosophy firmly planted in his mind did he grasp the coherence of Scripture. Chesterton was led to faith by the doubts of skeptics and agnostics, because he saw in them the inconsistencies for which they attacked Christianity. Swinburne accused Christ of making the world "grey"—unhappy. Yet, in *Atlanta* the poet gave this account of paganism, "I gathered that the world was, if possible, more gray before the Galilean breathed on it than afterwards." Even Swinburne said that pagan life was dark. Yet, curiously, he maintained that Christ had darkened it. He denounced Christianity as pessimistic, but was himself a pessimist. It appeared to Chesterton that "those might not be the very best judges of the relation of religion to happiness who . . . had neither the one nor the other."

Indeed, if his detractors claim that Christ was a pessimist, they had better be optimists. For if Christ brought unhappiness to the world, they must prove it was happy before he came. If faith in Christ raises problems, unbelievers must prove that disbelief produces answers.

INFLUENCE — of one person
1 Samuel 14:6, 45; Hebrews 9:15

The Influence of a Single Person

In January 1941, Viorel Trifa, leader of a Nazi-sponsored student movement in Romania, participated in the slaughter of one thousand Jews in Bucharest. American Jewish dentist Charles Kremer heard the name and vowed to remember it.

Trifa disappeared after the war, then materialized as a Romanian Orthodox churchman in America, becoming a bishop in 1952. He later became a citizen and an archbishop. Charles Kremer sent letters to congressmen and columnists seeking justice for Trifa's crimes, with no results. He sent photocopies of anti-Semitic documents signed by Trifa, the 1941 Romanian trial proceedings in which Trifa was condemned to life imprisonment at hard labor, and the names of eye witnesses who had seen Trifa take part in the slaughter—but nothing came from it.

Kremer poured out his story to U. S. Attorney Robert Morse in 1972. Again, promised action failed to come. More years passed, with no success. In 1979 Kremer and others went to Washington, walked the streets with placards, and chained themselves to the White House gate. Arrested, they were put on television and told their story. Suddenly, the story was news all over the country, and action quickly came: Trifa was stripped of his citizenship as a prelude to deportation proceedings.

One man relentlessly pursued a criminal and brought him to justice. And we feel we can accomplish nothing significant because we are only one person—unknown and unable? Ask Charles Kremer! The difference is dogged, unyielding commitment.

INGRATITUDE — examples of
Genesis 31:38–42; John 5:12–15

The Refusal to Appreciate

The Indians often aided the early Jamestown settlers, bringing them corn and bread in their desperate plight. Later, the settlers traded copper for corn—they offered the Indians an inch square of copper for a bushel of corn. When the settlers grew prosperous, they sold corn to the Indians, trading four hundred bushels for a mortgage on all their lands.

Both Generals Crook and Miles used Apache scouts to hunt and bring Geronimo to surrender. Yet, when the warring Apaches were sent to Florida, all the faithful scouts were sent with them, their faithful service to the government forgotten.

When David Livingstone died, his two faithful servants, Susi and Chuma, carried his decomposing body for nine months and a thousand miles. Yet, on arriving on the coast, they were rudely shoved aside as white men assumed responsibility.

God appreciates an attitude of gratitude. The presence of gratitude reflects our humility as certainly as its absence proves our pride and egotism. Jesus endured the cross for the joy set before him. But the shame he experienced should now be forgotten by the greater joy his disciples bring him, when they say thanks—and live like they mean it. It is time his disciples crown him in their personal lives.

INHERITANCE — all Christians share
Isaiah 53:11; 2 Thessalonians 2:14

Known to Be

A lawyer in Los Angeles serves some of the biggest stars in show business, but he never gets calls, complaints, or requests from them. He is an agent for dead celebrities. Among his clientele are Marilyn Monroe, W. C. Fields, and Elvis Presley. What he actually does is watch commercial markets for merchandisers who use the likenesses and names of the deceased stars to sell their products without reimbursing the heirs. The lawyer insists that the heirs of famous people retain a continuing right to the fame their relative developed while alive.

Jesus personified everything about the kingdom that he taught—light, life, love, salvation. That is why he wants us to follow and learn of him. If we understand and follow him—living as he lived, thinking as he thought—we possess him, having the salvation that he is. In appropriating Christ personally, we possess light, life, love, and salvation. We are temples of God, filled with God! Incredible: to have such treasure in these jars of clay!

INSTINCT — need to follow
Proverbs 8:19–21; Romans 2:14–15

That Little Voice

As usual, Jap Khalsa assembled and checked his equipment as he prepared to wash windows in the high-rise Imperial Bank building. Even though the rope he had was not the one he ordinarily used, he checked it carefully and decided to use it. Over the side he went in his bosun's chair, fluidly working his way from window to window.

Ninety minutes later, at the twenty-first floor, the rope snagged and refused to slip through the mechanism moving the chair. Unable to move, Khalsa banged on a window for help. When firemen arrived, a veteran of cliff rescues volunteered to be lowered to Khalsa, careful not to make the slight mistake that could drop both to the pavement. After several hours the grateful workman climbed over the rail to safety. "I should have listened to my instinct about that rope," he later said. By refusing to obey the "little voice," he had hazarded his life.

The twenty million laws legislators have written can't enforce even one of the Ten Commandments. But one conscience—one inner voice—forgiven, redeemed, and enlightened by God's Spirit, will keep a person from breaking any.

INTEGRITY — debased
Psalm 7:14; Mark 10:23–25

Unworthy Goals

On a salary of $7,500 per year, Jersey City's Mayor Frank Hague managed in ten years to pay $400,000 in cash for real estate. After thirty years as political boss of

New Jersey, he admitted to being worth $8 million—a broad underestimate according to a former attorney general of the state.

In his Senate diary the late Senator George Aiken noted that politicians, especially those seeking reelection or election to a higher office, will vote in committee for a measure they do not like, then trust the other members of Congress to kill it. That way they can truthfully say they favored the bill without worrying that it will actually pass.

Listening to a voice others will not hear, Christ's disciples rise to the level from which the Voice sounds. Embracing the absolutes the Holy Spirit enunciates, we scorn the numerous expedients available. In a world where discretion has gone to sleep and shamelessness has awakened, we remain circumspect. In a society where Christ's claims are no more welcome than his conclusions are acceptable, Christians adhere to both his claims and his conclusions.

INTEGRITY — example of
Amos 7:14–15; John 1:47

A High Class Person

When Elizabeth I called Robert Cecil as her principal advisor, she gave him an ultimate compliment: "This judgment I have of you, that you will not be corrupted by any manner of gift . . . and that without respect of my private will you will give me that counsel which you think best."

When Robert Morse died, his entire estate amounted to $59,000, after forty years as Director of Public Works in New York City. Billions of dollars had passed through his office.

Sam Rayburn refused to bill the taxpayers for trips other congressmen took for granted. He wouldn't even accept expenses for out of town trips. At his death, after decades as one of the most powerful men in the United States Congress, his savings account totaled $15,000. These men had, as the king of France said, "come not to woo honor, but to wed it."

Since God's Word is a spiritual integer, incapable of being divided against itself, Christians seek a biblical faith, its absolutes their spiritual infrastructure. We will cut our suit to fit the cloth the Bible provides rather than stretch the Bible to cover our distended values. Since what is relative cannot always be relevant, we choose the immutable as our model. We want to wed, not just woo, honor—and all the absolutes that define a Christian.

INTUITION — warning of danger
Jeremiah 6:16; Romans 1:9–10

A Sixth Sense

At Fort Lincoln, on June 25, 1876, the women of the garrison assembled in the quarter's of an officer's wife. They all felt strangely apprehensive. Someone prayed, and they started to sing "Nearer My God To Thee," but couldn't finish it. On July 5 they learned that at the very hour they had met, their loved ones were dying on the bluffs above the Little Big Horn River in Montana.

Golda Meir intuitively felt danger when Russian advisers evacuated their families from Syria in 1973, but her intelligence chiefs and generals dissuaded her. Her political contacts in other countries concurred, so she didn't order mobilization—and regretted it ever after. She should have listened to her heart, she wrote, and ordered her army mobilized. Nothing anyone could say afterwards in consolation would comfort her.

Christians should be ingeniously intuitive, enlightened as we are by the Holy Spirit. He enables us to distinctly resolve difficult questions; to perceive spiritual danger in an innocent temptation; and to see sin while it is still a principle, before it becomes a practice. However, while intuition can bring to our attention the facts needed to make a decision, we must will the decision.

INVENTIONS — key of century
Exodus 12:5, 13; John 1:29

Not the Same without Them

Three inventions came out of World War II that have characterized the military in each decade since: (1) the rocket, bequeathed by the Germans; (2) the nuclear bomb; and (3) the computer, the gifts of America to the world. The computer is the essential invention of the triad since it married nuclear power and rocketry, producing the ICBM, which guides the rocket as it carries the bomb. The computer also made possible in-depth space exploration and sophisticated military technology.

Jesus Christ remains the key figure in history. He accepted all Old Testament revelation, yet claimed superiority to it. He expressed an originality in every doctrinal essential, while he lived dependent on Judaism for his core spiritual values. He spoke of his absolute unity with God while completely identifying with the humanity he came to save. He perfectly married faith and works, perfectly balanced justice and mercy, and perfectly stabilized love and wrath.

INVENTIONS — necessity mother of
1 Kings 8:62–63; Hebrews 9:23

The Problem Demanded It

Europeans had to develop a ship different from anything known when they seriously undertook ocean travel and discovery. Prince Henry the Navigator's shipwrights built it—the *caravel*. It was big enough to hold the supplies for a crew of twenty, yet had a shallow enough draft to explore inshore waters. It turned quickly in the wind and thus saved weeks at sea. It could be beached for repair. Columbus' ships were of caravel design.

While content with merely remitting sins annually, God authorized the repeated sacrifice of animals for their blood. When God wanted to offer a completed, permanent forgiveness that emancipated sinners, he brought an entirely new idea into the world that would replace animal sacrifice—the death of Jesus Christ. Uncontaminated by sin, his pure and authoritative sacrifice forgave a humanity thoroughly saturated by sin. His sacrifice effected a perfect reconciliation between humanity and God.

INVESTIGATION — Christian life invites
Job 29:21–25; John 18:20

Out in the Open

A man in England disappeared the day after being questioned about the rape of an eighty-six-year-old woman. The police never gave up searching for him, making periodic visits to his home. On one of those visits, eight years later, they found him—hiding in a six-by-two-foot hole under the floorboards of his living room. He had taken refuge there the day he disappeared to avoid further questioning and arrest. He never saw daylight for the first two years of his self-imposed imprisonment. Then he felt it was safe to come out occasionally. Constantly terrified at the thought of arrest, he couldn't leave his wife and children. The children had no idea their father was there, sleeping in that miserable hole every night.

Christians do not hide in fear lest they be exposed. They welcome investigation and questions. Refusing to hide behind a privacy clause, we open all scriptural teaching and our personal life for study. The Christian experience is public domain, not a private preserve.

INVESTMENT — richly rewarded
Malachi 3:10–12; John 12:23

When You Give Your Life

Ray Kroc borrowed $1.5 million when he began expanding his McDonald's restaurants in the late 1950s. He took no salary at first and, in lieu of raises, gave his first employees stock in the company. His executive secretary, June Martino, received 10 percent of the company stock. Twenty years later it was worth $64 million.

Spending $1,650 for 100 shares of Wal Mart stock in 1970 multiplied into 51,200 shares worth $2.7 million by 1992. Many of the fifty original investors bought $5,000 shares in the revolutionary Price Club. Each $5,000 in 1993 was worth $43 million.

S. N. Behrman, who had backed many Broadway shows, had to be forced into financing "Oklahoma!" One of its supporters told him it was the least he could do for the Theater Guild after all it had done for him. His $20,000 eventually returned him $660,000!

Capitalizing on the power that enables him to bring everything under his control, Jesus multiplies every small investment into a colossal return. He weighs back to us in tons of spiritual benefits our every ounce of spiritual effort. He provides the wealth that secures what the heart needs and the soul desires. God has the intention and the resources to share all he possesses with those who remain faithful. If we don't want to be saved, no power on earth can make us. If we do, no power on earth can stop us!

INVOLVEMENT — penalty for not getting
Isaiah 42:6–7; Matthew 5:13

We Share the Blame

Aleksandr Solzhenitsyn decried the sheep-like submission of the Russian people to Soviet thugs. If they had only done something, he wrote in the *Gulag Archipelago*, to show their disgust at the oppression, it could have been reduced. "[W]e didn't love freedom enough. And even more—we had no awareness of the real situation. We spent ourselves in one unrestrained outburst in 1917, and then we *hurried* to submit. We submitted *with pleasure!* . . . We purely and simply *deserved* everything that happened afterward."

Regretfully, Christians can understand the great Russian's lament. We, too, stood idly by while spiritual miscreants stole the values we cherished and society respected. Now that those values are gone and vile ones are in their place, we complain bitterly.

Instead of rushing to submit, as the Russian people did to Bolshevism, Christians rushed to their church buildings, making attendance at services the standard of righteousness. By closing ourselves off from society, we made the unsettling discovery that since we failed to impress society with our values, unsaved people impressed it with theirs. Indeed, we deserve everything that has happened to us. However, we still possess the weaponry to storm Satan's castles. If we will wage warfare with the spiritual weapons of prayer, preaching, and evangelism, we can bring renewal to our society.

INVOLVEMENT — success from
Isaiah 49:6; Acts 16:20

Because She Cared

When his wife of forty years died, the elderly widower became a regular at the local restaurant. One teenage waitress waited on him regularly and called him if he didn't arrive at mealtime. When he died childless, he left most of his $500,000 estate to her. A part-time employee of the restaurant, she proved herself a full-time friend. She took time to show concern, not just to take his order. She gave him attention, and he gave her his gratitude in the one way no one could misunderstand.

There is an old saying that people won't care how much we know until they know how much we care. Christ's disciples need to cultivate friendships with non-Christians, not only because the unsaved need our values and perspectives but because it is the only way to keep our local congregations growing, involved in rescuing the community, renewing values, and begetting a spiritual renaissance.

JARGON — confusing communication
Job 13:17; John 8:43

The Problem with English

Even the British, experts in the King's English, can still make mistakes with it. A hospital sign read: Visitors—two to a bed and half-an-hour only. This sign was in a restaurant: Our establishment serves tea in a big bag like mother. A portrait studio advertised: Children shot for Christmas in the home.

Non-English speaking people have special difficulty with the English language. An Istanbul dentist's sign read: American Dentist, 2nd floor—teeth extracted by latest Methodists. In a Yugoslav hotel a notice stated, "Let us know about any unficiency as well as leaking on the service. Our utmost will improve." A Taiwan tailor's sign announced: Ladies can have fits here; and a Leningrad restaurant cloakroom requested: Please hang yourself here. Most amiable was the sign in a Teheran restaurant: Eat the Middle East foods in a European ambulance.

Children easily misunderstand words. A toddler serving as ring bearer stopped every other step as he walked the aisle, curled his lips, and growled—all the way to the altar. After the wedding someone asked him why he had gone through such antics. "They told me I got to be the ring bear," he replied.

The goal of communication is to express an idea clearly to another. Christians, whose life's work involves communicating God's eternal Word, face an awesome challenge. First, we personally need a clear perception of Jesus, then we need a clear statement of that perception expressed in a winsome manner. The classroom, the work place, the pulpit all offer the opportunity to communicate Christ. We need to carefully, articulately, and powerfully seize it.

JARGON — masquerading as language
Isaiah 55:10–11; John 14:26

The Hilarity of Malapropisms

Malapropisms are often seen in newspaper headlines: Jerk Injures Neck, Wins Award; Navy Finds Dead Pilots Flying with Hangovers; Lower Age for Elderly Opposed; Fire Officials Grilled Over Kerosene Heaters.

A letter to Dear Abby revealed samples from letters to local welfare departments: Mrs. Jones has not had any clothes for a year and a half and has been visited regularly by the clergy; I am very annoyed to find that you brand my son illiterate. This is a dirty lie, as I was married a week before he was born; Unless I get my husband's money pretty soon, I will be forced to live an immortal life; I want money quick as I can get it. I have been in bed with the doctor for two weeks, and he doesn't do me any good.

Many errors exist in either communicating, translating, or understanding language. That has brought the Bible under close, critical, and sometimes unfair examination. Will Durant critiqued critics of Scripture, saying that if the rules applied to the New Testament by such scholars were applied to other ancient writings, they would have no integrity. Josh McDowell, able Christian apologist, quotes Geisler and Nix, who compared textual variations between the New Testament and ancient secular literature. The *Iliad* has 5 percent of its 15,600 lines of doubtful origin. The New Testament has one-half of 1 percent of its twenty thousand lines (forty lines of about four hundred words) in doubt—and nothing at all of an essential nature.

JEALOUSY — baseless terror
1 Samuel 18:28–29; Acts 8:18

The Illogic of Jealousy

Othello is the story of a man who deeply loved his wife, but saw that love destroyed by a bitter, baseless jealousy. An unconscionable villain originated a mere suspicion that consumed the Moor, finally destroying him and his beloved. In one scene, Desdemona says she never gave Othello cause to be jealous. Emilia answers: "But jealous souls will not be answer'd so. They are not ever jealous for the cause, but jealous for they are jealous. 'Tis a monster Begot upon itself, born on itself." The villain Iago understood that clearly, for he had earlier decided to leave Desdemona's hanky in Cassio's lodgings, knowing that "trifles, light as air, are to the jealous confirmations strong as proofs of holy writ."

To escape the terrors to which jealousy can carry us, to elude the punishment it exacts on friendships and marriages, to banish the green monster once it appears, we need a strong self-confidence, a positive, God-enforced self-esteem, and an overflowing flood of God's love within. Only then, and then barely, will we cheat jealousy of the powers it craves.

JEWELRY — famously expensive
Isaiah 46:5: Luke 16:19–31

The Romance of Jewelry

In April, 1987, Sotheby's auction house sold the jewelry owned by the late Duke and Duchess of Windsor. Twelve hundred buyers at the site, and others sitting by phones around the world, dueled fiercely to purchase specimens made by Cartier, Seaman Schepps, Harry Winston, David Webb, or Van Cleef and Arpels.

Buyers scattered $33.5 million over a wide range of purchases. A Japanese diamond merchant paid the highest price, $3.15 million for a thirty-one carat diamond ring. Liz Taylor paid $625,000 for a diamond clip. Divorce attorney Marvin Mitchelson paid $605,000 for a turquoise, amethyst, and diamond bracelet. The Cartier Museum in Paris paid $1 million for a diamond and sapphire panther seated on a large cabodion sapphire. An eighteen-carat gold cigarette case brought $293,000. The Duchess' emerald and diamond engagement ring brought $1.93 million.

As the Duke's love for his Duchess grew through the years, so did his desire to endow her with stunning, jeweled masterpieces. To prove that the romance of jewelry survives, present day buyers paid almost five times the amount auctioneers expected.

John's explanation of the new Jerusalem is built around precious jewels, gems, and minerals. Christians differ on how literally the language is to be taken, but its meaning cannot be mistaken. Our eternal experience with God will be as precious, as valuable, as mind-boggling, and as remarkable as the diamonds, sapphires, and emeralds that attract people today.

JOURNALISM — lasting influence
Exodus 24:12; Genesis 4:10; John 10:35; Hebrews 11:4

The Influence of Journalism

Charles Finney preached revivals for ten years, until his health broke. When a sea voyage failed to restore his vigor, he looked for a way to continue his ministry despite his convalescence. He decided to run a series of lectures in the periodical *The Evangelist.* Amazingly successful, the series ignited revivals in Europe and England. Somewhat astonished at the success of his effort, Finney thanked God that he had used them to promote spiritual renewal throughout England, Europe, and North America. Finney's pen had proved as mighty as his tongue.

Alexander Campbell published the *Christian Baptist* and *Millennial Harbinger,* periodicals that changed religious thought in nineteenth-century America. At the time, the *Harbinger* was the most widely read periodical though printed in the backwoods town of Bethany, West Virginia. William Holmes McGuffey has received fame that eludes men who were his educational peers— Horace Mann, Jonathan Turner, Caleb Mills—simply because McGuffey serialized his material in six graded readers that enjoyed repeated reprintings, selling over one hundred twenty million copies.

The written word outlasts those writing it, leaving a permanent record to influence others after them. Which explains why God took such care in recording his word through some forty spiritual men over a period of 1,500 years. The men who wrote, and those of whom they wrote, died, but the word God revealed through them continues to speak!

JOY — original, eternal state
Psalm 30:11; Philippians 4:4

Our Natural State

In *Orthodoxy*, Chesterton wrote that most humans rejoice over the insignificant and despair over the essential. However, that isn't the last word, Chesterton averred. "Man is more himself, man is more manlike, when joy is the fundamental thing in him, and grief the superficial. Melancholy should be an innocent interlude . . . praise should be the permanent pulsation of the soul."

Why does joy go deeper in humanity than pain? Because joy is at the heart of our relationship with God and was the basis of Adam's initial walk with God. One day that joy will be restored as the basis of our redeemed walk. So often now joy lies manacled by the equivalent, or excessive, sorrows of life. And while we can hear joy shouting its existence, even while imprisoned, it will one day break free and embrace all the saved in its delight. Pain is a viscious interloper that will one day vanish. In the new world, free from restriction, joy will once again prevail, rippling like waters through stony heights.

JUDAISM — spiritually obdurate
Exodus 19:3–6; Romans 11:28–32

They Never Understood

Abba Eban said that Ben Gurion considered Israel both the descendant of the biblical Israel and the harbinger of the messianic peace dream. Ben Gurion had his history right, but not present day Israel's purpose in the world. Golda Meir made a similarly vacuous statement: "As for the Jews being a chosen people, I never quite accepted that. It seemed, and it still seems to me, more reasonable to believe, not that God chose the Jews, but that the Jews were the first people that chose God, the first people in history to have done something truly revolutionary, and its was this choice that made them unique."

The Jews have always had a problem with God. Despite the personal attention he paid them, and his repeated revelations to them, God remained a mystery to his people. It was, as Pascal wrote, given to the Jews to love the Old Testament, but not to understand it. God revealed so much to the Hebrew nation, to have so little of it understood. Yet, they cannot to this day escape what Golda called the "religious question." "Suffice it to say that no easy way was ever found of getting around the place of religion in the Jewish state. It bedeviled us then, and to some degree it bedevils us now."

For sure. The Jews have never known quite what to do with God. But God knows exactly what to do with them. He will be finished with them only when he fulfills his promises to their founding fathers.

JUDAISM — value of circumcision
Deuteronomy 12:23; Philemon 15–16

God's Ancient Word Is Wise

Circumcision of newborns was considered routine in American hospitals until 1971. The American Academy of pediatrics then decided to discontinue the practice except for religious reasons. Years later, however, after surveys at several hospitals, it was discovered that uncircumcised boys were ten times more likely to suffer from urinary tract and kidney infections than circumcised boys.

Dr. Thomas Wiswell, of Walter Reed Hospital, who had previously opposed the practice, changed his mind after studying statistics that showed unmistakable proof that circumcision provides a high degree of protection against penile cancer. Only .02 percent of 50,000 cases of such cancer had been circumcised. Other studies from the past few years show that women whose sexual partners have been circumcised have a lower incidence of cervical cancer and lower rates of acute and chronic infections.

In circumcision we see the wisdom of God's ancient word. Required as a religious practice, it simultaneously offered hidden health advantages! So many Bible teachings have that effect. For example, Jesus' teaching on self-denial. Some have criticized Jesus for depriving us of our sense of self. However, as Christians have discovered, daily self-denial both begets maturation in discipleship and sharpens our awareness of self, bringing unity to our diversity. Only an infinitely wise God could provide such instructions long before science and psychiatry discovered them. Jesus promised a fullness of life now because the Word that brings God's kingdom to earth also improves human life on earth.

JUDGMENT — dangerous
Amos 4:12; 5:18; Matthew 18:28–30

Be Careful What You Request

In Shakespeare's *Merchant of Venice,* Shylock insists on getting a pound of Antonio's flesh, then finds himself trapped by his request when Portia adjudicates the case. She adheres rigidly to the justice he demands. A pound of flesh he can have, but no blood. A pound of flesh he can cut, but only a pound—no more, no less, or he will pay with his own possessions. Shylock demanded judgment, figuring it would be to his profit, but he got justice, finding it to be his loss.

Many today who personally refuse God's rule in their lives demand that he correct all the wrongs in society—the war, famine, disease, poverty—insisting his goodness is questionable if he doesn't. Do they realize what it means to have God put an end to all trouble and troublemakers? When that happens, humanity loses its choices and decisions. Judgment will have come and all human misdeeds will be punished. Will those who clamor for it be ready? Is that really what they want? We should carefully consider our desires and requests—we may get them!

JUSTICE — no one escapes
Ezekiel 18:4, 20; John 8:47–48

No Escape

Convicted in 1973 of trying to bribe a witness, one man remained free during three years of appeals. Finally, in 1976, all appeals exhausted, he should have begun serving a four-year sentence; however, no one notified him when to surrender, and he never bothered to report. For seven years, he lived in a twilight of fear and hope. Had he escaped oversight, he wondered? Or would the arm of justice finally reach out and snatch him away? Finally, perhaps on the tip of an informant, the court routed the offender from the crack he had fallen into and ordered him to prison at a specific time. He gambled on escaping the system—but failed.

Many in the world resemble that man spiritually. They somehow hope to escape divine justice, to be small enough to be overlooked, to have offended so little that no one will care. To no avail. There are no cracks to fall through in God's judgment. He exempts, overlooks, and excuses no one. His perfect knowledge thoroughly educates us in his expectations and renders conspicuous any imperfection in our obedience.

JUSTIFICATION — of one's life
Jeremiah 2:25; Luke 16:15

We Can Always Find an Excuse

Peruvian farmers plant the coca shrub in the thin soils of the Andes, then nurture it to maturity. They harvest the leaves, chew them freely as a stimulant, and sell their bounty to drug syndicates who extract the white alkaloid from the leaves to smuggle for sale around the world, particularly the United States.

One writer asked some Peruvians if they didn't feel badly for the harm done by the coca they produced. They didn't use it or supply it to addicts, they replied. It was just a business to them. Yes, they admitted, perhaps it was wrong "but how else can we make a decent living?"

Like the Peruvians, we justify nearly any behavior, attitude, or sin that we feel offers us an advantage. If it isn't economics, it's social, or relational, or even religious. Enough careers exist that pose no intentional threat to human welfare to free us from working in those that do. If friends don't let friends drive drunk, neither do friends impose illegal behaviors on friends just to prove their friendship.

JUVENILE — precocity not unusual
1 Kings 3:7; Mark 14:51–52

Juvenile Precocity

The violinist played from memory Bernstein's "Serenade for Violin and String Orchestra," with the maestro himself conducting. Suddenly, her E string snapped.

She calmly borrowed the Stradivarius of the concert master and resumed, only to break a second E string moments later. She once again borrowed from the concert master, who had himself borrowed from another musician. With her third instrument the soloist finished the composition. Bernstein hugged her and the audience gave her a standing ovation. She had turned the E string mishap into an international triumph. Later, when fifteen-year-old Midori Goto made her debut as a soloist with the Boston Symphony Orchestra, she commented on the episode. It was sad to her that her reaction to the E string rather than her music had been appreciated. She thought the E string "stupid" and the music "beautiful."

The depth of talent in a person isn't always gauged by advanced age. Such precocity, while rare, is often obvious enough. Pompey was eighteen and Octavian but nineteen when they led armies in the Roman civil wars. Pompey had received a triumph in Rome before he had a beard on his face. David was just a teenager when he contested Goliath, and even at twelve years of age Jesus understood his mission in life.

KIDNEY — nature's purifiers
Psalm 90:3, 10; Luke 1:13, 2:36–37

Nature's Purifiers

They lie on each side of the spinal column, at the back just above the waist. Shaped like the bean named after them, they cleanse the blood of poisons, regulate blood volume, recycle water, minerals, and nutrients and adjust the body's chemical compounds. They are the kidneys—less than five inches long and three inches wide, each weighs about five ounces. Every minute they filter a quart of blood. Each day they receive and pass two hundred quarts of fluid through their millions of nephrons. They filter the blood, reabsorb water, and produce urine to carry off wastes.

When the kidneys don't function, we die. If they function below par, the person has to undergo hemodialysis, the process whereby an artificial kidney cleanses the blood. In kidney transplants, the organ's sensitivity demands the closest possible match in tissue and blood type, usually from a relative. Since the body's immune system viciously attacks a transplanted kidney as an unwanted intruder, drugs to block the immune system must be taken for months or years. Despite the constant stress of possible rejection, kidney transplant patients can anticipate an 87 percent survival rate for three years.

Three thousand years ago the psalmist exclaimed, "We are fearfully and wonderfully made" (Psalm 139:14). Just now, at the end of the twentieth century, we are even more in awe of the Scriptures and the body they describe. Since we live in a body of exquisite design, shouldn't we each be interested in getting acquainted with the Designer?

KILN — life a fiery
Jeremiah 4:19; Acts 26:23

In a Fiery Kiln

Nemesis was the goddess Greeks assigned to visit the good fortunes of men with the reverses their sins demanded. From the cradle to the grave, humanity lives in a fiery kiln of adversity. Even if we are not under constant stress, our mortality mocks us. The English had enjoyed an enviable reign of victory until they fought the Revolution. Then, the victory that seemed within reach always eluded the next general and military campaign. American troops, considered unworthy of contesting a battlefield with British regulars, had a maddening way of fighting them to a standstill. In 1780, Horace Walpole tried to put all the anxiety, pessimism, and division in perspective. "One cannot be always in the year 1759," he wrote, "and have victories fresh for every post-day."

No, one cannot.

Not even the world's greatest atomic powers can defeat every foe they face. America learned that lesson in Viet Nam. The Russians, far less restrained than we in warring ferociously, found it true in Afghanistan. Defeat is as much a part of life as victory; failure as much a part as success. Adversity is inevitable. Through our mother's agony we come into the world, and in the matrix of suffering we live. Yet, as our Lord's own sufferings proved, enduring trials should make us stronger and overcoming them should give us confidence for the future.

KINDNESS — returns
1 Kings 17:1–6; Luke 8:1–3

Cast Your Bread

Herman Brown went into business in 1909, building roads in the Texas Hill Country. He worked hard and faithfully, becoming a foreman and then a contractor. Political patronage and legal connections brought him a road-building contract. Having borrowed to the limit to finance a project, he found himself broke when rains made further work impossible. He couldn't even afford feed for his mules. At that point a local merchant gave him feed on credit. Years later when Brown was a successful contractor, he heard that the merchant had gone broke in the Depression and lived in poverty. Within a few days the old man received a check in the mail big enough to erase money worries for the rest of his life. His kindness had been remembered.

We never know when a kindness shown will become a kindness returned. Given the vagaries of life, any of us could someday be the object, not the origin, of the generosity we now express. Those who faithfully help others in their distress seldom lack help in their own.

KINDRED — numerous
Genesis 9:1, 7; Mark 6:3

A Fertile Race

No one can doubt our proclivity to procreation. On his world cruise, Magellan's men found one Spice Islands sultan who had fathered 526 children. Another had sired 660. These figures surpassed Augustus the Strong of Saxony, Morrison wrote, who boasted only 364 bastards. Aristotle records that one Greek woman had 20 children in four births and that most of them survived. In Chile, South America, a lady had 53 children, 18 of whom were still at home. The 20 of them shared a two-room shack in a rural community north of Santiago. When asked why she had so many offspring, she explained. Abandoned as an infant and reared in a church orphanage, she had vowed to keep her children always and never to give them away.

The urge to parenthood remains irresistible, even among career women who once considered motherhood an unwanted relic. We may want fewer children, but few couples want to be childless. Begetting children is part of the God-built creator in us. Like him, we too want to share ourselves with someone like us.

KINGDOM — of God
Isaiah 62:2; Matthew 16:18

A Deathless Kingdom

Before falling into disuse and disrepair, the church along route 22, constructed in 1794, had hosted up to five hundred worshipers each Sunday. When citizens of the community learned that a nearby factory intended to buy the property, raze the building, and pave the land with asphalt, they intervened. They raised funds, cleared the cemetery grounds, overhauled the structure, and saved the building as a historical landmark. *Readers Digest* ran a story about it called "The Church That Would Not Die."

In the years when mercy died and cruelty lived, congregations of men assembled along the banks of the River Kwai. Those emaciated, threadbare prisoners called themselves a church—a church whose single requirement for membership was faith in Jesus Christ as Lord. This was God's kingdom, Ernest Gordon wrote, a spiritual fellowship that expressed Christ's love. The physical temple was absent, with most of the accouterments we think of as the church, but the fellowship of God's people survived and thrived.

Which is the church, the kingdom of God? That colonial building along route 22, or the men of the death camps? Which can exist without the other? Which one goes on and thrives in all changes, in even the most dangerous places, without human intervention or sustenance? Which is the militant kingdom of God, spiritually warring against all of Satan's strongholds? Which is, simultaneously and forever, the church devoted to God's purpose and at rest in God's love?

KLEPTOMANIA — obvious
Hosea 8:2–3; Mark 1:15; Luke 12

An Uncontrolled Vice

A pretty young woman worked as a security guard for a major retailer in an upscale shopping mall. When police searched her home and garage, they found items worth $500,000 that she had stolen from the store in nine years of employment—

much of it still with the store's price tags. Officers counted over 1,600 items in her bedroom alone, meticulously detailing the numerous articles of clothing that she had obsessively and consistently stolen.

She was apprehended when security cameras caught her stuffing her girdle on three occasions. The police figure she just got careless; she had always previously adjusted or disconnected the cameras. Perhaps she was finally requesting help by no longer concealing her thefts. Perhaps her uncontrolled urge to steal clamored for a solution that her own self-will could not provide.

When we sin against God, he demands repentance as a condition of spiritual rehabilitation. Repentance has been defined as a turning around—from going in the wrong direction to going in the right direction. Repentance comes as a process. We first acknowledge our lost condition, then assume personal responsibility for our spiritual failures. As a result, we grieve over our rejection of God's grace and willingly change our direction in life, turning to God's way from our way.

KNOWLEDGE — insufficiency
Deuteronomy 29:29; Matthew 16:16, 22–23

Knowledge or Life?

An observer of the nineteenth-century American education system noted that parents pressured teachers to stress reading, but not a comprehension of the words. Educators today theoretically dismiss that philosophy, but low scholastic scores among students indicate we may be repeating their mistake. Still, while ignorance curses many lives, advances in knowledge and technology haven't brought us corresponding benefits. We continue to eat from the tree of knowledge, but what happened to the tree of life? Like a surgeon who opens up a patient, takes out the intestines and discovers the problem, we can get a person apart, but can we put that person back together again?

Only when we understand humanity's spiritual nature. Knowledge can at best diagnose the problem; it has no ability to prescribe the cure. "He was skillful enough to have lived still," Lafeu said of the good doctor in *All's Well That Ends Well*, "if knowledge could be set up against mortality." It can't be. We believe, not think or reason, our way to life. Any spirit that demands perfect knowledge is just like the student who can say the words, but has no understanding of what he speaks. How God saves us has never been explained, but there is no doubt he has. God asks us to accept by faith what we cannot understand or explain. Knowledge is a useful ally, but in reaching perfection, it is only the handmaid of faith, not its mistress.

KNOWLEDGE — limits of
Genesis 11:1–4; Acts 17:21

Limitations of Knowledge

We know that the remarkable Inca culture began about 850 B.C. We also know they abandoned their cities 2,300 years later—but not why. We know they split granite blocks, hauled them up and down steep gorges to building sites miles away, and fitted them so tightly without mortar that not even a knife's edge can be inserted between them. How they achieved these incredible engineering feats without iron tools, draft animals, or wheeled vehicles we cannot say. We know they ruled a vast empire that could muster armies within days, and that they divided their population into twelve age groups, each with specific assignments. We don't know how they managed this Herculean task without a written language, numerals, or currency.

All human knowledge, however replete, pales before our greater ignorance. Nowhere is this truer than in the spiritual life. What we know about God is about the same as fifty cents worth of information out of a billion dollar mine. Not that we lack essential information. Whatever we need to know, God has revealed. In turn, he expects obedience, whatever our level of knowledge.

KUDOS — encourage excellence
Judges 6:12, 14; Luke 7:48, 50

The Worth of a Kudo

Abba Eban, the Israeli statesman, impacts the twentieth century as one of its most eloquent speakers. From his earliest days he developed a skill generally lost to our generation. Henry Steele Commager and the *London Times* literary supplement compared him to Charles Burke and even Cicero. In classic understatement Eban noted that one need not take the eulogies at full value to be impressed and encouraged by them.

Positive reinforcement appreciates present achievement and encourages greater achievement. What people are inside determines whether praise makes them shrink, grow, or merely swell; whether it thwarts or stimulates greater effort, or freezes them in self-adoration. Humble people accept kudos as a challenge to excel present achievement. They serve from love, in competition only within themselves, and appreciate the notice someone takes of their efforts.

LAUGHTER — our ally
Job 8:21; John 20:20

The Saving Grace

When he and his companions talked about the prison sentences they had received, they found themselves laughing hilariously, Solzhenitsyn wrote. It cleansed them. It was the salvation of their bodies. Laughter is indeed good medicine. For one thing, it stimulates like exercise, increases the heart rate and blood pressure, enhances blood circulation, and promotes movement of oxygen and nutritional components throughout the body. It also relieves pain, presumably by releasing endorphins into the bloodstream. Laughter also breaks the cycle of negative feelings that invariably produces tension, which in turn hastens negative feelings.

Different levels of laughter have a progressive effect on our body. A smile produces activity in the face, neck, scalp, and shoulder muscles. Add mirth to a smile and you work the muscles around the ribs. Explode with laughter and the whole system vibrates. It provides good exercise for the whole body.

God made us to laugh, after all. He himself has a roaring sense of humor; his creation of the orangutan is proof of that, as is the coelacanth (a fish that stands on its head),and the giraffe of such ridiculous, yet graceful proportions. We'll never die laughing, but it just might contribute to a longer, healthier, more positive life.

LAW — outrageous costs
Leviticus 18:4–5; 1 Timothy 1:9–10

Quick to Take Offense

British Loyalists bristled at the clamorous American appeal to law and the rights of free men. However, with more law commentaries ordered from England than any book but the Bible, many Americans read the law. Today, two-thirds of all lawyers practice in the United States, offering 5 percent of the world's population 66 percent of the available legal counsel.

Our zeal for law has developed a litigious society that has profit—not the public good—as its goal. A recent study showed that more civil lawsuits are filed in the state of Massachusetts than in the nation of Japan. Little wonder. Japan has less than twelve thousand lawyers, fewer than the number of licensed attorneys in Washington, D.C. With a 1,000 percent increase in lawsuits since 1975, we spend $30 billion a year suing each other.

Many Christians carry a litigious attitude into their interpersonal relationships, especially toward other members in the local church. We too quickly take offense with a brother, divide the fellowship into competing sides, and pull our membership to go elsewhere. Conflict in the church body isn't necessarily evil. It offers an opportunity to put the second commandment into practice: Love your neighbor as yourself. Don't we want acceptance and patience from others, whatever our views? Can we refuse to others what we desire for ourselves?

LEGENDS — retold
Judges 10:17; 11:13, 14–27; John 8:40

Let's See . . . Was It . . .

When William the Conqueror came ashore at Pevensey in England, he slipped and fell forward to the ground. A bad omen, his men thought. But not to worry. William arose and grandly declared, "By God's splendor, I have seized the soil of England in both my hands." As David Howarth pointed out, however, this was a perennial story retold by historians: in Caesar's landing in Africa nine hundred years before and in King Edward's landing in Normandy three hundred years later.

Christians should stir uneasily when they hear legend and Bible in the same sentence. However harmless or entertaining the word *legend* may be, it has nothing in common with the Bible. Legend is unverified possibilities; the Bible is verified truth in its history, prophecy, internal unity, subject matter, continuity of existence, and accuracy in related disciplines. Legend is universal: "once upon a time"; the Bible is particularized history, giving dates, names, events, nations, rulers, and geographical references. Legend builds a story or belief on a fragment of the hypothetical; the Bible begins with the eternal, sovereign, almighty God. Legend tolerates all beliefs, however fanciful, as equally true; the Bible, as uncompromising truth tolerates nothing else.

LIFE — God's Presence Needed
Psalm 27:8; Philippians 3:10–11

What Do You Want?

Jane Goodall loves chimpanzees and spent years in Africa studying the little creatures. A confirmed evolutionist, she delights in any communication, understanding, and affection between herself and the apes. In her book *In the Shadow of Man* she tells of such an experience. She and a chimp patriarch sat close to each other. Goodall picked up a palm nut and handed it to the chimp. He took it and simultaneously held her hand firmly and gently. Her heart soared. The gentle pressure of his fingers indicated to her that the barrier of untold generations of evolution had been overcome, if only for those few moments.

We get out from life what we expect; often, what we put into it. People satisfy themselves with little when they could have much; with the least, when they could have most; with self, when they could enjoy God. We can choose the results of faith or take the consequences of self-will. We can develop the most inordinate, fleshly appetites, or in surrender to grace find self-control. We make the choice.

LIFE — selling cheaply
Numbers 24:6–9; Galatians 5:1

Asking Too Little

Trusted with one of the most prestigious positions in the United States military, the sergeant served in counter-intelligence, infiltrating the Soviet Union's KGB spy network. He personally handled several double-agents, who ostensibly served the Soviets but in reality were U.S. operatives. Two years after leaving the army, the sergeant went to Tokyo, met with a KGB officer, and supplied him with information that compromised at least one U.S. double agent. Others could have been exposed. For this unbelievable intelligence windfall the man demanded and received $11,000 from the Soviets. Business failures had driven him deeply into debt, and he turned to perfidy to escape. But such astounding information for a mere $11,000? How little he thought of his position! He could have bargained only briefly and raised the offer several times beyond that.

Judas got thirty pieces of silver for his betrayal of Christ, and the sergeant got $11,000. The traitor represents us all spiritually. Satan would pay premium rates to secure our tremendous spiritual power and potential if we weren't so anxious to sell at bargain-basement rates. To have us in his service, with our skills at his disposal, our lives in his keeping, he would offer us fabulous promises and awards. But we don't think that highly of ourselves. We demand from him nothing equal with or even comparable to our worth. In that sense, we love ourselves far too little!

LIFESTYLE — differences in
Psalm 16:11; Ephesians 2:10

The Way People Choose

Michelangelo and Raphael had totally different perspectives on lifestyle. Michelangelo lived alone, with only a servant; Raphael traveled with a retinue. "You go about with a suite, like a general," Michelangelo stormed at him. "And you go about alone, like a hangman," Raphael sniped in reply.

City dwellers of the Renaissance urged escape to the country to enjoy its delights and pleasures. One farmer replied: "Had I not been born a rustic, I should readily have been touched with pleasure" by the descriptions of rural happiness. However, being a farmer "what to you are delights are to me a bore." Contrary to his brother's greed for multiplied possessions, Prospero declared, "My library was dukedom large enough."

God orders no single lifestyle for humanity. Instead, by stressing our individuality, he allows each person to determine how to dress, where to live, or what career to pursue. But we must not confuse personal lifestyle with the life God planned when he created us. When God envisioned beings to share his fellowship, he created a person in his own image.

LIFESTYLE — thrift in disastrous
1 Samuel 11:1; James 3:5

For a Dollar More

Heinrich Friedrich Albert came to New York in 1915 ostensibly as a financial advisor to the German ambassador, Count Johanann von Bernstorff. His real purpose, however, as a spy for the Kaiser, was to keep America neutral by judiciously scattering forty million dollars on sabotage and propaganda. Personal thriftiness led to his failure. He took the nickel Sixth Avenue El to his hotel instead of a taxi, which would have cost $1.25. As he hurriedly left the El that fateful day, July 24, 1915, he thoughtlessly left behind a suitcase containing information on his vast network of contacts. The U.S. Secret Service snatched the suitcase and exposed its contents.

A small mistake, but it was disastrous for Germany. Eve made a similarly small decision in Eden, taking Satan at his word when he promised that she would not die, despite God's warning that she would. But that is the nature of sin: it hardens us to its deceitful nature. It makes disobedience harmless and virtue treacherous. When God later queried her, she admitted, "The serpent deceived me." She didn't know when she ate the fruit that she would get shame, not wisdom, and knowledge, but at the cost of horrible guilt. Satan knows how to exploit our many small weaknesses in an effort to minimize our few great strengths.

LISTENING — need to
Jeremiah 7:21–26; Matthew 7:26–27

Listening

Lucy, of the Peanuts comic strip, tells Charlie Brown that she has to read a book but doesn't want to. Would he please read it to her? "Read it yourself," he says. She replies that reading takes effort and she hates anything that takes effort. Charlie wisely says that listening takes effort, too. But, Lucy retorts, she wasn't going to listen.

How often we are like Lucy. Shamefully, some of us don't want the Bible taught. Others want it taught, but not at a level that will provoke thought, action, or change. That is bad. But to want it taught while we sit and not really listen is worse still. The worst of all is to listen—and not obey. Jesus left no doubt. Only those who listen to the Word, obey what they hear, and produce its fruit are acceptable to him. Since we believe in his absolutes, we absolutely believe in hearing and doing the Master's will.

LISTENING — to others
2 Samuel 17:23; Acts 1:18–19

If We Listen

He received a B.S. degree from Penn State at age twenty and earned his M.D. at age twenty-five. He became one of the nation's youngest psychiatrists and at thirty-four taught law in one university and psychiatry in another. Deeply troubled, despite his success, he had a marriage he couldn't save. One morning he and his estranged wife argued in her house. As she ran outside, neighbors heard a gunshot. Police found his body, a shotgun at his side.

Another man taught at a community college. He had been brilliant, innovative, and controversial. When he failed to appear for a meeting one morning, someone called his home. The man's recorded voice answered, "Call the coroner. There's been a suicide." The police found him slumped in a chair, a bullet in his head.

For several weeks beforehand each man had signaled his intentions, mentioning or openly discussing suicide. Passing it off as temporary depression, friends and relatives failed to take action, thinking the men were too much in charge of themselves, too logical, too educated, with too much to live for to ever consider such action.

People are rarely in such charge of themselves as to never have self-doubt. Often, their self-sufficiency only masks a much deeper need of the Creator. We masquerade our inadequacies to keep from others our unmanageable anguish. Behind apparent maturity, all too often, is a child whimpering for a hug.

LONELINESS — our despair
1 Kings 19:14; Luke 22:28

The Despair of Loneliness

Henry Ford II ruled an automobile company, spent princely sums on whatever he fancied, and had the attention of everyone he met. Yet this often lonely man would regularly turn to his younger daughter, even awakening her from sleep to talk. Sometimes he was sad; sometimes he was happy. But, she noticed, he always seemed lonely, with no one to share his deepest thoughts. Numerous studies prove the disadvantages of living alone or being lonely: sickness comes more often and stays longer, and suicides and automobile accidents are more prevalent.

Yet, as one young adult explained, "It isn't easy to find meaningful fellowship." In melancholy eloquence he stated the problem about the single's bar scene.

"Your work keeps you busy," he said, "but it also keeps you from seeing anyone. You go to a bar for fellowship, but find the lights so dim you can't see anyone. You drink with companions only to find that what you drink keeps you from understanding each other. And the noise in the bars keeps you from hearing each other." Their cure for loneliness only adds to their feeling of isolation.

God made us communal creatures to live within a fellowship of others like ourselves. From the Trinity's eternal, joyous fellowship we derive all our yearnings for fellowship. Only by associating with God, and those called to him through Christ, do we find an end to the loneliness that otherwise haunts and harms us.

LOOKS — importance of
1 Samuel 10:24, 16:6–7; 2 Corinthians 10:10

A Man of Stature

At age thirteen, while on vacation with her family, actress Betty Davis had her first crush—on a soda jerk. Each day she walked to the drugstore and sat at the counter, looking at the handsome young man. He was the first boy she kissed. When summer ended, the family left, and she never saw him again.

Fifty years later, while doing a show in Boston, she heard again: "Do you want a soda?" and instantly knew the voice. She invited him backstage. "I was so nervous waiting for him," she remembered. "When he came into my dressing room, I didn't recognize him. There stood this little old, old man, the person I had loved so madly long ago. Maybe that's my biggest regret—not that I remembered his voice but that, fifty years later, I asked to see him again. In seeing the man, I lost the first boy I ever loved."

It works both ways doesn't it? He wasn't the only one of the two grown older in those fifty years! But how clearly her response distinguishes infatuation from love—or from mature love. A couple married those fifty years would look past the bodily ravages to appreciate the soul's beauty. Instead of being unbearable, the astonishing reality would bring delight.

LOSS — enormous in short time
Isaiah 53:4; John 16:33

Afterwards, Begin Again

Thomas Carlyle spent a year in research, gathering materials. Then he wrote for endless hours daily through many weeks to complete the first volume of his history of the French Revolution. He then submitted it to a friend for inspection. The manuscript was accidentally and ignorantly destroyed by a servant. Carlyle bore the loss with equanimity and never openly criticized his friend's carelessness. He wrote to Emerson that he had to recruit his resolve and return to work. "I began again at the beginning. . . ."

An 8.1 personal quake won't shake some people while a sonic boom unravels others. Some with every advantage fail when confronting disaster while others, with no advantages, succeed despite the disaster. Whether we recover from tragedy slowly, quickly, or not at all depends on our reaction to it. Seeing obstacles as unsought opportunities can unleash creative forces within to recover and surpass what was lost. Resilience in life—the ability to constantly bend without breaking— will protect us from self-defeating responses when we confront the inevitable monsters of mayhem.

LOVE — idea of romantic
Song of Solomon 1:20, 4:5; 1 Peter 3:1–7

Only Within Marriage

Roland Bainton correctly wrote that many in the Renaissance saw love as an ennobling passion but felt it was possible only outside of marriage because it could be given without any claim of one party on the other. Thus, romantic love became the source of adultery; it was anti-marriage and anti-home. Love until love dies, then stop living together! Very convenient, very modern. (As one set of vows said: "to live together as long as both shall love.")

The courts of the Renaissance embraced the ideals of twelfth-century French royalty, which viewed sexual dalliances with bemused tolerance. Matrimony to them was simply a convenience for uniting families and transmitting property.

Obviously, early Protestantism rejected so impious a view of love. It subordinated romance to duty but found love and romance coexisting in marriage, with love its ultimate grace. Like kindling, romance ignites the courting; like logs, love alone keeps the marriage fires burning. God designed human love to expand and deepen within marriage, and those who embrace God's view find their experience equaling his expectation.

LOYALTY — to one's own cause
1 Kings 18:20–21; Colossians 2:20–23

For Himself Alone

An opponent of the Burmese government, Aung San escaped from authorities in 1941, contacted Japanese officials, and organized his forces under their training, accompanying them in attacks on Burma. However, when Aung San saw that the Japanese wouldn't let him be an independent ruler, he organized a secret anti-Fascist organization while ostensibly supporting the Japanese cause. In December 1944, he contacted the British with a request for Allied assistance and then surprised the Japanese by joining and fighting with the Allies. He saw collaboration with either side as a means of gaining independence for Burma.

Sometimes people make bargains with whomever they feel offers them the greatest advantage. The relationship chosen might be terribly harmful, as was

Aung San's bargain with the Japanese, but they feel the temporary advantage is worth it. The devil is always ready to strike a bargain. He knows his power, even if those who deal with him do not. He will accept our delay in accepting Christ if he can't convince us to disown him. He will encourage us to give up one sin to assure our continued involvement in others. He will settle for our occasional doubt about God's love since he is unable to turn us into atheists. But make no mistake. Satan hates God and vilifies Christ in order to exalt himself, and he knows the increasing power of his persuasion once he is allowed to persuade. No bargain struck with him will ever harm him or help us.

LOYALTY — under duress
Genesis 39:6–9; Colossians 2:15

In Code

In addressing the Iranian hostages after their 444-day terror, President Reagan referred to the hardships they had experienced and the valor they had shown. He mentioned Sergeant Gomez, one of the Marine guards. He had put up a sign in his cell that would have been immediately removed by his captors had they known its meaning. But he wrote it in Spanish, so they couldn't understand: "Viva la roja; blanca, y azul." The Iranians didn't know what it meant, but Sergeant Gomez knew. And when we heard, we knew, and our hearts warmed and tears formed as the president translated the message: "Long live the Red, White, and Blue!"

It reminds us of the New Testament Christians—innocent, common citizens in extraordinary crises, expressing loyalty in uncommonly brave ways! Though not individually guilty of any wrong, they belonged to a group deemed corporately guilty by Jewish and Roman authorities. Leaving Jerusalem after Saul's violent repression, the lay Christians carried the apostolic message into the cities of the Empire. Refusing to flee when hunted or to compromise when found, they suffered imprisonment, beatings, and torture. But while the persecutors could imperil the messengers, they were powerless against the spread of their message.

LYING — endemic in man
1 Kings 22:11–12; Acts 5:3

An Endemic Vice

A poll on "Lying in America," released in February 1987, indicated that Americans consider honesty as rare as a temporary tax. Seventy-one percent of the 1,006 adults questioned expressed dissatisfaction with our dishonesty. Yet, how many of those asserting unhappiness over our dishonesty are themselves dishonest in some way? A 1984 IRS survey found 50 percent of Americans have a flexible standard of morality.

A New York firm that annually investigates thousands of resumes finds outright lies in 20 percent of them. Hotel managers learned long ago to decorate rooms with inexpensive items, hoping that guests will swipe them and leave more expensive items. The American Insurance Association says that 20 percent of insurance claims contain an element of fraud.

There are some who lie for the sake of lying, Pascal wrote. Yes, a great many someones. But we destroy ourselves, others, and society by lying. Little wonder that most people think honesty is rare—it is. Little wonder they think everyone cheats; what we feel about ourselves is often our evaluation of others. If the surveys are true, we all need to repent of this horrible sin before it destroys us. God will have no liars in heaven (Rev. 21:8).

MARRIAGE — partners reflecting
Ezekiel 16:6–8; 2 Corinthians 11:2

More Alike

Long-married couples often seem to develop into mirror images, having similar movements, habits, and thoughts. This is not an illusion, an ongoing study at the University of Washington reports. The longer people stay together, the more likely they are to reflect each other. They eventually share thoughts, perceptions, and even mathematical skills. However, and perhaps not surprisingly, wives usually do the changing. Women gain mentally if they marry intelligent men; they lose an edge if they marry below their own intelligence quotient.

The study is based on tests given every seven years to 175 couples over the past thirty years. Twenty-two couples have been tested regularly. The tests cover a wide range of measurable skills in addition to personality traits and reasoning ability. Through the years the couples have become one in many unexpected ways.

This is not surprising. Those who live together invariably reflect each other, with the stronger personality generally impacting the weaker. Christians experience this in their marriage to the Lord Jesus. The Master's powerful presence impacts his servants, who find themselves progressively losing their own traits and acquiring his. God's children try to express in their own lives the perfect beauty of Christ's.

MATURITY — growth without perfection
Ecclesiastes 12:12; John 15:2, 7

Never Reach the Goal

Robert Hutchins wrote that school systems usually take for granted that learning stops after formal education. That is unfortunate, he wrote, "because most of the important things that human beings ought to understand cannot be comprehended in youth. . . . The great books of ethics, political philosophy, economics, history, and literature do not yield up their secrets to the immature."

That perspective challenges church leaders and their teaching programs! Do we offer teaching that merely satisfies people, or teaching that encourages them to learn as they are satisfied? Some may content themselves with what another teaches, but true Christlike teaching incites a desire for increased knowledge that grows toward the teacher's level and beyond, becoming a teacher one's self, beginning the cycle again.

MEDICINE — take it carefully
Micah 2:11; John 5:39–40

Harmful If Swallowed?

The prescription a doctor scribbles should help our body's immune system fight off disease. Improperly taken, or taken with the wrong food and drink, however, it can be more harmful than helpful. Wrong combinations can render the medication useless or, in rare cases, toxic.

Those who take high blood pressure or severe depression drugs should avoid aged cheese, Chianti wine, yogurt, or bananas. Anticoagulants should not be taken with large amount of leafy vegetables. Those on thyroid medication should avoid cabbage and brussels sprouts. Milk is better taken with some antibiotics, water with others. Alcohol in combination with depressants can be fatal. We have to take our medicine carefully to assure that what should help us does not harm us.

Sin is so deeply ingrained in our souls that the medicine God prescribes must be accurately taken before it can work its wonders in forgiveness. We dare not carelessly ingest into our souls any nostrum prescribed by any teacher. If wrong medications can kill our bodies, false spiritual prescriptions will threaten our souls.

MEMORY — bringing justice
Joshua 22:21–28; John 11:51–52

A Mother's Memory

In 1961, a seventeen-year-old runaway who was serving time in a reform school surrendered the son born to her there. In 1980 she began a determined effort to find the boy who would have been nineteen years old. The search led to a welfare department, where she learned that her boy had died of peritonitis when he was four years old. No further information was available. Unwilling to give up, she began poring over old newspaper accounts that raised suspicions about the boy's death. She took her findings to the police. After experts had carefully studied the dead boy's autopsy report, they determined he had been beaten to death. In January, 1987, the lad's adoptive mother was indicted for murder.

An obvious question arose. Why wasn't the boy's death more critically examined, since welfare workers had subsequently removed other children from that household? Apparently no one felt concerned enough or thought to make the connection. But twenty-five years after her son had died without cause, a mother's persistent efforts kept his memory alive and brought him justice.

God audibly expressed his appreciation of Jesus on at least four occasions: his birth, his baptism, his transfiguration, and during the week of his crucifixion. God's approval of Christ's sacrifice has no bounds. He honored that sacrifice when he raised Christ from the dead and will never allow anyone else to dishonor it. Since he accepted Christ's sacrifice as the completed redemptive act, summarizing all Old Testament sacrifices and human desires, God constantly demands our obedience to Christ's will. He will never accept less.

MEMORY — innate
Genesis 9:15, 16; 2 Corinthians 1:8–9

Not Able to Forget

He stormed ashore on Utah Beach, June 6, 1944, a young infantryman, alert and frightened. In the village of Sainte Mere Eglise, he blundered into a German patrol and instinctively fired his submachine gun, killing two. Terrified, he ran and took refuge in a nearby house, hiding beneath curtains stretched around a child's crib.

In 1966, he returned to the village, found the corner where he had killed the enemy, and strode down a side street to the house where he had hidden. To his amazement, he recognized the woman who answered his knock: she had helped him to hide in 1944. Shown to an upstairs bedroom, he saw the same crib in a corner, curtains still hanging around the bottom. Twenty-two years, and he remembered it all. Twenty-two years, and he could never forget, if another forty years passed.

Some experiences stay seared into our memories, alive to the touch, in that strange area of the brain that chooses to just as completely forget others. For good or bad, these living memories remain, soothing or afflicting, assuaging or tormenting us. Whether for enjoyment or despair, memory rouses itself and leafs through our mental files, poring over all, keeping some, dismissing others . . . some bringing a smile, others a sigh . . . frozen instants from an unrepeatable past. We can delight in the past our future rehearses by filling the present with spiritual encounters with God.

MERCY — call for
Jeremiah 2:35; 3:13; Mark 10:13–16, 17

Each Person's Need

While his studies led Nicolaus Copernicus from a geocentric to a heliocentric perception of the universe, he retained an unaltered personal faith in God. And, in a spiritual humility many modern scientists find unacceptably embarrassing, the great astronomer subordinated himself to the mercy Jesus showed the dying robber. Scorning the pride that demands privilege, he begged only the benevolence that exalts grace.

In choosing the dying thief—not Paul or Peter—as his model, Copernicus expressed the childlikeness that Jesus demands in all Kingdom subjects! He clearly understood the apostolic emphasis on grace alone. Like the dying robber, Copernicus knew he had purposefully violated God's laws; he could contribute nothing to his salvation; he had no ability to spiritually influence or impress anyone; and he had to depend solely and completely on the merits of Jesus Christ in order to be saved.

MIND — power of
Nehemiah 4:6; Colossians 3:9–10

In His Mind

"Bat," or "Roman Nose," as the whites called him, stood six feet three inches. He claimed to possess great medicine in a headdress he wore in all battles. It repeatedly protected him from arrows and bullets, even as he rode daringly close to the enemy. One inviolable stipulation attended this medicine: eating anything from a pot with an iron instrument would destroy the bonnet's medicine and require long purification rites.

One day, in 1868, six hundred braves cornered fifty Army scouts under Colonel Sandy Forsyth on an island of the Arickaree River in eastern Colorado. The night before the battle, Bat dined in a Sioux lodge, whose owner did not know of the taboo. When she offered him fried bread from a skillet, he willingly ate until he spied the fork she had used. He retained his composure but was inwardly shattered—he knew his fate. The next day, he loitered as warriors mounted their ponies. Urged to lead the charge, he explained about the taboo and said, "I know I die today." He finally put on his war bonnet and led a charge against the entrenched scouts. Shot from his horse, he was carried to his teepee where he died at sunset.

We cannot dispute the power of the mind over a person's life, whether good or bad. That being true, Jesus committed himself to recapturing God's original intent of the mind: to discover God in all his works. Christians have the privilege of continuing Christ's ministry by having our minds renewed in his image.

MINORITY — the few receive most
Psalm 18:1–3, 16–17; Romans 8:17

Only a Few

Forty-six percent of actors and actresses live in Los Angeles and 36 percent in New York. In 1982 they earned an unevenly distributed $459 million. More than 81 percent of all Screen Actors Guild members made less than $5000. More than 40,000 performers earned less than $1,000. The big money, $50,000 plus, went to 1,841 actors and actresses—less than 3 percent of the Guild's members. Many careers have similar statistics; a few famous are overpaid while the rest scrape by.

How starkly different the spiritual life! Everyone in God's kingdom shares equally in its one possession—eternal life—and all equally reflect its one glory—the person of Christ. True, some Christians are more spiritually enriched than others, but only by availing themselves of the opportunities every Christian has to become spiritually rich. God invites all his children to an equal involvement in his glories.

MISFORTUNE — blame wrong things
Job 42:6; 2 Corinthians 7:8–10

Not That at All

Columbus' fortunes plummeted after his first voyage. When he returned under fire from his second, he decided that pride had led God to frown on his achievements. To curry God's favor, he removed his fine clothing, put on the coarsest garments he could find, and left castles for religious houses. Recovering a sense of humility did Columbus no harm, but it helped his fortunes none at all. For his administrative mistakes—and being a foreigner—were responsible for his disasters more than anything else.

What of the multiple, escalating disasters afflicting Western culture? Ours is not a problem of sound theology and poor methodology; of a faulty electronic component that we can replace and thus function perfectly. No, ours is so egregious a sin that it is soluble only by a bone-rattling repentance before God! Non–Christians don't want to hear that, but it's true.

MISTAKES — experts make
Joshua 7:2–5; 1 Corinthians 10:12

Even They

George Morar made his first parachute jump in Korea when his plane went down behind enemy lines. It saved his life. In 1983 he made his last jump from a small plane over northern California. It killed him. The plane he and three other sky divers shared flew from the field of the instruction school he owned. At 5,600 feet the divers were preparing to jump when, suddenly, Morar's reserve chute burst open, billowed outside the craft, and tangled in the plane's tail, instantly plunging it into a nose-dive.

He should have dived out instinctively after the chute, but instead he grabbed frantically for the chute, trying to pull it back in. Why this pioneer of parachuting panicked and ignored all his own teachings and experience we will never know. For when he finally jumped, the reserve chute ripped off, and a wind gust or contact with the plane tore away his main chute as well. After nearly 3,000 jumps, an incredible blunder cost his life.

It is a warning to us all. We never get so good, so intelligent, or so experienced that we are invulnerable to foolish, deadly mistakes. Just when we think we have grown beyond a certain temptation, we find ourselves falling to it. When we feel mature enough to capably handle any crisis, a small problem renders us helpless. David had reached the zenith of his career and seemed invincible; then, one fateful night, he walked out on his balcony . . .

MISTAKES — forgive
Ezekiel 18:21–22; Colossians 3:13

Not to Erase the Good

A couple enjoyed a wonderful twenty-year marriage. Compatible in every way, it seemed the perfect match. When he died, the widow proved inconsolable. Her life had come to an end, and she had lost her only hope for love in this world. Then her husband's secretary dropped off his personal papers, and in them the widow discovered his affairs with other women.

Instantly, the woman's grief turned to rage, and her love to hate. She despised her husband for his deception. She removed all memory of him from their home and refused to hear his name spoken, even by their children. When she wrote to Dear Abby she confessed that she wished him alive just so she could inflict on him the grief his immorality had brought her. Abby wisely urged her to vent her anger with a counselor. Further, she wrote, their marriage was no less wonderful though her husband had been unfaithful.

How often we hold friendships and relationships hostage to disagreements and disputes. We forget the good done, the virtue shown, and the worth proven, just because of a failure or an argument. We sometimes allow one mistake to wipe out a lifetime of love and friendship. Like fire consuming a museum, anger can destroy in a few minutes what it has taken years to collect. Pride will keep us from forgiving. All other feelings can be assuaged by reason, but pride alone remains adamant against grace.

MISTAKES — learning from others
Jeremiah 7:12; 1 Corinthians 10:11

Learning from Other's Mistakes

On October 25, 1983, United States forces invaded the island of Granada, in the eastern Caribbean. Hard-line Marxists had seized control of the government, assassinated the previous ruler, and welcomed Cuban and Russian military support. To secure the release of American students on the island, and to answer appeals from other nations in the eastern Caribbean, the United States intervened. The next day the Marxist leader of Surinam, fearing for his safety, expelled the Cuban ambassador and one hundred Cubans working in forestry, health, and agriculture projects. Knowing the Cubans had plotted the assassination of the Granadian leader, Surinam's leader resolved not to be the next victim.

Give him credit: he learned from another person's mistake. He didn't want to become another casualty of Russian and Cuban imperialism, so he ousted the people he was sure would kill him if he ever refused their orders. Sad to say, many of us refuse to learn anything from other people's mistakes and failures. Experience is the best teacher, we say, but do we have to experience the same failures, mistakes, and tragedies of others before us? Must we keep repeating, time after time, the failures that mar history in endless generations? Isn't it wiser for us to learn from the past, rather than to simply repeat its mistakes?

MONEY — a delusion
Deuteronomy 6:10–12; 1 Timothy 6:17–19

The Delusion of Wealth

A national survey, conducted by scientists at the Alcohol, Drug Abuse, and Mental Health Administration, found that over half of Americans feel at least moderate stress in their lives. What is surprising is that the more highly paid and educated report higher and more persistent levels of stress. Apparently, education may lead to a higher income, but not necessarily to a higher life. Indeed, stress soared with the level of income, a factor many economically pressed citizens can hardly understand. And, more bad news, those who can most afford to enjoy the high life often don't, missing meals and sleep, drinking more often, and getting less exercise. Perhaps even more unexpected, women, usually considered more tolerant of difficult situations, suffer more stress than men.

It seems that money becomes so important to people that all other aspects of life become secondary. When that happens, wealth becomes a vicious deity, inflicting an equally vicious penalty. Anticipating the problem from the first, God explained how we could have peace with him and financial security. God clothed Adam and Eve with skins, undoubtedly from the animal he sacrificed as an offering for their sins. God was teaching a lesson: he will be faithful to our needs if we are faithful to his forgiveness.

MOODS — dealing with
1 Samuel 25:10–11; 2 Corinthians 1:8–9

Having and Solving

The National Center for Health Statistics surveyed over 42,000 adults in 1991 and discovered that while depression was more common for women, men were more restless, and both felt equally bored and lonely. Almost forty million American adults frequently experience bad moods, three days out of ten being the average. Those most susceptible to foul moods are likely to be smokers. The moodiest men tend to be heavy drinkers. Two percent of people are cheerful nearly every day and 5 percent have bad moods on four of five days.

Given the violence in our society, research on moods is important since we seem to have an increasing inability to climb out of the black holes once we fall into them. Reacting productively to moods offers the challenge. Some effective tactics are to do something to solve the problem, bolster self-esteem, resolve to do better, and remind yourself that you are better off than others. Some people think that drinking or visiting with friends or eating sweets or taking drugs will dispel their somber thoughts. However, these are illusions pretending to be solutions. They leave us worse than they found us. Being alone is least helpful; it increases our sense of isolation and leads to more negation. Other least effective responses are watching television and movie shows, and, surprisingly, releasing the feelings by screaming, yelling, or crying.

Few methods work for the release of anger. What doesn't work at all is to immediately respond to the offender. That will intensify, not reduce, anger. What works well is taking the other person's place and seeing the situation from his or her perspective—but of course that is easier said than done.

MORALITY — absolutely necessary
Deuteronomy 1:17; 1 Corinthians 6:9–11

Even the Depraved

While working undercover for the FBI, Joseph Pistone found that even Mafia soldiers have strong moral feelings. What did they feel about Iran, while it held our embassy? Bomb Teheran. About rapists? Burn them. About females? Never swear in front of them. About another soldier's girl? Never mess with her.

Everyone has moral principles, even the sexually promiscuous. A heterosexual couple engaging in weekend swinging sex parties, contracted the AIDS virus. However, they were not going to tell anyone in their sexual community because they didn't want to lose their friends. Robert McGinley, President of the North American Swing Club, couldn't countenance such irresponsibility. "The best thing they can do is stop going to swing clubs. Where is their morality?" he asked.

In each case morality was defined outside the particular perversion practiced. To the Mafia soldier, stealing silver plate is business but messing with a boss's girl is heinous. To the swinger, morality is in spreading AIDS, not in having multiple sex partners. Morality is important to them only as it transgresses their customs. In their view, immorality is not a debasing act in itself; it must threaten traditions or health. What effect it has on the soul remains unimportant and irrelevant.

With such freedom of choice, can't we see the absolute need of an outside Authority to determine what is true or false, good or bad, moral or immoral? Left to the decision ourselves, we will argue, debate, and fight without ever reaching a decision—unless diseases and bullets get us first.

MORALITY — not spiritual
Genesis 3:2–4; Romans 7:24–25

Not Really Scripture

In his *Meditations*, Marcus Aurelius praised his father as a man who could appreciate, without pride or apology, whatever good came to him. What he possessed he enjoyed; what he couldn't have he never missed. Attributing to his father a compliment first made to Socrates, Aurelius said his father could abstain from temptations others couldn't resist and enjoy in moderation pleasures other sought in excess.

All this sounds very much like Paul's statements in Philippians 4:12 about knowing how to be abased and how to abound. Paul enjoyed his possessions but was never possessed by them. There is a difference, however, between Paul and Aurelius. Aurelius gained his personal views from stoicism and reason. Paul's source of peace was Jesus Christ, not his own ability to calmly adjust to the gains or losses in life. Aurelius would staunchly oppose any threat to his self-sufficiency. Paul would bless whatever shattered his self-sufficiency to make him dependent on grace. He would never claim for himself qualities that come only from God.

MOTIVES — accomplishment with mixed motives
Exodus 4:18; 14:13–14; Acts 9:1, 3

Not Where He Began

A penurious Charles Dickens returned to his London home in the fall of 1843. His house, the holiday abroad, and a growing family taxed his earning ability. In October, 1843, borrowing a subplot from an earlier novel, he began a short Christmas story that he confidently felt would make money. Working furiously, he produced the story in six weeks, in time for December publication. He called it *A Christmas Carol.*

But something happened to Dickens as he wrote the story, something that crept over and saturated him with its presence—the same Christmas spirit that overtook old Scrooge. His story became a work of love, not just of finances. He later wrote an American friend that he had wept and laughed over the story as he wrote it.

He wanted it priced cheaply so everyone could buy a copy. Expensive illustrations in the work, however, kept his profit to only 230 pounds instead of the 1,000 he needed. However, *A Christmas Carol* continued to sell yearly, and his enhanced reputation brought greater success to his subsequent works, several of which became classics. He had begun *A Christmas Carol* to make money. In writing the story, however, the spirit of Christmas seized, then obsessed him. It often happens that those who tinker with the Bethlehem story find themselves obsessed by its Christ.

MUSIC — even reaching animals
Nehemiah 12:27–28, 31, 38; Hebrews 10:25

Gone to the Dogs

Neighbors close to a large kennel began to complain about the disruptive noise. The owner decided to experiment with music piped through the kennels to see if it would soothe the fretful dogs. It worked! Canine stress was reduced and, naturally, so was canine barking. Incredibly, some mutts even got their own headsets. Most of the hundred dogs of every kind found Bach's music the most relaxing. Music isn't called the universal language without reason!

In a beautiful way music offers a parallel to life. Sometimes a melody occurs in the combination of orchestra instruments that no particular instrument is playing. This happened when the first violins of an orchestra played a part of Tchaikovsky's Sixth Symphony. Then the second violins played their part. Then they played together, and a strange thing occurred: the conjunction of the two produced a melody that neither played alone.

It is also true in the Christian life. We each praise God in our own way, in our own time. But when, in public worship, we join our bodies, souls, and voices, we make a sound for God we cannot make alone. God will always listen to the individual's adoration, but how desperately others need to hear the voice the entire Christian orchestra speaks!

MUSIC — the most popular Christmas carol
Isaiah 7:14; Luke 2:15

In a Few Minutes Time

The priests in St. Nicolas Church, Obendorf, Austria, panicked Christmas Eve, 1818, when the church organ malfunctioned. The assistant pastor quickly penned a six-stanza poem, beginning with the words "Stille nacht, heilige nacht." He took the verses to Franz Gruber, the church organist, who arranged a melody for two solo voices, a chorus, and guitar.

That might have been the end of it had not a serendipitous organ repairman learned of the song and taken a copy home. Two traveling singing families took it to more distant locales, singing it before the king of Prussia and in New York City. In 1834 the classic was heard in English: "Silent Night, Holy Night." It is the most popular Christmas carol in the world.

Perhaps the beauty of the message endears the song to us, the message of a love that brought God down to us and of a grace that lifts us up to God— luminous threads through every inch of the divine fabric that envelopes all who tie their lives to Christ. We hang the song on our hearts like an ornament on a Christmas tree, knowing it will illumine our life all year long.

MUSIC — preserving sanity
1 Chronicles 15:16; Luke 7:18–19

To Stay Out of Despair

The Green Beret prisoner crouched in a small shipping crate in which his Vietnamese captors forced him. The incredible heat, the infernal mosquitoes, and the constant poking from sharp bamboo poles nearly drove him mad. To escape his limitations, he sang. He pretended to be Elvis Presley and sang "Hound Dog," or other recording artists and sang their songs. Music was the answer to insanity, he said, and he surrendered himself to it instead of to the fears terrorizing him. In the month before he escaped he found in music a positive companion stronger than the negative forces closing around and threatening him with depression and suicide.

Christians face the temptation to qualify their faith, to rely on their own understanding, to claim God's benefits even when they are being unfaithful to him. The master's wilderness experience offers us three principles that enable us to escape all temptation unscathed and triumphant. First, we must have a sound knowledge of the Bible. Second, we must be willing to trust God for our provisions even when it seems he has overlooked us. Third, we must resolutely refuse to compromise any spiritual truth in exchange for some proposed gain. Applying the Master's three principles will blunt temptation's attack and allow the Holy Spirit to counterattack.

MUSIC — reaches deepest part of us
Isaiah 55:1–2; Ephesians 5:19–20

To Bring the Light

Returning to his hut late one night after Bible study, Ernest Gordon thought he heard singing from another hut. He stopped and listened. It was singing. To the accompaniment of a stick on a piece of tin, the men along the River Kwai were singing "Jerusalem the Golden."

Will Durant had a similar experience in Chicago. He wrote his wife that he had just heard church bells chiming some "touching old Protestant hymns." One had been so moving that he cried aloud, "O God, how beautiful!"

Gordon thought that the hymn he heard was symbolic—of man's ability to live in hope without worldly goods; of the light that shines in the deepest darkness, bringing life, banishing death; and of the victory humans have over weakness, disease, and loneliness. Even then, we can sing, we can worship.

Durant's response was markedly different. The bells soon stopped, he wrote, "and the world proceeds on its agnostic way. . . ." As if to say he could believe in God as long as beauty expressed itself, but not in ugliness—as long as the music played, but not when it stopped. Yet God has so designed the world that his music is always playing somewhere, by someone. And when the music stops where they live, God's people keep humming the tune!

MYTH — given substance
Isaiah 60:16, 19; Ephesians 3:10–11

The Influence of Myth

An English doctor found writing short stories more to his liking than writing prescriptions. After numerous rejections, Beeton's *Christmas Annual* delighted the doctor by publishing his murder tale in 1887. Although Dr. Conan Doyle was paid a miserly amount for the story, that single mystery launched one of the most successful literary careers in history: the arrogant, impatient, and brilliant Sherlock Holmes.

Read by devotees around the world, Holmes continues to be studied, analyzed, appreciated, and imitated. As one said, he's the greatest detective who never was. People quiz each other's knowledge about him. They accumulate Sherlockian memorabilia—and he never existed. A complete fabrication is the object of this intense devotion, the kind usually reserved for historical beings. Is it a measure of our desperate need of heroes that we create one from a myth?

Like everyone else, believers need heroes. We have many of them, but ultimately only One, and he is authentic, not mythical. He lived among us. He is not the creation of our imagination, he is the Creator making us in his image and revealing himself to us verbally and bodily. He intruded himself into history so boldly and remarkably that he divided it in two. He abolished sin as a principle instead of condemning sinners.

NAÏVETÉ — unbelievable
Judges 11:27; Mark 13:7–8

How's That Again?

In May, 1950, General Douglas MacArthur explained why he didn't feel that war with North Korea was imminent. The nature of warfare had fundamentally altered its acceptability to the common people of the world, the brilliant strategist declared. Perhaps it once served a useful purpose in settling quarrels when hand-to-hand combat killed only a few, but total warfare, afflicting millions indiscriminately, had rendered the idea so loathsome that people would neither seek nor allow it.

A general of the United States Army actually made these statements; a man widely read in human history, a warrior from his youth. For a full year North Korea had been stockpiling military supplies and troops on her southern border, and MacArthur had seen CIA reports forecasting war in June 1950. On June 25, 1950, five weeks after his comments, North Korea invaded South Korea.

Humanity and war go together like secrecy and paranoia. We find ourselves in constant conflict with each other because we all war with our Maker.

NAME — important
Matthew 1:21; Luke 2:21

What's In a Name?

AYDS, a diet-control candy, made great profits for its manufacturer from 1941 until the 1980s. By 1988, sales dropped as much as 50 percent. Nothing in the product changed, but something in society had. The words AIDS, the disease, and AYDS, the diet suppressant candy, became indivisible to people. They instinctively identified the candy with the dreaded killer.

The Apaches called him Goyakala—the Yawner. The Mexicans called him Heronimo, anglicized by Americans to Geronimo. Could anyone ever fear a yawner? But the very name Geronimo terrified residents of Mexico and Arizona in the 1880s. Besides, as one writer said, American paratroopers wouldn't leap out of planes in World War II screaming "Goyakala!"

Mark Lindsay, a British actor, chosen from a hundred actors to play John Lennon in a biographical movie, was fired shortly after he was hired—because his name wasn't Lindsay. He had taken that name only a few years before when he joined British Equity and found another actor there with his real name: Mark Chapman. Another Mark Chapman had murdered John Lennon in front of his townhouse in New York City, December 8, 1980.

In the Bible a person's name often expressed something particular about that individual: Moses, because Pharaoh's daughter drew him from the water; Adam, because God made him father of all. The name also represented the person's nature—which surfaces the greatest of all names: Jesus, Savior; Christ, anointed.

NAME — similar leads to problems
2 Kings 23:36; 24:8; Acts 21:37–38

Do You Have the Right Guy?

The Navy twice arrested William Finch and hauled him in as a deserter, though he is not in the Navy. Someone used his name and social security number when enlisting, then went AWOL. At Great Lakes Training Center, contradictions between the real culprit and Finch became obvious: Finch is five feet seven inches, the culprit is five feet four inches. Finch weighs 220 pounds; the culprit weighs 140.

Marine veteran Richard Cronin was baffled when the FBI arrested him on a drug charge. A day later the FBI decided they had the wrong Cronin. Had they checked the vital statistics of both men, they wouldn't have made the mistake. The Marine veteran Cronin was forty-nine; the drug dealer Cronin was in his twenties. The Marine veteran, while from Massachusetts, didn't have the same accent as the Massachusetts Cronin on the FBI tape. Their wives also had different names.

Our spiritual separation from God hasn't destroyed our inventive genius, but it has robbed us of infallibility. That is why we can compile complete dossiers on all known criminals, but we cannot keep law enforcement officials from mis-identifying suspects. When we bring back to God the mind he created in his image, we will immediately experience a sharpening of our senses and discover ways to unerringly express ourselves. That repentance will not occur in this world, but our reborn soul gives a hint of what the next world offers, when all our senses will be perfected and glorified, and totally at God's behest!

NAME — unusual
Genesis 16:13–14; Matthew 21:15–17

From Frivolous to Foolish

When Mrs. Virgin went to the doctor to see if she was pregnant, the doctor examined her, then went to a window and scanned the sky. What was he looking for, the woman asked. "For an angel." Why? "Because you're a Virgin about to give birth." They named one of their daughters Elizabeth A. Virgin.

A lady whose maiden name was Bytheway often laughed to hear its mis-pronunciations as All the Way, Part of the Way, and Half the Way. Others included By the Mill, By the Hills, and By the Sea.

Columbus insistently demanded his titles as Viceroy and Admiral of the Oceans. They affected his honor. He even ordered his son Diego to call himself and his heir after him "the Admiral," perpetuating it in the family.

A Bible school class of youngsters was asked "Who was Christ's mother?" All replied "Mary." "And who was Christ's father?" the teacher asked. No one said a word. Then a little voice answered, "His name was Virg. All I hear about is Virg and Mary."

Despite every effort to clarify terms, little children may not perfectly understand all they are taught about God. But when the disciples asked Jesus to identify the greatest in the kingdom, he chose a child. Perhaps the youngster did not understand what the strong voice meant, but undoubtedly he under-stood the touch of those gentle hands and the warmth of his embrace.

NATIONALITY — preserved

Exodus 6:7–8; John 9:5

An Unabsorbed Identity

William of Normandy conquered only English land, not English hearts. Nor did he ever enjoy his triumph. By giving English land to Norman gentry, he antagonized his subjects. By brutally oppressing them, he destroyed any hope of reconciling them. Five years after the conquest he was still extinguishing fires of revolt.

In a national denial of his aims, England retained its identity despite an importation of two hundred thousand Frenchmen and the death of three hundred thousand Englishmen by starvation and execution. The people yielded allegiance only to their values, identity, and culture, making captive their captors by absorbing them into their character and making them a new kind of Englishman.

In a world hostile to Christian witness and values, God's children must pre-serve the distinctions that separate them from the lost. The Christ who ineradicably impacted his generation impacts each succeeding generation by reproducing in his followers his Galilean life. By having the mind of Christ, we help unsaved mortals become a new kind of human being, creating from the corrupt a redeemed nature, from the wild a cultivated impulse, from the primitive a sophisticated partisan. When God through Christ opened himself to our need, he opened our hearts to his presence.

NATIONS — receive justice now

Habakkuk 2:4, 7, 9; Revelation 18:2–3

Punished Now

At the end of World War I, Germany's infrastructure, government, and properties were intact, untouched by the cataclysm. At the end of World War II, her infra-structure was nearly extinct, imperiled by Allied bombing and Hitler's mad demand that it be destroyed.

Perhaps the difference between the two wars lies in the respective moralities of the German governments. Stories of atrocities by the Boche in World War I had been circulated but afterwards usually proved unfounded. Few believed the stories of Nazi atrocities in death camps based on similar stories of World War I. With the Allied liberation, however, Nazi depravities shook the world.

Only four percent of Americans in European POW camps died. But 27 percent of American POW's in Japanese camps died—the number in the River Kwai camps was higher. Could God have visited Japan with a national calamity as punishment for her inexcusable barbarity towards captive peoples?

Or consider the collapse of Communism in 1989. It began to unravel in Eastern Europe after nearly forty-five years of Marxist-Leninism lies, decep-tions, and failures. The Berlin Wall came down, Stalinist dictators fell, and fledgling democracies flourished. Anyone who believes in God's providence has to conclude that God judged and condemned an ideology determined to uproot and trash God.

The words of George Mason of Virginia, spoken at the Constitutional Convention in 1787 may well be true: "By an inevitable chain of causes and effects providence punishes national sins, by national calamities."

NATURE — basic behavior
Deuteronomy 30:15; John 16:6, 20–22

A Study in Contrasts

The North Pole is in a sea two miles deep—the South Pole is on a plateau two miles high. The North Pole is in a sea, encompassed by lands—the South Pole is on a continent, surrounded by oceans.

That kind of basic difference exists between Christ and all humanity. He came from heaven, we from earth. He spoke the truth, we tell lies. He is spiritual, we are carnal. Origins determine the behavior of each, indicating our respective natures and affecting every aspect of our behavior.

Christians live in a world where that principle still rules. Opposites still exist, often side by side: the good and bad, the beautiful and ugly, pleasant things and abhorrent. We even see this in our own lives, ideally seeking to serve Christ but often finding ourselves doing evil.

NATURE — protected
Psalm 68:19; 2 Corinthians 1:9

A Natural Protection

A record snow melt in the Colorado Rockies in 1983 triggered disastrous flooding the whole length of the 1,400 mile Colorado River system. A potentially deadly encephalitis threat emerged in the aftermath from mosquitoes hatching in stagnant waters of the flood. Encephalitis attacks the nervous system and is sometimes fatal. To forestall the danger, public health officials spent $24,000 spraying. But it cost far less to establish a first line of defense. Six thousand two-inch mosquito fish, officially known as *gambusia affinis,* were netted and dumped into stagnant riverside pools. The fish gorged on mosquitoes' eggs and larvae, eating as much as their own weight in one day. In addition, their own fertility allowed a tenfold growth in a month.

This natural defense against disease, divinely constructed into creation, is but one example of the finely tuned balance in nature. Learning how to manipulate that balance saves lives and money. God builds just such protection to disaster and disappointment into our lives: our ability to grieve, mourn, cry, laugh, forget, and remember. Even the shock first experienced when hearing of a loved one's death shields us from the onslaught of pain and anguish. This says nothing of our infinite capacity to recover from and overcome even the bitterest circumstances and experiences. We cannot escape adversities anymore than earth can elude disasters, but when they come, within us rises the natural protection against harm the calamities would cause without it.

NATURE — returning to an ancient desire
Psalm 89:9, 11, 14; Romans 8:20

We See Only Ourselves

In Old Topanga Canyon, Southern California, dissimilar groups manage a peaceful coexistence: pot growers, a nudist colony, a sprout farm, and million dollar homeowners. The common factor is their relationship with nature. When the great fires of 1993 burned towards them, the counter-culture devotees looked to nature for help. "Can you feel the spirits closing in around us?" one whispered. "The harmonic convergence of nature will protect us."

As an Arctic explorer lay in his sleeping bag, the green eyes of a male wolf glowed in the dark. The wolf repeatedly paced, sat, and stared. The man said that seeing the wolf's eyes reminded him how humans are necessarily coupled with other beings. N. C. Wyeth, commenting on the natural world, said, "I feel so moved sometimes toward nature that I could almost throw myself down into a ploughed furrow."

What is this yearning in man, ancient and modern, to return to nature for spiritual values? What is this longing for something in our past that we call nature, that gives us peace and purpose? Is it a beauty that casts a spell and charms like Chinooks in winter? Or do we see in nature a permanence denied us? Or an endless mocking of our aging, wrinkled bodies? Nature has no answer, for it too is fallen, and fallen because of us. And since creation looks to us for its redemption, why would we look to it for peace? How can what depends on us for its renewal be simultaneously the source of our peace?

NATURE — use of sky at sea
Job 37:22; Matthew 16:2

Map in the Sky

Ancient Polynesian mariners traveled thousands of oceanic miles with only a knowledge of sea currents, sea creatures, and the heavenly bodies to guide them. Columbus' men knew a large land mass existed somewhere ahead of them many days before sighting land when sea birds known to live near shore and the flotsam of dead vegetation and trees drifted in the swells. The early mariners exploring in Arctic and Antarctic waters preferred an overcast to a clear sky when sailing in unknown seas. It would unfailingly mirror what lay beneath it, forming a map in the sky. On the clouds, ice or snow would show white, and open water or land areas, black.

The Bible provides a "map of the sky" for believers. We can determine the danger or safety of any activity, belief, or relationship by seeing its reflection against God's Word. Invariably, the pure shows white, and everything else, black.

NEED — meeting the first priority
Psalm 78:38–39; Matthew 9:2

Only That

It happened in Florida. A doctor fell from his golf cart and hit his head so hard he almost bit off his tongue. Rushed to emergency in the hospital where he had been a surgeon for thirty years, they first demanded "cash or appropriate credit documents." He couldn't believe what he heard. After some lusty screaming, despite his wound, he finally was admitted for treatment—which included receiving an X-ray of the wrong arm and being prepped for an electrocardiogram that no one administered.

It would be hilarious if the incompetence didn't portend mortally serious problems in health care. Unfortunately, it has become a rule in some hospitals, and avarice causes it. The government pays so much money for Medicare and Medicaid that many doctors and hospitals refuse to treat anyone without cash, credit, or insurance.

How differently we approach our divine doctor for spiritual healing. He subordinates our need to nothing save his grace and mercy. He addresses that need above all and ministers to it immediately, knowing full well that some will not pay him the debt of gratitude owed and will not keep the promises made. He helps from the depths of his love.

NEGATIVES — need to be strong
Genesis 2:16–17; Matthew 7:21–23

Make It Emphatic

In an article written for the New York Times, Pulitzer prize winning composer Gian Carlo Menotti said it took him nearly eighty years to learn the golden word "no."

He had earlier been an optimist, thinking that "no" was too negative. "Only in my old age have I finally discovered that a sunny 'yes' is deceptive; that it can be a cowardly word full of compromises and illusions, a tacit acceptance of the mediocre. How much stronger and more honest is the word 'no'! It is a liberating word that cleanses the soul, even if it may make you a less pleasant or acceptable companion and cause you to lose a few friends!"

A worthwhile point, meriting acceptance by parents, church leaders, government officials, university presidents, and business leaders. We'll never learn a shorter, or more important, word. God authored both no and yes. When God says "no," he means it as surely, as certainly, and as eternally as he affirms his positives.

NEGOTIATION — our need
Exodus 18:13–14, 17; 1 Corinthians 6:4

The Need to Negotiate

When American recalcitrance to pay taxes motivated the colonies to fight the English Crown, statesman Edmund Burke felt the time had come for accommodation. The American spirit couldn't be removed, he said, and criminal processes against them couldn't be implemented. The best response was to negotiate. Later, when the framers of the Constitution met in Philadelphia in the summer of 1787, they found compromise essential to success. Such stratospheric differences existed between the delegates that only a willingness to negotiate kept the convention alive. When the delegates signed the finished document, many did so reluctantly, sensing its shortcomings but feeling it the best possible product under the circumstances.

Cornelius Vanderbilt left the bulk of his $100 million estate to his son William. Cornelius, Jr. contested the will when he learned that he had received only $200,000 in a trust fund. The trial took two years and was finally settled in a compromise. Junior got a $400,000 trust fund and $200,000 in cash, but the lawyers got more than $500,000.

Christians cannot afford to be known as contentious obstructionists. Where nonmoral, nonspiritual issues become points of disagreement, negotiation is always an advantage. Only where God has specifically spoken are negotiation and compromise impossible. Where we speak to each other, negotiation should always be considered the alternative to harmful disagreement.

NOBILITY — seen in action
Galatians 1:11; 2 Peter 3:15

In Act and Word

Gouverneur Morris was one of our most important founding fathers. According to James Madison, the style and arrangement of the Constitution were his. Morris talked voluminously at the Constitutional Convention in 1787. But, as

Catherine Drinker Bowen wrote, he also "had the courage to change his mind publicly when he saw himself in the wrong." Having admitted his mistake, he then supported the measure that had convinced him of his error.

Christian leaders cannot surrender truth, but they can compromise opinions that are sometimes hastily formed or misinformed. Our homes, churches, and relationships would all benefit. Good opinions usually can exist side by side with better opinions. Where one must yield, good should surrender to better. Indeed, when better arguments demand abandonment of current opinions, only pride demands their retrenchment. We may not have Morris' giftedness, but we should pray to acquire his disposition. We must certainly avoid the criticism leveled at Teddy Roosevelt—that he was born with his mind made up!

NOISE — getting worse in cities
Isaiah 7:4; Luke 6:12–13

Can't Hear Each Other Now

Prolonged exposure to eighty-five decibels or more can cause damage to the inner ear and result in permanent hearing loss and extensive health problems in related areas including high blood pressure. Imagine, then, the dismay of a Lehman College psychology professor as she stood, decibel meter in hand, and registered ninety decibels at an Upper Manhattan intersection. As she crossed the street the rattling staccato of a jackhammer shot the decibel level up to one hundred.

New York is considered the nation's noisiest city because of a population density fourteen times higher than other cities. Increased traffic, construction, ill-tempered motorists, careless pedestrians, and the constant repair needed in the metropolis promise to make it worse, not better. It is the price paid by those who live and work in the city. Among other benefits denied their city cousins, rural dwellers tend to lose less hearing capability in their lifetime.

Prayer offers a busy Christian the quiet time needed to withstand the noisy distractions of life. Too often our spiritual values get buried under the clamorings of family, health, and career. In prayer's quiet time God energizes our soul with his peace. Then, when times are not quiet, when we stand at the Broadway's of life, we can express the spiritual graces with which the quiet time equipped us. Christians continue to compete in the daily grind, confidently modeling God's life, knowing that we stand tallest from a kneeling position.

NUMBERS — few contribute disproportionately
1 Samuel 14:1, 6; Mark 3:13–15

So Much Owed So Few

Stealth fighters comprised just 2.5 percent of the aircraft in the Persian Gulf War. Yet, on the first day of the air war, they flew 31 percent of the sorties, obliterating Iraqi air defenses. The reason? Stealth pilots could evade Iraqi radar, seek their targets, drop their bombs, and escape scot-free. When Iraqi antiaircraft fire streaked the sky full of tracers, they shot at the stars; the Stealth bombers had long since left the drop zone.

When Jesus wanted to assure a witness of himself after he returned to God, he recruited a few good men. In his three years with them he invited them to study him, knowing they needed to see in him what he wanted them to be. And what an education the doctor of eternal studies gave his students! He also sent them on preaching tours, giving them field experience, letting them teach others what they had learned from him. When they preached or healed, they enjoyed his success, proving themselves even then mere extensions of his glory and authority.

By the time Christ died, the disciples still lacked the profile of the great apostles, but the Master had in place his chosen few. When the Holy Spirit fell on them at Pentecost, he finished the education Jesus' own ministry had carefully advanced. In the lives of those men Jesus multiplied his grace to spiritually feed millions in every age.

NUTRITION — animal
Psalm 19:11; Acts 20:20–21

Only the Best

The guest on Johnny Carson's *Tonight Show* was chauffeured in a limousine from the airport to her suite in the Sheraton Premiere Hotel. Not bad accommodations when you consider the guest was none other than Mlinzi, a lowland African gorilla from the Cincinnati Zoo.

Providing exceptional nutrition for its animals, the San Diego Zoo's food warehouse resembles a wholesale produce outlet. Many of the items used daily are familiar to any shopper: apples, seafood, and carrots. Others are Zoo exotic: crickets, mealworms, and night crawlers.

Feeding a thoroughbred is even more involved. At a stable in Hot Springs, Arkansas, the thirty-five horses enjoy a daily diet of timothy and alfalfa hay, oats, molasses, bran, barley, corn, milk substitute, vitamins, sliced carrots, five vitamins, fresh garlic, and fresh lemon juice. Feedings occur at 4 A.M., noon, and in the afternoon. Garlic and lemon juice are added to the feed to stimulate the appetite. When a horse refuses to eat, the trainer puts a goat in the stall. The goat's omnivorous appetite irritates the horse, which then eats in defense of its territory.

God has revealed in one book all the spiritual food ever needed in any age. Leaders responsible for God's flock must carefully and systematically nourish them with the Bible's message. It can be done through personal counseling, applying God's principles after problems have developed; it can be done through corporate preaching, applying God's principles to prevent problems.

OBEDIENCE — willed
Exodus 3:18; Luke 12:50

Always Ready, If Not Eager

Thinking war would be a great adventure, John Gibbon's Black Hat Brigade went eagerly into battle at Second Bull Run. There they fought well while losing many of their men contesting Stonewall Jackson's gray-clad warriors. Their regimental historian later wrote that the brigade was always ready for action after that, but was never again eager.

Goethe finished the second part of *Faust* at eighty years of age, sorrowing over the deaths of his son and other loved ones. Still he kept to his task, willing himself to live until he finished the task. Duty sustained him, he wrote, only his pledge to duty. He died six months after completing the work.

We must bring willingness, if not always eagerness, to obedience. Athletes routinely hate the time spent training, but they train anyway because they know its importance to success. When we would rather not obey, duty must assume control of our lives and lead us on until obedience is as natural to us as herding is to a Border collie. We are never less obedient at such times. In fact, it proves that our commitment has excelled mere feelings to become convictions. Often we will be eager to obey God, but whether eager or not, we obey and find in the act the satisfaction we thought came only from enthusiasm.

OBSTACLES — overcoming
1 Kings 20:26–27; Acts 4:13

Obstacles

Calvin Peete leaped a number of obstacles to become a pro golfer: he was black, he had only an eighth-grade education, he didn't swing a club until he was twenty-three, and he had a crooked arm that limited distance when he swung. No matter. He won anyway, finishing ten times in the PGA's top ten.

The late Wilma Rudolph had an obstacle so basic to a runner she shouldn't have been able to run: as a child she had contracted chronic pneumonia, scarlet fever, and polio. She wore braces until she was ten years old. No matter. In the

1960 Olympiad she won gold medals in the one hundred- and two hundred-meter races and in the four hundred-meter relay.

Booker T. Washington stated it well: "I have learned that success is to be measured not so much by the position one has reached in life as by the obstacles overcome while trying to succeed." Indeed, some people face life laden with as many chains as Marley's ghost, but their achievements belie their difficulties. That is why we cannot judge a person's achievements purely on evident progress or success. Some may be only at the starting position when others are five miles into the race. More is expected of a person who has the advantage of "starting ahead" in life or from those especially gifted. Those who continue in the race, despite shortcomings, may not place as highly, but the effort to compete compensates for their lesser showing.

OCCULT — even using Barbie
Exodus 22:18; Acts 8:9–13

An Appropriate Symbol

Could any symbol be more appropriate for an occult practitioner than a Barbie doll? One woman considers herself the channel through whom Barbie speaks in response to inquiries. She appreciates and understands Barbie, she claims. She feels that Barbie has been maligned by being forced to be just a pretty face year after year.

Incredulously, people take the woman's advertisements in a psychic magazine seriously, enclosing a $3 fee with their requests. Letters, stacked in a big pile on the woman's floor, request information about careers, future events, and relationships. The channeler replies on pink stationery, all the while surrounded by a dozen Barbies, obviously badly worn from the maulings of youngsters unimpressed with her wisdom.

Can anyone be so frivolous as to represent a doll? Or so superficial as to consult one? The occult is among us, and more deeply entrenched than Christians would think. Television advertisements of psychics use famous singers, columnists, and actresses as spokespersons to give the practitioners credibility. The millions spent by adherents on psychic practitioners staggers the mind. Barbie is a symptom, really. That a people who established this nation by looking to God could become a people desperate enough to consult a doll or psychics for guidance offers proof of an irremedial malaise in our spiritual life.

OCCULT — used to create luck
Ezekiel 21:21; Philippians 4:19

To Choose a Horse

As welders' arcs showered sparks in the racetrack's new $80 million grandstand, a middle-aged man walked down an aisle seeking a lucky seat. He had been hired by a public relations firm to show reporters what he felt would be the luckiest seats in the renovated house. He identified a pair of blue seats where he "felt" the presence of a charmed couple from Orange County.

In another area of the grandstand another psychic flipped tarot cards to determine the luckiest seats. A third psychic, a numerologist, selected the best seat for anyone whose birthday was May 22, 1955, concluding that the winning seats four and seven in section eleven offered propitious signs. Numerology, she affirmed, is a way of looking beneath the surface of events.

When you bet the ponies, you figure any help is better than pure guess-work, even if it means following the opinions of handicappers. But a tarot reader? A numerologist? Psychics? Are we that desperate to win, to succeed, to be secure? All of which would be sad enough if people resorted to such frauds only to bet the ponies. But 900 numbers keep humming with the plaintive requests of ordinary people seeking help in dating, marriage, and careers from these clever shamans. Why would we honor unscrupulous opportunists in preference to the living, all knowing God, who graciously invites our audience with him for any need we have?

OCCUPATION — sacred, whatever the career
Genesis 12:1–9; Acts 10:34

It Is Really for God

Like a harvester, God gathers his people on Sundays for worship, to celebrate their common faith. Afterwards, like a sower, God broadcasts those same believers like seeds into the community. In a real sense, however, the believer is always at worship, whether gathered or scattered. A surgeon at Barnes Hospital in St. Louis understood that. He walked into the room of a patient preparing for surgery. "See these hands," he said to her. "They are the best in this hospital. And I want you to know that before I operate, I'll be on my knees for an hour."

Peter Drucker said that religion "lives off the excess of culture," meaning it is something people do in their spare time. Not that surgeon! He saw himself just as righteous when pursuing his career as when he was gathered in formal worship. The offer of his hands to God to prolong human life and reduce human suffering in Christ's name made his surgery as sacred as a minister's sermon. May God increase his kind!

OPINION — the one we seek
Exodus 19:5; Malachi 3:17; Mark 1:11

That One Person

Somerset Maugham's *The Social Sense* centers on a married couple. Mary Warton had been a concert singer in her day and remained an accomplished musician as a doyen. Her husband, Thomas, had once held promise as a great painter, but never fulfilled it. He loved her greatly and always spoke highly of her. She loved him too, but never failed to make disparaging remarks about his art. Though she felt free to undermine his confidence, she hated the critics who panned his works. In turn, Warton took offense at his wife's criticism simply because he valued her praise more than the public acclaim of the critics. For, as Maugham brilliantly says, nothing is worse for us than to be undervalued or criticized by the one person whose appreciation we need most of all.

We all cherish the opinion of that someone whose praise is more valuable than gold or fame. Should we please that person, we feel we are a success, regardless what others think. Knowing we fail to draw honor from that one depresses us beyond measure. Spiritually, we seek to please the Lord Jesus. Just a nod of recognition from him excels a bear hug of praise from any other.

OPPONENT — critical help from
1 Samuel 23:16–17; Ephesians 4:7; Hebrews 2:4

With His Help

Jessie Owens and Luz Long competed against each other in the 1936 Berlin Olympics. What Owens later called "an act of special grace and special courtesy to a fellow athlete" enabled him to win his fourth gold medal. Long had already qualified for the running broad jump, while Jessie had jumped short on his first qualifying attempt, then fouled on the second. Long had been watching his rival. He walked over and urged Owens to begin his third leap well behind the rubber mat. Jessie did so, qualified, and won the gold medal, establishing a new Olympic record. Long finished second.

After the competition, Long walked with Owens down the jump runway and, directly in front of Adolph Hitler's box, thrust his arms around the great black American. Hitler, who had refused to greet any black winners, turned away, enraged. Long died in 1943 fighting on the eastern front.

Christians subordinate personal success to develop skills in others—it is the community factor in brotherhood. While we endeavor to excel in our personal capabilities, we also encourage others in theirs. The advantage is obvious: regardless who succeeds, the whole body benefits!

OPPORTUNITIES — missed
Deuteronomy 18:15, 18–19; John 8:24

Missed Opportunities

Ben Franklin made a speech on the last day of the Constitutional Convention, urging harmony among the delegates. It astonished him, he said, that they had produced a constitution of such high quality since so many compromises had fashioned it. He would vote for it because he expected no better given the differences among the colonies. Had it not been for Franklin's and Washington's willingness to sign the Constitution, many delegates would have refused. Only their influence made possible its eventual passage. Still, sixteen men refused even then to sign the document we so cherish today. What an opportunity they missed!

Jesus said he will forgive the sins of all who accept his Lordship; but those who refuse him will die in their sins. No other chance will come to them. To deny Christ is to miss the one opportunity that makes the difference between spiritual life and death. Those who sin but trust in Christ's grace will live despite their sin. Those who sin and reject Christ will be punished despite their morality.

OPPORTUNITIES — seized and missed
Jeremiah 36:16–17, 23–24; Acts 16:9–10

Do What You Are Given

Actor Jamie Farr played the high-heeled, cigar-chomping Corporal Klinger in *M.A.S.H.* About two hundred fans attended the ceremony when he was added to Hollywood's Walk of Fame. Few knew that he was originally hired for one day's work as a phony transvestite bucking for a section-eight discharge, granted to those the military considers mentally unstable. Farr seized the moment and chewed that cigar with a panache the producers couldn't resist. He turned a day's work into a career!

Jesus met people from all economic, spiritual, and social ranks. They had many differences, but a single similarity: all could become children of God if they seized the opportunity his coming provided. Many of them did, such as Zacchaeus, who opened his heart to love and emptied it of greed.

Some of them did not, such as the rich young ruler who was thwarted by his own avarice, and the expert in the Law who, instead of accepting Christ's gracious interpretation of the great commandment, wanted to justify himself. We all have the same opportunity when the kingdom of God comes near. Will we seize it, or let it pass?

OPPRESSION — a flawed rule
1 Samuel 17:45–46; Matthew 26:51–54

A Fatal Flaw

Incredible warriors, the Aztecs intrepidly bludgeoned their enemies into subservience. They were also uncompromisingly bloodthirsty, worshipping stony-faced deities they believed demanded human sacrifices. At the dedication of one temple, a procession of victims two miles long was led to the slaughter. All scholars agree that thousands of all ages died annually in their religious rites.

To find ever-increasing numbers of victims, the Aztecs raided far-flung territories. Their oppressive mayhem, inflicted without mercy, alienated their conquered peoples. Hatred for the Aztecs seethed among the oppressed people who awaited only an ally to rise in revolt. The Spaniards became that ally. They found the captive people favorably disposed to them and looking for help. In fact, after first contesting Cortes and losing, they became faithful supporters in his conquest of Mexico City.

Jesus came to us as the God-Man to preach a spiritual message and to establish a spiritual kingdom founded on and fueled by divine love. He personally won converts by moral and spiritual persuasion and ordered his apostles to the same mission. Biblical Christianity remains faithful to the Master's original blueprint however widely Christians may stray from it in their attempt to build the kingdom of God on earth.

OPTIMISM — invariable in Christ
Psalm 27:1; Acts 5:41

Eternally Optimistic

In 1914 the French never contemplated defeat at the hands of Germany. The essence of optimism over Germany's eventual defeat is revealed in an apocryphal report to General Joseph Joffre from General Ferdinand Foch: "My center is broken, my right retreats, the situation is excellent: I attack." That optimism brought Allied victory in 1918.

The first generation of church leaders expressed a similar buoyancy. They baptized every adversity, creating a grace from disgrace. They gladly accepted and gratefully endured all setbacks and attacks. Their unconquerable merriment fills the New Testament. Paul is in jail, but not the Word. Peter is on the run, but the Word still conquers human hearts. Christians lose their possessions, jobs, and lives, but others fill in the emptiness, unable to resist the sway of the Christ who uses even suffering to proclaim his conquest of Satan.

Whatever happened to that primal optimism? Did we lose it in our haste to institutionalize the body of Christ, to gain respect in a community of unbelievers, to safeguard our reputations, to ease the requirements for discipleship? If we have lost it, we had better find it again. If we never had it, we must pray to receive it.

ORIGIN — man's
Psalm 33:6, 139:13; Acts 17:26

Getting It Straight

In his book *The Genesis Mystery,* anthropologist Jeffrey Goodman surmises that humanity emerged from apelike ancestors by intelligent intervention of an outside source. The gradual changes necessary in an evolutionary development aren't in the fossil records, he notes. Goodman said he favors some kind of intervention because it both fits the facts better and accounts for the high view of human purpose the race has always held. Since beliefs about our origin determine present behavior and future life, he said, we need to discover our origins.

How true. Human purpose can be understood only as we understand human origins. Only then do we find ourselves as more than bundles of electrical impulses, nerve endings, and chemical reactions—the conclusion reached by "The Astonishing Hypothesis." That all of these are the parts is beyond doubt, but something else is the catalyst, charging them into life when it comes and leaving a corpse when it is gone. Sooner or later we have to come back to morality, character, and spiritual nature. The biblical answer never fails to satisfy on all points. It sees us in all our dimensions and relationships, but always from the perspective of our first dimension and relationship—formed bodily of dust but suffused with God's image.

OTHERS — see us objectively
1 Samuel 23:22–23; Matthew 22:16

As We Really Are

In talking to Brutus in Shakespeare's *Julius Caesar*, Cassius says, "Therefore, good Brutus, be prepar'd to hear; and since you know you cannot see yourself so well as by reflection, I, your glass will modestly discover to yourself that of yourself which you yet know not of."

After studying in America for a year, a group of eight foreign exchange students gave their impressions of America and its citizens. A Japanese student was struck by our open, outgoing nature—we want to know everything immediately. A Belgian doctor was struck by the ease with which we share our lives. However, he noted, it was superficial; the same people who talked so freely with him on one occasion would see him another time and say nothing. Since American institutions have a poor reputation in Europe, a Finnish teacher worried that his degree would not be accepted as authentic back home, though he doubled his course load and completed his M.A. in one year.

No Brutus needs a Cassius more than the local church. The good opinions we hold of ourselves (few churches hold bad opinions of themselves) are generally discounted by strangers. Christians should not ask doctrinal questions of outsiders. We must do market research for information about ourselves from the people we are trying to reach for Christ. Christians need to be harmless as doves while they are wise as serpents.

PAIN — not all the same
Judges 6:36–40; Acts 20:28; 1 Peter 5:2–3

A Personal Threshold

Two kinds of athletes confront pain, according to a study in *Athletic Training Magazine*. One focuses single-mindedly on the goal and is impervious to pain during competition; the other focuses on personal image, refuses to project a false impression of personal talent, and cannot compete unless in optimum health. Two athletes can have the same injury yet will recover at different speeds, trainers say, perhaps because each person's perception of pain is different. Trainers study the background of athletes to determine their approach when injury occurs. An athlete pampered as a child will not be as tough as one who was encouraged to confront pain in youth, including restrictions and refusals. Often the trainer's own approach to the injury will impact the athlete. If the trainer tells him the shoulder looks better, the athlete quite possibly picks up the positive message. A negative attitude by the trainer generates a similar response in the athlete.

Christian leaders who are responsible for a host of potentially powerful spiritual athletes cannot afford to overlook the implications of these studies. They need to have, or acquire, the facility of appreciating those they lead—valuing their strengths, overlooking their disabilities. Understanding personalities is certainly essential to leading others. Some need a spur and others a bridle, some thrive on encouragement while others need to be bullied, and some accede to minimal while others demand maximum proof of need before serving.

PAST — memory keeps us humble
Psalm 78:39; 1 Peter 1:16–18

Humility in Memory

Someone wrote the editors of a leading magazine asking if Tom Selleck's image was real or celluloid. He seemed so unaffected with stardom, but was he? He seemed so down-to-earth, but was it a charade? Judging from interviews with his friends, the editors replied, Selleck remained modest and unassuming. Unlike many stars, he remembered the rejection and failure of his earlier days (he couldn't even win a date on the *Dating Game*), and he realized that success in show business is frequently the result of luck, not talent.

Egotism is as natural to us as the tango to Argentina. Cultivating the memory of a less fortunate past will keep today's felicity in perspective. Our present fame or prosperity offers no excuse for arrogance. Prominence and abundance are no more permanent than obscurity and indigence. We can be forgiven our ignorance of an unknown future, but not the amnesia of past experiences.

PATIENCE — example of
Joshua 14:7; 1 Corinthians 15:49; 2 Peter 3:10–13

An Elusive Virtue

In 1404, twenty-five-year-old Lorenzo Ghiberti won a commission to build and adorn a pair of bronze doors for the north side of the baptistery in the cathedral of Florence, Italy. He took twenty-one years to design and cast the masterpieces, dividing the doors into twenty-eight New Testament panels. They cost $550,000. The donors then asked him to make corresponding double doors for the baptistery's east side. This endeavor took twenty-seven years and featured the Old Testament in ten panels. He spent forty-eight years one just two projects, but his time and effort left artistic masterpieces for generations to admire.

Building spiritual lives challenges us to a perseverance that defies even Ghiberti. The free will, prejudice, stubbornness, and pride that mocks God are all obstacles to change and growth. The life produced by the Spirit in the Word seldom comes easily or quickly. People are never as easy to mold as bronze and wood. Although a skilled craftsman can predict how basic elements will react under given stimuli, the spiritual leader never masters the moods and reactions of people.

PATIENCE — necessary
Jeremiah 25:11; 2 Timothy 2:24–26

Not Done Quickly

Counseling Luther to move more temperately, Erasmus judged that ancient institutions could not be quickly changed and would yield more easily to persuasion than condemnation. We can agree that Luther, not Erasmus, "understood the times," and still appreciate the truth Erasmus stated.

Benjamin Rush disgustedly resigned after he repeatedly failed to get needed medical reforms through Congress for the Revolutionary Army. John Adams begged him to stay and fight the abuses from within. "Patience! Patience! Patience!" Adams said. "The first, the last, and the middle virtues of a politician." Wasn't the wicked Iago correct when he said, "How poor are they that have not patience. What wound did ever hear but by degrees?"

By it's very nature, success in spiritual work is as elusive as the missing link. Workers feel they may as well plough the seas as to plant gospel seed in human hearts. The work of integrating faith and practice demands such firm, dogged efforts that many seek easier toil elsewhere. Spiritual work takes time—fast-profit entrepreneurs need not apply.

PEACE — none lasts
Isaiah 9:6; Luke 2:14

The Elusive State

From November, 1921, to February, 1922, Britain, France, and the United States met in Washington, D.C. and agreed to limit naval armaments. European statesmen followed that conference with their own at Locarno, Italy in 1925, to guarantee Germany's sovereignty against *French adventuring* (emphasis added). They sponsored German membership in the League of Nations and pledged further disarmament. The "spirit of Locarno" enthralled optimists who believed a new milestone had been reached on the road to peace. Still aglow with hope, statesmen met again in Paris in 1928 to sign a pact outlawing war. After ages of conflict, twentieth-century statesmen had deciphered the combination to peace on earth!

Really? Over a hundred wars have been fought since World War II ended. No state is more elusive in humanity than the state of peace!

When angelic hosts praised God in the presence of the shepherds, they promised that Bethlehem's baby would reveal the glory of God and bring peace to those on earth who accepted his favor. Even as the angels spoke, the *pax romana*—Roman peace—existed. But God rejected that peace, human in origin and enforced with weapons, and offered lasting peace within to all who accept Christ. Pax romana is Lucarno and Paris and Geneva and Washington—all the world's capitals whose goal is military peace. "Peace among those on whom his favor rests" is God's peace—the peace of forgiveness, reconciliation, and right-eousness. This peace military might can never give!

PEOPLE — used
Exodus 22:22; Romans 12:15

People as a Means

Robert Caro noted that the men President Lyndon Johnson used in his climb to political power resented only that his manipulative skills exceeded their own. The idea of using people as a means to an end did not bring remorse or surprise to either side. Each simply wanted to weigh the scales in its favor: use more than it got used and intrigue to be ahead at the end. Exploitation is the world's way. People concentrate on self-aggrandizement, not service; of taking from others, not giving.

It is a violent betrayal of Christ's life and teaching. He demonstrated the importance of individuals as an end in themselves, not as a means by which others can prosper. This has significant consequences for each Christian. Can we rejoice in the wealth of another, even if we don't prosper? Can we thank God for another's success, even if we fail? Can we delight in the advancing career of another, even if ours languishes?

PERSEVERANCE — example of
Matthew 10:22; Hebrews 10:35–36

They Showed It Can Be Done

When he first began playing his guitar and singing, Elvis Presley's schoolmates derisively coined a term to describe its bad quality: "Elvised it." Later the teenage Presley repeatedly drove a company truck past the Memphis Recording Service before scrounging the courage to record a song he had written for his mother.

Eighteen years elapsed from the time Columbus conceived his voyage of discovery and fulfilled it by weighing anchor in Palos Bay. Eighteen years of poverty, ridicule, and disappointment.

Elena Bonner typed and edited as her husband, Andrei Sakharov, wrote his memoirs, which they smuggled from the Soviet Union. As he wrote, the KGB often stole the writing. It would simply vanish. On one occasion, when he learned of a particularly severe loss, Sakharov "had the expression of a man who has just learned of the death of someone close to him," Elena wrote. After a few days, however, he sat at his desk and rewrote the material.

Why then would we refuse our faith just because it makes demands on our time, talent, and treasure? Or refuse a new challenge because "we have never done that before"? Or get discouraged because we sang or taught badly, or it seems we are no closer to our goals than we were years ago? If Christians have a talent for anything, it should be to finish what they begin. Jesus did.

PERSEVERANCE — God demands
Nehemiah 9:7–8; Ephesians 1:19–20

To the Extreme

In 218 B.C. Hannibal invaded Italy in the second of three Punic Wars that determined the fate of Rome and Carthage. From her own people Rome raised an army, animated it with patriotism, and ordered it to fight. The wealthy devoted their treasure to the cause, and all classes sacrificed everyday amenities for troops in the field. For fifteen years the Romans defended their homeland against the brilliant Carthaginian—and could never drive him out. But their willingness to persevere assured victory, for Hannibal could never conquer them. He finally disembarked his troops from a lack of support at home.

God demands that we obstinately oppose Satan, as those Romans untiringly harried Hannibal. Victory is ours! We may not be able to conquer Satan all at once, but he cannot conquer us at all. No, not at all. We shall conquer him eventually, for God has willed his truth to triumph through us.

PERSEVERANCE — when it is hard
Numbers 11:4–6, 10–15; 1 Corinthians 16:8–9

Staying When Quitting Is Easier

Coastwatcher Donald McFarland fled to the hills when the Japanese invaded Guadacanal in 1942. Pursued, he receded deeper into the jungle and higher into the mountains. He had been ordered to remain in place because the Navy needed his intelligence reports on Japanese ship movements.

On July 28, 1942, he wrote to another coastwatcher that Japanese patrols sniffed dangerously close to his lair and he didn't intend to stay until the tiger pounced. "But of course, he stayed," Walter Lord wrote. "Every once in a while a man discovers he can go beyond the limits he sets for himself. . . ." His self-set deadline for leaving came, went, and found him in place. "We'll hang on a few more days," he wrote his friend again. "I suppose we must have faith."

Serving Jesus in any capacity sometimes becomes burdensome. Immovable obstacles prevent growth, or people clamor for growth but refuse to change the traditions that prevent growth, or leaders with a Diotrophes complex resist change. At such a time Jesus may want us to remain in place when we would rather move, to stay and offer solutions. He may ask teachers to keep Bible school classes they consider tiresome. He may ask lay leaders to remain in positions that have no future. Can we resist our heavenly Lord when others obey a secular ruler? Isn't the awareness of his devotion to us, despite our ingratitude, enough to motivate us to serve him, despite the difficulty?

PERSISTENCE — necessary
Micah 5:2; Acts 19:29, 34

Dare to Trust

In 1975 a young couple bought a small paper in California. Almost immediately the husband unearthed a scandal involving a foundation that had served in rehabilitating former alcoholics and dope addicts. He persevered in his research even when major newspapers refused to run his exposé and when local law enforcement officials covered for the foundation. He ran down leads and former members who were willing to talk. When the foundation's leaders tried to kill an opponent by putting a rattlesnake in his mailbox, the newsman's efforts paid off. The leaders were brought to trial and convicted, and the newsman received a Pulitzer Prize for responsible, effective journalism.

We Christians sometimes despair at the problems confronting us. We wonder if we—small, weak, helpless—can survive against stronger powers. We feel that giving up is the only alternative to the frustration of trying and constantly failing. *Sursum corda!* Those destined to lose cannot win, and those destined to win cannot lose if they persist in faithful service! We succeed against all the Goliaths confronting us because God has willed for us to win and for them to lose. Nothing will defeat us!

PESSIMISM — debilitates
Jeremiah 10:19–20; 2 Corinthians 11:29

To the Rear

A major fighting in Normandy during World War II said that he was being mauled by "the manic-depressive atmosphere of war." He knew he had to conquer his feeling, or be destroyed by it; while he had seen soldiers advance under many conditions, he had never seen them "follow gloom in any direction other than to the rear." His appraisal reflected what happened to the American leadership in both the North African and Anzio campaigns. The American general who led the attack in each battle was later replaced and sent home due to "fatigue." The term indicated his inability to motivate himself, leading to a deadly malaise among the troops and an inability to reach military objectives.

Gloom never leads a life in any direction but to the rear. Depression is a silent assassin because it often masquerades as other illnesses. It can also be caused by illness or medication taken for illness. Those overwhelmed by depression need the understanding and active involvement of family and friends. Christians burdened by it need the support network of their local congregation. The depressed need, above all, active association with people whose zeal for living offers an alternative to their gloom-filled impasse.

PLEASURE — always have time for
Deuteronomy 10:16; Colossians 3:5–10

Energy Enough for That

General James Gavin wrote that the Army Air Force made paratrooper training as difficult and exhausting as possible. Nevertheless, the troopers always had enough energy to get into fights in surrounding towns. Even after punishing a group by marching them out all night and back the next day, many of those punished were back in town brawling on Sunday night.

This predisposition to pleasure—especially carnal pleasure—grows in us like barnacles on a ship. We have a legendary capacity to play and party. Duty we fulfill; pleasure we relish. We reluctantly yield to obedience but abandon ourselves to amusement. If Adam and Eve broke the one command God gave them, why would it surprise us that we break the ten God gave to Moses? Jesus intentionally made self-denial the heart of his teaching. He who gave his life to secure salvation offers discipleship only to those who surrender theirs to his direction.

PLEASURE — not in things
Ecclesiastes 12:1; Philippians 3:20–21

Only in Their Maker

Augustine once saw a beggar drunk with wine but enjoying himself. At the time

Augustine felt miserable and hypocritical because he had to make a flattering speech about the emperor. In his *Confessions,* he commented on the difference between himself and the beggar. Both aspired to security, he said, and it seemed the beggar had found it, while Augustine vainly sought it. "True it is that the joy which he had was not the true joy," the great confessor continued, "but yet I, by my ambition, was seeking after one more false by far. And certainly he was merry while I was melancholy, and he was safe while I was full of fear."

Neither ambition nor alcohol has any positive answers to establish self-worth and success. We are miserably misled if we feel that our best hope is simply between two evils, not between the right and the wrong—the good and the evil, God and Satan. That is part of our problem. We get accustomed to accepting something less than total victory or complete defeat. God has a better idea: absolute success for us and obliterating defeat for Satan. In God alone are the things that C. S. Lewis calls "the scent of a flower we have not found, the echo of a tune we have not heard, news from a country we have never yet visited." Even now, however, the scent, the echo, and the news embolden and empower our lives!

POLITICS — alcohol in elections
Deuteronomy 1:16–17; 1 Timothy 2:1–4

A Swig on Me

In colonial America, politicians were expected to provide liquor for the voters on election day. Even George Washington provided one and a half quarts of liquor for each of the 361 supporters who voted him a seat in the House of Burgesses. (He learned his lesson from an earlier rejection by the voters for not providing decent drinks.) When he ran for the House of Burgesses, Patrick Henry spent over eight pounds sterling to get elected. Seven pounds purchased twenty-eight gallons of rum and one pound hired the men who carried it to the polls.

It seems undignified to buy votes with drinks, yet politicians today use their own brand of liquor to win votes. They simply call it by more refined names: welfare, entitlements, and subsidies. Whatever it is called, it beguiles the electorate into thinking they get something for nothing. They do not realize that they are paying themselves for all those gratuities the government so freely dispenses. We demean ourselves and our representatives when we equate a person's worth to govern by his or her personal promises to us.

POLITICS — no good choices
Ezekiel 2:4–7; Revelation 4:2–3

Not a Straight Line

In reading *Conflict and Crisis,* the account of Harry Truman's presidency, one appreciates Sir Edmund Burke's statement that most political decisions are choices "between the disagreeable and the intolerable." How thoroughly politics impacts

American life! Politically profitable stances, even if wrong, are assumed; politically questionable positions, even if right, are abandoned. Truman wanted a vigorous civil rights platform in his campaign, but he said little about it to avoid offending Southerners. In the latter part of the campaign, he vilified Hoover for causing the Depression. Later, he confided to an aide, "I didn't mean a word of it. Hoover didn't have any more to do with the Depression than you and I did." But it was politically expedient, so he rode the charge like a pony at Santa Anita. Unfortunately, that is the nature of the political animal: find the opponent's weak spot and slug him there until he drops. Politics can never be a straight line, for it invariably moves like a river, following the path of least resistance. The purpose of the politician is to have maximum success with minimum offense.

God's Word is always a straight line. He won't make scurrilous charges just to make the enemy look bad, or comprise his purity to make the enemy look better and less horrible than he really is. And God certainly won't reduce his require- ments to win converts. Our questions to God are always different; God's answers to us are always the same.

POLITICS — doctrine of effective occupation
Psalm 119:89; 1 John 5:4–5

There First

To combat the New World claims of her European opponents, Elizabeth's England said they would avoid any area actually occupied by the Spanish or Portuguese, but felt free to sail where no national colonies existed. This was called the doctrine of effective occupation—if you get there first, you can have the place.

Satan untiringly lies that he has effective occupation rights on earth. Yet the biblical message is one of recovering for God what his creative powers first estab- lished. Satan is the interloper whose opposition remains historical, not eternal. Satan will be cast into hell at the end, and God's truth, more ancient than Satan's lies, will continue after the end, eternally.

POSSESSIONS — mean nothing at last
Deuteronomy 4:5–6, 14; Philippians 3:7–11

Trade Them All

Lee Atwater wanted to reach two goals before he was forty: manage a winning presidential campaign and head the Republican party. He accomplished both—the first by managing the 1988 Bush campaign, the second when the president-elect asked him to become chairman of the National Republican Committee. During a speech at a fund-raiser in 1990, Atwater's goals changed. Suddenly unable to finish his speech due to uncontrollable shaking, he was taken to a hospital and was diag- nosed with cancer—an egg-sized tumor was on his brain. Radiation killed it, but could do nothing for a second tumor.

Before has death on March 29, 1991, Atwater wrote about the 1980's as the decade of acquiring wealth, power, and prestige. He had subscribed to it wholeheartedly. "But you can acquire all you want and still feel empty," he wrote. "What power wouldn't I trade for a little more time with my family? What price wouldn't I pay for an evening with my friends. . . ."

Our vaunted ability to face life with equilibrium vanishes when we are eye to eye with our mortality! That inescapable time bomb came with our conception and will inevitably explode our plans and goals. Tell us again; maybe we will listen this time—"Do not store up for yourselves treasures on earth" (Matt. 6:19). "A man's life does not consist in the abundance of his possessions" (Luke 12:15). "What good will it be for a man if he gains the whole world, yet forfeits his soul? Or what can a man give in exchange for his soul?" (Matt. 16:26).

POSSESSIONS — having many
1 Chronicles 29:14–16; 1 Timothy 6:6–10

Whatever Money Could Buy

Liberace lived garishly, spending more than $2 million a year on clothes for his Las Vegas acts. He would drive on stage in a mirrored Rolls-Royce, or pop out of a giant pink egg, or soar across the stage in a swirl of purple feathers. Offstage, he dressed conservatively, but thoroughly enjoyed spending money. He owned eighteen pianos, including instruments owned by Chopin and Gershwin; dozens of antique cars; a desk owned by the last Russian Czar; a collection of Napoleonic pieces; and a reproduction of the Sistine Chapel ceiling in his bedroom. He stored the overflow in three warehouses. He owned twenty-one dogs, a Las Vegas restaurant, and had plans for an expanded park with a piano-shaped museum at its center.

Whatever money could buy! Except continued life. What are people missing who crave possessions? Who buy in extravagance? Is it security? Self-esteem? Spiritual purpose? Confidence? A sense of achievement and self-worth? Eliminating private property as a means of controlling greed is the socialist's dream— but it is also impossible. Neither property nor possessions is wrong. Prosperity is no more intrinsically evil than impoverishment is virtuous. The Bible everywhere recognizes the right to private ownership. Possessions pose a danger only when we trust them to provide our self-esteem, security, and confidence. To identify these needs with anything or anyone but God is idolatry. He alone offers us our sense of worth. We are made in his image, and no amount of money can buy, replace, or restore that.

POSSESSIONS — small but essential
1 Samuel 14:25–26; 2 Corinthians 11:29

A Treasure to Her

When James Reed was banished from the Donner party for killing one of its members, his wife, Margaret, was left to care for their four children, including eight-year-old Patty. After three harrowing, cannibalistic months in the Sierra Nevada mountains, the survivors emerged from their holes in the snow when the first rescue party arrived. When they were finally safe at Fort Sutter, Patty pulled a bundle from her ragged dress. It held a lock of her grandmother's hair and a four-inch doll. She had carried them all the way from Springfield, Illinois, keeping them with her through the horrors of starvation in the mountains. Small as they were, the items represented hope to a little girl who had experienced in a few months more terror than most adults experience in a lifetime.

Possessions that relate to an important event or person in our life take on a priceless value—we say sentimental—whatever their original cost. Christians have such a possession—the Lord's Supper—and because we know what it cost, we treasure it and revere the Lord who instituted it.

POSSIBILITIES — seeing
Genesis 46:26; Exodus 12:37; Mark 4:30–32

Seeing, Not Just Looking

Someone said that Samuel F. B. Morse had the genius to search for corner lots while others walked the neighborhood gazing at the view. Carl Graham Fisher was another entrepreneur who saw "corner lots." As he walked along a swampy coastline in 1912 he constantly swatted at mosquitoes. The land looked ugly and was full of pests and predators. Its only redeeming quality was a beautiful white sand beach washed from the Atlantic swells. "Look, honey," he exclaimed to his wife, "I'm going to build a city here! A city like magic, like . . . you read and dream about but never see." That beach site became Miami Beach, Florida, a Mecca of high-rise hotels. The dream sometimes cost its promoters fifty thousand dollars a day, without a return, but they shared Fisher's vision and lived to see their "corner lot" built.

Jesus expects "corner lot" faith in his people. Abraham had that kind of faith. After waiting twenty-five years for Isaac's birth and seeing him grow into a fine lad, God asked Abraham to offer the boy as a sacrifice. In response, Abraham took Isaac to Moriah. Through faith Abraham saw that the boy could be both a sacrifice to God and a man reproducing himself to maintain the messianic line. How God would accomplish it, Abraham did not know; but that God would, he had no doubt. That is "corner lot" faith!

POTENTIAL — unfulfilled
2 Kings 17:6; 25:21; 1 Timothy 4:14–16

Unused Potential

The Germans had two powerful weapons in World War II that never repaid their investment. The *Tirpitz*, one of the most powerful battleships of her time, fired her eight fifteen-inch guns only to reduce shore batteries at Spitsbergen, Norway. Gustav, the largest gun ever manufactured, had to be shipped in sections on railroad cars. When assembled, its mounting straddled two sets of standard gauge tracks, with eighty wheels supporting it. Though it could propel a seven-ton shell twenty-three miles, the Germans used it only in the siege of Sevastopol, Russia.

When Jesus ascended to heaven, he gave gifts to his children. To some more, to others less, but to each something. He gave them for a single purpose—to be used. He loaded his people with all the armor, weaponry, and ammunition needed to live victoriously. Having done so, he now expects us to do it. Any refusal insults him and mocks his purpose.

POVERTY — amidst plenty
1 Samuel 25:2–3; 1 Timothy 6:19

With All That Wealth

When Edgar Degas was in his seventies and nearly blind, he spent his days pacing the boulevards of Paris, following funeral processions. Financially secure, he lived as if burdened with debt and dressed so shabbily that a tobacconist offered him free cigarettes. His friend Mary Cassatt despaired. He exasperated her continually, ignoring her advice and spurning her care. "What a state he is in!" she wrote a friend. "He scarcely knows you, he neglects his clothes, he takes no interest in himself. It is dreadful! With millions of francs still in his studio, they can do him no good; he is consumed with old age."

He had painted brilliantly but had no future. He had become famous but couldn't enjoy it. He could buy whatever he pleased but desired nothing. While still living he had lost the capacity to appreciate life! There are others like him—those who make the best of their careers, professions, or businesses, but leave undeveloped the best in themselves.

POVERTY — extreme national
Leviticus 25:19–22; 1 Peter 4:1–5

Not Even the Least Expense

Congress finally voted pay for the soldiers who so faithfully served the nation in the Revolution. Yet, they had no money to give them. What was worse, Congress could offer only certificates that promised three months pay. Most veterans valued the certificates so lightly that they left for home before they were issued.

Truth to tell, our present-day Congress still can't afford to pay the huge demands made on the U.S. Treasury. Undeterred, Congress simply borrows more. Whatever happened to the simple but effective economic belief that if you don't have money, you shouldn't spend it?

Easy plastic money, twenty-four-hour tellers, and home equity credit lines have fueled a runaway consumerism. We buy what we want but don't need; we pay for pleasures that we can't afford and don't appreciate. Then we work like machines at high speed to create income to catch our runaway expenses. Of course, our net income never exceeds our gross habits. We would think Paul's wise economic philosophy out of touch—being content whatever the circumstances, in need or in plenty. His perspective speaks of a spiritual wealth whatever his financial condition; ours of a spiritual poverty whatever our wealth.

POVERTY — insoluble by government programs
Deuteronomy 15:4, 11; 2 Thessalonians 3:11–13

Can't Support Them to Prosperity

America spent three hundred billion dollars to wage and win World War II. In 1992, the U.S. Congress spent three hundred six billion on welfare, trying to support people out of poverty. We have lost this war; poverty remains intractable precisely because government cannot spend people to prosperity. After spending five trillion dollars in a thirty-year war on poverty, the Census Bureau lists thirty-seven million as poor—though some of the statistics are certainly skewed. (Nearly 40 percent of the poor own their own home, worth $50,000; three-fourths of a million poor own homes worth more than $100,000.)

The government cannot pay our way out of poverty. By example and teaching, Scripture solidly backs the concept of labor equals capital, both economically and spiritually. Where people can, God expects them to earn their own living. Jesus made the principle equally distinct in discipleship. The master gave talents to be used while he traveled. The apostles worked at their tasks and taught their congregations to engage in honest labor. The Christian who hopes for an eternal reward but will not presently serve the Master's cause, should take heed: God is not Uncle Sam, and the Trinity is not Congress.

POVERTY — relative
Jeremiah 33:3; James 2:1–7

It Depends on Your Perspective

To the Romans, poor was a relative term. "The poor were the rich who were not very rich." Horace, who made a virtue of his poverty, said he had only a "life raft" in reserve, consisting of two estates, one whose house covered six thousand square feet.

Poverty also remains relative in America. Many families who fall beneath the government's official poverty line—$13,924 for a family of four—receive noncash assistance that significantly increases public monies spent for the poor. Food stamps, public housing, and Medicaid accounted for three-quarters of all public assistance in 1991. Almost half of poor households have air-conditioning; nearly a third have microwave ovens; more than 60 percent own a car; 14 percent own two or more cars. As long as government bureaucrats define poverty, we will discover increasing numbers of the "poor." We'll also find fewer and fewer "rich" people to support them. Giving economic aid without requiring labor in turn eventually bankrupts the benefactor without enriching the recipient.

Spiritual poverty inside the Christian faith is also relative. Every one who is reborn immediately falls heir to all of the Kingdom's spiritual wealth. However, the individual's willingness to invest time, energy, and finances determines the enjoyment of that wealth. Economic equality is an illusion; spiritual equality is a potential reality. While we cannot have equal access to lucre, all Christians have equal access to God and an equal opportunity to be spiritually affluent.

POWER — small but great
Isaiah 41:14; Revelation 3:2

In Small Packages

The bee hummingbird weighs less than a penny and hatches eggs the size of coffee beans in a nest no bigger than a doll's teacup. Notwithstanding, the wings of this pugnacious little creature beat eighty times a second, too rapidly for the naked eye to see. It is usually a loner, is very territorial, and will brazenly attack hawks that could swallow it whole. It has the highest metabolic rate per unit of body weight in the avian world and requires disproportionately large amounts of food.

Kinetic energy, that which is in motion, versus potential energy, that which is unused, distinguishes the value of believers in their discipleship. Believers who have significant knowledge and faith but do not express it are relatively useless to God. They betray the purpose of their faith. Those with limited knowledge and faith but zealous to share what they know have significant value, though they may incorrectly interpret the faith. God won't have us harboring our spiritual energies in the barracks when he equips us to serve in the line.

PRAYER — longing for spiritual realities
2 Chronicles 7:14; Colossians 1:9–14

Reaching Out to Reality

Kevin Klose went to Moscow in 1977 as bureau chief for the *Washington Post.* Over the next four years he made friends with many Russians. Back in Chicago, he maintained the friendships because the people had sacrificed so much to make them and faced retribution for continuing them. Whatever other factors motivated them, the Russians conversed with the American to fill a spiritual vacuum in their lives. They reached out to one who embodied the freedom, choice, values, and personal creativity they craved but their government callously denied. So they stood against what they abhorred to express a longing for what they admired.

Christians understand that search for reality. We seek God to find the truth and absolutes that this life advertises but never delivers, the values and ideals that philosophy, psychology, and society seek to produce but cannot. However good life is, we sense it is but a shabby imitation of true life in God's son. Whatever pleasures we enjoy, we instinctively know they are but a shadow of the substance from another place. This is not our home however much we feel at home. We reach out through prayer, Bible study, and the quiet communion of the soul with the infinite God to that world where all is as it seems to be.

PRAYER — spend time in
Psalm 63:1; Romans 1:9–10

Only in Leisure

National Park officials welcome 250 million people to our treasured parks each year. Most visitors are day-trippers, coming to look and run. In 1983, the average time spent for all forty-eight national parks was four and one-half hours. For Isle Royale it was four days, perhaps due to its remoteness. Yosemite or Sequoia, Yellowstone or Glacier National Park in four and one-half hours? To so heatedly race in and out of these stunning temples of granite offers no time to pause, let alone stop and look, listen and smell the delights of mountains, rivers, and high country.

Unfortunately, prayer fares far worse than our National Parks. Though God invites us to sit and enjoy time in his presence, we hasten in and out of prayer like we do a fast-food establishment. Yet the more we pray, the more we enjoy it and receive from it. When we rise from prayer we are always more keen for it than when we first knelt. God's answers come to all who seek his presence. He doesn't time the length of our prayers, but it is for our own soul's delight that we spend time with him, finding in spiritual leisure the grace that haste denies.

PREJUDICE — always blinds
Exodus 7:23; Acts 6:9–10

They Didn't Want It That Way

John Wilkes, a radical in Britain during the American Revolution, fell from royal favor and went into exile. When he returned, he ran for and won a seat in the House of Commons—not once, but three times. Each time he was elected, the House expelled him on orders from George III. Each time he was expelled, he won reelection. The House finally seated his opponent, stating that the latter "ought" to have been elected.

How prejudice blinds, rendering us incapable of objectivity. It will deny, twist, argue, or talk truth to death, but it will never accept truth. This can happen in our personal relationships, where we see only negative aspects in a person who actually has many redeeming features. It can adversely affect our view of the local church, causing us to see its shortcomings and to miss its contributions. It can happen more ominously in our interpretation of the Bible. We may prefer what it "ought" to mean; however, we will all be judged by what it says, not by what we wish it had said.

PREPARATION — benefits of
Psalm 90:12; 1 Peter 3:15

To Pay the Price

Alexander Campbell, the brilliant leader of the Restoration Movement in the nineteenth century, often studied sixteen hours a day, rising at 4:00 A.M. to work uninterrupted in his study. He spoke without notes but never without preparation. With only two hours notice, he preached his famous sermon on the law to a group of Baptist pastors. One pastor later said that Campbell had broken more light from the book of Romans than any man he had heard preach.

In his debate with skeptic Robert Owen over the nature and historicity of Christianity, Campbell spoke for twelve hours on the evidences for Christianity as a supernatural religion after Owen had exhausted his objections to Christianity. One who heard him at the time declared, "I have been listening to a man who seems as one who has lived in all ages." Mr. Owen, hitherto unchecked by religious leaders, went back to Scotland, taking his infidelity with him.

Our life with God is as enjoyable, fruitful, and educational as we determine. Our knowledge of God is as deep as we desire. We can rise early, or retire later, in order to read the Bible and pray. Perhaps we will never be called to Alexander Campbell's significance, but we are challenged to set Christ apart as Lord so we can give an accounting to those who ask about our faith.

PREPARATION — too much taken
1 Corinthians 5:11; Titus 3:10–11

Prepared to Death

On picket duty during a forty-day punitive expedition against Comanches in the Texas Staked Plains, a trooper lassoed his horse and wrapped the lariat around his body. He remarked to a fellow trooper that if he went to sleep the horse couldn't stray. His excessive precaution cost his life. During the night an approaching buffalo herd spooked his horse, and it ran away, dragging the sleeping cavalryman to his death.

Why did that soldier even think of sleep? The very nature of a watchman (in this case called a *picket*) means wakefulness. As the first line of defense, he had to stay alert to protect his sleeping comrades.

Christians are too often like that trooper. We fall asleep at our tasks by failing to discharge them promptly, if at all, or by giving only half-hearted efforts. And where are our fellow Christians at such a time? The buzz word in too many congregations is unconditional, not accountable. Unconditional is a comforting word since it erects no standards, imposes no expectations, and makes no demands—and leaves us each to determine when and how much to change. Accountability rouses us from our spiritual somnolence, raises expectations for us, and holds us to the high calling of God.

PRESENT — all we have
Psalm 61:8; Matthew 6:34

Energies for the Moment

May 26, 1805. Captain William Clark gazed westward from a summit to see the Rocky Mountains blanketed in snow, shining brilliantly in the sun. To have them so near brought a sense of accomplishment. To know they remained so distant brought a sense of dread. He momentarily reflected on the difficulty they posed. "But," he wrote in his journal, "as I have always held it little short of criminality to anticipate evils, I will allow it to be a good, comfortable road until I am compelled to believe otherwise."

Isn't that the essence of Christ's teaching on living today and not worrying about tomorrow? Habitual practice offers the key to triumphant discipleship: serving Christ one day at a time. The life we surrendered to Jesus yesterday will be in rebellion against him tomorrow unless it is surrendered today. That is the nature of our stubborn will, thinking to retain our self-respect by asserting self-will. But while God doesn't obliterate our self-awareness, he simply demands the consecration of that awareness to him.

PRESENT — bad for future
Genesis 17:6–8; 1 John 3:3

Too Late to Change

For all the good Otto von Bismarck accomplished in uniting Germany, his rule was marked by a conspicuous failure. He brought absolutism, not democracy, to the German people. His twenty-seven year autocratic rule led to Kaiser Wilhelm; then, after World War I, to an ineffectual Weimer republic that had no basis in German history. After that it led to Hitler. Before he died, Bismarck said that even good kings can be bad if they hold uncontested power. Unfortunately, it was too late to remake Germany.

God has established an unfailingly complete sufficiency for us in Christianity. It has a benevolent, all sovereign Lord. It provides the perfect sacrifice for sin and an infallible guide for principles of good behavior in each generation. It consists of a forgiven constituency of saints who complete God's mission in each generation. It promises a righteous, eternal kingdom ruled by almighty God and inhabited by forgiven, perfected saints.

PRESSURE — necessary for growth
Matthew 4:18–19; Mark 10:21

Applied Just Right

The lady observed the airplane mechanic testing plane parts to certify their serviceability. He picked up a nut and screwed it on a bolt that protruded from a piece of metal. Then he took a torque wrench, set the gauge for the necessary pressure, fit the wrench over the nut, and began to turn. Exactly the right pressure was necessary, he told her. Too little and the nut would come loose; too much and it would crack. When the wrench reached the right torque he looked to a large pendulum hanging behind the metal. "That's a torque meter," he said. "It's accurate and reliable—it never changes. It double checks the amount of pressure applied by the wrench."

What is the spiritual principle? God knows the exact amount of pressure we each need to make us function accurately, productively, and safely. We can trust him to apply just the right stress to each of us to assure our maximum productivity.

PRESSURE — peer
1 Kings 22:13–14; 2 Corinthians 10:12

Everyone Did It

Women of the Enlightenment showed little illumination about the clothing they wore. They bound themselves with corsets, then flounced around in hooped skirts so big staircases had to be redesigned to let them "float" down in style. Fashionable ladies also wore their hair in colossal three-foot coiffures, with horsehair padding, wire foundations, ribbons of ostrich feathers, and models of farms, ships, or battles. They kept it styled for several months without washing it, giving insects and even mice places to build nests. Fashions for females do occasionally defy good judgment.

God may tolerate the purchase of elaborate clothes and the application of high fashion makeup so we can feel at ease around our peers, but he will not tolerate accepting any authority but his for doctrine, morals, and values. He has spoken to us through his Word. That means we are not alone, but it also means we are not free to choose our own spiritual truth.

PRIDE — brings harm
2 Samuel 1:13; 2 Corinthians 2:5–11

Two Are Involved

In *The Force of Circumstances,* Somerset Maugham tells of a man who lives ten years in the Far East, during which time he cohabits with a native woman. He then returns to England where he meets and marries "a proper English girl." When she discovers his previous alliance, she cannot bring herself to forgive. Rage consumes her, and though she loves her husband, she cannot forget his past. So she leaves him, knowing that she is punishing herself as much as him.

Jan Rubens, the father of the great artist Peter Paul Rubens, committed adultery and was put in jail. His wife assured him of her willingness to forgive. Intensely guilty because of his betrayal, he had a difficult time accepting her forgiveness. She continued to assure him of her affection. How could she fail, she said, "to pardon a slight trespass against myself, when I have to pray to God to forgive the many grave trespasses I commit against Him every day?"

How often, like the woman in Maugham's story, we harm ourselves as much as others when we let pride dictate our decisions. We cannot disassociate ourselves from our intimates; and our treatment of them automatically impacts our own life. How we admire the humility that would prompt Mrs. Rubens to forgive her husband's infidelity. By comparing carnal with spiritual sins, she rose above a natural human reaction to attain a spiritual grace.

PROBLEMS — new solutions
Jeremiah 29:13; Matthew 17:19–20

The Same Old Way

A 4.6 earthquake tore through the ocean town and shook the residents awake. A sharp crack like a giant rifle sounded in the night, followed by ominous rumblings that flowed in waves across the metropolitan area. When he felt the shaking, police officer Dennis Johnson rolled out of bed and instinctively grabbed his service revolver. "Dennis," his wife said calmly, "not even you can stop an earthquake with a gun."

Humanity expresses an insufferable arrogance. We are convinced we can solve human problems if enough intelligent people work at it for long enough. All the solutions, however, reduce themselves to the same few: government spending, stiffer laws, more prisons, harsher sentences, more police on the streets. Jesus forgives sin and rehabilitates lives. Only fasting, prayer, humiliation, and tears can solve our problems. There is no need to keep grabbing for the same old answers—we need to reach out to Jesus.

PROGRESS — theme of humanity
Habakkuk 2:13; Acts 4:12

We'll Always Get Better

At the end of the seventeenth century, French philosopher Bernard Fontanelle predicted unbridled progress for humanity in science and learning. So greatly would the race advance in these ways "we might almost be tempted to let our hopes for the future rise too high," he wrote. Thus was born the theory of progress that sailed unobstructed through the next two centuries, until the second decade of the twentieth. Then an assassin shot the Archduke Ferdinand, and that unbridled optimism died in the trenches of France and buried its victims in Flanders field.

If advancements in science and learning indicate progress, then humanity in the last half of the twentieth century is remarkably superior. But can technological progress be a suitable compensation for moral decline? After World War II some churchmen said they wanted to find answers to the disparity between military achievements and human atrocities, especially of the Nazis against the Jews. In seeking answers, many were led to doubt God's existence. Other churchmen questioned whether their compatriots were seeking answers, or escaping conclusions. Should they have been led to doubt God's existence, or human ability to live and govern without God?

PROMISES — broken
1 Kings 8:56; 2 Peter 3:9

With His Fingers Crossed

In 1492, Ferdinand granted Columbus great titles, vast privileges, and a tenth of the riches his explorations materialized. By 1500, when the size and wealth of the new world actually dawned on Ferdinand, he broke the agreement, though he had promised it by solemn treaty.

In the early 1950s, the Russians opened sixty million acres in Kazakhstan to grain farmers. They imported trainloads of Russians, Ukrainians, and Byelorussians to work the state-owned cooperatives, planning to be self-sufficient in grain by 1954. The Communist Party promised to bring the future to its people. The people believed . . . in vain. Today, several millions of those acres have reverted to pasture. The Party made promises and brought hope, one man said, then the Party vanished, leaving broken promises and ruined lives.

God understands that we live in hope and that, deprived of hope, our spirit diminishes, then dies. He has encouraged us to believe in his promises, which never fail; but we are intent on believing our own, which seldom succeed. Greed, false economic theory, political or social collapse can destroy even well-intentioned assurances. God's promises will not fail, for they are founded on him.

PUBLICITY — changes people
Deuteronomy 13:11; Acts 5:6, 11

Just Show It On TV

In its report on the Los Angeles riots in 1992, the Webster Commission concluded that live television coverage exacerbated the looting and violence. It was an unintended message, the Commission concluded, but seeing law enforcement officials respond slowly to the emergency emboldened those who would have been reluctant to steal had an alert police presence been in the riot areas. A media feeding frenzy sizzles with any catastrophe, war, or sensational murder. It happened at the Lindbergh trial, it happened in the big city riots of the 1960s, the Los Angeles riots of 1992, and reached perhaps its highest temperature in the trial of O. J. Simpson.

The main problem with media coverage is that it offers no value judgment on what it portrays. The cameraman shoots what is happening and the anchor people may feel free to offer an editorial comment. But it is outside the ability of the media to offer condemnation or acquittal. Only a constituted authority can do that—the police, the courts, and the Bible. Long ago God ordered his people to quickly execute his judgments against lawbreakers so that others, seeing the swift retribution, would be afraid, not emboldened. Given the nature of the media, the lengthy judicial process, and our poor memories, how do we expect to restrain criminals today?

PUBLICITY — of product
Isaiah 40:25; 43:10; John 10:8

What Is Cyclamen?

Before the 1920's, cyclamen was considered the traditional Christmas plant for Americans. Then a Californian named Paul Ecke, who knew how to publicize his product, began to actively promote the poinsettia plants he raised. The flower was not new. Originally it grew wild in Mexico and was widely used by padres in earlier centuries as Christmas decorations. All it needed to become the Christmas flower of America was an energetic advocate.

The devil has been fashioning false gods since his successful encounter with Eve—where the first imitation god he offered was Eve herself. He shamelessly creates counterfeits of the true God and convinces entire nations that they are just as good as God. They look like God, they have some of God's attributes, they can be worshiped as God, so why shouldn't they be accepted as God? Satan's imitations cannot substitute for God—God is one of a kind.

PUBLICITY — value of
Matthew 21:45–46; Acts 16:37

The One Everyone Saw

On February 19, 1945, Marines landed on the beaches of Iwo Jima, fighting by inches to secure a beachhead. After four days of knock-down-drag-out battle, they finally cleared the southern end of the island, climbed Mount Suribachi, and planted a small flag. The commander wanted a larger presence on Suribachi to encourage the Marines still fighting at the northern end of the island, so he ordered a larger flag raised. The first flag over Iwo Jima flew early on February 23, 1945. Three hours later the larger one went up. The second flag-raising was the one Joe Rosenthal photographed. No one saw the first flag—Rosenthal's photograph guaranteed that no one would forget the second.

God made sure that Christianity would have generous publicity. It started the night of Christ's nativity, with the world's most brilliant corps of press agents declaring his epiphany. John the Baptist publicly declared Jesus the Lamb of God. Jesus himself maintained a high public profile throughout his years of ministry. He was crucified publicly before a watching crowd, and after he arose was seen by many witnesses.

PUNISHMENT — God threatens
Isaiah 37:26–29; Hebrews 4:12–13

Exert the Authority

William Buckley is that rarest of combinations: an Ivy League conservative with the brains, wit, and will to defend his positions. In a column written in the mid-1980s, he insisted that a sovereign nation must rattle its sabers so the other guys will know it still has and is willing to use them. Far from contributing to war, weapons preserve peace. If, indeed, we have power and show a willingness to employ it when challenged, lawless rapine will be severely curtailed in our world.

Couldn't churches use a little saber-rattling to terrorize flagrant, impenitent sinners who claim fellowship with the Holy Christ? To claim that such action only drives the offender to another church misses the point. What church wants to be known as the church where you can be a drunkard, an adulterer, a murderer, or a prostitute—with full honors of membership?

PURPOSE — different from original
Psalm 119:11, 105; Hebrews 12:1

Where Are Those Old Charts?

A British yachtsman sailed the waters around the Falkland Islands, mapping landing areas, harbor depths, and beach conditions. He hoped to sell a book that vacationers and picnickers could use. In the Falklands War, May 1982, the British used his book and drawings to achieve total surprise when they invaded to reclaim the Islands the Argentines had seized. Had it not been for that book, the British would not have known about the beach.

No generation ever completely repays its debt to those who have gone before. We are always in the process of becoming ourselves from the contributions made by others. We may advance the position of those in the past, perfecting a theory or applying it in a new invention, but the connection remains. At a particular time in the past, a specific event occurred that helps us reach a goal now. That kind of event occurred on Mount Calvary. Jesus fulfilled the Old Testament as he began the New, uniting both in himself. Removing sin from between God and man, he reestablished the perfect divine-human relationship.

QUACKS — in medical practice
Leviticus 10:2–3; 1 Timothy 5:3

Still at It

How many incompetent doctors are practicing, diagnosing, and writing indecipherable prescriptions? The small percentage the American Medical Association
admits may be as high as 10 percent, according to Menninger Clinic studies. That
translates into 64,000 out of 645,000 doctors in this country (1989 figures). They
are afflicted by drug addiction, alcoholism, mental illness, senility, or incompetence. One of every three thousand persons in the general public is a drug addict;
one of every hundred physicians is.

Multiplied disasters lurk in hospitals and operating rooms where incompetent personnel labor. A diabetic had the wrong leg amputated. Two boys, with
similar names, but of different ages, had the surgery needed by the other. A
physician prescribed medication in nearly illegible handwriting. An inexperienced
nurse misread it, administered too powerful a dosage, and killed the patient.
Another man, scheduled for surgery to remove a cancerous tumor from his hip,
instead had healthy bone tissue removed, leaving the tumor intact.

What is really disturbing about this is . . . if at least 10 percent of doctors
are maladroit, with all the testing and schooling they must endure, could the percentage of incompetent pastors be worse, since no one tests them? How much
greater the responsibility of those whose mistakes can kill the soul.

QUAKE — danger
Acts 15:26; Philippians 2:30

The Coming Quake

It slashes across California like a ragged trench—the San Andreas Fault, stretching
south from the Baja Peninsula northwest through the state, east of Los Angeles,
under San Francisco, and north along the coast until it plunges into the cold
waters of the Pacific. For seven hundred miles it threatens any building or inhabitant in the state with a disastrous quake. The San Andreas Fault is particularly
dangerous because it is the boundary between the two great plates of the earth's

crust. East of the fault lies the North American plate, containing more than 99 percent of the North American continent. West of the fault lies the Pacific plate, supporting most of California's population and extending into the Pacific as far as the Philippines.

The apostles faced the certainty of opposition as they proclaimed the resurrection of Christ. They sometimes faced open threats of abuse, beating, and death if they persisted. But persist they did because they had previously counted the cost of serving against the benefits of knowing Jesus and had determined that the benefits far outweighed the costs. They had made their decision. In the peace that only such commitment to purpose gives, they served, forgetting the danger their commitment forced on them.

QUALITY — tells

Exodus 13:21–22; John 1:5

Light That Overcomes

When bandleader Lawrence Welk signed with the ABC network in the mid-1950's, he received a small trailer dressing room. Soon after, the network hired Frank Sinatra and gave him a lavish dressing room. About a year later Sinatra was gone, and Welk inherited it. Jerry Lewis came next on ABC, and they built him a dressing room superior to Sinatra's. In a year Lewis was gone, and Welk inherited that one. Some years later Welk returned to ABC for a taping and walked into a magnificent dressing room, thinking it was his. They apologetically explained that it was Sonny Bono's. Six weeks later Bono was gone too—and Lawrence Welk inherited another dressing room. He had outlasted them all, though each was reputedly better than he.

Scripture affirms that Christ is greater than all who oppose him, outlasting all who compete with him, who claim to have taken his place, and who claim to have the answers he failed to give. He is the only true light and will go on shining after he has eclipsed all the darkness and after all other lights have been extinguished.

QUARANTINE — sin put under

Ezekiel 18:31–32; Romans 8:3–4

Contain It

Bubonic plague killed half the population of Europe in the Middle Ages. Deadly even now, it grows more slowly in the body and can be cured with antibiotics. Pneumonic plague, the same disease, but infecting the lungs, is even now fatal 95 percent of the time. Unless diagnosis is made almost immediately, and antibiotics administered on diagnosis, the victim dies. Pneumonic plague offers no forgiveness.

Sin is our soul's pneumonic plague. It instantly deals death, though it may not be evident. That is the specious difference between our lungs and our soul.

We die instantly if we cannot breathe, but we can be dead spiritually for years without even realizing it. To guarantee that sin will not be fatal to us, we must immediately quarantine and eradicate it. No sin is acceptable just because it is "harmless," "small," or "under control." Sin is to the soul what pneumonic plague is to the body—a fast growing assassin that kills if not destroyed immediately.

QUARRELS — lead to violence
Genesis 13:8–9; Philippians 4:2

Where It Can Lead

Two elderly brothers regularly argued over which television show they would watch. It would seem that a solution would be to purchase a set for each one to watch as he pleased. Unable or unwilling to do so (perhaps such a purchase would have led to more endless quarreling), they continued to dispute, week after week, month after month. Later, telling police he just got tired of all the bickering, one brother fatally shot the other after an argument. More than one quarrel, even between friends, has led to violence. One family complained to a neighbor about his noisy dog. He continually ignored their appeals, so they finally called the police. When the officers arrived, the neighbor pulled a gun and shot the policemen as they stood in his driveway.

Arguing, quarreling, disputing—all such verbal jousting should be limited and contained. For, once out of control, even decent people find anger carrying them to extremes reason would never allow. Each congregation should establish a conflict resolution procedure. In this way, when disagreements occur, the procedure to address them is in place, ready to be implemented. In establishing the procedure, each church should distinguish the absolutes from the negotiables. This will restrict truth to Scripture and free opinions for compromise. Truth that cannot be relinquished without compromising faith will be retained; opinions that could be surrendered to maintain unity will be abandoned.

QUARTERBACK — leadership
2 Samuel 23:8–23; 1 Thessalonians 5:12–13

The One In Charge

Dan Fouts quarterbacked the San Diego Chargers for eighteen years. In that time they rewrote the meaning of offensive football in the NFL, a legacy still impacting pro football in the 1990s. The impact of Fouts' leadership was felt throughout the team. No one questioned his authority. His leadership in the huddle and in executing plays was unassailable. Quarterbacking demands a person like Dan Fouts. He must be confident of his abilities, be willing to take risks, and be willing to fail 50 percent of the time. He has to be willing to make all the calls, the bulk of which will not result in yards or points. Above all, he must initiate the course of action to be taken and must lead in its execution.

Leadership is getting out in front, maybe only a step, and urging others to follow. It puts the leader, as Foster Dulles said, at the powerhouse, not the transmission point, of decisions. God appointed leaders for his church: pastors, deacons, teachers, evangelists, and prophets. Scripture urges Christians to follow, honor, pray for, and emulate their spiritual leaders.

QUESTIONS — raised by adversity
Psalm 13:1–2; John 1:14

Questions

A confirmed bachelor, C. S. Lewis married late in life only to find love doomed when his wife was stricken with cancer. He plummeted into despair following her death, raging against the God about whom he had so coolly and confidently written when not personally afflicted. His little volume *A Grief Observed* is a testament to his agonizing endeavor to find meaning in the incomprehensible. He said that he would listen to anyone who spoke of the truth of religion. He would even listen if told of the duty of religion. But he would suspect the individual of not understanding who spoke of the consolations of religion.

We understand intellectually that God loves us even when it seems he does not. But faced with a despair we could not handle, haven't we all felt abandoned, even if we did not express it? Haven't we occasionally accused God of not caring, of overlooking our concerns, of being too busy to notice us? Lewis shared the thoughts he experienced while working through his grief. Some of his ideas offend gospel truth; they might even offend the untouched Christian. But God was never threatened by Lewis' grief, nor did he hold Lewis responsible for the charges grief conceived and agony shrieked. God understands. He too was once a man afflicted with the agonies of our existence.

QUIETNESS — need times of
Isaiah 30:15; Philippians 1:4–5

In Quietness

When the Air Force officer called his subordinate in and complained of office procedures, the engineer suggested that they might find a solution by going fishing. Perplexed, the officer agreed, wondering how a fishing trip would relate to everyday office problems.

As the weekend progressed, the engineer explained that at one time he had routinely worked fifteen-hour days. However, when he discovered he had malignant hypertension, he cut back on his hours and began to go fishing. He then led the officer to a point of the cove where the waters were mirror-still. "Look carefully," the man directed. Just beneath the surface they saw huge salmon swimming slowly. Others lay on the bottom, their only motion the fanning of gills and fins.

The man then called attention to the salmon in the channel. They were fighting upstream to obey their primal need to deposit eggs in the gravel where they were hatched. Turning once again to the salmon in the cove, he remarked that these fish were different. It was almost as if some instinct brought them to this quiet place to rest before leaping the falls.

He discovered he had been like the salmon in the channel—constantly thrashing to get ahead, immediately attacking the obstacles facing him. Seeing the salmon at rest helped him understand that sometimes peace and quietness offer the strength we need to face the challenges of life.

RACE — nomenclature of changing
Exodus 12:38; Acts 13:1

Nomenclature

In 1927, the opening lines of *Showboat* began: "Niggers all work on de Mississippi, Niggers all work while de white folks play." In 1936, the lines had become: "Darkies all work"; in 1946, "Colored folks work"; and in 1951, "Here we all work." The original score was used again in recording the music in 1993. From outright racist slurs, the writers of *Showboat* adapted more acceptable ethnic terms; then whitewashed, politically-correct nonterms; and finally returned to the original racist slurs.

We cannot correct the mistakes of the past by ignoring them. Revisionist historians always find an appreciative audience among those who will not face their past. A better answer than specious revisionism is an open acceptance of past mistakes, buttressed by a fixed determination not to repeat them or others equally fallacious.

RACE — racism
Numbers 16:3; John 12:32

Depends on the Prisoner

Racial prejudices intensify in wartime. World War II studies proved that when seeing Japanese POW's, a near majority of American soldiers felt "all the more like killing them." When soldiers in the European theater saw German POW's, more than half felt "it is too bad we have to be fighting them, they are men just like us." John Keegan rightly says that fighting is more ferocious between out- than in-groups. It is easier to hate someone different from you!

The Master's ministry proved that he tolerated differences in personalities, politics, and piety. That proscribes prejudice based on diversity. Diversity, meanwhile, runs the significant danger of splintering, not uniting, those with distinctions. The answer is to accept all differences in the body—political, social, or religious—with the diverse parts integrated into and subjected to the whole. By focusing the energies of his followers on spiritual issues, Jesus defused other issues that contentiously divided them.

RACE — racism inherent
Romans 15:20

Back to the Beginning

Trobriand Islanders, who live at a minimal subsistence level, nevertheless have little interest in or respect for other people and nations. Their word for an outsider is *dim-dim*—someone of little consequence. They consider outsiders as lower beings. This is nothing new. Wherever explorers found Indians in America, each band considered itself "the people" and the next Indian tribe up or down river as barbarians. Caucasians have been among the worst offenders, as U.S. Immigration figures from 1924 prove. Southern European, Slavic, Middle East, and Far Eastern countries could send from 100 to 4,000 people to America annually; Northern European countries could send from 34,000 to 51,000 people. America's immigration policies have certainly shifted since the 1970s.

Nationality is instinctive to humanity. Christians need to seize each group's awareness of itself as a means of expressing its importance to God. God loved each ethos—each fragment of the human race—so much that he gave his Son to die for it. Jesus died for each of the persons in every ethos. Christianity magnifies the individual as the object of God's love. That individual is then added to other individuals to create a church—the body of Christ!

REALITY — our goal
Jeremiah 32:8–9, 25; Romans 15:7

Putting on a Face

General George Patton, an incredible complexity of vice and virtue, of heartfelt prayer and bone-chilling profanity, of harshness and tenderness, felt that his public face had to be unyieldingly stern. He looked and acted the cold, ruthless warrior because he felt it cultivated the correct attitude for battle. This produced soul-wracking problems for him since, despite his unabashed egotism, he experienced painful self-doubt. To develop the right profile, he would practice his public persona like an actor. To overcome the sensitivity he felt was incompatible with a military profession, he forced himself to wear a harsh, vicious mask.

Are we not occasionally like Patton? Don't we sometimes put on a mask so we can make a desired impression? Occasionally we may need to restrain our feelings behind a mask, but it is a behavior we don't want to prolong, for we can become the victim of our delusions. In addition, if we keep putting on masks, we run the risk of losing ourselves in them, forgetting who we really are—whether we are kind or mean, intelligent or stupid, good or evil. Having hidden behind a mask so long, it may become our puppeteer, and we the puppets.

REASON — God wants us to use
Numbers 16:12–14; Acts 18:27–28

That Is Why We Have It

In the second century of our era, Ptolemy, an Alexandrian astronomer/mathematician, concluded that the heavenly bodies revolved around the sun. In the sixteenth century, Copernicus, the Polish astronomer, advanced the solar-center theory of the universe. In the century after him, Galileo, the first to study the universe through a telescope, concluded that Copernicus, not Ptolemy, had drawn the right conclusion. He fearlessly defended his position, bringing himself into conflict with the Roman Catholic Church, which had accepted the Ptolemaic theory. Galileo was persecuted and imprisoned by the Inquisition. Forced to recant his heliocentric theory, he was nevertheless adamant about our need to use the mind God gave us. "I do not feel obliged to believe that the same God who has endowed us with sense, reason, and intellect has intended us to forgo their use."

We sharpen our mental skills by accepting Christ. He quickens every part of our being, including our mind. Loving God with all our mind stands on an equal footing with loving him with our heart, soul, and strength! The pursuit of knowledge is an ally, not an adversary, of biblical revelation. God welcomes in-depth study of every discipline, for all study, in every discipline, ultimately leads to God. Knowledge is dangerous only when divorced from faith.

RECONCILIATION — value of
1 Kings 14:30; Romans 12:18

To Put an End to War

Robert E. Lee considered his surrender at Appomattox an unmitigated, but unavoidable, disaster. By forbidding a continuing guerrilla warfare, favored by some of his generals, General Lee wisely refused to inflict an even greater disaster on succeeding American generations. Lee knew that such an action would render reunion impossible and would bring perpetual military occupation of the South, with its unspeakable scandals. Enough blood had been shed, and the great Rebel Chief called for the complete surrender of all Southern troops. With all the racial problems still plaguing America—increased with the massive immigration from Third World countries—can't we appreciate General Lee's decision to accept the defeat he couldn't avoid, to avoid the disaster he couldn't accept?

How many families and churches have waged war long enough? How many have been wounded by exploding words? A war of words will see every good intention disappear. Now is the time to stop the fighting and wage peace. Our families are important to us. And if they, how much more essential to us our Christian friends? We trusted the Holy Spirit to effect our reconciliation with God. Won't we let him save relationships based on our common reconciliation?

RECREATION — needed in every age
Deuteronomy 25:24–26; Ephesians 5:15

From Earliest Days

Amasis, King of Egypt, spent part of his busy day in apparently unseemly levity. This scandalized some of his courtiers, who criticized him, complaining that he demeaned himself. He replied that bowmen bend the bows to shoot but unbrace them when not in use. Should the bows always be strung they would break in time of need. "So it is with men," he said. "If they give themselves constantly to serious work and never indulge in past time or sport, they lose their senses, and become mad or moody." To permit long-term productivity in serious work, a person needs to temporarily indulge in trivial matters.

Time-use specialists today see the wisdom of saving a lot of time by wasting a little of it. Companies and businesses give coffee breaks to their employees for the simple reason that it is advantageous to productivity. This won't surprise the believer. Our Creator foresaw our need to rest one day in seven. He also provided celebration feasts throughout the year so people could relax and enjoy the fruit of their labor. His Son took his disciples away from the crowds to relax. We need to apply ourselves while at work, but enjoy times of refreshing relaxation.

REDEMPTION — another must do it for us
Leviticus 4:13–15; Galatians 4:4

Someone to Step Forward

By 1921, a counter-revolution had begun in Russia to protest Soviet actions against the people and the agreed agenda of the original conspirators against the Czar. Lenin ordered the arrest of all counter-revolutionaries, so they went into hiding. Many could not be found because sympathizers willingly endangered themselves to protect them. Not to be denied their prey, Lenin's secret police arrested the families of the fugitives and threatened to exile them if each fugitive did not appear within three months to exchange his life for theirs. Of course the rebels surrendered.

Every form of government—the kindest, the harshest, the most benign, the most malignant—experiences revolt among some of its subjects. Even God's perfect government saw its first two subjects rebel though they had but one law imposed on them. We come as naturally to resistance against constraint as a wolf to its howls. We must take credit for our best instincts as well as the blame for our worst impulses. When we found ourselves in bondage to sin, with no escape, God punished himself, not us. He sent Christ from heaven to overcome the entire kingdom of darkness. He offered the unavoidable sacrifice that rescued us from an inevitable doom. We have no place to go but willingly out of our sins, and no place to come but joyfully into God's service.

REJECTION — has many faces
1 Samuel 8:7–8; 1 Peter 5:8

The Many Faces of Rejection

Andrea Darvi, at age seven, earned as much as $1,500 a week (in 1962) acting in numerous television shows. Seven years later her weekly salary had disappeared and studio executives would not return her calls—she had become outdated and unwanted. In a 1983 book she recalled the glory and deplored the rejection.

In December, 1993, The Jesus Seminar, a group of theologians and scholars, claimed that Jesus said only 18 percent of what the four Gospels claim for him. A year later they decided that Jesus was not born of a virgin. One felt that Mary was probably impregnated by a Roman soldier.

Such rejection is nothing new to Jesus. He found himself out of fashion with the Jews within two years. That unbelieving theologians would attack him is not surprising. Rejection of Christ even now takes at least one of the ten forms it took while he preached. The citizens of Chorazin and Capernaum rejected Christ through indifference; the Pharisees through blasphemy; the people of Gadara through fear; Pilate and Herod through politics; the Pharisees through traditional religion; the Capernaum crowd through carnality; the Athenians through intellectual pride; the Samaritans through prejudice, and the apparent disciple through procrastination. We can all find ways to dismiss him, for denial assumes many forms. Whether it is an indifference bordering on contempt, or an active opposition that seeks to slay him, even his devoted disciples can find a way to reject him.

REPENTANCE — stay free
Isaiah 58:6–7; Romans 6:1–2

More Would Mean Less

Comic strip character Andy Capp walks along, obviously tormented by dark thoughts. We learn it is his conscience. He has done something disgraceful even for him. On he walks, under a cloud of guilt. But, not to worry, he will always be a worthless layabout. For, in the final frame, he gloats that his conscience never kicks up a fuss until after he has had his fun.

Shades of us all! Like the Israelites, we easily become weepers after we sin; we dejectedly drag ourselves into penitent prayer; grief afflicts our conscience; self-accusation roars to life, lacerating our soul.

True repentance, however, demands resistance to further temptation! More resistance to sin automatically means less repentance. God is certainly as anxious to activate the Holy Spirit's power within us to overcome sin, as he is willing to exercise his grace forgiving us once we have fallen. Christ's overcoming life should be as real to us as his sacrificial death. As we laud his death for sin, we must strain to follow his resurrected life. He is as interested in creating his new life in us as in continually forgiving our old one.

REPETITION — of truth essential
Deuteronomy 6:7–9; Titus 3:1

Again and Again

Joseph Goebbels, the crippled Nazi propaganda genius, lied so easily he had to have received it from his mother's placenta. He did understand clearly the necessity of repeating whatever teaching you wanted people to believe. Furthermore, the same message had to take different forms to achieve maximum efficiency. Constant repetition in varying forms: this was his successful scheme to delude the German people.

American leaders have not succeeded as well. Polls showed that ignorance of basic geography was behind the opposition most Americans felt towards U.S. involvement in Central America. People had no idea where Nicaragua was, how close it was to our borders, or what nations surrounded it. They didn't even understand the difference between a Contra and a Sandanista.

How much more astonishing is humanity's spiritual illiteracy. Church members know so little about the Bible that cults easily prey on their ignorance. Well-fed sheep cannot be stolen; informed ones cannot be misled. Yet it is difficult to communicate truth to a generation that lacks a basic acceptance of truth.

REPUTATION — power of
1 Samuel 21:10–15; John 6:38

A Predictable Behavior

On Easter Sunday, April 16, 1865, Secretary of State William Seward lay physically crippled and emotionally shattered after being repeatedly stabbed by Lewis Paine. He had not yet heard of President Lincoln's death.

Wanting a better view of the trees that were just blooming, he asked to have his bed moved closer to the window. He looked through vagrant eyes at the signs of resurrection in the natural world—until he spied a flagstaff at the War Department. There he riveted his gaze. He stared, squinted, furrowed his brow and blinked away the tears. "The President is dead!" he suddenly exclaimed, his firm voice a mixture of unbelief and anguish. When the nurse tried to deny it, Seward insisted. "If he had been alive, he would have been the first to call on me. But he has not been here. Nor has he sent to know how I am. And there is the flag at half-mast." He said no more, but great tears rushed from his eyes and soaked the bandages that covered his gashes.

Jesus quickly established a predictable pattern of behavior that people came to expect and trust. He treated everyone equally. He always had time for children. He had an unappeased sympathy for any human need. He openly welcomed women as disciples. He always talked about God. He fearlessly expressed his independence of every authority except God's—an authority he not only claimed to obey, but to be!

REPUTATION — preceding one
Romans 1:8; 1 Thessalonians 1:7–8

No Doubt Who It Is

Dwight Moody regularly asked complete strangers about their spiritual life. One day he stopped a young man and asked, "Are you a Christian?"

"It is none of your business."

"Yes it is."

"Then you must be Dwight L. Moody."

What a splendid reputation to precede any Christian! What would others say of us if what we were best known for became public knowledge? If the letters of our life would form one word to describe us, what would it be? Better still, rather than describe ourselves, with what one word would others describe us? *Evangelistic* was the word that characterized Moody. What do we say, or do, that as quickly identifies us?

RESERVES — necessary
Joshua 1:2; John 7:15

In Reserve

Susan Butcher had won four Iditarods by the early 1990s, successfully overcoming the pulverizing thousand-mile dogsled race from Anchorage to Nome, Alaska. Among the reasons for her phenomenal success were her choice and number of sled dogs. She raised and ran only Alaskan huskies, bred to trot at twelve miles and to lope at eighteen miles an hour. Their padded feet reduce the accumulation of snowballs that cripple other dogs. The second reason was equally important. Even Alaskan huskies have different temperaments and constitutions, so she raised and trained with fifty dogs in order to have fifteen ready to go and thirty-five reserved for resupply.

The principle applies in any endeavor: we should always marshal personal resources beyond what we seek as our consistent peak performance. Without the reserve, life's natural deterioration will drag us below our consistency.

RESPONSIBILITY — individual
2 Kings 2:9, 13–15; 1 Timothy 4:12

Everybody Does It?

The underground economy in America thrives. At least $200 to $450 billion in income each year goes unreported to the IRS and, consequently, untaxed. One man began his deception in 1976, receiving $1,000 in unreported income. By 1983 he had pocketed another $5,000 the same way. A gnawing fear of discovery tormented him the first year, but saving $200 on his return encouraged him to perpetuate the lie until he saved at least $7,000 annually. He used the money to pay for his family's vacation and other personal possessions. It was a contribution to the national economy after all. He now feels a duty to keep the extra cash from the IRS. "I've never felt a pang of guilt," he said. "After all, everybody does it."

What complacent self-justification people use in cheating! To use "everybody does it" as an excuse for our personal misbehavior is one of the oldest, weakest means of justifying misbehavior—and it is a lie. Some may do it, many may do it, most may do it, but not everybody. God has seven thousand stalwart disciples in every lying age, in every lying crisis, in every lying situation who do not and will not do it.

RESURRECTION — Christ's own our hope
Exodus 12:10; Matthew 28:2–4

He Also Came Back

Ocean journeys by Polynesian, Chinese, and Viking seamen proved that ancient mariners could successfully sail long distances without sighting land. Most ancient sailors, however, kept land in sight to assure their ability to return to it. Since a return was always essential to the success of an enterprise, as well as the enrichment of its sponsors, the sailors chose the safe course.

Before Christ, millions had experienced death. They all left, but none came back. What it was like out there, beyond life and human experience, no one ever returned to say. The world stood awestruck before the mystery behind the veil. The Jesus came . . . though at first disappointingly, for he died like all the rest. But death couldn't contain, let alone conquer him. He surrendered to death's power to victimize it. Into its stifling depths he went to free all trapped inside their fears of it. From death's grip he freed himself, and up from the grave he arose, exposing its emptiness and proving his victory over it!

REVENGE — growth of
Exodus 21:24; Romans 12:17–21

Overkill

A man took it personally when the IRS refused to refund his fourteen dollars. He decided to get even. He began to make and plant bombs near IRS offices in several local counties. At first his inexperience kept the damages to a minimum. The bombs either malfunctioned or were too weak to cause harm. But it soon became obvious that the bomber had increased in his expertise and rage, for he planted devices to kill people, not just to damage buildings.

On February 22, 1990, when the bomb disposal team got a call about a suspicious pickup parked in downtown Los Angeles, they found that the bomber had planted four hundred pounds of explosives in each of five, fifty-five gallon drums. The detonation would have blown a crater seventy-five feet wide and twenty-five feet deep, and broken windows in the fifth floor offices.

Revenge grows like a rumor—from a small desire . . . to a large need . . . to a bloated obsession. The Law of Moses limited revenge, and Jesus Christ abolished it. Restricted revenge served a useful purpose under the Law, but revenge of any kind is unacceptable where grace reigns. Indeed, beyond not seeking revenge, Christians are to pray for their offenders and do them so much good that it will be like coals of fire melting their opposition. God will avenge us if that becomes necessary. What is necessary for us is to be gracious to the offender.

RUMOR — as basis of fact
Genesis 1:1; John 1:19–21

It Couldn't Be

The Japanese High Command in 1941 planned their Pearl Harbor attack in leak-proof secrecy. No one knows who conveyed the plan, but within a mere twenty days after Admiral Yamamoto developed it, the Peruvian Ambassador to Tokyo had the information in hand. He sent word of it to Joseph Grew, the American Ambassador. Grew read it, noted where he received it, and forwarded it to Washington. State Department authorities read, discussed, and denigrated it. To each other they openly wondered how a man of Grew's qualifications could take such a rumor seriously.

When Jewish authorities in Jerusalem heard rumors of a man who might be the Messiah, they lost no time sending a delegation to interrogate him. The man admitted his prophetic role, but dissuaded them of the rumor. If they wanted to see the Christ, they would have to look elsewhere. Interestingly, another delegate came one night from the same leadership to another man. His first statement to the young preacher offered a compliment and posed a question. We know you are from God . . . but exactly who are you?

With both John the Baptist and Jesus at work in Israel, messianic rumors flourished. Once John died, Christ became the focus of all speculation. It never ended; it hasn't to this day. Exactly who is Jesus? We must each answer for ourselves; and on our answer hangs our eternal fate. For make no mistake—Jesus is not a rumor; he is real!

SACRIFICE — keeps returning good
Numbers 12:1–2; Ephesians 3:20–21

Always Returned More

When President Ulysses S. Grant reached the end of his second term in office, he reminisced about cost and gain in public service. He would, by some philanthropy, thank the American people for the honors they had given him. But he had found that any sacrifice brought an equivalent, or greater, reward. Every "contribution turned out to be an additional reward," he said.

So declares the Christian of life in God's Son. We are always able to discern the difference between cost and benefit. We know that, like advertising, discipleship doesn't cost; it pays. Sometimes, however, God's treasure comes in chests loaded with rocks, not rubies. Would we have served God for a lifetime just to catch a glimpse of a tiny infant? Simeon and Anna did, and soared into ecstasy when they saw the God-child in their arms. Would we exchange honor from the people we plundered for mistreatment by the people we enriched? Moses did, and his glory at the Transfiguration was excelled only by Christ's. Would we trade a place of honor in the nation's recognized religion for a steady habit of shipwrecks, hunger, danger, and sleeplessness in what they called a sect? Paul did, and appearing before Agrippa, regretted only that everyone could not have known Jesus Christ as he!

SALVATION — accept it late
Joshua 14:6–12; Acts 23:6

Never Too Late

One hundred twenty-eight people, from twenty-nine different countries took the oath of allegiance to the United States. Having done so, the judge granted them citizenship. Two of those inducted, Henry and Rose Konstat, had waited for that moment for more than forty years. He left Poland after World War I and emigrated to Mexico because Polish quotas in the United States here were full at the time. Once in Mexico he applied for an American visa. While there, he met Rose, who had been born in Philadelphia but moved to Mexico City as a child. When they married, she lost her U.S. citizenship.

Henry built a profitable textile business in Mexico City, but continued to long for U.S. citizenship. After retirement he decided to apply for a visa. It was approved in 1976, and they moved to San Diego. They immediately applied for citizenship, then waited the mandatory five years. The big day came in December, 1983. At long last they had become American citizens.

It is never too late if we want to pursue a goal. No one can plead old age as an excuse for not changing, not learning a new habit, or not becoming a Christian. We still eat in old age, and sleep, and think. Why can't we change habits in our senior years? If increasing age had been an excuse for inaction, the Konstats would still be in Mexico.

SALVATION — accept while offered
1 Samuel 28:16–19; 2 Corinthians 6:2

Salvation at Present

Government annuities to the Indian tribes in the nineteenth century were ordinarily paid in June. Usually late, the tribes patiently waited their arrival. But in 1862 the money—$71,000 in gold coin—did not arrive at the Indian Agency in Minnesota until August 18. Just the day before, four hungry Indians had stolen eggs from a farmer, who killed them in retaliation. This led to reprisals from the tribes and to the great Sioux uprising, which resulted in the deaths of over seven hundred whites and forty-six Indians before the uprising was quelled. The time for peace had come and gone—by only one day.

So many people plan to accept Christ sometime, but not yet. They intend to later, but not now. Maybe when they are sure where they will settle down, or when vacation is over, or a new job begins, or the new house is purchased. Many promise to do it at Easter or Christmas. How casually we promise God the future—which isn't ours to give—and selfishly keep the present—which is all we have to give. How many have intended to accept Christ at such and such a time, only to have others weeping over their death before that time!

SALVATION — action required
Psalm 122:1; 2 Corinthians 5:28

Execute!

Through a series of tactical blunders in September, 1863, General William Rosecrans forfeited the gains his brilliant flanking movements had brought the Union in July and August. He suddenly found his starving army invested in Chattanooga, with the closest supply depot sixty miles through the mountains of east Tennessee. Cashiered for his failure, Rosecrans went north and met the south-bound Grant at Stevenson, Alabama. Rosecrans apprised Grant of the desperate situation and gave detailed, excellent plans to rectify it. Grant's only wonder, he wrote in an account of the siege, "was that he had not carried them out."

The best ideas are only as good as their persistent application; a project only as good as its execution! Nowhere is this more important than in becoming a Christian. Many know the steps to salvation, but have not taken them. They know that being close to Christ is different from being in Christ, yet they stay outside.

We should come to God, because nothing is worse than staying away. Come reluctantly, if you won't come willingly. Come with doubts, if you can't come in full faith. Come in a crisis, if you won't come in good times. Come from fear, if you won't come from love. Whatever, come to God.

SALVATION — almost not enough
1 Kings 13:20–22; Acts 24:25

Almost Isn't Enough

George Barber worked two years as a security officer at a local hotel. At 2:00 A.M. that morning he was going to quit to become supervisor in a security company. At midnight, as he roamed the buildings and grounds of the vast complex, he encountered a suspicious vehicle on the third-floor parking lot. Suddenly, his call for assistance crackled over the security office radio, then . . . gunshots. Officers rushed to help and found him lying on the pavement, several gunshots in his chest and shoulder. Six bullet holes in the door of an abandoned car offered mute testimony that he had gone down only after trading shots with his assailant.

After ten years as a city policeman and two years at the hotel, one hundred twenty minutes before he would have left his job—George Barber was dead! Life shouldn't happen that way. When you get that close you should be able to finish your term, your job, your plans. But not in this case; and, sad to say, not in many cases.

Many people get close to God's kingdom, but not in. They are almost, but not quite, convinced. They nearly accept Christ, but never do. However near they come, they fall short. Whatever effort they make to gain entrance, they remain outside grace. What an imponderable disaster for those who nearly or almost become Christians—for close doesn't count. Near is not in.

SALVATION — everyone needs
Numbers 16:28–34; Matthew 25:21, 23, 28

No Favoritism

By 1986, 92,921 former Nazis had been prosecuted in West Germany for crimes against humanity. In East Germany, by that same time, 12,861 had been sentenced. Obviously, the former Nazis in East Germany had become too valuable to the Soviet Union to be prosecuted.

Mastery of the environment and incredible engineering breakthroughs highlight civilization wherever you open the door on history. Yet boasting of significant achievements blinds us to our monstrous failures in morality and our helplessness before our mortality. Indeed, what should hasten humility all too often breeds a roaring arrogance—despite God's repeated, adamant warnings not to trust ourselves for what he entrusts only to himself—the conquest of sin, death and judgment. Spiritual insubordination activated our fall from grace; only unconditional surrender to God can activate our restoration.

SATAN — power of deception
Deuteronomy 4:2; Matthew 4:6

Twisting His Words

Jeane Kirkpatrick, then U.S. Ambassador to the United Nations, blasted the Soviet Union as "master falsifiers," determined to interpret words to their own advantage. They debased language by redefining all the key terms in our political vocabularies. Peace to almost everyone meant a chance to live without war; to the Soviets it meant a world dominated by communism. Freedom to us meant the right to choose; to the Soviets the right to dominate all under their rule. Mrs. Kirkpatrick also accused the Soviets of continuing their dialectic deception by attributing to America precisely the qualities displayed in their own behavior—repression, lies, and imperialism.

Genesis 3:4 was the source of the Soviet's criminality. There the master deceiver changed but one word God spoke and completely altered the meaning! Satan follows the same procedure throughout history. He attributes to God a callous hatred for humanity, a desire to hurt and destroy, deceit, and untruth. Then he assumes for himself all the virtues only God possesses—beauty, compassion, eternality.

SATAN — uses the pleasant
Judges 19:12–13; 2 Corinthians 2:10–11

Sin Isn't Particular

A man and his wife customarily soaked in their mountaintop hot tub, relishing the lights, freeways, and canyons of the great city below. Then the man fell victim to a rare parasite that thrives in hot tubs. It resists chlorine and lives on the bacteria present in warm water. It also damages eyes—the man lost sight of his left eye—and can be fatal.

California offers agricultural germs and parasites a buffet of possibilities. That is why officials expressed concern that world athletes coming to Los Angeles for the 1984 Summer Olympics might unknowingly host varmints in their suitcases or clothes. After all, the 1981 Mediterranean fruit fly infestation is thought to have begun with one fly from Hawaii.

Sin is like that. It uses even the good, ordinarily harmless thing to gain entrance into our lives, where it corrupts completely. Satan isn't particular how he penetrates our lives. He uses the sex drive to prompt fornication or adultery.

He infiltrates our need of self-esteem to turn us into egomaniacs. He distorts our love of victory into soul-destroying ambition. Satan knows that all misdirected good can become an instrument of evil, and he knows that his easiest victims are those who think they are safe.

SCIENCE — not always exact
Psalm 24:1–2; Matthew 19:4

In Everyday Details

In 1964, a new volcano erupted into existence off Iceland's southern coast. Volcanologists called it Surtsey. By 1967, nearly a square mile had emerged from the sea. Surtsey surprised scientists in important details. It was the first time they had seen the formation of a submarine island. Following their uniformitarian theories, they figured it would take thousands of years for the volcanic ash to harden into rock. They were wrong. New minerals quickly fused the particles of ash, hardening and forming rock within a few years.

It was also their first time to study how life colonizes a completely sterile environment. Biologists believed that lichens would be the first plants on the island, followed by mosses, then higher plants (same evolutionary theories in place). Again, they were wrong; the opposite happened. In 1965, Surtsey's second summer of existence, a sea rocket was found, apparently sprouted from a seaborne seed. Birds came even during the eruptions, warming their feet on the hot rocks. Cliff dwelling fulmars and guillemots were the first to nest on the island in 1970, soon followed by kittiwakes and black-backed and herring gulls.

Scientists wrong? Biologists wrong? Yes, in such everyday factors. Since they didn't get right something so familiar to them, why should we trust them to verify the origins of the worlds? Only the One there at the genesis of life can offer that information.

SCIENCE — opportunity for gospel
Isaiah 55:9–11; 1 Corinthians 3:5–9

A Matter of Time

Jesuit priest Matteo Ricci went to China in 1578 hoping to establish a Catholic mission. He made a good first impression by offering the Emperor a clock. (The Chinese loved western clocks.) Little came thereafter of his endeavors. As the court busied itself with politics, Ricci stayed, taught where he could, and waited his opportunity. It finally came in 1629, when Chinese astronomers mistakenly forecast an eclipse of the sun for two hours on June 21, beginning at 10:30 A.M. The Jesuits knew it would occur at 11:30 A.M. and last for two minutes. The dispute became public, and everyone anxiously awaited the outcome. When the churchmen were proved right, and the astronomers wrong, the Emperor welcomed the westerners to his court.

Mission fields are often so resistant to the gospel that a huge deficit occurs between expenditure of effort, time, money, and converts. God's servants must then be patient, sow seed where they can, cultivate however they can, and pray for an increase. It took fifty-one years for Matteo Ricci's breakthrough. He obviously had been preparing in the interim. God's Word will be fruitful to its intended purpose, but in his, not our, time. God's servants must remain faithful in their work even when few successes accrue. It takes time for an acorn to grow into an oak.

SCIENCE — possible through belief in orderly God
Isaiah 40:22; 1 Corinthians 1:27–29

Because God Is

Non-Christian scientists Whitehead and Oppenheimer rightly said that the earliest scientists—Galileo, Newton, Farrady, Copernicus—could be scientific because they believed in an ordered system of a sovereign, orderly God. "Men became scientific because they expected Law in Nature," C. S. Lewis wrote, "and they expected Law in nature because they believed in a Legislator."

Humanistic scientists accept the validity of the early scientists' faith in an orderly system, based on an orderly God, but personally reject that God, preferring to see life as the result of blind, mechanistic, indiscriminate chance. How inexcusably inconsistent! Unbelieving scientists study creation as if God exists, but personally live as if he doesn't. Since they personally refuse God's existence, how can they explain an orderly universe based on chance?

SECRETS — keeping
Isaiah 45:3; 2 Corinthians 5:5

No One Knew

After the German battleship *Bismarck* sank the *HMS Hood* on May 24, 1941, she disappeared into the Atlantic Ocean. For three days she eluded British search planes. Then the *Modoc,* a United States Coast Guard cutter, spotted her in the Bay of Biscay. The British dispatched a plane, piloted by a United States Navy pilot, to sight and radio Bismarck's position. This led to the sinking of the great ship. The role played by the Americans, even then Britain's neutral ally, was kept secret for thirty years.

God has arranged for allies to stand by his people so they can constantly be assured of spiritual aid. The creation is our ally: it encourages us by longing for our redemption. Christian experience is an ally: our suffering sharpens our desire to have Christ return so we can be redeemed. The Holy Spirit is our ally: he helps us pray, and when prayer is beyond our ability, he prays for us to God. In the darkest times or in our greatest joys, when words fail, even then we are in touch with God!

SECURITY — breached
Deuteronomy 4:19; 1 Corinthians 5:9–11

Doing Other Things

The defecting Cuban pilot, flying his MIG-21 fighter, not only had to outwit Cuban reconnaissance to escape but had to alert American authorities of his intentions. He had little trouble eluding the Cuban watchdogs, and had even less flying into American air space. He slipped into Florida completely undetected, because the only working radar blimp in the Florida Keys was busy transmitting television programs to Cuba. Air Force officials in Colorado Springs, Colorado, quickly explained that the jet avoided radar by flying 518 miles per hour at fifty feet. However, after a similar defection in 1991, the Air Force installed a radar system in the Keys designed to detect such low-flying aircraft.

Hmm! Next explanation?

God's people have not been too careful about keeping Satan out of their churches. Many Bible-believing Christians attend churches where God's existence is openly disputed or subtly questioned; and where the Gospels and New Testament writings are considered the creation of men, not the revelation of the Holy Spirit. Who is standing guard against falsehood? Immorality among the members weakens the church's witness. Won't anyone stand in the breach for God's holiness? Human nature being what it is, and Satan's deceptions so clever, doesn't the kingdom of God need an internal affairs department, manned by the chosen congregational leaders, to keep watch over people's souls?

SELF — can consume us
Genesis 4:23–24; Philippians 2:3; James 3:14

Never Secure Enough

Sugar Ray Leonard won an Olympic gold medal in Montreal in 1976, then won the junior middleweight and welterweight titles in professional boxing. His record stood at 32-1, and that loss he avenged in his famous 1980 bout with Roberto Duran. Then he quit in 1982. When he returned to boxing a year later, he explained that his previous success had been insufficient. He was only twenty-seven, in his prime, and he wanted to assure his place in boxing history. He wanted no one to question that he was the best in his era.

The appetite for rule, competition, or power distends as it is fed; it increases with its achievement; it needs continual nourishment to be satisfied. Sugar Ray wasn't the first or last boxer, sports figure, corporate executive, or political leader to fall prey to personal ambitions. The flesh originates and gorges on these cravings. It always feels the need to climb one step higher in the corporation, fight one more fight, make one more deal, rule one more country. Then, flesh assures itself, it will be secure in history, have enough money, or sufficient power.

Wrong! If we cannot find security in what we presently are, we will never find it in what we might become. We will find, after sacrificing time, talent, family, and life in pursuit of our added goals, that they are mirages just beyond our next victory, goal, or success. They are shooting stars, incinerating themselves even as we reach for them.

SELF — looking after
Daniel 4:29–30; Acts 9:36–41

Looking Out for Self

When, in June 1544, Philip the Prudent sailed to wed Mary Tudor in England, his father ordered him to go with a "minimum of display." So he took only 9,000 nobles and servants, 1,000 horses and mules, three million ducats in gold, and a mere 125 ships. Carl Graham Fisher, the first successful promoter of Miami Beach, once sold a plot of land for $86,000. He wired the money to his wife in Paris. In four hours she had "invested" the entire amount in jewelry. W. W. Halstead, an early physician at John Hopkins Hospital in Baltimore, had expensive tastes in clothing and laundry. He bought suits only from London clothiers and dress shirts from Paris, then he sent his shirts back to Paris to have them laundered.

Ostentation, self-extravagance, indulgent pretense! It is amazing how many ways we find to exalt self. Whether we have the means of Philip the Prudent, or of Graham Fisher's wife, or of Dr. Halstead, we certainly find self-aggrandizement natural and self-denial exasperating. Christians need not dress in burlap and go barefoot to prove they are not materialists. They should, however, be recognized for modesty in dress and generosity in charity, not vice versa. Beyond the tithe we owe to God is the mercy we owe to those less fortunate or in great need. The love that cost Christ everything should cost us something.

SELF — problem between God and us
Jeremiah 31:3; Acts 13:46; 14:1

Still We Reject It

Imperial Beach, California opened the second week of February, 1984, after being closed since the latter months of 1983. It opened in spring of 1994 after being closed the winter of 1993. The problem: sewage that poured down the Tijuana River valley from Mexico and washed ashore in California. Federal officials twice offered to have United States crews fix the broken Tijuana sewers, but the Mexican government refused. When a city councilman said that he could send a crackerjack crew and fix it in a few days, Mexican officials irately criticized our interference in their personal affairs.

Humanity's problem with sin is like Mexico's with sewage. By ourselves we cannot overcome the injustices, hatreds, and wars that plague us. Yet all the while, God offers his help in correcting the situation, promising to do the job quickly because he has a "crackerjack" who is all-wise, all-sufficient, all-capable. We continue to reject his offer, however, because we would rather fix the troubles ourselves—proving that our pride grows even as our ponderous bungling expands. We are determined to prove our capability even as we prove our incompetence. All we prove is that no matter how incapable we are, we are far more stubborn still; that whatever failure we have, we will never consult and request God's help.

SERVICE — render when possible
Jeremiah 5:30–31; 2 Corinthians 5:20

To Be Unable

The desperate shriek *mayday! mayday!* pierced the headset of a Trans-America captain flying his cargo jet over South Carolina. He immediately relayed the information to Myrtle Air Force Base. A few minutes later a Piedmont Airlines captain reported hearing a frantic female garbling a message about the pilot being unconscious, someone trying to fly the plane, and no one knowing what to do. The pilots urged the small plane to stand by on that frequency so they could communicate. They urged the people to turn on the plane's transponder, an automatic signaling device that can be used to locate an aircraft. They encouraged them to retain their altitude.

The only response was indecipherable, confused hysteria. For twenty agonizing minutes ground trackers and pilots tried desperately to establish communication, hoping to locate the plane, to calm the victims, and to offer guidance. Nothing! The craft plunged vertically to earth in a field about twenty miles from Myrtle Beach, killing all four aboard and ploughing a hole three to four feet wide.

While time exists, and while our efforts can make a difference, Christians must give themselves to their Master's service. Life is too short for anything but God's work. Eternity is too long to live with anyone but God. While we have the time, let's teach and live the spectacular and substantial realities of God in Christ. While we have time; before it is too late and the end comes!

SILENCE — not always best
Zechariah 2:13; Revelation 8:1

The Need for Life

The radio and public loudspeakers broadcast music, poetry, and news items to Leningraders during the horrific winter of 1941–1942. When the musicians grew too weak to perform, the state played the dull, monotonous sounds of a metronome—anything to give people hope. When the metronome once fell silent, people shuddered in dismay at the quiet. To their immense relief it started again after three hours. Any sound—even the stupefying tick of a metronome—any sound rather than silence, for silence meant death.

Silence can be a blessing in one context and a curse in another. We can sit with a loved one in silence all evening, every moment a feeling of security. But if a loved one lies in a coma, or is recovering from surgery, the silence can be terrifying.

God's child can value the silences he experiences. There is a silence of inquiry, when we read God's Word and let it saturate our soul. There is a silence of faith, with our heart suddenly unburdened of incarcerating fears. There is a silence of introspection, when we mentally interrogate our motives and goals in the light of Christ's expectations. There is a silence of intensity, when a worship leader directs our prayer thoughts, focusing them like lasers. There is a silence of awe, when we struggle to comprehend God's majesty, Christ's love, and the Spirit's gentle counsel. What a joy to be still and know that he is God!

SIN — abolish
1 Kings 9:16; 11:1; James 1:13–15

Dash It Out

George Keenan served as adviser to U.S. diplomats and ambassadors to Russia from the 1930s to the 1950s, then as ambassador to Russia in the 1950s. His writings on Soviet aims and ideals were widely accepted. He became noted for advocating containment of Communism, meaning that wherever it appeared, the democracies would counteract it. Containment didn't work well against communism; it died under the weight of its own inadequacies.

Containment never works in the spiritual life. Either we conquer Satan or he conquers us. If we attempt accommodation, Satan wins. We fail to understand that he has more willpower than we, and that he has far more openings into our lives to develop than he ever exploits. The only answer to evil is annihilation. It must be obliterated, because the alternative is its horrendous growth, our gradual acceptance of its presence, and our eventual downfall. The best time to get rid of sin is *now*.

SIN — always fatal
Ezekiel 33:10–11; John 17:12

Always Fatal

The average person's fat carries fifteen to twenty parts DDT per billion. One Alabama man's body fat contained 2,300 parts DDT per billion, one of the highest concentrations ever recorded; second only to a man whose tests ran 3,100 parts per billion. The two tested lived many years.

Germs and carcinogens are strange, unstable, inexplicable powers. We can't understand why some kill that shouldn't, and others don't that should. When Robert Koch, the great German scientist, stated that bacteria caused disease, including cholera, others in his profession scoffed. One dared Koch to send him some of his so-called cholera germs. Koch did, and the man drank the entire vial. Millions of cholera germs lurked in that little tube, but the man did not catch the deadly disease. Others, however, who accidentally swallowed small doses of the virulent microbes, died horribly. We cannot yet account for the fact that highly fatal germs invade our bodies daily, yet only some people are harmed, not all. It is assassination at random, not by design.

Diseases and germs aren't always fatal, but Satan is! One hundred percent of the time! Sin always pays in death. The soul that sins dies every time—you can count on it. Sin never ends in anything but destruction of the soul. It is a 100 percent deadly force, destroying 100 percent of the time, 100 percent of the people who remain unforgiven.

SIN — always wrong
Jeremiah 6:16–17; Luke 16:15

That Doesn't Make It Right

A psychologist in Los Angeles conducted weekly seminars for women who had experienced—or were considering—extra-marital affairs. The purpose of the seminar was: (1) to develop covering-excuses that a husband couldn't check, (2) to resist the temptation to confess the infidelities, (3) to carefully choose the partner in the affair, and (4) to enjoy the relationship without feelings of guilt. The last point was particularly important to those involved. One lady confessed that her guilt had nearly ruined her mental health. After the seminar she felt nearly guilt-less, because she too had a "right to happiness."

Strange, to what absurd lengths people will go to encourage sin; and, equally strange, what explanations others will embrace to justify it. As if educating a person in the art of adultery makes it right; as if soothing the conscience eliminates the guilt. You can always make sin palatable, but you can never make it right! You can profit from it financially, but never spiritually. You might even make it guiltless in the person, but not without penalty. The concept of right and wrong comes from God, not from us, and no psychologist or seminar will ever displace God's eternal Word.

SIN — ban it
Deuteronomy 31:16–18; Galatians 5:19–21

Giving Sin an Education

A study by the Alan Guttmacher Institute not surprisingly suggested that teenage pregnancy in the United States could be reduced if sex education and contraceptives were offered to young girls. It cited statistics of ninety-six pregnancies in every thousand female teenagers in the United States, compared to forty-five in one thousand in England, forty-four in one thousand in Canada, and fourteen in one thousand in the Netherlands. The Institute felt that information and prophylactics would stem the rising tide of pregnancies and abortions here.

A striking omission characterized the study: the refusal of governments to take any responsibility in discouraging sex among teens. They see their duty only as addressing the problem of child bearing. They feel that parents, churches, and teens should relate to questions of the sex act itself. But who says government has a voice in any of the matter? How can bureaucrats casually define the role they will play? By refusing to stress morality, don't they become quiescent partners to immorality? Politicians say they cannot legislate morality, yet they do it all the time. Saloons cannot be open past a certain hour in most states, drunk drivers are under increasingly oppressive legal action, and vice squads regularly raid brothels and suspected drug labs. How convenient to insist that government has a right to regulate some sins—and not others!

SIN — hiding it
Genesis 34:31; 1 Corinthians 5:1–2

Sinning and Getting Paid for It

In Tulsa, Oklahoma, a woman won a $390,000 award from a church, claiming invasion of her privacy and consequent emotional stress when the church ordered her membership voided because of an adulterous lifestyle. In San Jose, California, a man who was excommunicated by his church after confidential details of his marriage and sex life became public, sued the church and a family counselor for $5 million. He claimed breach of confidence that destroyed his marriage, strained relations with his children, and threatened social and business ostracism by friends and clients in the church.

Both suits portend difficulty for churches and raise disturbing questions. First, if government says that churches cannot get into public schools, how can the government get into the churches? Second, do people who claim to be Christians have a legal right to sin and expect their church to tolerate it, and the government to defend them and see that they get paid for any exposure of it? Churches have been notoriously slow to discipline any of their offending members. With a possible lawsuit for such an effort now looming on the horizon, will any church have the nerve to break fellowship with the sexually immoral?

SIN — condemn ourselves
Psalm 51:16–17; Hebrews 2:17–18

The Disease Ourselves

Critics have subjected Sigmund Freud to some withering broadsides. Freudian scholars willing to critique his theories and personal life find a rich source of inflammatory information. Accusations against Freud's impregnating his sister-in-law, then having her child aborted, and his murder of a best friend provide merely the opening statement of a long indictment. Freud himself admitted, in letters to a friend, that some of the treatments he had given patients led to their deaths, through the use of cocaine and sexual, hypnotic drugs.

Whatever the truth or fantasy of the accusations, there is little doubt that some of the Freud family members were prime candidates for analysis. They, and certainly Freud, had difficulty identifying reality and separating fact from fiction. He viewed people as basically sexual beings—a fatal delusion since we are basically spiritual beings. He missed the essential factor in undisciplined sexuality: sexuality advances as the spiritual nature recedes.

Efforts such as Freud's to solve human problems are doomed to failure for one reason, if no other: we all have the disease we are trying to cure. There is only one who can help us, for he overcame the disease—Christ our Savior.

SIN — continually reconquered
Jeremiah 34:17; 1 Peter 5:8

Continually Fought

In 1976, with border violence in epidemic proportions, the San Diego Police Department organized an undercover detail to counter it. Of Hispanic descent, the men dressed as aliens and walked the desolate canyons at night. Acting as decoys, they hoped to attract attention from thugs who preyed on helpless aliens as they crossed into the United States. In eighteen months the squad made many arrests, shot suspects, and were shot in return.

To no one's surprise, in the next six years border crime increased. So back to the border the police went, this time openly and in uniform, not in disguise or undercover stealth. Rather than walking the canyons as potential targets, they actively patrolled in vehicles as enforcement officials.

The battle against crime is never won. Neither is the spiritual war over our souls. There may be occasions when we fight and win—titanic battles that decide the war—but even those battles must be defended. We have to repeatedly win our victory against Satan. He never reaches a point of collapse; he always has the ability to regroup and strike again. Like the border criminals, he is always alert for opportunities to raid our lives, then fade away into the wilds of life. If we remember that spiritual victories are never final, we will not be surprised by Satan's sudden attacks.

SIN — dangerous when small
Joshua 9:14; James 4:7

Just a Small Sin

Toddling about his grandparent's home, a small boy discovered a bottle of lye and swallowed a single mouthful. Nine years later, after numerous surgeries, his digestive tract could function once again. Nearly nine years of restorative and reconstructive surgery were necessary to compensate for a small mouthful of lye.

And we think small sins are harmless? That no one needs to worry over "insignificant" wrongs? It was only a mouthful of lye! But it was enough to endanger his life and bring years of misery to him and his family. Even the smallest wrong can be destructive.

SIN — hard to surrender
Jeremiah 2:25; Galatians 6:7–8

Many Won't Accept

Fires in the coal-rich veins under Centralia, Pennsylvania, finally forced the residents to consider relocating to another area. Some decided to leave though it meant surrendering lifelong possessions and memories. Others couldn't bring themselves to make the break. It was the only home they had known, and they couldn't imagine life without it. Really, there was no choice. Fires continued to burn uncontrolled, flinging smoke, gases, and dirt into the air. Twice, the flames had broken through the surface and buckled the only highway into town.

Spiritually, many have difficulty surrendering old, discredited, useless ways! God's offer of new life in Christ—the chance to start again, without the hardships, guilt, and emptiness of the past—is readily refused. Why would anyone reject God's offer of forgiveness? Why do they hang on to what they have had, useless as it is? God offers a whole new life, with all the resources to enjoy it. How much he values us to care for us when we prefer our lust to his love, our evil to his forgiveness, and our ego to his presence.

SIN — massively afflicts
Genesis 9:12–13, 24–25; Romans 1:26–27

A Long Time Before

In 1968, a young man suffering from several illnesses came to a clinic in St. Louis. He had swollen lymph nodes and swelling in his legs and genitalia. The doctors had no clue to his condition. He admitted to being sexually active, but denied being gay, though evidence indicated otherwise. Despite fifteen months of treatment, he died of bronchial pneumonia. Tissue samples from his body were frozen for later study, and in 1987 a virologist at Tulane University analyzed the tissue and found it positive for AIDS.

Many doctors think that the AIDS virus appeared at least once, perhaps twice or more, in society before invading the general population. The virus was present in American society over a decade before it became a lethal threat. It was not a threat earlier because there was no appropriate sexually active population to transmit it. Heterosexual intercourse was not the vehicle, or it would have reached epidemic proportions almost immediately. No, it needed the freewheeling male homosexuality of the 1970s, when homosexuals openly practiced their sexual preferences. Bathhouses offered the freedom to engage in orgies of homosexual behavior. One man claimed to have up to seventy partners in a single week. But even some gays saw the inherent danger in that uncontrolled sodomy and demanded restraints. In an act that shamed other cities for their reluctance, San Francisco gays closed their bathhouses to prevent the spread of the disease.

SIN — swindles
Proverbs 5:3–6; Romans 6:23

Not in the End

Several years ago, investors in a West Coast mortgage firm received 18.5 percent return on their money. When the firm went bankrupt, fifty of the investors retrieved all the funds invested. The rest hoped to get ten cents on the dollar. The case took an unusual turn when a lawyer for the mortgage firm sued the investors who had withdrawn their money, accusing them of abusing usury laws. Strange indeed. The firm that enticed investors with promises of quick, high returns sued those investors lucky enough to regain their money before it collapsed.

A madam (later arrested for organizing a prostitution ring) assured all willing hookers of at least $3,000 a month from their work. But would any self-respecting woman want to prostitute her body for that, or any amount of money? A police sting operation in 1983 recovered nearly $24 million in stolen property—but what decent human being would sell his soul to be a fence for thieves? A drug dealer who made huge profits from his illicit traffic was arrested. At his home, police found eight vehicles, a diamond-studded bracelet, and the deed to a lot worth $50,000. Want to join him in prison?

Living in sin can pay handsomely in the freedom imagined, the money to spend, the unlimited opportunities—but it is never profitable in the end. Whatever profit Satan offers is an illusion, for he pays in counterfeit bills.

SIN — unforgiven punished
Numbers 32:23; Romans 2:9–10

No Exceptions

The son of a famous American was arrested for driving under the influence of alcohol. He pleaded guilty to reckless driving, a plea bargain that saw the drunk driving charge dropped. Two policemen, one an eighteen-year veteran and former vice detective, were arrested for using an escort service as a prostitution ring. They pleaded guilty only to obstructing justice, a result of plea bargaining that saw the more serious charges dropped. It is amazing what serious violations of the law can be overlooked in the prosecution of lawbreakers. What is an affront to even a primitive sense of justice—allowing felons to plead guilty to lesser charges—mocks the entire judicial process.

No plea bargain can be made with unforgiven sin. It is never forgotten, minimized, or excused, and no allowances will be given for position, fame, or wealth. With the Judge that none can corrupt or impress, all unforgiven sins will be punished. Those who refuse to surrender their sins will pay a penalty. That is the threat of the cross when its forgiveness is refused.

SLEEP — getting tired enough
1 Kings 19:5–6; Matthew 26:41

The Urge to Nod

A Lieutenant in World War II got so tired he went to sleep while talking on a field telephone—not when he was listening, but in the middle of his sentence! A professor told a class he once got so tired he nodded off while he lectured. Dozing is not uncommon in American courtrooms, among judges, attorneys, lawyers, bailiffs, court clerks, jurors, and clients! Often without windows, poorly lighted and deprived of necessary oxygen, the courtrooms offer tired, tense, and sometimes bored participants an irresistible invitation to nod. A court clerk was surprised to find the judge furiously scribbling on notepads during closing arguments. She laughed later when she looked at the message: "Don't go to sleep, don't go to sleep! Don't go to sleep, do NOT go to sleep!"

The Master understood the need to sleep. Exhausted the night the disciples sailed across the Sea of Galilee, he would have slept through the gale and its dangers if the disciples had not awakened him with terror in their eyes. But in the greatest crisis of his life he mastered the urge to sleep by his greater need to pray. Knowing that spiritual disaster loomed, he prayed through it to success. The disciples, far less tired than he, but unaware of spiritual disaster, slept through it to their disgrace. How thankful we are that Jesus prayed through to victory.

SPIRITUAL LIFE — real, if different
Deuteronomy 3:23; Acts 17:32

A Different Life

Coronado's men explored the Great Plains from the south. Zebulon Pike explored them from the east. They all labeled those millions of acres "The Great American Desert." It was an illusion, of course, for they seethed and swarmed with a staggering multiplicity of life. Numerous grasses sustained fifty million buffalo and millions of other wild creatures, and nomadic peoples lived well on the limitless vistas. The critics did not comprehend what they were seeing.

Likewise, the secular mind cannot comprehend the Spirit-filled life. It sees faith as a compensatory hallucination of those who are unwilling to compete in life. How poorly the Christian life is understood, especially its two greatest implications: forgiveness and eternal life. In Christ, all faith is credited to and no sin is charged against our account. When life is over, an eternal life of activity in ceaseless rest begins, of labor in ceaseless ease.

STRENGTH — how to achieve
Joshua 10:24–25; Ephesians 6:10–18

Who Would Pay It?

Some of the Alta Indians of California made themselves "invincible" to arrows by being whipped with nettles until they couldn't walk. Carried to the hills, they were laid on ant hills and left to the mercy of the insects. The bystanders stirred the ant colony to make their attacks more vicious. The warriors endured this torment because they felt it enabled them to resist enemy arrows.

To withstand Satan's attacks, we equip our soul with the armor God provides. He outfits us completely for our task. Having every weapon and piece of armor available, God orders us to stand and contest the evil one. Satan counts on us to be afraid—Jesus counts on us to have courage.

STRESS — antidote for
Psalm 22:9; Matthew 23:15

To Overcome and Recover

"I want you to do nothing and do it slowly," a physician once told a patient suffering from stress. Appropriate advice and worth following! In American society, however, being idle is often interpreted as laziness; a lack of ambition or initiative or, perhaps, of character. It smacks of insufficient motivation. Certainly those who pride themselves on being busy all the time feel suspicious of those with free time. Those focused on constant activity say they work hard and play hard. Every activity is taken full-steam and head-on. They need to learn how to "do nothing and do it slowly"—perhaps watching a sunset, talking to a child or spouse, or reading a relaxing book.

Christians must avail themselves of spiritual reststops—worship services, Bible studies, church socials—for these gear down the souls that have often been revved to the max. Let Christians consider themselves soldiers on the front line. They can only remain there so long before being relieved and sent to the rear for rest and relaxation.

SUBMISSION — beauty of to Christ
Jeremiah 10:6–7; Romans 11:33–36; Hebrews 13:20–21

To Live in Christ

"So I hold out my arms to my Redeemer," Pascal wrote. "By his grace, I await death in peace, in the hope of being eternally united to Him. Yet I live with joy, whether in the prosperity . . . it pleases Him to bestow . . . or in the adversity . . . He sends for my good, and which He has taught me to bear by His example." Kepler, as great an astronomer as he was a Christian, studied the heavenly bodies as a ministry to God, believing that their Creator wanted a personal relationship with each human being. And the great explorer David Livingstone said, "May God so imbue my mind with the spirit of Christianity that in all circumstances I may show my Christian character."

Christian testimony is the enduring love song of the saved for the Savior! A testimony that starts deep in the soul, where God meets and loves the person with his everlasting love. Though words may fail, the loved soul must express its gratitude. Worship flows from an appreciation of the Master. Praise is the fruit of a heart renovated by grace.

SUCCESS — too high
Psalm 4:7; 1 John 2:15–17

Not Worth the Effort

Even Andy Capp has something positive to tell to us. Here is a guy who finds breathing hard too much effort—unless he is playing football. He and a friend are hard at billiards, when the friend leaves in the middle of the game. Andy cannot grasp that, and as the friend drives off in his new car, Andy hollers after him to get his priorities straight. (Playing snooker is high priority to Andy Capp.) In the last frame he makes a telling point: "Some people work day and night so they can drive between jobs in a nicer car."

Good point! Sometimes people work so hard getting ahead that they are behind when they arrive. They make such an effort to improve their living standard that they have no time to appreciate the improvement. They spend time climbing the ladder of success, only to spend enormous amounts of energy just hanging on once they get there. They have suffered a Pyrrhic victory; it brings more anxiety and problems than their previous life brought in poverty and anonymity.

Working for Christ has an unalterably true result: no matter what you invest, it repays handsomer dividends. Whatever you give him, he returns more; and his service rewards not only the achievement but the effort. When we give our best to Jesus, the Master responds in a pandemonium of generosity!

SURVIVAL — incredible
Psalm 16:8; John 15:5

The Great Survivor

On November 23, 1942, the British merchant ship *S. S. Ben Lomond* sank after being torpedoed by a German sub 565 miles off the west coast of Africa. A lone seaman, Poon Lim, survived. He swam in circles for a couple of hours before finding a small raft rising on the swells. To his relief the items he found aboard gave him hope: a few tins of biscuits, a container of water, a flashlight, and a rope. By carefully rationing his supplies he survived sixty days. When his rations ran out, he made a hook from a wire spring in the flashlight, attached it to the rope, and caught small fish. He occasionally lured sea gulls aboard by placing bits of food on the raft. He used his life jacket as a reservoir when it rained, and he swam daily for exercise. On April 5, 1943, more than four months after the sinking, some Brazilian fishermen found the lonely voyager off the coast of Brazil. He had lost only twenty pounds and could walk without help.

We too must keep ourselves in spiritual trim as we serve Christ. To remain spiritually fit, we need the nourishment of his Word and the exercise of prayer. We call it our devotional time, but it is really our lifeline, our spiritual umbilical cord to life in Christ. It provides the spiritual vitality we need to be victorious and to reach out to others.

SYMBOLS — necessary
Ezekiel 4:1–3; Hebrews 13:10

Relating to Symbols

Radio station KGB in San Diego conceived a brilliant stunt and hired Ted Giannoulas to dress up as a chicken and entertain at promotional events. He expressed himself so imaginatively in the outfit that the one-night stand became a career. For several years he represented the station as the KGB Chicken, regularly appearing at Padres baseball games and even traveling overseas. When a lawsuit broke the original relationship, the station got back its chicken outfit and Ted Giannoulas had to hatch another.

It happened in the San Diego Stadium, June, 1979. A giant egg rolled out of an enormous, gift-wrapped box. Something inside thumped against the shell, a few cracks appeared, and suddenly, before 47,000 screaming fans, the San Diego Chicken was rehatched. He made his fans believe that a real chicken lived in that suit.

God has often used symbols to strengthen his promises and teachings: to Noah he gave the rainbow; to Abraham, circumcision; to Moses, a lamb; to Gideon, the fleece; to Christ's death, the Lord's Supper. Symbols relate abstract truths in a visible form. The symbol is a type representing its reality—the anti-type. It is a shadow of the form it represents. It contains something of, but lacks the essential nature of the thing it represents. The radiance it symbolizes is the essence of the source from which it came. A lamb's blood in Egypt was a symbol; the Lamb of God's blood on Calvary was the reality.

TALENT — each develops
Numbers 13:30–31; 1 Corinthians 15:10

According to His Ability

In dismantling Mao Tse-Tung's commune system, the Chinese communists allowed individuals to develop their own businesses, and farmers could grow and sell much of their own produce on the private market. Since the reorganization, a logical thing has happened: some peasants earn as little as $50 a year, while others make more than $50,000 a year. The Chinese shrugged away this oddity, saying that while some got rich first, others would get rich later and, sooner or later, all would get rich.

This will not happen with two universal laws of economic life in effect: (1) where people are free to choose, invest, work, and plan for themselves, some always make more than others; and, (2) there will never come a time in such a free economy when everyone will be rich . . . or poor, for that matter. God allows the same freedom in the spiritual realm. According to Luke's account of the talents (19:12–26), the lord gave all three servants the same amount of money. Each in turn gained a different proportion on his bequest: five, three, and none. So it is possible that people with the same basic gifts and capabilities will produce differing results. Some will be more productive, some less. The difference is not in the basic skill, but in the zeal and industry with which it is applied.

TALENT — looks not important
Isaiah 53:2; Acts 6:8; 8:5

An Odd Choice

Leo Tolstoy's beauty resided in his brain, not in his face. Looking every inch the peasant instead of the patrician he actually was, he invariably disappointed those who saw him. His broad nose and thick lips offended many who had developed an idealized profile from his novels. Visitors would wait for hours to see him, only to wish they hadn't. Socrates was said to be the homeliest of Greeks, yet was perhaps the wisest of his nation. Ulysses S. Grant was a markedly unmilitary-looking general; he was very ordinary-looking, in fact. Yet he fought like a Bengal tiger.

God considers two factors in recruiting servants: (1) the particular ministry needs; and (2) the person who perfectly fits the servant profile. God chose Abraham because he was the only man alive who would outwait unbelief to gain his patrimony. He chose Noah because only he could see thunderstorms in skies that had never floated a cloud. He chose David because although king-designate, he was willing to serve as public enemy number one. He chose Hannah because she freely surrendered her only hope of happiness just as she had promised she would. He chose Ezekiel because no one else would act like a lunatic in order to bring Israel to her senses. He chose Mary because she alone believed that God could outwit the law of human regeneration.

God has numerous ministries that need to be serviced. Which one of us would be willing to offer our résumé to check against the servant-profile?

TALKING — as catharsis
Isaiah 26:3: Philippians 4:6

I Feel Better Already

Despite the deprivation of daily necessities and comforts, Elijah Fisher wrote, he served honorably and faithfully in the American Revolutionary army. To his bitter regret, economic injustice marred his return to civilian life. Yet, as he wrote, optimism replaced heartache. Other soldiers had even less food and clothing, more perilous health, and fewer economic opportunities. In verbalizing he found relief from his miseries.

Catharsis, a cleansing of one's emotion by merely talking, offers a necessary release for the stresses we face. Murderous rage can erupt when those who have been deeply offended act out instead of talking out their grief. Unbidden, unwanted accusations and dilemmas can roil our peace of mind into a foaming collision of converging mayhem. If, on those occasions, we pray until we have prayed through the difficulty, we will reclaim our peace of mind. Why would we forfeit peace we could easily keep, and bear pain we could easily lose? God stands ready to bless our lives with his presence.

TALKING — warned against
Proverbs 13:24; Ephesians 6:4

Be Still!

In a Navajo puberty ceremony, the child lies on blankets placed on the ground. He has his legs and arms pulled straight, to grow tall. Then his mouth is slapped four times so he will not talk too much. Each culture has its own approach to child rearing. The permissive American approach is shocking to many other cultures. Having bombastic, know-it-all kids on our television programs has only exacerbated that perception.

God's Word takes a firm stand on rearing children. They must be valued, loved, taught God's precepts, and punished when disobedient. Hardly any child-behavior expert denies that parents need to clearly define and enforce rules for children. Parents who refuse to discipline their children and punish them when discipline fails, stifle their learning skills. Only children who learn accountability and who suffer for irresponsibility can constructively handle pain, disappointment, and failure as they mature. In responding to parental penalties, children learn how to manage greater rejections later. Children will grow older naturally but will mature only as parents prepare them for adulthood—where few are willing to indulge childish whims.

TEACHING — false is still false
Deuteronomy 6:4; Matthew 15:13

Other Benefits Notwithstanding

Page Smith rightly said that the Mormons forged a religious/economic combination that appealed to the nineteenth century. They provided a vision from God that built the foundation of an autocratic religious faith, and their active welfare provisions offered otherwise unavailable economic security. Mormonism guaranteed that no church member would be alone when sickness, accident, or death removed the family breadwinner. Then, with a whimsy characterizing secular scholars, he added, "The belief in the golden tablets was a small price for converts to pay for the healing of the wounds inflicted by a competitive, individualistic society."

But it wasn't just golden tablets that converts accepted when they became Mormons. It was an entire creed inherently hostile to biblical teaching—and growing more so as Mormon theologians speculated blatantly anti-Christian theories. The Mormons have long endeavored to make themselves more clearly understood by other churches. They want to be seen as just another Christian group. To achieve this goal they even added a new twist to the Book of Mormon, calling it The Book of Mormon: Another Testament of Jesus Christ.

Those who clearly understand Mormonism know that it is a spiritual nightshade, deadly to the soul. Its theology contradicts New Testament teaching. As long as Mormons claim that Joseph Smith had a revelation beyond New Testament teaching, they remain a cult and stand outside historical Christianity.

TEACHING — results differ
Ezekiel 2:5; John 11:45–46

Different Responses

At different times, both Alexander Kerensky and Nicolai Lenin studied under Kerensky's schoolmaster father. While learning the same historical facts and economic theories from their teacher, Alexander and Nicolai interpreted them quite differently. Both men opposed Czar Nicholas II and conspired to overthrow him.

When the Czar abdicated in July, 1917, the revolutionary council appointed the younger Kerensky over Lenin as head of the government. Three months of ideological warfare between the two men and their supporters led to open warfare. Both envisioned socialism as the incoming tide in economic and political life. The Bolsheviks, under Lenin, demanded class warfare to achieve the goal; the Mensheviks, under Kerensky, chose gradual victory through parliamentary procedures. The Bolsheviks grew stronger, while the Mensheviks grew weaker. In October, 1917, Kerensky was overthrown by the radicals, and Lenin's star ascended. Kerensky went into exile as Lenin assumed control of the revolution.

The gospel message always has multiple results, as Jesus clearly taught in the Parable of the Sower. Christ's messengers cannot predict how their message will be heard, received, or obeyed. They can only be faithful to communicate it clearly and forcefully. The hearers then stand accountable for how they receive the message. Careful listening is as necessary for the hearer as clear instruction is from the messenger.

TECHNOLOGY — only so successful
Ecclesiastes 2:4–5; Revelation 18:2, 10–11

Needs Only God Can Fill

H.M.S. Queen Mary ruled as sovereign of the seas when launched in 1936. A thousand magnificent feet long and 81,000 tons in weight, she possessed every possible convenience and appointment. Shipbuilders reached the zenith of their craft in her construction. Yet, that great ocean liner nearly capsized in December, 1942, while carrying 15,000 soldiers from America to England. A rogue wave, formed when three or four giant waves synchronized their strength, struck her vertically to starboard, then pounded on her broadside with mountainous fury. She listed until her upper decks were awash and her safety margin was no more than five degrees. Had she listed just inches more to port, the *Queen Mary* would have gone to the bottom of the Atlantic.

Human ability, however brilliant, and human resources, however enormous, have a limit. We sometimes forget that when we consider our dazzling technological advances since World War II. We find ourselves ruling land, sea, and space, but not our own depravities and frailties. We are awash in our sins and nearly drowning in our corruption. We who rule everything God's hands made must yield to him to bring ourselves under control.

TECHNOLOGY — two-edged
Isaiah 40:6–8; 1 Timothy 6:7

With the Advance of Knowledge

Humanity thankfully hails medical advances that have brought an end to smallpox, diphtheria, measles, and polio epidemics. Microsurgical techniques now being developed and used, along with laser technology, promise unbelievable benefits for the future. However, advances have two sharp edges: the built-in possibility of abuse and danger. Knowledge has brought us innumerable benefits. It has chartered the way to a better, safer life, but it cannot take us into that life. The laser can heal, but can we keep it from becoming a death-ray weapon? We splice genes, but can we eliminate a social tyranny from abusing the information, killing "unwanteds and inferiors"? We build super computers, but can we keep hackers from plundering their secrets?

There is always a limit to our ability. Humanity glows with pride and expectation over its past and present accomplishments. But a somber, sobering limitation still confronts us: all of our knowledge tears apart on the reef of our mortality.

TEMPTATION — overcome
Judges 2:4; 1 Corinthians 11:1

Always After, Seldom Before

Civil War horses quickly mastered the steps of drill. When bugles sounded march, halt, or wheel, the animals responded instinctively, before troopers pulled the reins. Infantrymen and cavalrymen then often bivouacked together. Yet, bugling that called the horse soldiers to duty never awoke the foot troops, and the long roll of drums for the foot troops never stirred the horse soldiers. If Union and Confederate batteries exchanged volleys, the soldiers slept undisturbed. But they fell out immediately if their pickets fired a few musket shots.

For all we can say against it, there is some value to obedience by reflex or conditioning. Following the Master's example, Christians could use more intuitive obedience. For how often we find repentance of sin better than resistance to it! How easily our remorse comes afterward and our resistance so reluctantly before! Christ's redemptive death aims to free us from both temptation's presence and power. He gives grace to overcome temptations, not just penitence after we have fallen. Forgiveness is ours if we seek it humbly, but victory is ours only when we thwart temptation beforehand—not when we repent of it afterwards.

TENSION — caused by unused energy
Exodus 18:17–18; Mark 3:13–15

Unused Energy Harmful

The term *horsepower* originally referred to the load-weight a single horse could pull. Not content with that simple definition, the U.S. Customary System defines it at 745.7 watts or 33,000 footrounds per minute.

Individually, we can generate fourteen horsepower over a limited time with a maximum effort. We generate only 0.1 horsepower while at rest. What happens to all that unused, potential energy? Some physiologists suggest that without exercise and expenditure in work or play, the accumulated, unused energy will produce tension and build greater fatigue and related complaints. A catch-22 results. We will feel worse and not want to expend energy when the only way we will feel better is to expend energy.

How true in the body of Christ. Most of the spiritual vitality in the lives of members goes unused. That vitality accumulates until, with no outlet, it explodes in complaints, criticisms, and divisions. Leaders face no greater challenge than to discover and channel the energy, interest, and spiritual giftedness of their people. If leaders don't challenge and channel the energy in their people, those individuals will find ways to express it—possibly to the consternation of their leaders.

TESTIMONY — not everyone accepts
Jeremiah 1:17; Acts 5:20

Not All Will Believe

Convicted of robbing a fast food restaurant, the man received a life sentence. Over a year later he received his freedom because the state decided a mistake had been made. The victim had been jailed on the testimony of five eye-witnesses, but the court ignored the testimony of nine co-workers, who claimed he was working with them when the robbery occurred.

God's commission to his people always has a steel-cold warning in it: not everyone will believe our testimony. Being an eye-witness to the resurrection of Jesus couldn't empower the apostles to convince everyone that he was alive. Convincing the Jews that he had experienced a personal encounter with Jesus Christ did not bring Paul widespread success in winning Jews. Our Christian witness will face the same obstacle: human intransigence against God's grace. No testimony, however true, guarantees its acceptance—not then, not now, not in spiritual or secular matters.

THANKSGIVING — for a whale
Psalm 150:1–6; Luke 7:44–46

Not Like Jonah

On finding a whale washed up on the Oregon coast by huge waves, Captain William Clark noted with satisfaction the small but important quantity of oil it provided. "Small as this stock is," he wrote in his journal, "I prize it highly; and thank Providence for directing the whale to us. And think Him much more kind to us than He was to Jonah, having sent this monster to be swallowed by us, instead of swallowing of us, as Jonah's did."

Little things do mean a lot, positively or negatively. Small oversight or remembrances make relationships and marriages difficult or delightful. Small, apparently insignificant attitudes towards our faith also produce significant results. By refusing to grant the small but expected acts of hospitality for his guest, Simon the Pharisee proved that he was prepared to entertain, but not to honor Jesus. In the same house, at the same time, the former streetwalker expressed her complete delight in Jesus by wetting his feet with her tears and wiping them with her hair. We can entertain Christ by calling on him only when we are desperate for his help, or we can honor him by inviting him into our lives and letting him have the run of the place.

THANKSGIVING — precedes gifts from God
Daniel 9:22–23; 1 Thessalonians 1:2–3

Before, Not After
Mary Chestnut's father-in-law had the enduring habit of returning thanks after his meals. As he left the table he would invariably say, "I thank God for a good dinner." When asked why he didn't pray prior to eating, he replied "My way is to be sure of a thing before I return thanks for it."

Christians never fear that giving thanks involves a gamble. Their experience verifies that nothing will ever be more certain than God's provisions for life. The feeding of the four and five thousand people offers a parable of God's provisions. After everyone had eaten to complete satisfaction, seven and twelve basketsful remained. Left over! Ready to serve to others! That's what Jesus accomplishes with those who commit themselves to him. For the use of Peter's boat, Jesus filled the nets so full of fish they began to tear and the boats nearly to sink. The divine bounty proved so lavish it threatened disaster! If that for the use of a boat, what will God give for the use of a life?

THEFT — by employees
Joshua 2:1; Luke 16:8–9

Those Paid and Trusted
A 1989 survey revealed that employee thefts accounted for seven times more revenue loss than shoplifting. More than two billion dollars was reported in losses in 1989 by the 160 companies responding to the survey. The average recovery per theft by employee was $1,350, compared to the average $196 recovered from each customer arrested. Forty-five percent of the thefts occurred at the cash register, with clerks manipulating the entries. Ten percent were in the stock room. Not surprisingly, drug abuse figured prominently in the employee arrests: 25 percent of the employees had previous drug-related arrests.

Research can uncover problems and potential in any group or organization. To be useful, however, programs aimed at solving and exploiting the problems and potential must follow. Christian leaders need to carefully study their congregation and compare its up-to-date demographics with the community's. After the demographic studies are complete and the congregation has perused and understood the facts, leaders should offer proposals for action to the congregation, with their recommendations. Such procedures offer restart possibilities in new areas for many congregations or simply an awakening to overlooked ministry opportunities in an existing area.

THEFT — harsh penalties for

Leviticus 20:21; 22:14; 1 Timothy 4:6

Definitely Not Worth the Pain

Ninth-century Europeans highly prized their hunting dogs and falcons. They considered theft of them nearly tantamount to a capital crime. The Burgundians allowed the stolen falcon, once recaptured, to peck and tear five ounces of flesh from the offender's chest. A dog thief had to pay a fine to the owner or be disgraced by publicly lifting the dog's tail and kissing its behind. Hopefully, dog thieves had a cash reserve!

At the dawn of our history, God promised rewards for obedience to his Word and threatened penalties against transgression. The Old Testament details the kinds of crime to be expected in any society, with appropriate punishments. At least two principles accompanied the statutes: (1) punishment should fit the crime; and (2) the punishment should be swiftly administered. In this way justice is served, and the community is spared the expense of harboring the criminal. In addition, it intimidates other would-be felons. If outlaws today knew that every time they crawled from their hole they would see far more than their shadow, they wouldn't be so aggressive and innocent citizens wouldn't need to be so defensive.

THINGS — unexpected

Hosea 9:7–8; John 6:66

Appearances Can Be Deceptive

When General MacArthur waded ashore in Leyte Gulf, October 1944, he had the grim look of a man fulfilling a vow. Actually, he was scowling at the beachmaster who had made him walk through the water from fifty yards out. Later, however, when the General saw the dramatic effect of the picture, he intentionally waded ashore at the next beach.

Things are not always what they seem. Even widely known pictures can be deceptive. Christ's entire life proved different from what people expected. He came as a root from a stump, as something apparently weak from a presumably dead tree. But how remarkably his achievements belied his humble beginnings! From a rebellious people he derived—to perfectly obey God. In a fervently political and nationalistic atmosphere he grew—to embrace spiritual concepts. With the weakest possible appeal he inaugurated his work—love one another—and conquered the imagination and hearts of millions. His life proved that God's ways and wisdom are strangely humble, but overpowering; that success isn't in appearance, but in substance.

THINKING — too much can ruin
Psalm 119:5; Philippians 1:21–22

Don't Want It Anymore

In his short story "Episode," Somerset Maugham tells about a man who was jailed for eighteen months for stealing. His girlfriend promises to wait for him. When first incarcerated he thinks of nothing but the girl—the shared good times, the marriage they will solemnize on his release, their future life together. As time passes, however, and he continues to pore over their relationship, a change occurs, of which he is not even aware until a fortnight before his release. In his isolation, obsessed with only her, he has grown tired of her. He has exhausted himself thinking about her and has come to despise her. As a result, he has no alternative but to dissolve their relationship.

Sometimes fixation on a particular object can have an adverse effect, but riveted concentration on Jesus brings excitement, not boredom; delight, not remorse. It stimulates as it sates our senses. We find his every disclosure to us a bridgehead and our every insight into it a breakthrough to more. He speaks a spiritual language, and we suddenly crave a fluency with words. He calls for holiness, and we suddenly feel the need for purity. He speaks of commitment, and we suddenly want to prove our faith.

THOUGHT — influence of ancient
Daniel 1:3–4; 1 Corinthians 1:20–21

Even Now

Greek philosophers live today in the influence they have had on Christianity, Judaism, and Islam. The ninth-century translation of Aristotle's scientific and metaphysical works into Arabic compelled Moslem thinkers to reconcile Greek philosophy with Moslem doctrine. Aristotle's influence on Hebrew scholars in the twelfth century had the same effect on Judaism, as Ibn David and Moses Maimonides led in a reconciliation. Aristotle's works in Latin brought a synthesis between Greek philosophy and Christianity in twelfth- and thirteenth-century Europe.

Wherever philosophy touches belief, it leaves an indelible print. Where scholars combine it with Scripture, it becomes a "microbe with ink stains on its feet," marring and defacing Scripture. By itself, divorced from the Greek philosophy of the world into which it was born, God's Word came to holy men. By itself, separate from that philosophy in every generation, God's Word must remain. Scripture and philosophy are opposites: truth and theory, reality and supposition. Any effort to combine Scripture's truth with philosophy's theories renders the truth less definite without making the theories more distinct.

TIME — signs of
Deuteronomy 28:43–44; Romans 11:28–29

Signs of the Times

A Shinto priest flown in from Japan stood before assembled dignitaries and an invited gaggle of newsmen and photographers. He waved a cloth-tipped stick across the ground and through the air, "purifying" the ground of the new $125 million Emerald-Shapery Center in San Diego. That just didn't seem right. Shouldn't American capital have constructed that Center? Shouldn't an American pastor have been praying the benediction of Almighty God on the building?

Governments endlessly repeat the cycle of nations: from struggle to achievement to luxury to corruption to destruction. No one frustrates God's determination to rule as he chooses. God is the incalculable mystery; we are the readily explicable fact. He is the Creator; we are the object of his creative purpose. Without our knowledge and against our will his righteousness condemns national iniquity. Here we are, then, for the first time since the Revolution, the world's largest debtor nation and going constantly deeper into debt. The wonder is not that Japan would be so strong but that we should have become so weak.

TITLES — don't make the person
Psalm 147:10–11; Galatians 2:20

That Didn't Improve Him

Kaiser Wilhelm of Germany was not only emperor, but twice a grand duke, eighteen times an ordinary duke, ten times a count, and three times a margrave. However, those titles did not keep him from being the chief villain of World War I. He could never overcome the inferiority he felt, symbolized in his crippled arm. Short on self-esteem, but monstrous with an ego that masked it, he encouraged his cousin, Czar Nicolas II of Russia, to wage war against the Japanese, promising Germany's assistance. When Japan upset Russia in their brief conflict, the Kaiser did nothing but conceive the term "Yellow Peril" to describe Japan's threat to Europe. He saw enemies against Germany everywhere, especially in England and America. With each premonition came a vision to prove German superiority. With him as Kaiser, and with his constant meddling in other nations' affairs, worldwide catastrophes were inevitable.

Christian discipleship begins with the assassination of our ego, since in it we concentrate all our vehement opposition to God. Our ego stands between us and what God wants for us: the humility necessary to serve him and the righteousness necessary to see him. The death of our ego deprives us of being Kaisers, but who would want to be? It empowers us to be Christlike, and who wouldn't want to be?

TOLERATION — urged, rejected
Exodus 22:21; John 10:10

First One, Then Another

In 1520, Martin Luther urged Christians to "vanquish heretics with books, not with burning." In 1530, in a commentary on Psalm 82, he advised governments to execute all heretics who preached sedition or false doctrine. The different positions may reflect nothing more than his personal life in each decade. In 1520, very much the hunted and hated heretic, he naturally urged toleration. By 1530, in charge of his own reform efforts, he no longer called for restraint on those whose ideology and theology seemed as dangerous to him as his earlier teaching had to the Roman Catholic Church.

William Penn, of all colonial founders, succeeded in establishing a community based on equality and toleration, welcoming all races and religious persuasions. It was at the time held as a model government. The few exceptions to the rule only reinforced Pennsylvania's effort to give equality and justice to all.

The Pennsylvania experiment, like the Plymouth and Jamestown colonies, proved the worth of the Christian faith despite the inadequacies of its adherents. By managing and empowering the otherwise intractable and powerless apostles, Jesus offered proof of his claim to save the world. Wherever undisguised biblical faith has flowed, it has been the rising tide that lifts all life. In an amazing divine contradiction, the Christian faith that unerringly makes its emphasis from an eternal perspective vastly improves daily life on earth. But, then, Jesus did promise an abundance of life to all who followed him.

TRADE — unusual way to conduct
Exodus 24:3–4; Galatians 3:2–3

Give and Take

When the Carthaginians traded with other people in Lybia, they brought their wares to a beach along the ocean, spread them out on the sand, and retired to the ships. There they raised a smoke signal alerting the villagers to their presence. The natives came to the beach, looked over the goods, and put beside each article the gold they thought it was worth. They then withdrew to a distance. Back to the beach the Carthaginians came to look. If the exchange seemed fair, they gathered the gold and left. If not, they returned to the ships and waited. The tribe approached the beach again and added to the gold until they felt a fair trade had been made. "Neither party deals unfairly by the other" Herodotus said, "for they themselves never touch the gold till it comes up to the worth of their goods, nor do the natives ever carry off the goods till the gold is taken away." It seems an agreeable method of transacting trade, showing honesty, business acumen, and appreciation of privacy.

Many people think a similar method exists between them and God: each one makes an offer, one ups or lowers it as the other resists or yields, bargaining until a fair deal is struck. Never! We deal with God as inferior beings to the Supreme Being, on his terms, taking or leaving the offer he makes. He never gives us the right to barter for discipleship and salvation. The former comes only through our self-denial, the latter only by his grace.

TRADITIONS — too important
Genesis 17:9–10; Matthew 15:2–3

Too Much Tradition

Recruiters for American businesses and corporations value a person who earns a graduate degree from abroad. They feel it enriches and broadens. In Japan, however, higher education from abroad hinders the applicant because it is considered too independent and individualistic. Teachers stress that their pupils must adhere to Japanese ways if they expect to succeed. All this stems from a basic cultural distinction between the two countries. Americans stress individual achievement; Japanese stress the group. We believe the individual is most important; they, the organization.

Custom! It is the accepted way individuals and groups perform functions. In Japan, conformity to the group is essential. In America individual effort and leadership are essential. Both would swear to the propriety of their ways and the inadequacy of any other. Yet both are cultural, adapted by the citizens to what works for them. Each has assets and liabilities. Neither is perfect.

The Pharisees fought Jesus tenaciously over the sacredness of customs that had only tradition behind them. They swore allegiance to those traditions, persecuting anyone who deviated from them. However, Christ refused to be intimidated. Knowing the difference between truth and culture, he always embraced the former and, at will, disregarded the latter. His disciples followed his example then, and should follow him now. We should accept customs where possible, but not place our faith in them. Then, when it is better to abolish the custom, its passage produces no turbulence. As it is, changing the traditions of a church is often far more disruptive than correcting false teaching in the body of believers.

TREACHERY — name synonymous with
Psalm 41:9; Matthew 26:24

Infamy Itself

Of Benedict Arnold, Trevelyan wrote "It would have been well for him if the memory of his existence upon earth could have perished with him. . . . The Revolutionary heroes, great and small, received each of them his allotted meet of national gratitude; while the name of Benedict Arnold, which once promised to be only less renowned and honored than that of George Washington, was regarded by three generations of his fellow countrymen as a by word for treachery."

There is another, more infamous name synonymous with treachery: the wretch who double-crossed his Master. Allowed to be treasurer even though known as a thief, allowed to sit at the seat of honor at the Upper Room though awaiting only the signal from Satan to betray, he dishonored the only friend he had. We don't condemn Judas hoping to exonerate ourselves. We don't make him a blacker to make ourselves a lesser spiritual criminal. We plead as guilty to weakness of conviction and to strength of self-will. But our betrayals come from just that: weakness of conviction and strength of self-will—not from a calculated, cold-blooded intention to make merchandise of our Lord! Intention is the key to Judas' condemnation and our forgiveness. We fail Christ when we have every intention of succeeding; he betrayed Christ because he had every intention of deceiving.

TRIUMPH — Roman style
Jeremiah 17:24–25; 1 Corinthians 2:14, 4:9

Only to the Splendid

A Roman Triumph was a spectacle reserved for those whose campaigns killed five thousand of the enemy. The procession formed outside the city, where the general and his troops disarmed themselves. Through a triumphal arch they rode, led by heralding trumpeters. Floats representing the captured cities followed. Then wagons rolled, wheels groaning under the weight of the plunder, followed by seventy white oxen, the sacrificial victims. After the animals came the chained enemy chieftains.

Preceding the commander came musicians playing gaily and incense bearers holding their braziers aloft. Then, regal in a purple toga and a crown of gold, and standing ramrod straight, the general passed in his chariot, pulled by sleek Arabians. Behind him, in other chariots, followed his aides and behind them, in faultless formation, his legions. At the capitol, the general stepped down and, followed by his family, ascended the steps to the Temple of Jupiter, Juno, and Minerva where he laid his treasures, sacrificed an ox, and usually ordered the captive chief slain as a thank-offering.

With the Roman triumph processional in mind, Paul contrasted the price he had paid to be a Christian leader with the rich confectionery of spiritual gifts in the Corinthian church, and he exulted in his role as a participant with Christ in his final victory parade. In either role Paul was content. He would rather be in Christ's procession, slain by him, than be the earthly conqueror slaying; he would rather be recognized as a servant in an eternal kingdom, than be a ruler in a dying kingdom.

TROUBLE — affects long after
Daniel 9:1–3; Luke 14:1–6

The Fallout Continues

Russia sent 115,000 troops into Afghanistan in December, 1979, to prop a puppet government on the verge of collapse. After years of failure and humiliation, the Soviets withdrew in 1986. Yet, by 1993, conflict in Afghanistan continued among Mujahiden gangs. War casualties from 1979 to 1992 included a million Afghanis killed, two million driven from their villages, and over five million in exile. How can the nation survive, with half its population casualties of continual warfare?

Many churches, now at peace, betray the existence of previous divisions whose bitter legacy includes decreased attendance, small offerings, a crippled spirit, and no effective community outreach. Like volcanic eruptions, trouble is soon past—but the fallout continues for a protracted time. We need to pick our spiritual fights carefully; to wage them over scriptural absolutes, not personal opinions, and, even there, to concentrate on issues, not personalities. This allows a vigorous defense of truth while keeping intact our personal relationships, whatever our differences. If Jesus maintained personal contact with the Pharisees, with whom he had irreconcilable differences, shouldn't Christians keep dialogue flowing with skeptics, liberals, and atheists who deny the values and doctrines we hold dearer than life itself?

TROUBLE — coming from afar
Isaiah 65:2; 1 Corinthians 1:23–24

From Out of Nowhere

University of Cambridge Professor Jim Benton walked the mile and a half shoreline of the Island of Ducce Atoll in 1991. It is one of the most remote islands in the world, three thousand miles from any continent. On the beach he counted nearly a thousand objects: plastics in all shapes and sizes, shoes of every kind, wooden crates, glass bottles, even light bulbs—all the refuse of more than fifteen countries!

Since few visitors go to the island, the trash floated there, the rubbish thrown overboard from ships hundreds, perhaps thousands, of miles away. If that much trash washed ashore on Ducce Atoll, Benton exclaimed, what massive debris is floating on the ocean, looking for a lonely beach where it can land?

Sin in the human heart resembles that debris. There is always more where that came from. Expressing itself wherever possible, it waits for new openings where none exist now. Cleaning up the environment may once again offer clean water and pristine beaches, but it will not eliminate sin.

TROUBLE — friends causing
Isaiah 52:5; Acts 5:13

Friendly Fire

Friendly fire in the Gulf War brought unnecessary casualties to both American and British troops, accounting for a fourth of all Allied casualties. In 1994, with the Gulf War long over, American jets shot down two American helicopters over Iraq, mistaking them for the enemy. Friendly fire is a danger in war or in a war zone, despite intentional procedures to prevent it.

In Hawaii, December 7, 1941, three shipyard workers, on their way to Pearl Harbor, died from friendly fire. Five-inch shells shot at Japanese planes from the U. S. fleet hit the men's car, destroying it and leaving them dead inside.

It is a short step from friendly fire casualties in battle to the needless suffering Christians inflict on one another. In a kingdom ruled by the Prince of Peace, to whom each subject yields allegiance, interpersonal mayhem should be the exception where it is all too often the rule. Christians seem to forget when with their peers the manners they sensibly show when with the unsaved. Forgiveness, tolerance, and patience should as clearly characterize our feelings for each other as for the lost. We cannot hide our private wars from the public forever. In fact, our inability to love one another has been as deadly as the breath of Rappaccini's daughter. Sadly, it has made skeptics of those who hear us say that God loves them.

TRUST — essential
Genesis 24:2; 1 Corinthians 4:2

When Trust Ceases

A California attorney was convicted on twelve counts of grand theft and four counts of perjury for looting a wealthy client's estate. Trusted to oversee the client's possessions, he systematically siphoned almost a million dollars from it in eight years. The judge who heard the case rejected the defense appeal for probation, sentencing the defendant to eight years in prison and fining him $80,000. The betrayal of that trust, the judge said, would make probation a mockery of justice.

Trust is absolutely essential to our life. Only when we have to doubt everything we hear, see, buy, or experience do we understand the magnitude of its loss. Our relationship with an ever-faithful God demands an ever-faithful life from his people. Others should be able to bank on our promises and entrust to us any important matter, with no further thought. We need to be known for our integrity as Tiffany's is known for jewelry. We are called to be moral absolutists in a society of moral relativists. We need to be responsible and to act responsibly. We need to integrate our faith in the God we trust with a personal integrity that can always be trusted.

TRUTH — absolute
Deuteronomy 32:39; John 17:17, 18:37

There Must Be Truth

Veteran actor Vic Morrow and two Vietnamese children died when a helicopter crashed while flying over them during the filming of the movie "Twilight Zone." A preliminary hearing in January 1984 resolved into a single question: Could the explosives used have thrown a six foot bamboo pole into the helicopter rotor, destroying it and causing the crash? An FBI explosives expert said no; a UCLA engineering professor said yes.

Two experts, looking at the same evidence, drew different conclusions. Both had the same qualifications on which to base their decisions. So which was right? The decision was critical, especially to the prosecution's contention that recklessness in planning the set brought the disaster. The judge decided the issue. An impartial observer, he determined that the prosecution offered the more impressive, convincing evidence. The accused were later acquitted in a trial.

The search for truth . . . the irreducible fact that can judge all other matters because it is unimpeachably so! There must be such a source of authority in this world, beyond which we cannot go, beyond which we cannot appeal, whose word is final and perfect, whose judgment is infallible, whose decision is unassailable, which can discern between all the claimants to truth to ascertain the one, single truth that exists. For if truth exists at all in the parts, it must have its origin in the united whole. It is nonsense to say truth can exist only where we claim it. If there is truth anywhere, in anything, it came from Someone in particular, somewhere specifically.

TRUTH — by inches
Genesis 1:2; John 3:7–8

Crawling Toward It

Pinchas Lapide, an Orthodox Jewish professor of Scripture, wrote *The Resurrection of Jesus: A Jewish Perspective.* He concludes that Christ's resurrection is authentic, because the rise of the church, filled with Jewish converts and soon spreading to the Gentile world, along with the change in the disciples from the terrified sheep of Gethsemane to the bold lions of Pentecost offers indisputable proof of the resurrection. Despite his sensational advance, however, Lapide protects his flank, for he insists that the resurrection does not prove that Jesus is the Messiah or the Son of God. He claims that Christ rose from the dead to save Gentiles not Jews, who were already saved through Abraham.

The good doctor, like most of us, does not leap into truth. He crawls toward it, step by agonizing step, and sometimes backtracks when the way looks too ominous. We all have many restrictions and limitations in our lives and many prejudices against new truth. The Holy Spirit has his own means of encouraging and developing faith. The Spirit continues to blow where he wills, witnessing to, convicting, and convincing unbelievers of Jesus Christ's deity. Wouldn't it be just like the Spirit to use an unbelieving Jew to bring faith in their Messiah to other unbelieving Jews?

TRUTH — damaged
Jeremiah 44:15–19; John 7:11–13

Making Truth Subjective

Columbus' knowledge of winds and waves brought him to the New World and took him back to the Old. But if he knew the elements, he never escaped his illusions about the New World being the Indies. On the contrary, he found in every discovery new evidence to support his contentions. A shrub that smelled like cinnamon he called "cinnamon." The aromatic gumbo-limbo in the West Indies he considered the equivalent of the mastic tree of the Mediterranean. The common garden rhubarb of the West Indies he mistook for the valuable Chinese rhubarb. The scent of the far east floated in the Caribbean's tropical air and Columbus equated odor with geography.

People do that religiously. Anything resembling truth becomes truth. They call it truth and immediately draw parallels to truth. The mother of heaven becomes the pagan ideal of the Virgin Mary; the ancient Egyptian trinity of Atum, Shu, and Tefnut becomes the biblical trinity; and various saviors in heathen writings are not unlike Christ in many ways. Whatever the Bible teaches, these seekers of their own objectives weave any thread of possibility into an unyielding rope of evidence. It is all part of Satan's deception. He unremittingly works to produce as genuine a counterfeit as he can. He confuses the unwary and insensitive. They call true even the poorest imitations of truth. Worst of all, they even consider outright lies to be truth.

TRUTH — rejecting
Psalm 2:1–6; Acts 4:27

An Unimpeachable Standard

Two homosexuals, one a psychiatrist and the other a psychologist, had been a pair for twelve years when they published a book called *The Male Couple*. Among the interesting conclusions they reached from interviewing 156 male couples for the book is their casual attitude towards sexual fidelity. Most of the couples interviewed began their relationship with sexual exclusivity, but only 7 of the 156 couples had remained monogamous. To disarm those disturbing statistics, the authors define fidelity in purely emotional, not sexual, terms. Gay men expect to have sex outside their relationship, they state.

The dreadful partner-hopping of the homosexual isn't at all surprising to those who embrace the heterosexual relationship, which deepens in time. The cheap homosexual imitation disappoints and seeks to replenish itself with new lovers. The authors represent many who approach truth with grenades in both hands, ready to lob them at whatever they disdain. Since they claim that no independent, unimpeachable benchmark of truth exists, they define it for themselves—and woe to even the Bible if it disagrees with them.

They are wrong! A singular, unassailable truth exists that makes liars of us all. It remains intact even if the entire human race swears it has been obliterated. God remains faithful to himself, to his Word, to his promises, and to his threats!

UNDECIDED — many remain
1 Kings 18:21; John 7:40–43

Indecision

Buridan's Ass, ascribed to French philosopher Jean Buridan, dramatizes a person's inability to make a decision between two equally potent choices. In the figure, the unfortunate animal stands midway between two identical stacks of hay and starves because it cannot choose which to eat.

Human behavior makes the figure all too real and disturbing. General Friedrich von Paulus had the problem at Stalingrad in World War II. He knew his sixth Army could not hold the gains it made there and that its only hope lay in a breakout. Yet, his devotion to Hitler kept him in the city because Hitler fanatically refused to surrender it. Because von Paulus stood between the options, looking but doing nothing, he accomplished neither. He lost both Stalingrad and the sixth Army, the critical loss of the eastern campaign.

All too often, indecision afflicts people spiritually. Liberal religionists find themselves there. They have an insatiable addiction to knowledge but none for decision. They summarize the meaning of existence as the search for—not the discovery of—truth. They unfailingly temporize, not finalize, truth. Since they don't want to hear it, they feel no one does. Though they have an irresistible attraction to truth, it is only to flirtatiously dance around it. Indecision is an ally of Satan. Deciding to remain undecided is an affirmation of evil.

UNDERSTANDING — others
1 Kings 3:16–38; 2 Corinthians 8:20–21

In Order To Help

The First Continental Congress, meeting in 1774, offered no solution to the English absolutism that had aroused the colonies. It could not agree how to resolve the growing menace of war, but it did serve to acquaint the delegates with each other, an indispensable element in understanding different views, intentions, and backgrounds. It led, in 1776, to the Declaration of Independence.

In the Civil War, few officers could hide their inadequacies or strengths from the enemy since most of them had attended West Point and had fought in the Mexican War. When Grant demanded unconditional surrender of Simon Buckner at Fort Donaldson, he knew Buckner would collapse. When, at Chancellorsville, Lee divided his army and passed half of it before Hooker's vastly superior force, he knew Hooker would not attack. When Lee heard that Meade had succeeded Hooker as commander of the Army of the Potomac, he correctly surmised that Meade would make no mistake on his front.

God's servants must do for his cause what politicians, businessmen, and generals do for theirs. Since understanding one another is the first step in offering positive help, we should carefully plan our approach to ministry. Studying the target group we want to influence is essential to winning them. How best to present the message, what methods work best, how to fruitfully recruit and inspire workers for the project are all considerations that reduce the chance of failure and increase the chance of success. Working smarter as well as harder enables us to offer both effort and victory to our Savior.

UNITY — of God's people
Joshua 7:10–11; 2 Corinthians 9:2

From Afar

A March 1984 malfunction in a 500,000 volt Pacific Gas and Electric Company line in Northern California triggered a chain reaction that eventually darkened lights for millions in six Western states. The blackout came at rush hour, with motorists backed up at traffic lights in cities of California, Arizona, Nevada, New Mexico, and Texas. The trouble originated at the Round Mountain, California, substation, about one hundred miles south of the Oregon border. A circuit breaker tripped, and the concatenation shut down circuits all over the West as machinery protected itself from damage.

How dramatically that breakdown expressed the interdependence of our country's power, transportation, and food production! One little circuit breaker tripped in a remote rural substation, and hundreds of miles away people's lives instantly changed. We are one people in more ways than we think. What affects one affects many, perhaps all. Interdependence characterizes us.

The unity of the church is no different. An interlinking of interests, goals, and influences exists in which we all share. The good one person does makes righteousness easier for all. The bad example one sets negatively affects us all. God's people, wherever they live on earth, are linked into a grid of community interdependence from which they can never escape. Inextricably bound to one another as separate parts of the whole, what affects one becomes part of all.

UNIVERSE — immensity
Psalm 8:1, 3; Romans 1:25

Incredible Dimensions

In 1983 an infrared astronomy satellite detected more than two hundred thousand new objects in the heavens, including twenty thousand galaxies. In 1987, astronomers discovered the largest structures ever seen in the universe—mysterious, glowing blue arcs approximately two million trillion miles long. It took eleven months for the Viking I spacecraft, traveling at fifty-seven thousand miles an hour, to reach Mars, two hundred twenty million miles away. But that is a trip next door compared to the infinitesimal distances between earth and other stars. Consider that a light year is nearly six trillion miles, the distance light travels in a year at 186,282 miles per second. The closest star to earth, Alpha Centauri, is four and a half light years away. The most remote objects now known in the universe are ninety-eight light years from earth. The colossal geometrics of creation!

Modern astronomers did not invent the universe's expansiveness. More than 1,700 years ago Ptolemy taught that the earth should be regarded as insignificant compared to the vast distances in the universe. Long before Ptolemy speculated, God called Abraham from his tent one night and challenged him to count the stars if he could. Our telescopes have simply sensitized us to distances previous generations could not measure—but before which they stood baffled and dazzled. Why hasn't the Creator received awe equal to the awe given his creation? If what he made staggers our imagination, how unimaginable is his majesty!

USEFULNESS — need of
Isaiah 55:10–11; 1 Thessalonians 1:1–3

Feeling Useful

Nearly 30 percent of Americans serve in some volunteer capacity. That is almost seventy-five million people, serving in seven million jobs without pay. Interestingly, church members are twice as likely as unchurched people to volunteer, and those with a strong commitment to their church are the likeliest of all to serve. In the fall of 1987, the five hundred volunteers from Seventh Day Adventist, Mennonite, Catholic, and Amish churches who poured into Saragosa, Texas, proved the reality of the statistics. They went to rebuild a community that a tornado had demolished in the spring.

Pastors should appreciate the implications of these statistics. If church members are the most willing to serve and their faith prompts it, can't that enormous energy be harnessed for local evangelism, teaching, conservation, renewal, and community work? Many disciples would consider such service an honor, not an obligation. Will ministers possess enough confidence in the gospel to expect significant results when it is preached and be delighted, but not surprised, when their members express them in daily life?

VALUES — lasting
Jeremiah 9:23–24; Acts 16:25

That All Depends

A young couple in California remodeled their home, installed a swimming pool, and settled in to enjoy their $70,000 investment. A few weeks later that same couple stared in disbelief at the big white sign posted on a porch pillar of their house: "Notice, this building has been inspected and . . . is hereby declared unfit for human occupancy." The house stood erect. It had no holes in the walls or in the foundations. It looked neat and attractive; yet the lack of running water had reduced the desirable property to a condemned wreck. One Thanksgiving Day the well supplying the development went dry and faucets in the area sputtered only air and sand into sinks.

How conditions change—and change values along with them. In this case, a lifetime investment was threatened because a well failed. What we possess may now have value because circumstances permit or favor it. But will it have value if circumstances change? Can the loss of health imperil it? Or a financial reverse? Or a natural catastrophe? Or death? God wants to give us values that remain unshaken, whatever circumstances we face. He chooses to grant possessions that no cold, warmth, stock market crash, business failure, personal crisis, or death can disrupt or devalue. He will give them if we seek them in Christ.

VALUES — lesser
Jonah 4:9–11; Mark 6:30–34

Lesser Values

One man advertised himself as America's premier pet detective, hiring himself at $50 an hour to search for pets who had been lost or stolen. People whose pets are dear to them willingly unload valuable keepsakes and possessions to retrieve them. A Seattle, Washington, lady left her $500,000 estate to her cat. It is to remain in the apartment with the caretaker. When it dies, enough money will be set aside to provide flowers on its grave at Easter and Christmas.

Jonah's simultaneous concern for a shriveled vine and his apathy toward the residents of Nineveh offers a shocking parallel to people and their pets. How could he be so upset over the death of a plant and so apathetic over the coming judgment of eternal souls? His misdirected zeal proves that even God's people can mistake their interests for his and can wrongly direct their energy to unworthy goals, away from God's concerns to their own.

VANITY — everyone has
1 Corinthians 3:16–17; Revelation 3:20

The Last Thing
During the Renaissance women wore corsets they could tighten with a key. With a key! This led Petrarch to pity tummies that suffered pain from vanity equal to martyrs for religion. Nineteenth-century American women maintained that silly custom, buttoning themselves into slender vials of flesh, suffering courageously while enduring horrendous pain. Contemporary ladies spurn that custom, then suffer equal pain by wearing sharp-toed, high-heeled shoes that squeeze their toes, warp their bones, and shoot agonies through their legs.

But not to worry. Fashion demands it. Vanity is really the innocent edge of ego and a necessity for social life. It encourages baths, combed hair, and the use of deodorant. Without it, we would all dress like unmade beds. Controlled and disciplined, vanity is an asset to our daily lives; only when undisciplined does it become an egotism hostile to our discipleship. In self-denial God provides that delicate balance. We remain conscious of ourselves but more so of the God we love and serve.

VENGEANCE — refuse
1 Samuel 24:8–13; Mark 11:25

That Heartless Cry
Custer employed Osage Indians as allies when he attacked Black Kettle's village on the Washita River. All but one painted themselves in their hideous war colors and donned their war costumes. That one couldn't because tribal custom demanded that no warrior don paint or costume while the death of a relative at the hand of an enemy had gone unavenged. That brave had befriended a Cheyenne the previous summer, and while he was away, the guest had killed his squaw and destroyed his lodge. Until he had killed, the Osage would not dress in his usual finery. Later that cold November morning he galloped through the smoking ruins yelling and waving a bloody scalp. He disappeared but quickly reappeared, dressed as the warrior his avenged wrong permitted and demanded.

Though some Christians still believe in getting even, not mad, Christ taught against both—and with good reason. Vindictiveness darkens the mind and breeds despicable behavior. Not a few people, supposedly enlightened by the gospel, should heed the Master's counsel. What must be avenged in the unsaved becomes, in the Christian, something to be forgiven. That is Christ's pedagogy, and only as we have the courage to obey his difficult demands do we have the right to claim his great and precious promises.

VICTIM — killing
Genesis 47:7; Hebrews 2:14–15

Turning the Tables

Who would have thought it: a harmless mouse felling a venomous serpent? An Inland Taipan, one of the world's deadliest snakes, whose poison ducts pack enough venom to kill 1,200 humans, was itself hospitalized by a bite from its dinner—the mouse. The supposedly stunned victim bit the snake on its left cheek while being swallowed.

How naturally symbolic of Christ on the cross! Jesus died, like all the rest, a son of Adam, paying for Adam's sin. But appearances deceive. For while he seemed a helpless victim in death, he gave Satan "a bite" from which he will never recover—a bite that neutralized his death-venom and rendered him powerless to kill even one more soul. All this is seen in Revelation 5:5–6. John was told that the Lion of Judah had conquered. Yet when he looked, he saw a Lamb, "looking as if it had been slain." Jesus submitted to death to prove that it had no power over righteousness. He proved that while death is fearsome and forbidding it is not final!

VICTORY — hard-fought
Judges 7:12,; 8:10; Matthew 26:39; Luke 4:13

From Victory to Victory

The Russians fought tenaciously in the fall and winter of 1944 to wrest Budapest from the German defenders. Savage house to house, hand to hand conflicts occurred in the streets, in the rubble, and in the city sewers. The conquest consumed Russian troops, bringing a victory hardly distinguishable from defeat. However expensive to the Russians, the battle proved fatal to Germany. It so critically weakened Hitler's army that it had no strength left to contest the Russian spring offensive. As a result, Vienna and Berlin fell quickly in 1945.

Not every victory comes easily; but sometimes the most expensive one offers significant long-term benefits. Confronting and defeating temptation is like that. It may seem too difficult for our resources, and sometimes we shy from contesting a harder, preferring to confront a lesser temptation. But conquest of a tough, brutal temptation promises easier conquests of others.

VIOLENCE — increasing
2 Kings 23:29–30; Matthew 24:3

Violence Into Violence

Periods of ferocious violence have generally been mere preludes to even greater catastrophes in history. Volatile permutations characterized the decade leading to the fall of Jerusalem. In one eighteen-month period four emperors suffered violent deaths, leading to insurrections in the provinces. Three uprisings of Gentiles against Jews occurred, a number of famines in the empire created unrest, and pestilence killed thirty thousand in Rome.

In the decade prior to World War I, no less than six heads of state were assassinated, including President McKinley. Hundreds were killed in bombings as buildings were destroyed by nihilists, acting on the socialist advice to protest whatever they couldn't accept; but they did it recklessly and with no regard for life. The grievances and hostilities, the shameful mistakes of those twenty-five years, all smoldered until igniting the malignant catastrophe of World War I.

With the intuitive wisdom and insight God offers, Christians must carefully study historical events and draw conclusions from them. History can teach us; only God can prepare us for the End!

VIRTUE — exercise
Haggai 1:2–4; Ephesians 6:10, 13–14

Exercise It

Many settlers in Washington and Oregon during the 1850s and 1860s expressed virulent anti-Indian behavior. Against their antipathy, many who were sympathetic to the Indians hid them from enraged settlers. The problem was the inertia of the pro-Indian compared to the truculent energy of the anti-Indian settlers. Those who wanted them removed actively pushed for their removal, while those who sought accommodation with the red man remained quiescent. Inevitably, the critics moved policy makers.

In the years preceding World War II, the virtuous motives of European statesmen, combined with military and political timidity, loosed a monster on the nations. Decrying their naiveté, and worse, Churchill bellowed that a sincere love of peace was no excuse for muddling the world into total war.

No marshaled virtue has value until it is exercised on behalf of its object. Good thoughts never saved anyone, rescued anyone, resisted any evil, or accomplished any good. More than one ministry has failed because a handful of critics withstood an army of supporters. On the other hand, evil cannot overcome virtue if virtue asserts itself, gets involved, speaks up, and takes action. We in the church do not need greater powers to succeed; we need only the vigorous exercise of spiritual powers now latent within the body of Christ.

VISION — necessary
Proverbs 29:18; Acts 1:8

Able to See

Frank Dugan came to San Diego from Long Beach in 1933, after losing his office and home in the Long Beach earthquake. He immediately began touting his dream of an international fair in San Diego. Few listened. No one got excited. Some people in high places became annoyed with the stranger and his even stranger visions. Then, gradually, as he kept talking, the less chimerical and more realistic his vision seemed. Dugan eventually sold the Chamber of Commerce on the idea, and a finance committee raised $700,000 from investors. Civic leaders began to enthusiastically share Dugan's dream.

New buildings were added to Balboa Park, and its existing structures, first built for the Panama California Exposition in 1915, were refurbished and restored. On May 29, 1935, the California Pacific International Exposition opened in the Park. When it closed November 11, 1935, nearly five million people had attended. It cost the city $20 million to stage; it reaped a profit of $315,000.

Only one person needs to have a vision before other people begin to see it too. But at least one person must. Without a vision, the people perish, Scripture says. Only when someone possesses, sharpens, and augments the vision can it take a shape that others can see, accept, promote, and work to achieve.

VOICE — evolutionary explanation
Genesis 9:3–4; Romans 1:18

What Will It Be Next?

According to an article in *Natural History Magazine,* a wife shouldn't complain about her husband's snoring,. A group called the Institute of Human Origins speculates that male snoring is not a random noise but a planned defense system developed by our ancestors to safeguard their sleep. Knowing that sleep made them especially vulnerable, our early human ancestors mimicked the sound of their most common predators: cats and hyenas. Snoring thus warned the predators that humans were alert and tough.

Well . . . why do females snore, then? Did they like the sound so much that they imitated it to perfection? What about males who don't snore? Did they unlearn this important defense mechanism? Why did only the males develop the defense? Surely mindless evolution would have indiscriminately scattered it, with even infants and children snoring like foghorns in the night!

Indeed, to what futility our thinking can deteriorate when we separate God from thought! How dark our foolish hearts become when not illuminated by God's love.

WAR — costs of
Deuteronomy 20:5–7; Revelation 9:20

High Cost of War

In 1976, the Federal government paid $528,000 to the 459 surviving beneficiaries of the Civil War. It paid nearly $100,000 to the dependents of Indian fighters. It also paid $33,000,000 for 1,200 veterans and 27,000 surviving dependents of the Spanish-American War. The last pension claims of the Revolution were paid in 1911, 130 years after Yorktown; the last claims of the War of 1812 in 1946, 131 years after the treaty in Ghent, Belgium; the last claims of the Mexican War in 1962, 114 years after the battle for the City of Mexico.

Benefits to participants in and beneficiaries of World War I, World War II, Korea, Viet Nam, and the Persian Gulf War will not be fully paid until well beyond 2075. Who can say what future catastrophe will plunge us deeper into debt for a much longer time?

The nation must pay its debt to its soldiers and their dependents. Any refusal would be an inexcusably callous disregard of the sacrifices made. But what an appalling financial price humanity pays to wage war! How we obligate generations yet unborn to pay the responsibilities acquired just because some satanic tyrant seeks to rule the world! We have learned that the cost of war goes on and on, long after the peace is signed. When will we learn that the cost of personal surrender to the Prince of Peace will save us untold millions of dollars and lives?

WATER — shortage
Exodus 17:6; John 4:14; 6:35; 7:33–38

Not a Drop

Water composes three-fourths of the globe yet remains desperately deficient in much of the world. A water shortage does not exist, but relocating it from where it falls to where it is needed is prohibitively expensive. Antarctic ice contains three-fourths of the world's fresh water, but that doesn't make it convenient to water a lawn in Los Angeles or to irrigate a field in Ethiopia. The American Southwest has as critical a shortage as any place in the world. The Plains and

Midwestern states pump from the vast Ogallalla Aquifer much faster than it is resupplied. The Jordan River, shared by Jordan and Israel, now flows at a billion cubic feet a year from a thirty-eight million cubic feet per year in the past. The African droughts continue to jeopardize millions of people in at least fifteen nations, and China struggles to keep the Gobi Desert from encroaching on its expanding population.

We can survive only two or three days without water. While a 5 percent loss of body water debilitates, a 15 to 20 percent loss is fatal. What water is to the body, Jesus is to the soul. But he offered living water—living because God gave the Holy Spirit as a deposit on our future state. What will one day be an overflowing is even now an abundant life within.

WEAKNESS — everyone has a
Judges 1:1–3; Ephesians 2:19–22

Even They

Jack Nicklaus was a Kodiak bear on the golf course, impervious to pressure while huge galleries and television audiences watched his every shot. But put him in the maternity waiting room and he became weak as a newborn cub. Four of five times he fainted on hearing of his children's births. The first time he hit his head on the floor. The second time he was fortunate enough not to hit his head. The third time they caught him going down. The fourth time he sniffed smelling salts—and fainted anyway. The fifth time he narrowly escaped fainting.

Individual weakness can be compensated by corporate strength. That is the mystery of all the members forming the body of Christ. With God mercifully ignoring our personal liabilities to magnify our assets, each Christian contributes essential cells to each bodily function. Incompetence in one area offers no reason for guilt; what one member can't, another can do—each one is essential to the whole. If all serve, no one's disability disables the body!

WEAPONS — positive and negative
1 Kings 19:8; Luke 4:13–14

Especially Deadly

George Whitefield, frail in body and weak in lungs, nevertheless had an astounding range in voice. He preached to a crowd in Scotland estimated at one hundred thousand. Ben Franklin claimed to have heard him at a mile's distance. He was perhaps the second greatest open-air preacher ever, specifically endowed by God for the work.

Ward Hill Lamon, Lincoln's friend and marshal of the District of Columbia, almost killed a man with his bare hands when arresting him. Lincoln wrote him, only half-jokingly: "When you have occasion to strike a man, don't hit him with your fist; strike him with a club or crowbar or something that won't kill him."

Our spiritual life exists apart from either the frailty or potency of the body. We always live on two planes of existence, neither essential to or prohibitive of the other. Samson, though strong in body, never developed strength of soul. Jesus' soul burgeoned even as his body shrank after forty days and nights of hunger in the wilderness. From sources deep within him light shone in his eyes like arcs in the night. He met Satan spiritually energized, alert, powerful . . . determined to slay the dragon. determined while disadvantaged in all but one way, to utilize that way to overcome!

WEATHER — cold!
Joshua 13:1–7; Acts 27:33–36

That's Cold!

The lowest atmospheric temperature ever recorded was logged at a Russian research outpost in Antarctica: -128.6 Fahrenheit. Brrrr! The Wright Brothers didn't experience such bone-cracking cold at Kitty Hawk, North Carolina, but they found its severity worse than any they had experienced in Ohio. They wrote home that they had one-, two-, three-, and four-blanket nights. They also had five-blanket nights. They had five-blankets-plus-two-quilt nights. They had five-blankets-two-quilts-and-a-fire nights. The cold deepened and the brothers used five blankets, two quilts, a fire, and a hot water bottle. When they were still shivering, they slept with all of the above and in their clothes.

Outside forces sometimes threaten to cancel the completion of our spiritual work, but planning for problems can turn them into assets when they occur. They inspire alternative strategies that can be superior to the original or can be used in another project. God knows our limitations. They don't concern him, but not using our giftedness to strategize a compensation of our limitations does.

WELFARE — a class dependent on
Jeremiah 31:17; 32:44; Revelation 22:3

Get Off the Rolls

Deciding that welfare should be a system, not a state—a temporary aid in misfortune, not a lifestyle—California legislators finally took action in 1993. Their proposals included the following: (1) recipients who work will get to keep a third more of their earnings; (2) to encourage thrift, welfare families can accumulate up to $7,000 in savings if it is put aside for education or buying a home; (3) teen mothers who return to school after giving birth and maintain a C average receive a bonus $100 each semester and a $500 bonus if they graduate.

God's Word teaches the value of work. Even in Eden's perfection Adam and Eve "worked and took care of it." With sin came the curse of continued labor but without ease, of sometimes unrewarded effort or hard-earned success, but never again in this world laboring in ceaseless ease. Such a time will come, however, in the New Jerusalem. The curse of Eden will be removed, but the labor begun there—studying, learning, growing in our understanding of God—in rebirth will continue, never to be disrupted again.

WELFARE — problem in other ages
Genesis 47:13–19; Romans 6:22

A Similar Problem

In his "Address to the German Nobility," Martin Luther decried the proliferation of begging in Germany. Any large city in the world today offers a striking parallel. Many, unwilling to work, make a living off those so busy working they have little time to live. Luther urged the princes to provide for the beggars from public revenues—then carefully hedged his advice in words we would find profitable today. The support need not insure total comfort for the beggars. "It is enough if the poor are decently cared for, so that they do not die of hunger or cold. It is not fitting that one man should live in idleness on another's labor or to be rich and live comfortably at the cost of another's discomfort."

Overcoming humanity's natural distaste for labor has historically challenged the creative genius of government, business, and church leaders: how to make duty so attractive people think it is pleasure; how to make what they ought to do become what they like to do. Calling us to spiritual tasks multiples the problem. God must overcome not only our natural laziness but our native perversity. Many people who willingly work for a living will not give an ounce of effort for spiritual tasks. God's answer is a challenge: take Christ's yoke on you, work at being obedient to him, and he guarantees that your work will restore you.

WILL — the difference
Jeremiah 26:7–8, 12–15; Acts 5:40–42

Was a Will

Off Flamborough Head, September 23, 1779, by 10 P.M. the *Serapis* and *Bonhomme Richard* had embraced in a three-hour death grip. John Paul Jones' *Richard* gradually sank, five feet of water in her hold. Freeing the prisoners, Jones ordered them to man the pumps. One jumped ship into the *Serapis* and informed Captain Pearson of the *Richard's* jeopardy. By 10:05, with nearly everyone wanting to abandon ship and his own officers bellowing, "Quarter! Quarter!" Jones still refused. "Sir, do you ask for quarter?" Pearson roared. "No sir, I haven't as yet thought of it," Jones bellowed in return, "but I'm determined to make you strike." Victory for Jones came quickly. The main mast of the *Serapis,* shot through, began to tremble, and Pearson lost his nerve. He struck, pulling the colors down himself. Two commanders, two ships, two countries at war, but in this titanic struggle the difference was "measured by the margin of a will." Pearson fought to win until it cost too much; Jones fought to win, whatever the cost.

Christians must undertake their spiritual struggle to be Christlike with Jones' indomitable tenacity. True, our life compared to Christ's looks like a thread spool placed beside a telephone cable spool, but the difference should excite, not depress us. Exactly like Jesus Christ we will one day be. Let that assurance prompt us to pursue it now. We will achieve, if we persevere in our goal, for God has built irrepressible spiritual success into discipleship for anyone determined to have it.

WITNESS — need of
Isaiah 42:6–7; Luke 4:42–43

Discoverers

The Portuguese, Spanish, and English kept secret their first discoveries on the West African, and South and North American coasts. An essentially economic decision, each country wanted to preserve a monopoly on whatever resources it found there. To protect their findings, maps and charts of the voyages were often kept in a lockbox aboard ship with two locks and two keys. When the mariners returned home, their documents went into state archives to shield them from prying eyes. The records from Francis Drake's epochal world cruise were hidden from the public for ten years. They were so well hidden, in fact, that they have never been found.

Christians have been like the explorers: we have kept secret the knowledge of our discoveries in Christ. Truth must be shared, not hoarded. It reaches its greatest victory in sharing, not in acquiring. Christians cannot withhold Scripture from the unsaved hoping everyone will somehow get to where we are in faith. That might work in geography, but not in spiritual life. God must reveal himself before we can understand him. Thus Christians must communicate what God has revealed in Christ. Very few people will ever find out about God on their own. How will they ever find their way to heaven unless they have Christ's map?

WITNESS — successful
Isaiah 52:7; Acts 13:42, 44

Convert Turned Witness

David Brainerd had spent seven unsuccessful years preaching when he came to his post at Crosswicks, New Jersey in June, 1745. His ministry among the Indians there began as others had ended—with a few in attendance and little interest shown. He wished himself elsewhere.

Then one day he preached to a few women and children. They went great distances and shared their joy in the Lord Jesus. Thus began a nine-month revival. The converts of one day would repeatedly return to their unsaved friends and bring them to the next meeting. In the end, nearly ninety Indians were baptized, and it all started with a few women and children!

Christ converted only one person in Samaria—a woman, and a dishonored one at that. But, as it turned out, that was enough, for the woman immediately turned into a witness, went back to her village, and invited everyone to hear Christ. Her willingness to witness shames our reluctance. A disliked member of the community, she could have taken revenge by remaining quiet. She was a woman, to whom few men would listen and certainly not in public; a dishonored person, whose experiences would naturally be suspect. Yet she allowed no excuses to keep her from speaking. Something wonderful had happened to her, and she took a chance and said so. What great blessings came because of it! Who is to say whether our personal witness will provide the same benefit to others?

WORDS — basis of life
Genesis 28:20–22; Luke 22:60

What Words Reveal

Some cannot afford the luxury of a nap even if they find themselves exhausted: an engineer directing a locomotive down steel-ribbed rails; the pilot of a 747 on take-off or landing, and controllers in the flight tower. They must be alert constantly. The Russians developed a computerized warning system for their controllers at Sheremetyevo Airport in Moscow. It checks the patterns of human speech for signs of fatigue and sets off an alarm when sleepiness is indicated. It detects the slightest difference in the vowels of certain words that occurs when fatigue staggers the controller's mind. The system monitors those specific words and blares its warning at the first intimation of fatigue.

Speech! It can sound like mechanical birds popping from a cuckoo clock, or like rain charming flowers from desert sands. Just listen as people speak of God, the Bible, Christ, and the church. They may sound like a novice or a concert violinist, but their speech will never misidentify their skill, experience, and commitment to spiritual values or their secular, irreligious, profane disposition. Little wonder Jesus said we are condemned or acquitted by our speech. Out of the overflow of our heart, our mouth speaks.

WORDS — reveal much about us
Malachi 1:6–7; John 9:15;

Famous People

The *New York Times*/CBS News poll asked a number of celebrities to summarize themselves in one word. Among them, Pat Riley, coach of the New York Knicks—*traditional*—because he doesn't believe in fads. Ed Koch, former New York Mayor—*candid*—because he doesn't equivocate. Norman Mailer, writer—*improvisational*—because he feels we should treat life as a novel just begun, with no conclusions drawn. Eileen Ford, chairman of Ford Modeling Agency—*busy*—because she doesn't even have a Sabbath rest. Rush Limbaugh, political analyst—*misrepresented*—because he is different from the media reports. David Lynch, film director—*confused*—because that is how he feels when he looks at life.

Words communicate us. They show whether we are familiar with or a stranger to a responsibility; whether we are conversant with the subject or just getting introduced; whether we are comfortable or discomfited by the discussion. Nowhere is this more obvious than among God's people. You can listen to any number of disciples and instantly determine their spiritual ranking. The halting, faltering vocabulary of new Christians, sincere in faith, but unacquainted with Christian terms, marks them, as does the more developed knowledge and speech of growing Christians. In a category of their own are the speech, terms, and usage of those at ease with their faith and thoroughly familiar with their relationship with God. Words do all that.

WORRY — useless
Zechariah 8:20–22; Acts 27:25

The Uselessness of Worry

When John Jacob Astor heard of the loss of his ship *Tonquin,* and the disaster it augured for Astoria, on the Pacific Coast, he knew his investment was lost and his western fur enterprise endangered. He still went to the theater the day he received the bad news. When a friend who knew of the disaster asked how he could receive such news then attend light amusement, as if nothing had happened, Astor replied, "What would you have me do? Would you have me stay at home and weep for what I cannot help?"

That businessman, who had only his wits to guide him, took an unexpectedly rational position when facing disaster. Shouldn't we, who serve the eternal King in charge of all history on behalf of the church, be far more calm when experiencing challenges, disappointments, and losses? Through prayer we can put everything in life under God's direction. Through prayer, we can enjoy personal peace even while experiencing travail.

WORSHIP — devotion to
Joshua 14:7; Acts 2:42

All That Far

A couple lived twenty miles from Munich, Germany, where they attended Sunday services. To arrive for Bible School at 9 A.M., they arose at 4 A.M. They ate quickly and walked forty-five minutes to the station, getting there at 6:55 A.M. to take the train for Munich at 7:45 A.M. From the station in Munich a streetcar took them to the church building for the 8:30 A.M. prayer service. They reversed the transportation schedule after services and arrived home around 1:30 P.M.— every Sunday; without fail.

What good reasons prompted such inconvenience to worship among God's people at an appointed time and place? Perhaps it was the fellowship among friends in Christ, or the chance to teach a Bible school lesson, or a Bible message they could ponder for nourishment through the week ahead. Whatever inspired them, they challenge us to emulate their example.

WORSHIP — use of exact forms
Amos 4:4; Romans 4:13–15

Whatever the Content Is

The early Roman religion, around 800 B.C., was essentially pantheistic. Exact forms of worship had to be followed nonetheless. Divine favor was thought to depend upon performing all ceremonies and uttering all prayers with exactitude. The slightest mistake in word or gesture could nullify the entire proceedings. Sometimes the same rite was repeated thirty times before it was acceptable. Obviously, this greatly increased the power of the priestly class. If forms allowed no deviation, only those conversant with them could be trusted to lead in offering worship.

The entire Old Testament sacrificial system risked the loss of personal faith to a priestly class. To prevent that, God's prophets taught that sacrifices would be acceptable only if accompanied by the spiritual integrity of the worshiper. Nevertheless, formalism plagued the Jews in their preexilic life, unleashing the wrath of the prophets. The Romans had an excuse: they were mortals seeking a way to placate unknown gods. The Jews had no excuse. Their immortal God had revealed certain forms and regulations to discipline their worship experience; but always, in every way, the Word that defined forms also defined spirit, and its vastly greater importance.

WRATH — real
Lamentations 1:1; Ephesians 2:1–3

A Real Threat

A. B. Earle, a nineteenth-century evangelist, insisted on preaching the judgment of God against sinners. He did so, he said, because people have to see themselves as lost before they seek salvation. They won't escape from the wrath to come until they believe it exists.

Two hurdles must be overcome in convincing people that God is angry with unrepentant sinners. One, the very idea that God has communicated with humanity is unacceptable in "sophisticated" company. They feel that we are nobodies who came from nothing; the little whimper left from the Big Bang. How could nobodies need to repent? Two, human pride resents being called sinful. In this regard, the apostles had an easier task, as C. S. Lewis said. They preached to a people aware of their sins, while we preach to a people adamant in their self-righteousness.

YACHTING — demands teamwork
Nehemiah 2:17–18; Hebrews 13:17

All For One . . .

Dennis Conner recaptured the America's Cup when he skippered *Stars and Stripes* to victory over Australia in 1987. The press lionized Dennis, but success came from the combined efforts of the crew. The sixty-five-foot craft has no engine, is not a good sea boat, and is not made for rough seas. To make the America's Cup the toughest possible test of boat and crew, only eleven of the sixteen men needed can sail her. Each member fills at least two or three positions, and serves as backup for those on either side.

The ten thousand moves that go into a race are orchestrated in sequence to achieve maximum speed. Tasks demand muscle, finesse, or acrobatics. At the rear, where the captain stands at the wheel, commands originate and race forward for execution. He is the somebody who knows what everybody is doing.

Sailing the *Stars and Stripes* offers parallels to the church. God designed the church to sail in rough seas, oblivious of danger. The church has always been undermanned, with too few workers and too little money. Christians need to serve knowledgeably as God has gifted them, and anywhere in an emergency. They must be steadfast in their work, even when it is hard, dangerous, or costly. They must listen to directions from their leaders, who have devoted their lives to bringing people to Christ and edifying them so they can continue winning others to Christ.

YANKEE — different meanings
Isaiah 56:5; Acts 21:12–13

The Same Always

The term *Yankee* has a number of meanings, depending on time and era. A Yankee was originally a native of New England. In the Civil War, a Yankee was either a Federal soldier or an inhabitant of the Northern states. In World War I and II the term *Yank* meant an American GI. The term also refers to a large sail used by yachtsmen. Words in all living languages change, adapted by each generation to its own uses.

One word, and its meaning, has never changed: *Christian*. In whatever generation, from the day in Antioch of Syria when it was first used, to our own, the word Christian has always meant "someone belonging to Christ, therefore, Christlike." Christlikeness is the essence of the term: to honor in life him who honored us in death.

YARD — our need
2 Kings 4:10; Luke 10:38

Someplace That Is Mine

The United States no longer leads the world in home ownership, though it remains one of our greatest longings. Until 1980, the percentage of citizens owning homes kept increasing, reaching 65.6 percent. Since then the percentage has declined until, in 1994, 64.2 percent own their own home. In Australia, 70 percent own homes. New Zealand, Great Britain, and the United States have programs to assist first-time buyers.

Our home doesn't have to be in Beverly Hills, California or Sands Point, New York to be important to us. It doesn't have to appreciate 5 to 10 percent a year to be valuable. The human race needs a yard, a house, a few feet of privacy—a place to call home, a place to return to at the end of a long day, where we can feel at ease and be ourselves. Wherever we are, home seems a better place. Whenever we go away, it is always a pleasure knowing we will be able to return.

YELLOWSTONE — renewal
Genesis 2:8–9; Revelation 7:9–17

Room to Breathe

Securing his release from the Lewis and Clark Expedition as they neared the settlements in 1806, John Colter returned upriver with trappers Forrest Handcock and Joseph Dickson. In 1807, as Manuel Lisa's trapper-traders toiled up the Missouri, they found the same Colter at the mouth of the Platte. Alone, after wintering with the duo of the year before, he again signed on to roam the mountains.

That winter he performed one of the prodigies of western exploration, traveling more than five hundred miles across several mountain ranges, with only thirty pounds of supplies. He may have reached South Pass in Wyoming. He definitely saw the thermal springs and sulfurous gas vents of Yellowstone that later trappers called Colter's Hell. In 1872, over two million acres in Northwest Wyoming, with adjacent areas of Montana and Idaho, were set aside as Yellowstone National park, the first of its kind in the country. The Park has been a national treasure of magnificent waterfall, geysers, petrified forests, wildlife, forests, and flowers.

Where humans have not corrupted it, the natural world retains astounding beauty and fecundity. Even in a fallen world, God permits a remnant of its lost resplendence. Perhaps he cheers us with hints of greater glories, once lost, but one day to be repossessed—and never again lost!

YOUTH — no answers
Isaiah 55:6; I Timothy 6:20

No Answers There

Dr. Jonas Salk was one of the premier scientists of the twentieth century. He discovered the polio vaccine that made a casualty of that former crippler. Perhaps dazzled by his scientific knowledge, he pontificated on other subjects. He insisted that the world would, because it must, find new ways to deal with aggression and conflict. Humanity would fashion progress out of its own evolution, he believed, or would become victims of the process of evolution. The young were our hope, he said, because they were not yet conditioned to destructive aggression as were the earliest humans in the evolutionary struggle.

Young people have no answers because they are saturated with the same academic, social, and religious misinformation that Salk learned in his youth. Only when the race leaps over all succeeding history and lands squarely in Day One, in the opening chapter of Genesis, will there be hope for the youth of tomorrow. Until then, the youth of today will keep repeating the mistakes of yesterday, simply because they are the products of a false yesterday.

ZEAL — fact based
Jeremiah 37:14–17; Romans 10:2

A Misplaced Zeal

Adolf Hitler always placed zeal for Nazism above giftedness when choosing his deputies, cabinet ministers, and generals. The generals were usually the first to be dismissed, as the Fuhrer had a maddening way of superseding expert military advice with his intuitions. Early successes emboldened his every decision as the war broadened and Nazi armies stamped out production line victories. As setbacks came, his zeal for ideology continued unabated and his confidence in intuition soared. When generals such as Franz Halder offered strong military reasons against Hitler's plans to hold fast at Stalingrad, he brushed them off, saying "we need national socialist ardor now, not professional ability." When others joined the general voicing their concern, Hitler dismissed them. Nazi zeal would conquer, he said.

Zeal is the essence of commitment, and commitment the means to success. Thus, better is one whose mistake is zeal, not lethargy; who must be reined in, not spurred on. But a disordered, baseless zeal offers no answer to crises that demand truth and objectivity. In religion, zeal has often brought harsh persecution, needless sacrifice, and inhumane brutality. It has also encouraged sacrifice, generosity, and love. Each negative result has originated in submission to a false ideal as each positive result in submission to a true ideal. For zeal to be useful it must originate and end in truth. Truth disciplines and empowers zeal, making it constantly relevant and necessary.

ZEALOT — Jewish
Lamentations 4:12–13; Romans 8:31–34

To the Last

Herod slipped out of Jerusalem in 40 B.C., escaping his enemies by fleeing to Masada, the 1,300 foot bastion in his home territory. Atop that gaunt, rocky outcropping in sight of the Dead Sea, he built a tri-level structure, with two of the levels built into the cliff face and reached by stairs cut from the rocks. To soften the harshness of exile, he embellished the site with luxuriant baths and stately administrative offices.

Masada came to be ineradicably associated with a tenacious Judaism when zealots captured it in A.D. 66, at the beginning of the Jewish-Roman War. In A.D. 72, Flavius Silva led the Tenth Legion and thousands of prisoners of war to reduce the fortress. After building a wall around the mountain to prevent escape, he constructed an earthen ramp from the valley to the rim of the summit. After battering rams breached the walls, the Romans took possession of the twenty acre site. Jewish tradition—which even some Jews question—says that 960 men, women, and children committed suicide to escape capture.

World peace remains a mirage that not all the wisdom of its brilliant statesmen can finesse into reality. But personal peace is an established fact for all who lay their sins—the burden that oppresses—at the foot of the Cross and take upon themselves Christ's righteousness—the burden that brings and maintains peace in the soul.

ZENITH — reaching brings fall
Isaiah 40:6–8, 15; Matthew 24:1–2

From Zenith to Nadir

In the fall of 1959, John, Allen, and Eleanor Dulles held high positions in President Eisenhower's administration. In two years John was dead, Allen fired, and Eleanor released because she was a Dulles. They had climbed to the zenith of political success, only to fall.

Cardinal Wolsey seemed destined to assume the authority of King Henry VIII. He had systematically worked his way into that position, and none could interfere. Then came Anne Boleyn, who changed everything. In Shakespeare's Henry VIII, Wolsey mournfully complains to a servant, "The king has gone beyond me: all my glories in that one woman I have lost for ever." He had climbed to the heights of a church career. He seemed destined to take the final step in political ascendancy. Then he fell irretrievably.

Imperial Rome, arrogant, invincible, frightening, ruled her world with an iron-fisted disdain of mercy. It seemed the one kingdom too strong to fall, or even decay. Yet it shrank from the isles of Britain and the gates of Asia to a provincial town unable to defend itself, its once regnant Forum lost in wheat fields.

God always challenges us to the zenith of service, holiness, and spiritual grace. Attaining these assures a lasting reputation and honor. To reach the heights of any other endeavor guarantees an eventual fall from it. Tacitus was right: political power, for all its influence, rarely lasts indefinitely. For that matter, what power does except that generated by the Holy Spirit?

ZIONISM — ages-old dream
Deuteronomy 31:3, 6; Ephesians 3:14–19

A Longing for Home

As a boy in Germany in the 1930s, Henry Kissinger suffered the beatings perpetrated on all Jewish children. After emigrating to America with his family, young Henry quickly discovered the security of his new homeland. One day, while walking the sidewalks of New York, he saw a group of boys coming toward him. He instinctively thought of crossing the street to avoid them—then he remembered where he was.

Zionism began with the fall of Jerusalem in A.D. 70, when Jews dreamed of reconstituting the Jewish state in Canaan. Modern Zionism had its origin in the life of Theodor Herzl and the first World Zionist Congress in 1897. In 1917, the British issued the Balfour Declaration to help establish a homeland in Palestine for the Jews. Great Britain received a mandate of Palestine in 1923, partly to implement the Declaration. After World War II, the support of allied governments led to the establishment of the state of Israel in May, 1948. After nearly nineteen hundred years the Jews again had a place where they did not have to cross the street to avoid a beating.

In God's house, where all are welcome, all who come should find refuge, friendship, and tolerance. Whatever dangers we face in the world, in God's house we should feel safe. Where others fail to understand us, those in God's house should perfectly interpret our feelings and moods. Whatever emotional or spiritual beatings we take from others, in God's house we should find recovery and healing.

ZODIAC — ancient error
2 Kings 23:4–5; Acts 19:18–20

First One, Then Another

The Greeks, Babylonians, and Romans worshiped the stars, dividing the sky and naming days after planets. The Greeks developed the Zodiac and assigned a particular force to each part of the body. Julius Caesar regularly used astrology to plot political and military campaigns. Adolf Hitler used an astrologer, which encouraged Winston Churchill to hire one to predict Hitler's possible moves. Indira Gandhi was thought to consult astrologers regularly. And our national press had a feeding frenzy when Donald Regan revealed that President and, especially, Mrs. Reagan, would hardly have breakfast before consulting their astrologer. An entire industry has flourished in America, with some 185,000 practicing astrologers.

Even secular astronomers and physicists deride astrology, however, critiquing the selectivity of facts used to enforce the concept. Many ancient critics also attacked the whole dogma of the Zodiac. The Bible bitterly and scathingly denounces astrology. Moses warned against the use of the Zodiac. Isaiah heaped scorn on its practitioners. Josiah exiled astrologers and burned all their accouterments. Those who believe in the God who controls the universe ridicule astrology's basic tenet. How can inanimate heavenly bodies control historical events when awareness, intelligence, judgment, and decisions are all necessary factors to control? Many consult the planets because astrologers charge what they are willing to pay: money. They will not consult God, because he charges what they will not pay: obedient faith.

APPENDIX

Ability
Discipleship – challenges best of us
Absolutes
God – is absolute
Accidents
Loneliness – our despair
Mistakes – experts make
Accountability
Economy – of Roman steward
Truth – rejecting penalizes
Achievements
Body – is limited
Heaven – disproportionate to now
Heaven – God's endowment
Knowledge – limits of
Kudos – encourage excellence
Obstacles – overcoming
Success – too high
Survival – incredible
Vision – necessary
Weapons – positive and negative
Yellowstone – renewal
Action
Reputation – preceding one
Salvation – action required
Undecided – many remain
Virtue – exercise
Adultery
Love – idea of romantic
Mistakes – forgive
Morality – absolutely necessary
Sin – always wrong
Sin – hiding it

Adventure
Habits – need daily
Adversity
Choice – affects destiny
Christ – his life challenges us
Crisis – response to
Experience – sets you apart
Experience – value of personal
Joy – original, eternal state
Kiln – life a fiery
Laughter – our ally
Listening – to others
Music – preserving sanity
Music – reaches the deepest part
of us
Pain – not all the same
Questions – raised by adversity
Will – the difference
Advertising
Aging – vigor
Alcohol – weak penalty
Aging
Christ – a never-ending experience
Looks – importance of
Poverty – amidst plenty
Salvation – accept late
Agriculture
Bible – set it free
Discipleship – commitment
Distance – relative
Earth – leave it intact
Failure – without knowing it
Nature – protected

Satan – uses pleasant

Aids

Name – important

Sin – massively afflicts

Alcohol

Christian faith – works positively

Future – present habits determine

Help – arriving too late

Integrity – debased

Medicine – take it carefully

Money – a delusion

Pleasure – not in things

Politics – alcohol in elections

Sin – unforgiven punished

Ambition

Goals – necessary

Pleasure – not in things

Self – can consume

America

Awards – for outstanding achievement

Law – outrageous costs

Others – see us objectively

Zionism – ages-old dream

Ancients

Humanity – always the same

Knowledge – limits of

Morality – not spiritual

Oppression – a flawed rule

Poverty – relative

Recreation – needed every age

Theft – harsh penalties

Thought – influence of ancient

Trade – unusual way to conduct

Triumph – Roman style

Universe – immensity

Worship – use of exact forms

Zealot – Jewish

Anger

Looks – importance of

Mistakes – forgive

Moods – dealing with

Quarrels – lead to violence

Talking – as catharsis

Animals

Bible – faith must accompany listening

Bible – spiritual engineer

Change – some things don't

Conversion – miraculous transformation

Conversion – speaking God's Word

Discipleship – lived daily

Discipleship – no limitations

Fear – of one thing

Form – without content

God – listen to

God's Image – on our soul

Habits – changing

Habits – force of

Life – God's presence needed

Music – even reaching animals

Nutrition – animal

Occult – used to create luck

Patience – example of

Possessions – having many

Preparation – too much

Reserves – necessary

Science – not always exact

Temptation – overcome

Thanksgiving – for whale

Theft – harsh penalties

Undecided – many remain

Values – lesser

Victim – killing

Voice – evolutionary explanation

Anxiety

Worry – useless

Appearances

Brain – capacity of

Danger – lurking close by

Evangelism – incumbent on Christians

Form – without content

Generosity – God's gauge

Homosexuality – not as many as claimed

Ideas – more attractive than reality

Illusions – exist in what seems
Journalism – lasting influence
Looks – importance of
Motives – accomplishment with mixed
Name – important
Poverty – amidst plenty
Reality – our goal
Resurrection – Christ's own our hope
Sin – always fatal
Spiritual life – real, if different
Talent – looks not important
Things – unexpected
Time – signs of
Truth – damaged
Victim – killing
Weapons – positive and negative
Yellowstone – renewal

Appreciation
Ingratitude – example of
Opinion – one's we seek

Archaeology
Humanity – always the same

Architecture
Zealot – Jewish

Arrogance
Looks – importance of

Art/Artists
Beauty – inability to grasp
Bible – a work of art
Bible – endless spiritual insight
Bible – most effective in original form
Bible – undiscovered treasure
Evidence – essential
Experience – sets you apart
Grace – saved by
Inconsistency – in the religious
Opinion – one's we seek
Patience – example of
Poverty – amidst plenty

Astronomy/Astrology
Heaven – resplendent grandeur
Science – opportunity for gospel

Universe – immensity
Zodiac – ancient error

Atheism
Beginnings – great events from small beginnings

Athletes
Discipleship – growth in necessary
Forgiveness – available for asking
Heaven – not everyone belongs
Knowledge – insufficiency
Obstacles – overcoming
Pain – not all the same
Quarterback – leadership
Satan – uses pleasant
Self – can consume us
Weakness – everyone has a

Atomic Bomb
Fame – you want to miss
Inventions – key of century

Authority
Confidence – self-confidence is necessary
Truth – absolute

Automobiles
Bargain – mutual
Christian life – excellence requires time
Heaven – God's endowment

Average
Nature – basic behavior
Reserves – necessary

Awards
Fame – not desiring
Honor – coming late

Awareness
Listening – to others
Satan – uses pleasant

Backsliding
Conversion – miraculous transformation
Discipleship – lived daily

Balance
Thinking – too much can ruin

Bankruptcy
Sin – swindles
Banks/Banker
Humility – example of
Baptism
Patience – example of
Baseball
Heroes – kids need
Bath/Bathing
Hygiene – varies in cultures
Beauty
Prayer – spend time in
Behavior
Bible – spiritual engineer
Conviction – develops behavior
Future – present habits determine
Habit – changing
Habit – need daily
Help – from unexpected source
Homosexuality – not as many as claimed
Inconsistency – in behavior
Justification – of one's life
Listening – to others
Salvation – accept it late
Betrayal
Treachery – name synonymous with
Bible
Beginnings – great events from small beginnings
Christian faith – demands informed members
Christian faith – nothing hidden
Conviction – develops behavior
Economy – of Roman steward
Evidence – compelling
Evidence – essential
God – as Creator
Gospel – communicate clearly
Humanity – always the same
Listening – need to
Morality – absolutely necessary
Morality – not spiritual

Origin – man's
Politics – no good choices
Prejudice – always blinds
Repetition – of truth essential
Science – not always exact
Teaching – false is false
Thanksgiving – for a whale
Universe – immensity
Voice – evolutionary explanation
Bible Translation
Beginnings – great events from small beginnings
Birds
Discipleship – lived daily
Discipleship – service
God – love, enjoy
Power – small but great
Blood
Christ – only his blood cures sin
Christian life – glimpses of what shall be
Kidney – nature's purifier
Body
Brain – capacity of
Christ – only his blood cures sin
Conscience – listen and obey
Discrimination – in things seen
Discrimination – practice it
Dreams – energy used
Heart – physical and emotional
Judaism – value of circumcision
Kidney – nature's purifier
Laughter – our ally
Mind – power of
Nutrition – animals
Others – see us objectively
Sin – always fatal
Sleep – getting tired enough
Temptation – overcome
Tension – caused by unused energy
Weapons – positive and negative
Boxers/Boxing
Self – can consume us

Brain
Dreams – energy used
Habits – changing
Memory – innate
Reason – God wants us to use

Bureaucracy
Poverty – relative

Business
Bargain – mutual
Christian life – excellence requires time
Counterfeit – always imitating reality
Law – outrageous costs

Calendar
History – renewal needed

Calvary
Christ – came, knowing his fate
Christ – one died for all
Christ – only his blood cures sin
Christ – the sure cure
Christian life – glimpses of what shall be
Death – means of reconciliation
Experience – sets you apart
Fame – not desiring
Fear – of one thing
Redemption – another must do it for us
Resurrection – Christ's own our hope
Victim – killing predator

Candy
Name – important

Capability
Listening – to others

Career
Aging – vigor
Christ – among us but separate
Christ – is life-changing
Christian – behavior betrays Christ
Christian faith – demands informed members
Christian life – excellence requires time

Christian life – success despite failure
Discipleship – challenges best of us
Failure – career from correcting others
Goals – necessary
Grace – saved by
Grace – value of
Integrity – debased
Kindness – returns
Kleptomania – obvious
Listening – to others
Loneliness – our despair
Minority – the few receive most
Occupation – sacred, whatever career
Opportunity – seized
Perseverance – example of
Success – too high
Weapons – positive and negative
Words – basis of life

Celebrities
Divorce – costly
Inheritance – all Christians share

Ceremonies
Triumph – Roman style

Challenge
Sin – always fatal

Chance
Death – close calls
Deeds – good returned
Humility – example of
Influence – of one person
Juvenile – precocity not unusual
Symbols – necessary

Change
Fortune – from good to bad
Government – excessive costs
Habit – changing
Habit – force of
Journalism – lasting influence

Cheating
Fraud – based on greed

Children
Divorce – children hurt
Family – why risk failure?

God – tragedy without
Heaven – endowments
Heroes – curious about
Heroes – kids need
Humility – forced on one
Kindred – numerous
Knowledge – insufficiency
Loneliness – our despair
Memory – bringing justice
Negotiation – our need
Possessions – small but essential
Punishment – God threatens
Sin – dangerous when small
Weakness – everyone has a

Christ
Authority – be careful which you follow
Christian life – be consistent
Conversion – speaking God's Word
Counterfeit – always imitating reality
Creation – enormous energy in
Creation – no answers to our questions
Experience – sets you apart
Extremism – get their attention
Failure – career from correcting others
Fame – not desiring
Holy Spirit – always at our side
Honor – ultimate German military
Inconsistency – of skeptics leading one to faith
Inheritance – all Christians share
Joy – original, eternal state
Marriage – partners reflecting
Motives – accomplishment with mixed
Nature – basic behavior
Numbers – few contribute
People – used
Quality – tells
Redemption – another must do it for us
Rejection – has many faces
Resurrection – Christ's own our hope

Sacrifice – keeps returning good
Sin – we condemn ourselves
Submission – beauty of to Christ
Temptation – overcome
Things – unexpected
Treachery – name synonymous with
Worry – useless

Christian
Christian faith – demands informed members
Christian life – glimpses of what shall be
Christian life – practiced by Christians
Christian life – successful results
Division – natural
Evangelism – incumbent on Christians
Fame – not desiring
God's will – his aims, our interest
Gospel – communicate clearly
Honor – coming late
Inconsistency – in the religious
Inheritance – all Christians share
Involvement – penalty for not getting
Maturity – growth without perfection
Nationality – preserved
Nature – basic behavior
Need – meeting first priority
Occupation – sacred, whatever career
Perseverance – God demands
Potential – unfulfilled
Pressure – necessary for growth
Submission – beauty of to Christ
Trust – essential
Usefulness – need of
Weapons – positive and negative
Worry – useless
Yankee – different meanings

Christianity
Bargain – mutual
Bible – most effective in original form
Christ – is life-changing
Christian faith – nothing hidden
Christian faith – works positively

Church – no compromise
Church – the body of Christ
Extremism – get their attention
Inconsistency – of skeptics leading one to faith
Optimism – invariable in Christ
Preparation – benefits of

Christmas
Church – the body of Christ
Motives – accomplishment with mixed
Music – the most popular Christmas carol
Publicity – of product

Church
Bible – most effective in original form
Christian faith – nothing hidden
Christian faith – works positively
Fellowship – value of
Potential – unfulfilled
Punishment – God threatens
Purpose – different from original
Sin – hiding it
Tension – caused by unused energy
Thought – influence of ancient
Toleration – urged, rejected
Trouble – affects long after
Unity – of God's people
Weapons – positive and negative

Circumstances
Values – lasting

Cities
Ancients – urban society
Bible – a work of art
Bible – it remains
Evangelism – limited
Fame – you want to miss
Ideas – more attractive than reality
Lifestyle – differences in
Noise – getting worse in cities
Possibilities – seeing

Citizenship
Salvation – accept it late

Climate
Weather – cold!

Clothes
Pressure – peer
Understanding – others
Vanity – everyone has

Coal Mine
Sin – hard to surrender

Commerce
Trade – unusual way to conduct

Commitment
Christian faith – works positive
Church – no compromise
Obedience – willed
Zeal – fact based

Communication
Ancients – urban society
Bible – in plain language
Christian faith – nothing hidden
Evangelism – limited
Gospel – communicate clearly
Silence – not always best
Talking – as catharsis

Companionship
Loneliness – our despair

Competition
Failure – but still competitive
Nutrition – animal
Opponent – critical help from

Compliments
Kudos – encourage excellence

Compromise
Conviction – develops behavior
Negotiation – our need
Opportunities – missed
Trade – unusual way to conduct

Computers
Brain – capacity of
Inventions – key of century
Technology – two-edged
Words – basis of life

Confidence
Courage – how it develops

Jealousy – baseless terror

Conflict

Traditions – too important

Congress

Bible – no alterations to truth

Government – excessive costs

Understanding – others

Conquest

Nationality – preserved

Oppression – a flawed rule

Conscience

Extremism – get their attention

Instinct – need to follow

Repentance – stay free

Conservatives

Punishment – God threatens

Consistency

Christian life – practiced by Christians

Constitution

Opportunities – missed

Conversion

Beginnings – great events from small beginnings

Discipleship – lived daily

Earth – leave it intact

Nature – returning to an ancient desire

Salvation – almost not enough

Sin – we condemn ourselves

Conviction

Extremism – get their attention

Obedience – willed

Corporations

Honesty – absence of

Lying – endemic in man

Theft – by employees

Cosmetics

Aging – vigor

Appearances – lift our morale

Counterfeits

Bible – evidences of divine origin

Counterfeiters – always imitating

Truth – damaged

Couples

Marriage – partners reflecting

Truth – rejecting

Courage

Experience – sets you apart

Courtrooms

Sleep – getting tired enough

Creation

Brain – capacity

Bible – endless spiritual insight

Bible – set it free

Bible – spiritual engineer

Christ – one died for all

Christian life – unending value

Conversion – advantageous

Earth – leave it intact

Expectations – unfulfilled

God – love, enjoy

Heart – physical and emotional

Nature – use of sky at sea

Science – not always exact

Science – possible through belief in orderly God

Zodiac – ancient error

Creeds

Bible – it remains

Bible – most effective in original form

Crime

Christ – among us but separate

Fraud – perpetrators caught

Sin – continually reconquered

Theft – harsh penalties for

Crisis

Heaven – God's endowments

Mistakes – experts make

Critics/Criticism

Opinion – one's we seek

Virtue – exercise

Culture

Aging – welcomed

Diet – of almost

Division – natural

Divorce – children hurt
Hygiene – varies in cultures
Prayer – our longing for spiritual realities
Pressure – peer
Custom
Morality – absolutely necessary
Pressure – peer
Traditions – too important
Vengeance – refuse
Danger
Animals – their instinct to save
Christ – came, knowing his fate
Growth – by doing what hasn't been done
Quake – danger
Darkness
Bible – faith must accompany listening
Death
Disaster – immense
Disease – deadlier than war
Dreams – coming true
God – tragedy without
Humor – part of good health
Involvement – success from
Memory – bringing justice
Memory – innate
Mind – power of
Mistake – experts make
Nature – protected
Origin – man's
Possessions – having many
Preparation – too much taken
Quarantine – sin put under
Questions – raised by adversity
Reputation – power of
Resurrection – Christ's own our hope
Silence – not always best
Trouble – affects long after
Values – lasting
Victim – killing

Deception
Christian faith – nothing hidden
Christian life – increasing in worth
Christian life – personal relationship with Christ
Investment – richly rewarded
Mistakes – forgive
Responsibility – individual
Satan – power of deception
Sin – always wrong
Truth – damaged
Decision
Quarterback – leadership
Undecided – many remain
Defeat
Kiln – life a fiery
Pessimism – debilitates
Reconciliation – value of
Defection
Events – symbolic of
Security – breached
Treachery – name synonymous
Depression
Moods – dealing with
Music – preserving sanity
Pessimism – debilitates
Descendents
Kindred – numerous
Desert
Choice – affects destiny
Detectives
Myth – given substance
Values – lesser
Devotees
Myth – given substance
Occult – even using Barbie
Dictators
Alternatives – none good
Differences
Division – natural
Disarmament
Peace – none lasts

Temptation – overcome
Trade – unusual way to conduct
Values – lasting
Values – lesser
Vanity – everyone has
Virtue – exercise
Weapons – positive and negative
Words – reveal much about us
Worry – useless
Worship – devotion to
Yankee – different meanings

Discipline
Conversion – advantageous
Conversion – miraculous transformation
Punishment – God threatens
Sin – committing, wanting no exposure

Discovery
Promises – broken

Disease
Christ – the sure cure
Conscience – listen and obey
Expectations – unfulfilled
Experience – value of personal
God – tragedy without
Humor – part of good health
Judaism – value of circumcision
Laughter – our ally
Possessions – mean nothing at last
Quarantine – sin put under
Satan – uses pleasant
Technology – two-edged

Disguise
Character – shows through a disguise

Dispute
Mistakes – forgive

Division
Trouble – affects long after

Doctors
Deeds – good returned
Experience – value of personal
Need – meeting first priority
Quacks – in medical practice

Doctrine
Medicine – take it carefully
Thought – influence of ancient

Dogs
Animals – man's best friend
Animals – their instinct to save
God's image – on our soul
Quarrels – lead to violence
Theft – harsh penalties for

Doubt
Questions – raised by adversity

Dreams
Vision – necessary

Drugs
Animals – man's best friend
Christian faith – works positively
Future – present habits determine
Kidney – nature's purifier
Persistence – necessary
Quacks – in medical practice
Sin – swindles
Theft – by employees

Duty
Ingratitude – example of
Obedience – willed

Earthquake
Problems – new solutions

Easter
Resurrection – Christ's own our hope

Economics
Change – some things do
Honesty – absence of
Responsibility – individual
Talent – each develops
Witness – need of

Education
Change – some things do
Christian faith – works positively
Goals – necessary
Journalism – lasting influence
Knowledge – insufficiency
Money – a delusion
Others – see us objectively

Preparation – benefits of
Repetition – of truth essential
Sin – ban it
Teaching – results differ
Youth – no answers

Effort
Christ – came, knowing his fate
Christian life – excellence requires time
Christian life – greater effort—greater success
Christian life – successful results
Failure – a lesson
Failure – chance one takes for trying
Influence – of one person
Juvenile – precocity not unusual
Listening – need to
Loss – enormous in short time
Obstacles – overcoming
Service – render when possible
Success – too high
Virtue – exercise

Egotism
Boasting – mocked by defeat
Kudos – encourage excellence
Reality – our goal
Self – looking after

Elections
Politics – alcohol in elections
Prejudice – always blinds

Electricity
Conversion – advantageous
Unity – of God's people

Eloquence
Kudos – encourage excellence

Embarrassment
Lying – endemic in man

Emotions
Humor – part of good health
Laughter – our ally
Moods – dealing with

Empires
Triumph – Roman style

Encouragement
Christ – his life challenges us
Kudos – encourage excellence

Enemies
Conscience – listen and obey
Consistency – needed in relationships
Discipleship – needs forbidden zones
Nobility – seen in action
Satan – uses pleasant
Triumph – Roman style

Energy
Bible – set it free
Christian life – greater effort—greater success
Creation – enormous energy in
Crisis – can cause incredible achievement
Dreams – energy used
Goals – necessary
Pleasure – always have time for
Tension – caused by unused
Usefulness – need of
Virtue – exercise

English
Jargon – confusing communication
Jargon – masquerading as language

Entertainment/Entertainers
Change – some things do
Heaven – disproportionate to now
Name – important
Past – memory keeps us humble
Quality – tells
Rejection – has many faces

Enthusiasm
Zeal – fact based

Environment
Christian faith – works positively
Trouble – coming from afar

Espionage
Character – lack of
Consistency – in relationships
Enemies – admitted

Mistakes – experts make
Naïveté – unbelievable
Name – similar leads to problems
Rumor – as basis of fact
Truth – absolutes
Youth – no answers

Explorers/Exploration

Authority – be careful which you follow
Body – is limited
Christ – his life challenges us
Christ – only way to God
Evangelism – limited
Example – power
Expectations – unfulfilled
Humanity – always the same
Hunger – obliterating other feelings
Invention – necessity mother of
Misfortune – blaming wrong things
Perseverance – example of
Politics – doctrine of effective occupation
Race – racism inherent
Thanksgiving – for a whale
Truth – damaged
Witness – need of
Yellowstone – renewal

Exposure

Investigation – Christian life invites
Sin – hiding it

Extremes

Weather – cold!

Facts

Bible – cuts to the bone

Failure

Chance – wishing for a second
Christ – came, knowing his fate
Christian life – be consistent
Christian life – success despite failure
Crisis – response to
Discipleship – growth in necessary
Exploration – success even in failure
Goals – falling just short of

Juvenile – precocity not unusual
Kiln – life a fiery
Mistakes – forgive
Motives – accomplishment with mixed
Quarterback – leadership

Faith

Bible – faith must accompany listening
Christ – his life challenges us
Christian faith – works positively
Christian life – a revolutionary life
Christian life – practiced by Christians
Church – no compromise
Confidence – self-confidence is necessary
Discipleship – investigated first-hand
Discipleship – personal experience
Evangelism – public witness
Experience – sets you apart
Form – without content
Inconsistency – of skeptics leading one to faith
Kingdom – of God
Knowledge – insufficiency
Maturity – growth without perfection
Present – all we have
Quietness – need times of
Salvation – action required
Worry – useless

Fame

Fellowship – value of
Heroes – curious about
Illusions – exist in what seems
Inheritance – all Christians share
Jewelry – famously expensive
Loneliness – our despair
Past – memory keeps us humble
Poverty – amidst plenty
Quality – tells

Family

Children – blessedness of

Christian faith – works positively
Death – means of reconciliation
Divorce – children hurt
Goals – necessary
Heroes – curious about
Negatives – need to be strong
Possessions – mean nothing at last
Poverty – insoluble by government
programs
Poverty – relative
Quarrels – lead to violence

Fantasy
God – as Creator
Myth – gives substance

Farmers
Christian life – increasing in worth
Events – symbolic of a movement
Generation – building from previous
Justification – of one's life
Lifestyle – differences in
Salvation – accept while offered
Satan – uses the pleasant

Fashion
Pressure – peer
Vanity – everyone has

Fathers
Family – fathers in leadership
Loneliness – our despair

Fear
Alternatives – none good
Failure – a motivation
Guilt – haunts
Investigation – Christian life invites
Justice – no one escapes
Laughter – our ally
Listening – to others

Feelings
Obedience – willed

Fellowship
Loneliness – our despair
Worship – devotion to

Figure Skaters
Discipleship – growth in necessary

Fire
Sin – hard to surrender

Fish
Nature – protected
Quietness – need times of

Flag
Publicity – value of

Flowers
Beauty – a necessity
Publicity – of product

Food
Diet – of almost anything
Discrimination – in things seen
Expectations – unfulfilled
Hunger – obliterates other
feelings
Hunger – visceral
Medicine – take it carefully
Nutrition – animal
Thanksgiving – precedes gifts from
God

Football
Prayer – spend time in
Quarterback – leadership

Forgiveness
Christ – the sure cure
Christian life – overcoming the past
Guilt – haunts
Help – from unexpected source
Medicine – take it carefully
Sin – hard to surrender
Vengeance – refuse

Formality
Kingdom – of God
Knowledge – insufficiency
Worship – use of exact forms

Fortune
Kiln – life a fiery
Loneliness – our despair

Frauds
Lying – endemic
Morality – not spiritual
Responsibility – individual

Freedom
Habit – force of
Law – outrageous costs

Friendship
Christ – among us but separate
Enemies – admitted
Fellowship – value of
Holy Spirit – always at our side
Others – see us objectively
Possessions – mean nothing at last
Treachery – name synonymous with
Trouble – friends causing

Funeral
Death – means of reconciliation

Future
Chance – wishing for a second
Choice – affects destiny
Christ – a never-ending experience
Fortune – from good to bad
Generation – building from
previous
Kindness – returns
Present – all we have
Present – bad for future
Progress – theme of humanity
Salvation – accept while offered

Gambling
Fortune – from good to bad
Future – present habits determine
God – listen to

Generation
Expectations – unfulfilled
Failure – one generation afflicts
the next

Geography
Failure – without knowing it
Spiritual life – real, if different
Witness – need of
Zealot – Jewish

Germs
Sin – always fatal

Giftedness
Potential – unfulfilled

Goals
Christian life – success despite failure
Discrimination – practice it
Life – God's presence needed
Salvation – accept it late

God
Christian life – success despite failure
Discrimination – practice it
Evidence – compelling
Expectations – unfulfilled
God's will – his aims, our interest
Grace – helps though we offend
Heaven – resplendent grandeur
Ideas – more attractive than reality
Judaism – spiritually obdurate
Life – God's presence needed
Pleasure – not in things
Politics – doctrine of effective
occupation
Salvation – action required
Science – possible through belief in
orderly God
Trade – unusual way to conduct
Truth – rejecting
Universe – immensity

Golf/Golfers
Divorce – costly
Obstacles – overcoming

Gospel
Evangelism – limited

Government
Bible – insists we face reality
Christ – only his blood cures sin
Consistency – in relationships
Evangelism – public witness
Experience – sets you apart
Grace – helps though we offend
Ideas – more attractive than reality
Illusions – many build on
Kiln – life a fiery
Lifestyle – thrift in disastrous
Mistakes – learning from others
Negotiation – our need

Heirs
Inheritance – all Christians share
Hell
Punishment – God threatens
Quarantine – sin put under
Salvation – almost not enough
Heroes
Myth – given substance
History
Christian faith – nothing hidden
Evangelism – limited
Events – symbolic of a movement
Humanity – always the same
Kingdom – of God
Legends – retold
Others – see us objectively
Punishment – God threatens
Rumor – as basis of fact
Teaching – false still false
Treachery – name synonymous
with
Violence – increasing
Home
Yard – our need
Zionism – ages-old dream
Homeliness
Talent – looks not important
Homosexuality
Sin – massively afflicts
Truth – rejecting
Honesty
Integrity – debased
Integrity – example of
Lying – endemic
Promises – broken
Trade – unusual way to conduct
Honor(s)
Titles – don't make the person
Horseracing
God – listen to
Occult – used to create luck
Hospital
Need – meeting first priority

Hospitality
Mind – power of
Humanism
Church – the body of Christ
Morality – not spiritual
Humanity
Boasting – mocked by defeat
Creation – no answers to our questions
Division – natural in
Expectations – unfulfilled
God – listen to
Illusions – many build on
Nature – basic behavior
Nature – returning to an ancient
desire
Origin – man's
Peace – none lasts
Pleasure – always have time for
Progress – theme of humanity
Race – racism inherent
Recreation – needed in every age
Service – render when possible
Technology – only so successful
Weapons – positive and negative
Youth – no answers
Human Nature
Body – is limited
Humility
Body – is limited
Crisis – response to
Forgiveness – available for asking
Ignorance – of the impossible
Kudos – encourage excellence
Past – memory keeps us humble
Humor
Laughter – our ally
Hunger
Diet – of almost anything
Hypocrisy
Character – necessary
Ideas
Discrimination – practice it
Dreams – giving insight

Morality – not spiritual
Sin – abolish

Identity
God – love, enjoy
God's image – on our soul
Nationality – preserved

Idleness
Money – a delusion
Quiet – need times of
Stress – antidote for

Idolatry
Zodiac – ancient error

Ignorance
Repetition – of truth essential
Sin – massively afflicts

Illness
Loneliness – our despair
Nature – protected
Obstacles – overcoming

Illusions
Sin – always fatal
Spiritual life – real, if different
Truth – damaged

Image
Name – important

Imagination
God – as Creator

Immigration
History – renewal needed
Race – racism inherent
Sin – continually reconquered

Immortality
Illusions – many build on
Inconsistency – in the religious

Immunity
Kidney – nature's purifier
Sin – always fatal

Impenitence
Self – problem between God and us

Imperialism
Awards – for what true purpose?

Imprisonment
Conviction – develops behavior

Incarnation
Character – shows through a disguise
Christ – his life challenges us
God's image – on our soul

Incompetence
Quacks – in medical practice

Inconsistency
Hypocrisy – flagrant
Opinion – one's we seek

Independence
Unity – of God's people

Indians
Bible – no alterations to truth
Diet – of almost anything
Failure – means of success
Ingratitude – example of
Intuition – warning of danger
Mind – power of
Name – important
Race – racism inherent
Salvation – accept while offered
Strength – how to achieve
Understanding – others
Vengeance – refuse
Virtue – exercise
Witness – successful

Individuals
Grace – value of
Survival – incredible
Traditions – too important
Unity – of God's people
Vision – necessary

Influence
Christian life – overcoming the past
Jewelry – famously expensive
Myth – given substance
Persistence – necessary
Vision – necessary

Informality
Others – see us objectively

Information
Secrets – keeping
Witness – need of

Ingratitude
Humiliation – abject
Need – meeting first priority
Injustice
Salvation – almost not enough
Innocence
Ignorance – of the impossible
Testimony – not everyone accepts
Insects
Diet – of almost anything
Nature – protected
Insecurity
Confidence – self-confidence is
necessary
Insight
Dreams – giving insight
Instinct
Crisis – response to
Intuition – warning of danger
Mistakes – experts make
Temptation – overcome
Insurance
Law – outrageous costs
Lying – endemic
Integrity
Honesty – subject to conditions
Humility – example of
Politics – no good choices
Intelligence
Origin – man's
Secrets – keeping
Intercession
Holy Spirit – always at our side
Interpretation
Bible – plain to everyone
Intuition
Zeal, fact based
Invention
Failure – means of success
Investment
Christian life – increasing in worth
Expectations – unfulfilled
Exploration – success even in failure

Jewelry – famously expensive
Lying – endemic
Responsibility – individual
Revenge – growth of
Sin – swindles
Values – lasting
Worry – useless
Jewelry
Self – looking after
Journalism
Discipleship – centered in self-
denial
Fame – with preferential treatment
God – as Creator
Myth – gives substance
Naïveté – unbelievable
Persistence – necessary
Judaism
Heroes – kids need
Truth – by inches
Worship – use of exact forms
Zionism – ages-old dream
Judgment
Bible – it remains
Blame – casting on others
Christian faith – has basic structure
Discrimination – practice it
Fraud – based on greed
Heaven – not everyone belongs
Investigation – Christian life invites
Listening – need to
Mercy – call for
Nations – receive justice now
Opportunities – missed
Salvation – accept now
Sin – unforgiven punished
Time – signs of
Wrath – real
Justice
Extremism – get their attention
Judgment – dangerous
Law – outrageous costs
Sin – unforgiven punished

Knowledge
Help – from unexpected source
Maturity – growth without perfection
Naïveté – unbelievable
Others – see us objectively
Reality – our goal
Rumor – as basis of fact
Science – opportunity for gospel

Language
Christian life – glimpses of what shall be
Education – answers from college
Education – things they learn at school
Jargon – confusing communication
Jargon – masquerading as language
Satan – power of deception
Words – reveal much about us

Laughter
Humor – part of good health
Name – unusual

Law/Lawyers
Fraud – perpetrators caught
Punishment – God threatens
Sin – unforgiven punished
Testimony – not everyone accepts
Theft – harsh penalties
Trust – essential
Welfare – a class dependent on

Leadership
Bargain – mutual
Christ – among us but separate
Christian faith – demands informed members
Example – power
Integrity – example of
Investment – richly rewarded
Juvenile – precocity not unusual
Maturity – growth without perfection
Misfortune – blaming wrong things
Negatives – need to be strong
Pain – not all the same
Patience – necessary
Perseverance – when it is hard

Preparation – benefits of
Present – bad for future
Quarterback – leadership
Recreation – need in every age
Repetition – of truth essential
Reputation – preceding one
Reserves – necessary
Tension – caused by unused energy
Understanding – others
Vision – necessary
Yachting – demands teamwork
Zodiac – ancient error

Liberalism
Rejection – has many faces
Truth – by inches

Libraries
Ancients – urban society

Life
Bible – spiritual engineer
Character – lack of
Christian faith – works positively
Conviction – develops behavior
Death – close calls
Economy – of Roman steward
Effort – what purpose?
Hope – absolute need
Illusions – exist in what seems
Investigation – Christian life invites
Nature – use of sky at sea
Pessimism – debilitates
Possessions – having many
Poverty – amidst plenty
Thinking – too much ruins

Life, Eternal
Disaster – immense

Lifestyle
Divorce – costly

Light
Bible – faith must accompany listening
Creation – enormous energy in
Quality – tells
Universe – immensity

Limitations
Obstacles – overcoming
Listening
God – let him prescribe
Litigation
Change – some things do
Law – outrageous costs
Negotiation – our need
Sin – hiding it
Sin – swindles
Love
Experience – sets you apart
Jewelry – famously expensive
Kingdom – of God
Mistakes – forgive
Opinion – one's we seek
Luck
Past – memory keeps humble
Luxury
Generosity – God's gauge
Lying
Counterfeit – always imitation of reality
Promises – broken
Repetition – of truth essential
Satan – power of deception
Youth – no answers
Mafia
Character – shows through a disguise
Management
Bargain – mutual
Manifest Destiny
Exploration – success even in failure
Marriage
Divorce – costly
Heroes – curious about
Listening – to others
Love – idea of romantic
Mistakes – forgive
Marxism
Mistakes – learning from another's
Maturity
Aging – compensations

Medicine
Ancients – urban society
Christ – only his blood cures sin
Christian life – practiced by Christians
Christian life – success despite failure
Conscience – listen and obey
Goals – necessary
God – let him prescribe
Judaism – value of circumcision
Knowledge – insufficiency
Listening – to others
Occupation – sacred, whatever career
Medieval Europeans
Hygiene – varies in cultures
Memoirs
Perseverance – example of
Memory
Aging – compensations
Fame – evanescent
Mental Illness
Laughter – our ally
Merchandising
Inheritance – all Christians share
Methods
Form – dismissed in crisis
Military
Achievements – not given their due
Bible – insists we face reality
Christ – one died for all
Christian life – be consistent
Conviction – develops behavior
Crisis – can cause incredible behavior
Disaster – immense
Discipleship – commitment
Fame – not equal to faithfulness
Fame – you want to miss
Generation – building from previous
Honor – coming late
Honor – ultimate German military
Hope – absolute need of
Illusions – many build on
Ingratitude – example of

Intuition – warning of danger
Inventions – key of century
Juvenile – precocity not unusual
Kiln – life a fiery
Life – selling cheaply
Loyalty – to one's own cause
Loyalty – under duress
Memory – innate
Mind – power of
Mistakes – learning from others
Music – preserving sanity
Naïveté – unbelievable
Name – similar leads to problems
Nations – receive justice now
Numbers – few contribute
Optimism – invariable in Christ
Perseverance – example of
Pessimism – debilitates
Pleasure – always time for
Potential – unfulfilled
Poverty – extreme national
Publicity – value of
Purpose – different from original
Reality – our goal
Reconciliation – value of
Rumor – as basis of fact
Salvation – action required
Secrets – keeping
Security – breached
Talking – as catharsis
Technology – only so successful
Things – unexpected
Triumph – Roman style
Trouble – affects long after
Trouble – friends causing
War – costs
Zeal – fact based

Mind
Christ – a never-ending experience
Conscience – listen and obey
Conversion – speaking God's Word
Effort – what purpose?
Reason – God wants us to

Minister/Ministry
Christ – is life-changing
Discipleship – service
Fame – not equal to faithfulness
Ignorance – of the impossible
Need – meeting first priority
Patience – example of
People – used
Quacks – in medical
Service – render when
Talent – looks not important
Usefulness – need of

Miracles
Evidence – compelling

Misery
Talking – as catharsis

Misinformation
Education – answers from college
Education – things they learn at school

Missiles
Inventions – key of century

Missionaries
Understanding – others

Mistakes
Apology – unusual
Chance – wishing for a second
Failure – career from correcting others
Family – why risk failure?
Forgiveness – available for asking
God – tragedy without
Jargon – confusing communication
Jargon – masquerading as language
Misfortune – blaming wrong things
Naïveté – unbelievable
Name – similar leads to problem
Nobility – seen in action
Preparation – too much
Present – bad for future
Race – nomenclature
Science – not always exact
Sin – dangerous when small
Trouble – friends causing

Money
Aging – vigor
Alcohol – no emphatic penalty
Bible – a work of art
Bible – evidence of divine origin
Bible – undiscovered treasure
Character – lack of
Christian life – increasing in worth
Christian life – successful results
Counterfeit – always imitating reality
Discipleship – commitment
Discrimination – practice it
Divorce – costly
Expectations – unfulfilled
Exploration – success even in failure
Fame – evanescent
Fame – with preferential treatment
Fortune – from good to bad
Fraud – based on greed
Fraud – perpetrators caught
Future – present habits determine
Generosity – God's gauge
God – listen to
Government – excessive costs
Heaven – disproportionate to now
Heroes – curious about
Illusions – exist in what seems
Integrity – debased
Integrity – example of
Investment – richly rewarded
Jewelry – famously expensive
Kindness – returns
Kleptomania – obvious
Law – outrageous costs
Life – selling cheaply
Lifestyle – thrift in disastrous
Loneliness – our despair
Minority – the few receive most
Motives – accomplishment with mixed
Nature – protected
Need – meeting first priority

Negotiation – our need
Others – see us objectively
Possessions – having many
Possibilities – seeing
Poverty – amidst plenty
Poverty – extreme national
Poverty – insoluble by government programs
Responsibility – individual
Revenge – growth of
Self – looking after
Sin – swindles
Trust – essential
Vision – necessary
War – costs
Yard – our need

Morality
Bible – spiritual engineer
Integrity – debased
Lying – endemic

Mountain Men
Exploration – success even in failure
Humility – example of

Movies
Truth – absolute

Murder
Memory – bringing justice

Music
Achievements – not given their due
Christian faith – demands informed members
Fame – missing it
Goals – necessary
Juvenile – precocity not unusual
Opinion – one's we seek
Race – nomenclature

Mystery
Dreams – coming true
Heaven – resplendent grandeur
Knowledge – limits of
Sin – always fatal

Name
Treachery – name synonymous

Nationality/Nationalism
Race – racism
National Parks
Prayer – spend time in
Yellowstone – renewal
Nations
Punishment – God threatens
Time – signs of
Traditions – too important
Violence – increasing
Zenith – reaching brings fall
Nature
Change – some things do
Hunger – obliterating other
feelings
Prayer – spend time in
Quake – danger
Science – possible through orderly
Spiritual life – real, if different
Yellowstone – renewal
New Testament
Beginnings – great events from
small beginnings
Bible – message never revised
Obedience
Discipleship – no limitations
Discipleship – service
Fear – of one thing
Temptation – overcome
Objectivity
Crisis – response to
Others – see us objectively
Prejudice – always blinds
Obscurity
Fame – missing it
Occult
Zodiac – ancient error
Ocean
Self – problem between God and us
Technology – only so successful
Trouble – coming from afar
Will – the difference
Yachting – demands teamwork

Opinion
Distance – relative
God – listen to
Naïveté – unbelievable
Nobility – seen in action
Occult – used to create luck
Spiritual life – real, if different
Opponents
Zenith – reaching brings fall
Opportunity
Chance – wishing for a second
Organs
Heart – physical and emotional
Kidney – nature's purifier
Others
People – used
Pride – brings harm
Understanding – others
Pain
Experience – sets you apart
Experience – value of personal
Humor – part of good health
Joy – original, eternal state
Laughter – our ally
Parachutist
Mistakes – experts make
Parade
Triumph – Roman style
Parents
Family – fathers in leadership
Family – why risk failure?
Knowledge – insufficiency
Negatives – need to be strong
Past
Chance – wishing for a second
Christ – a never-ending
experience
Guilt – haunts
Memory – innate
Publicity – of product
Patience
Christian life – excellence requires
time

Peace
Reconciliation – value of
People
Events – symbolic of a movement
Fame – not equal to faithfulness
Moods – dealing with
Name – unusual
Noise – getting worse in cities
Perfection
Christian life – success despite
failure
Persecution
Christ – is life-changing
Church – the body of Christ
Experience – sets you apart
Optimism – invariable in Christ
Perseverance
Influence – of one person
Loss – enormous in short time
Memory – bringing justice
Obstacles – overcoming
Persistence – necessary
Salvation – accept it late
Personality
Character – necessary
Character – shows through a
disguise
Perspective
Crisis – response to
Distance – relative
Kiln – life a fiery
Lifestyle – differences in
Others – see us objectively
Pessimism
Inconsistency – of skeptics leading
one to faith
Pesticide
Grace – saved by
Pests
Hatred – indiscriminate
Philosophers/Philosophy
Death – final words
Thought – influence of ancient

Pilots
Growth – by doing what hasn't
been done
Service – render when
Pleasure
Satan – uses pleasant, good
Poetry
Experience – sets you apart
Poison
Sin – always fatal
Sin – dangerous when small
Victim – killing
Police
Animals – their instinct to save
Christ – among us but separate
Fraud – perpetrators caught
Name – similar leads to problems
Publicity – changes people
Sin – continually reconquered
Politics
Bible – cuts to the bone
Christ – only his blood cures sin
Experience – sets you apart
Failure – one generation afflicts
the next
Holy Spirit – always at our side
Honesty – subject to conditions
Integrity – debased
Integrity – example of
Kindness – returns
Lifestyle – thrift in disastrous
Loyalty – to one's own cause
Lying – endemic
Nations – receive justice now
Negotiation – our need
Nobility – seen in action
Patience – necessary
Peace – none lasts
People – used
Possessions – mean nothing
Poverty – extreme national
Poverty – insoluble by government
programs

Prayer – longing for spiritual realities
Present – bad for future
Prejudice – always blinds
Punishment – God threatens
Sacrifice – keeps returning
Salvation – everyone needs
Satan – power of deception
Self – problem between God and us
Things – unexpected
Titles – don't make the person
Understanding – others
Virtue – exercise
Zeal – fact based
Zealot – Jewish
Zenith – reaching brings fall

Population
Discipleship – commitment

Possessions
Jewelry – famously expensive
Kleptomania – obvious
Pleasure – not in things
Success – too high
Values – lasting

Potential
Discipleship – challenges best of us
Evangelism – limited
Future – present habits determine
God's will – his aims, our interest
Heaven – God's endowment
Ignorance – of the impossible
Life – God's presence needed
Opinion – one's we seek
Opportunities – missed
Possibilities – seeing

Poverty
Past – memory keeps us humble
Welfare – a class dependent on
Welfare – problem in ages past

POW's
Children – blessedness of
Music – reaches deepest part of us

Practice
Discipleship – growth in necessary

Juvenile – precocity not unusual

Praise
Grace – helps though we offend
Opinion – one's we seek

Prayer
Christ – among us but separate
Evangelism – public witness
Experience – value of personal
Occupation – sacred, whatever career
Quietness – need times
Temptation – overcome
Thanksgiving – precedes gifts
Worry – useless

Preaching
Christian faith – demands informed members
Gospel – communicate clearly
Repetition – of truth essential
Reserves – necessary

Pregnancy
Sin – ban it

Prejudice
Opponent – critical help
Race – racism
Toleration – urged, rejected

Pride
Boasting – mocked by defeat
Mistakes – even experts make

Privacy
Investigation – Christian life invites

Privilege
Obstacles – overcoming

Problems
Misfortune – blaming wrong things

Promises
Illusions – exist in what seems

Proof
Evidence – compelling

Property
Nature – protected

Prophecy/Prophets
Christ – came, knowing his fate

Judgment – dangerous
Talent – looks not important
Values – lesser
Prophets, False
Counterfeit – always imitating reality
Psychics
Occult – using Barbie
Occult – using to create luck
Psychology/Psychiatry
Sin – always wrong
Sin – we condemn ourselves
Publicity
Influence – of one person
Prayer – longing for spiritual realities
Punishment
Alcohol – weak penalty
Blame – casting on others
Forgiveness – available for asking
Joy – original, eternal state
Judgment – dangerous
Laughter – our ally
Thinking – too much ruins
Time – signs of
Quality
Bargain – mutual
Failure – a lesson
Racing
God – listen to
Racism
Opponent – critical help from
Reality
Bible – insists we face reality
Experience – sets you apart
Form – without content
God – as Creator
Ideas – more attractive than reality
Illusions – many build on
Spiritual life – real, if different
Reason
Mistakes – forgive
Reconciliation
Death – means of reconciliation
Enemies – admitted

Recovery
Nature – protected
Redemption
Nature – returning to ancient desire
Reformation
Church – the body of Christ
Toleration – urged, rejected
Regret
Christ – a never ending experience
Rejection
Discipleship – needs forbidden zones
Relationships
Mistakes – forgive
Negotiation – our need
Quarrels – lead to violence
Trust – essential
Relaxation
Prayer – spend time in
Recreation – need in every age
Stress – antidote for
Renaissance
Church – the body of Christ
Renewal
History – renewal needed
Repentance
Authority – God is absolute
Belief – understand clearly
Blame – casting on others
Christian life – overcoming the past
Discipleship – needs forbidden zones
Forgiveness – available for asking
Problems – new solutions
Salvation – action required
Wrath – real
Reputation
Character – necessary
Counterfeiters – always imitating
Fame – evanescent
Fame – not deserving it
Kiln – life a fiery
Titles – don't make the person
Rescue
Evangelism – incumbent on Christians

Instinct – need to follow

Resources

Kindness – returns

Respect

Fame – with preferential treatment

Opinion – one's we seek

Responsibility

Apology – unusual

Blame – casting on others

Chance – wishing for a second

Kleptomania – obvious

Truth – rejecting

Results

Talent – each develops

Truth – rejecting

Resumés

Lying – endemic

Resurrection

Inheritance – all Christians share

Truth – by inches

Revelation

Bible – in plain language

Bible – message never revised

Revenge

Mistakes – forgive

Vengeance – refuse

Revival

History – renewal needed

Journalism – lasting influence

Revolt

Nationality – preserved

Rewards

Deeds – good returned

Heaven – disproportionate to now

Honor – ultimate German

Immortality – exceeds all our anticipation

Kindness – returns

Sacrifice – keeps returning

Triumph – Roman style

Romance

Jewelry – famously expensive

Royalty

Self – looking after

Sacrifice

Christ – came, knowing his fate

Christ – one died for all

Oppression – a flawed rule

War – costs

Sailors/Sailing

Christ – one died for all

Division – natural

Fame – evanescent

Yachting – demands teamwork

Salvation

Authority – God is absolute

Christ – one died for all

Christ – only his blood cures sin

Christ – only way to God

Earth – leave it intact

Evangelism – incumbent on Christians

Grace – helps though we offend

Mercy – call for

Trade – unusual way to conduct

Satan

Christ – his life challenges us

Christian life – be consistent

Christian life – greater effort— greater success

Christian life – increasing in worth

Christian life – overcoming the past

Counterfeit – always imitation of reality

Discipleship – needs forbidden zones

Help – from unexpected source

Kingdom – of God

Life – selling cheaply

Loyalty – to one's own cause

Occult – using Barbie

Perseverance – God demands

Politics – doctrine of effective occupation

Politics – no good choices

Sin – abolish

Sin – continually reconquered

Testimony – not everyone accepts
Truth – damaged
Victim – killing

Scholarship
Awards – for what true purpose?

Science/Scientists
Conversion – speaking God's Word
Conscience – listen and obey
Creation – enormous energy in
Creation – no answers to our
questions
Humility – example of
Progress – theme of humanity
Sin – always fatal
Youth – no answers

Secrets
Rumor – as basis of fact

Security
Bible – evidences of divine origin
Heaven – not everyone belongs
Illusions – exist in what seems
Kleptomania – obvious
Technology – two-edged

Self
Confidence – self-confidence is
necessary
Justification – of one's life
Loyalty – to one's own cause
Optimism – invariable in Christ
Pride – brings harm

Self-Control
Emotions – hidden at critical
Emotions – overcoming

Self-Denial
Conversion – miraculous transfor-
mation
Discipleship – centered in self-
denial
Failure – career from correcting
others
Habit – need daily
Self – looking after
Self – problem between God and us

Self-Preservation
Christ – one died for all

Serendipity
Failure – means of success
Motivation – accomplishment with
mixed
Music – the most popular Christmas
carol
Purpose – different from original

Service
Fame – not equal to faithfulness
Zenith – reaching brings fall

Sexuality
Christian life – practiced by Christians
Homosexuality – not as many as
claimed
Love – idea of romantic
Morality – absolutely necessary
Sin – massively afflicts

Ships
Humanity – always the same
Invention – necessity mother of

Sight
Discrimination – in things seen
Evangelism – incumbent on Christians

Sin
Bible – insists we face reality
Blame – casting on others
Christ – only his blood cures sin
Christ – the sure cure
Christian life – overcoming the past
Hatred – indiscriminate
Help – from unexpected source
Homosexuality – not as many as
claimed
Jealousy – baseless terror
Justice – no one escapes
Morality – absolutely necessary
Nature – returning to ancient desire
Occult – using Barbie
Quarantine – sin put under
Redemption – another must do it
for us

Wrath – real

Slaves/Slavery
Extremism – get their attention
Failure – one generation afflicts the next
Hypocrisy – flagrant

Sleep
Humility – forced on one
Humor – part of good health
Money – a delusion
Voice – evolutionary explanation
Words – basis of life

Snakes
Animals – their instinct to save

Socialism
Ideas – more attractive than reality

Society
Distance – relative
Involvement – penalty for not getting
Trouble – affects long after

Sorrow
Reputation – power of

Soul
Medicine – take it carefully
Origin – man's

Space
Creation – no answers to our questions

Speech
Conversion – speaking God's Word
Voice – evolutionary explanation

Spiritual Life
Experience – sets you apart
Knowledge – insufficiency
Zenith – reaching brings fall

Sports
Alcohol – weak penalty
Chance – wishing for a second
Christ – only way to God
Christian life – greater effort—greater success
Consistency – relationships
Discipleship – growth in necessary

Evangelism – incumbent on Christians
Failure – a motivation
Fame – evanescent
Forgiveness – available for asking
Future – present habits determine
Grace – value of
Heaven – not everyone belongs
Hope – absolute need of
Knowledge – insufficiency
Need – meeting first priority
Prayer – spend time in
Symbols – necessary
Words – reveal much about us

Stress
Christ – among us but separate
Emotions – overcoming
Kiln – life a fiery
Listening – to others
Money – a delusion
Pressure – needed to grow
Quietness – need times
Success – too high

Style
Christian life – successful results

Success
Christ – is life-changing
Christian life – greater effort—greater success
Christian life – success despite failure
Courage – how it develops
Exploration – success even in failure
Failure – a lesson
Failure – a motivation
Failure – chance one takes for trying
Failure – means of success another way
Goals – falling just short of
God – listen to
Kiln – life a fiery
Motives – accomplishment with mixed
Nationality – preserved
Obstacles – overcoming

People – used
Quarterback – leadership
Self – can consume us
Will – the difference
Witness – successful

Suicide
Listening – to others
Music – preserving sanity
Zealot – Jewish

Sun
Creation – enormous energy in

Symbol
Discipleship – center of self-denial

Talent
Animals – man's best friend
Expectation – unfulfilled
Failure – a motivation
Juvenile – precocity not unusual
Potential – unfulfilled
Poverty – amidst plenty
Yachting – demands teamwork

Taxes
Responsibility – individual

Teaching
Maturity – growth without
perfection
Repetition – of truth essential

Teaching, False
Christ – his blood alone removes sin

Technology
Security – breached

Television
Homosexuality – not as many as
claimed
Prayer – spend time in
Publicity – changes people

Temptation
Christ – his life challenges us
Christian life – greater effort—
greater success
Christian life – overcoming the past
Danger – lurking close by
Discipleship – centered in self-denial

Discipleship – needs forbidden zones
Perseverance – kind God demands
Repentance – stay free
Satan – uses pleasant
Sin – continually reconquered
Victory – hard-fought

Tension
Discipleship – challenges best of us
Potential – unfulfilled
Quarrels – lead to violence

Terrorism
Possessions – small but essential

Testing
Marriage – partners reflecting

Theft
Crisis – response to
Honesty – absence of
Inconsistency – in behavior
Kleptomania – obvious
Lying – endemic

Time
Body – is limited
Chance – wishing for a second
Habits – changing
Help – arriving too late
History – renewal needed
Humanity – always the same
Humor – part of good health
Loss – enormous in short time
Marriage – partners reflecting
Optimism – invariable in Christ
Prayer – spend time in
Present – all we have
Publicity – value of
Salvation – accept while
Salvation – almost not enough
Science – opportunity for gospel
Vision – necessary
Zionism – ages-old dream

Tongue
Conversion – speaking God's Word

Torture
Strength – way to achieve

Toxicity

Medicine – take care ingesting

Tradition

Bible – it remains

Bible – most effective in original form

Form – dismissed in crisis

Form – important, if costly

Morality – absolutely necessary

Truth – by inches

Tragedy

God – tragedy without

Traitor

Events – symbolic of a movement

Life – selling cheaply

Treachery – name synonymous with

Treaties

Bible – no alterations to truth

Trust

Investment – richly rewarded

Life – selling cheaply

Lifestyle – thrift in disastrous

Truth

Authority – God is absolute

Bible – cuts to the bone

Bible – most effective in original form

Bible – no alterations to truth

Christ – only his blood cures sin

Christ – only way to God

Counterfeit – always imitating reality

Extremism – get their attention

God – as Creator

Teaching – results differ

Undecided – many remain

Witness – need of

Unbelief

Bible – faith must accompany listening

Effort – what purpose?

Evangelism – incumbent on Christians

Evidence – compelling

Preparation – benefits of

Unity

Yachting – demands teamwork

Values

Beauty – inability to grasp

Bible – a work of art

Change – some things do

Family – fathers in leadership

God – tragedy without

Nationality – preserved

Prayer – spend time in

Victims

Hatred – indiscriminate

Oppression – a flawed way

Victory

Christ – came, knowing his fate

Christ – his life challenges us

Christian life – success despite failure

Failure – means of success

Perseverance – God demands

Repentance – stay free

Triumph – Roman style

Vitality

Morality – not spiritual

Vocabulary

Words – reveal much

War

Achievements – not given their due

Alternatives – none good

Apology – unusual

Appearances – lift our morale

Awards – for outstanding achievement

Bible – insists we face reality

Choice – affects destiny

Christ – one died for all

Christian life – be consistent

Conviction – develops behavior

Crisis – can cause incredible achievement

Deeds – good returned

Disaster – immense

Discipleship – commitment

Discipleship – need forbidden zones

Disease – deadlier than war

Effort – what purpose?

Emotions – overcoming
Enemies – admitted
Example – power
Fame – not equal to faithfulness
Fear – of one thing
Generation – building from previous
Guilt – haunts
Honor – coming late
Humility – forced on one
Illusions – many build on
Kiln – life a fiery
Kingdom – of God
Memory – innate
Mind – power of
Mistakes – learning from others
Naïveté – unbelievable
Nations – receive justice now
Obedience – willed
Optimism – invariable to Christ
Peace – none lasts
Perseverance – when it is hard
Potential – unfulfilled
Reconciliation – value of
Salvation – action required
Secrets – keeping
Survival – incredible
Temptation – overcome
Things – unexpected
Treachery – name synonymous
Trouble – affects long after
Trouble – friends causing
Undecided – many remain
Understanding – others
Victory – hard-fought
Violence – increasing
Will – the difference
Yankee – different meanings
Zeal – fact based

Water
Animals – their instinct to save
Christian life – unending value
Conversion – advantageous
Evangelism – incumbent on Christians

Fear – of one thing
Humanity – always the same
Nature – basic behavior
Nature – protected
Nature – use of sky at sea
Values – lasting

Weapons
Consistency – needed in relationships

Weather
Fame – you want to miss
Kindness – returns
Nature – protected
Yard – our need
Yellowstone – renewal

Weeping
Emotions – hidden at critical time
Emotions – overcoming

West, American
Bible – spiritual engineer
Yellowstone – renewal

Will
Conscience – listen to and obey

Winter
Weather – cold!

Women
Money – a delusion
Pressure – peer
Vanity – everyone has
Witness – successful

Words
Christian life – personal relationship with Christ
Death – final words
Education – answers from college
Education – things they learn at school
Listening – to others
Name – important
Name – unusual
Negatives – need to be
Promises – broken
Quarrels – lead to violence

Race – nomenclature
Yankee – different meanings
Work
Christ – among us but separate
Discipleship – challenges best of us
Loss – enormous in short time
Pleasure – always have time for
Salvation – almost not enough
Theft – by employees
Words – basis of life
Yachting – demands teamwork
World
Nationality – preserved
Worry
Present – all time we have
Quake – danger
Worship
Ancients – urban society
Evangelism – public witness
Form – dismissed in crisis
Intuition – warning of danger
Music – reaches deepest part of us
Occupation – sacred, whatever career
Prayer – longing for spiritual realities
Zodiac – ancient error
Youth
Juvenile – precocity not unusual
Zoo
Nutrition – animal

INDEX

ABOUT THE AUTHOR

Virgil Hurley, M.A., B.D. has served as a pastor in various churches in Illinois, Colorado, Nevada, and California. He received M.A. and B.D. degrees from Lincoln Christian Seminary. He is a sought-after speaker and has published numerous articles in various religious publications. He lives with his wife Judy in Oceanside, California. Their sons Lance, Brooks, and Scott are all in Christian ministry.